The Innovation Marathon

For Joe, at long last, with all my love
M. J.

For Jer and Scott, in appreciation for their love and support
C. B. S.

The Innovation Marathon

Lessons from High Technology Firms

Mariann Jelinek
and
Claudia Bird Schoonhoven

Basil Blackwell

First published 1990

Basil Blackwell Ltd
108 Cowley Road, Oxford, OX4 1JF, UK

Basil Blackwell, Inc.
3 Cambridge Center
Cambridge, Massachusetts 02142, USA

British Library Cataloging in Publication Data
A CIP catalogue record for this book is available from the British Library.

Library of Congress Cataloging in Publication Data
Jelinek. Mariann.
    The innovation marathon : lessons from high technology firms /
Mariann Jelinek and Claudia Bird Schoonhoven.
        p.   cm.
    Includes bibliographical references (p.   ).
    ISBN 0–631–15392–6
    1. Microelectronics industry—United States—
    Technological innovations. I. Schoonhoven, Claudia Bird.
    II. Title.
    HD9696.A3U5627   1990
    338.4'562138l'0973—dc20   89–18614   CIP

Cover photographs courtesy Intel Corporation, reprinted by permission. From left to right: the world's first microprocessor, the Intel 4004 with 2,300 transistors on a single chip (1971); the 80286 microprocessor with 128,000 transistors on a single chip (1982); and the *i*486™ microprocessor, with 1,180,235 transistors on a single chip of silicon (1989).

Typeset in 10½ on 12 pt Plantin
by Photo·graphics, Honiton, Devon
Printed in Great Britain by
T.J. Press Ltd, Padstow, Cornwall

Contents

Acknowledgements

This book exists because of the authors' mutual interests in the semiconductor and electronics industries, and in the dynamics of managing innovation in science-based, technology-intensive environments. We were introduced at a meeting thousands of miles from our home universities by colleagues who knew of our interests, initially pursued independently. Jelinek was first fascinated by TI Chairman Patrick E. Haggerty's compelling description of innovation management in his company in direct contradiction of organization theory accounts of how innovation occurred. Haggerty kindly agreed to extensive discussions of innovation management himself, and Jelinek also spent many hours interviewing managers at TI during research for her dissertation at Harvard.

Schoonhoven's interests were similarly aroused by contradictions in managers' accounts. First while studying for the PhD at Stanford University, and then later when conducting research in high-technology firms, Schoonhoven had met and interviewed scores of Silicon Valley executives and managers. The descriptions they provided of their electronics firms were simply not consistent with prevailing notions in organization theory about organizational change and adaptation. While their firms were remarkably dynamic, organization theory did not adequately capture this dynamism, substituting instead static comparisons of organizations in general.

From two very different but highly comparable sets of data, then, the authors independently concluded that the world of high-technology firms was not sufficiently well represented in organization theory. This book was created out of our desire to systematically capture the dynamism and change inherent in high-technology companies' rapid rates of innovation, and also to understand how these firms simultaneously achieve predictable, consistent, high-quality volume output.

The preparation of the manuscript stretched over more years than we had at first envisioned, and the world has changed since we began our inquiry. However, if anything, the insights seem to us even more cogent and important than before: not only are the high-technology firms we studied still battling, but the circumstances of their struggle have become far more widely generalized. Today, virtually every business faces rapidly changing technology, an increasing science base, and intensified competition in the global marketplace. A great many industries once thought "mature" are experiencing the sorts of change we saw originally in the high-technology firms we studied.

Any book that is rooted in field data depends in great measure on the willing co-operation of those who are its subjects. Because of the intensive nature of the interview process, our research took up many hours of managerial time. Our special thanks go to David Packard and John Young of Hewlett-Packard, Dr Goordon Moore and Les Vadasz of Intel, William Howard of Motorola, Charlie Sporck of National Semiconductor, the late Patrick E. Haggerty and Jerry Junkins of Texas Instruments.

While the support of these pivotal players was critical to gaining an entrée to the managers and engineers we met and interviewed in their companies, senior managers in no way limited our access to their employees, nor did they attempt to influence the conduct or conclusions of our research. To state that we had outstanding co-operation from the participating companies understates the significant contributions which these corporations and their leaders have made to our understanding of the management of innovation. Without their willingness to take technology risks, there would be no story to tell; without their willingness to discuss with us their experiences with these multi-million dollar risks – both their successes and some embarrassing failures – the story would be less detailed and far less interesting. We are particularly grateful to these leaders of innovation as well as to the almost 100 managers, executives, engineers, and scientists whom we interviewed for this book.

Special thanks are also due to Jack Kilby and Charles Phipps, who read the manuscript in draft, as did Joseph Litterer of the University of Massachusetts, John Aram of Case Western Reserve University, Robert Burgelman of Stanford University and Dorothy Leonard-Barton of the Graduate School of Business at Harvard University. Sarah McKibben read several early chapters. The manuscript was improved by these colleagues' comments, but of course all responsibility for any errors remains entirely with the authors.

Jelinek began this project at McGill University, where Henry Mintzberg's esteemed colleagueship encouraged her interests. The book was finished at Case Western Reserve University in Cleveland, where three years as the Lewis-Progressive Chair assisted in the completion of the work.

Throughout this project Schoonhoven has received the support of the Department of Organization and Management of San Jose State University's School of Business. In 1984–5, a sabbatical grant from San Jose State University created the opportunity for more intense research and writing on this book. During that year, Stanford's Graduate School of Business provided institutional support. Schoonhoven would especially like to thank James G. March, Associate Dean Eugene J. Webb, and Dean Robert K. Jaedicke for the intellectual hospitality of the Graduate School of Business at Stanford.

A special thanks to the Apple Corporation for creating the Apple III and the MacIntosh computers. The authors worked through numerous drafts of each chapter on our Apples without a whimper of complaint from the machines. Because Apple's technology was our mainstay, we have no secretaries to thank for their assistance: the machines became our late night companions and workhorses, secretaries without equal.

Finally, a heartfelt thank you to our families. Joe's interest survived discussions of innovation management from off the coast of Maine, while sailing, to Singapore, and many places in between. Deep thanks from Kaye to Jer and their son Scott. While they sometimes questioned when the book would be done, they never doubted that it would be. Scott assumes that all mothers take computers and drafts of books along on skiing vacations.

Mariann Jelinek
Cleveland Heights, Ohio

Claudia Bird Schoonhoven
Los Altos, California

1

Electronics Competition: A New Game

Commodore Perry's famous black ships opened up Japan in 1853, and the Japanese surrendered unconditionally to General MacArthur aboard American ships in Tokyo Bay in 1945. Since then, seemingly, all the ships have been traveling the other way.

Robert Sobel

An Economic Challenge

Americans once prided themselves on American management, but recent marketplace results have been disquieting. Enormous US trade deficits have continued to soar almost without respite since 1971. In 1987 and 1988, the dollar reached a series of post-war lows against major currencies, falling by 50 percent and more against the yen. Nevertheless, American customers continue to prefer expensive imported goods, while many foreign buyers have a lessening appetite for our exports. The lower dollar has helped to a certain extent, but not much: despite a 33 percent decline against the Deutschmark and a 50 percent decline against the yen since 1983, even "expensive" German and Japanese products continue to sell well in the US.

Market after market has fallen to foreign competitors. Japanese firms in particular are widely offered as a new model, and books on "Japanese management style" have even invaded the best-seller lists. Other countries' government policies, trade practices and tariff barriers appear to assist emerging new foreign competitors, like Brazil and Korea, for example. Even older competitors seem to have some edge we lack: a recent issue of *Fortune* headlined lessons to be learned from German managers (Richman, 1987). Foreign companies are now seen to practice the same sort of organized, efficient management that frightened the Europeans twenty years ago as "The American Challenge" described by Servan-Schreiber (1968) – but this time, it is the US that is threatened.

One frequent diagnosis is that American management has failed to adapt, allowing others to succeed. Henry Sharpe, chairman of Brown & Sharpe Manufacturing, the oldest independent machine tool manufacturer in the US, is blunt about the losses:

> It would take a generation – maybe more – to retool and recapture what has already slipped through our fingers. It's very sobering to realize that there are more and more types of machine tools that apparently can't be made in this country at all any more and that the national capacity to make many other types of machine tools in quantity is growing extremely limited.
>
> Farnum, 1987

Where once American industrial might was the stereotype, now it is American rigidity, low quality, and manufacturing problems that are on everyone's lips. Automobiles offer a pertinent example. Foreign competition (principally Japanese) holds a persistent quarter of the US domestic automobile market, and has also captured a share in important foreign markets. Productivity, cost, and quality are the sticking points. Mighty GM manufactures automobiles at $2,000 or so more than the *landed* cost of comparable imported Japanese cars, not to mention Hyundai or Yugo. Meanwhile, Honda has begun to produce cars in Ohio with US personnel at costs low enough to justify export – to Japan. After almost a decade of intense effort to improve quality, "Detroit's Cars Really Are Getting Better," says an early 1987 *Fortune* headline. The text cites expert Robert E. Cole, however, who is less congratulatory: "The best of ours are about as good as the worst of theirs, and that is a tremendous achievement. But there is still a significant gap."

Numerous "causes" of the American failures in manufacturing have been identified: foreign government subsidies, unfair tariff barriers abroad, and burdensome US government regulation, pollution controls, unionism, and high wages at home among them. But these frequently seem more like excuses than causes.

Our research leads us to believe that the problem is a lack of effective innovation. Economic competitors succeed by embracing new approaches, new technology, and above all, more efficient practices to get new products to market. They succeed by responding to change more quickly, or even precipitating new conditions. Their innovations force American firms to dance to their tune in industry after industry – just as American innovations formerly gained advantages for American firms against their competitors. Today, because they innovate more readily, it is foreign competitors who control the game.

An American Success Story

With so many foreign successes, and so many US failures, it is sometimes difficult to comprehend what has gone wrong, or how it is that once-vaunted US management cannot seem to compete today, despite its past successes. It seems easier to focus only on the gloomy, unrelieved picture of failure, blaming "unfair" foreign practices, or "unacceptably low" foreign wages. But to understand truly, and to act effectively to solve the problems, a more complex view is essential. Not all US firms are bureaucratic, organizationally rigid, inefficient, or technologically backward. US successes are not limited to protected niches, small companies, or simple markets. Some of those successes inhabit a complex and highly demanding industry cluster where tough foreign competitors employ abundant financial resources, protective tariffs, and constant technological change: micro-electronics.

This book explores management strategies and practices in a selected set of outstanding firms in the US electronics industry. We closely examine five firms of that very demanding industry, and comment more briefly on others. Hewlett-Packard, Intel, National Semiconductor, Motorola, and Texas Instruments are all highly respected by their competitors. They are well run; they innovate constantly; and, despite the competition, they have generally prospered in an industry strewn with the wreckage of many failures.

Like the rest of their industry, these firms have also experienced difficulties – sometimes, as during the electronics recession of 1985–6, severe difficulties. Since the early 1950s, they have competed in a global industry characterized by targeted government support of their foreign competitors, and even US government support of technology transfer abroad in support of military and diplomatic ends (Prestowitz, 1988). Nevertheless, the US firms' reputations as tough competitors

Table 1.1 The sample electronics firms

Company	Products type of business	Employees	Structure	SIC classi-fication(s)	1988 Sales $ billion
Hewlett-Packard Company	Electronics equipment for measurement, analysis, and computation	82,000	52 divisions	3573, 3825, 7379, 3693, 3674, 3832	9.8
Intel Corporation	Semiconductor components and systems	18,700	3 groups	3674	2.9
Motorola, Inc.	Electronic equipment, systems, and components	94,400	3 sectors, 4 groups 31 subsidiaries	3662, 3661, 3674, 3679, 3694, 3651, 3573, 3693, 3559, 3822, 3825, 3824	8.2
National Semiconductor Corporation	Semiconductor components and systems; computer systems	30,800	3 operations, 1 subsidiary	3679, 3674, 3573	2.4
Texas Instruments, Inc.	Semiconductor materials and devices; electric and thermostatic controls; calculators; geophysical and environmental services; radar, infrared, and other electronic systems	77,270	8 operations	1382, 3399, 3573, 3362, 3674, 3679, 3822, 3823	6.3

Source: Compiled from company annual reports, IOK, and various business directories.

persist among their peers – including both domestic peers and substantial foreign competitors with deep pockets and government support. Even more importantly, these firms are survivors: they have emerged from each electronics recession repositioned and prepared to cope with change, not weakened and further behind. If they have not won every battle – and they certainly have not – they have given excellent account of themselves against odds that have defeated many other US companies.

Amidst persistent US industrial difficulties, electronics seems to offer a glimmer of American success. The lessons from electronics are deceptively simple and easily summarized: technology is essential, but technology alone is not enough. Innovation is absolutely central to survival, especially in high-technology industries. To maintain innovation requires much effort, constant attention (and some selective "benign" neglect, upon occasion), as well as consistent support. Managing technology is not simply a technical matter: managing human interactions, organizational structures and infrastructures, support systems, and information, and above all people's involvement in the work of the firm are at least as important – and at least as difficult.

Translating these lessons into specifics for broader practice is more difficult still, and requires a closer look at electronics company successes, and at how insights from electronics might be applicable to other industries. Some of the translation seems obvious: virtually any industry, including those long considered mature or "low-technology," is vulnerable to creative high-technology attack. Thus the electronics industry's successes in fending off competitors may suggest useful models. Electronics industry difficulties are also instructive: worthy adversaries confront our sample firms, and they increasingly employ methods that seem more characteristic of "mature industries" than those more usually anticipated in high-technology industry. At the same time, change remains endemic.

Electronics industry experience now incorporates both a continued high rate of change in technology, and growing insistence upon "mature industry" skills and factors such as manufacturing mastery, efficiency, and close customer links. In this experience we can see the outlines of future competition taking shape in very much the same way as for US firms in automobiles or textiles, machine tools or consumer products – with some important differences, most notably a continued commitment to innovation.

This inquiry is a field study, based on extensive recorded personal interviews with over 100 insiders in companies in the electronics, computer, and semiconductor industries. (The formal description of our approach is deferred to a methodological appendix, where interested readers may find details.) We interviewed company founders, managers, engineers, senior executives, and technical specialists. Interviews were supplemented with systematic data of various sorts, including quantitative data on company performance and economic conditions. However, the interviews are the core of our data. The voices and views of practising managers and engineers in the electronics industry are the "battlefield accounts" that tell how these managers accomplish continued innovation, and what they think is important in managing it.

Electronics offers an entry point to an understanding of the complexities of both past US industrial successes and current difficulties. The micro-electronics industry carved out its successes in the midst of competitive realities only now being shared by older American industries. The electronics experience provides important insights because changing competitive realities are themselves a part of what must be understood. A whole set of competitive conditions was first experienced in electronics – but is increasingly characteristic of contemporary businesses in general. Chief among these is the growing need for widespread, repeated, consistently successful innovation.

Although everyone pays lip service to "innovation," electronics firms have lived it, throughout a 40-year history of new products, scientific achievement, and technical breakthroughs. Their task has not been easy, and they remain locked in intensive struggle with highly competent competitors from around the world. Such constant challenge is another new reality for virtually all firms, as is global competition. But the electronics firms' successes are notable. This book explores how five successful firms manage the dominant challenge of constant innovation. Their success at innovation is directly related to their continued survival.

From its earliest days, the US electronics industry has experienced foreign competition in a global marketplace. Production quality and technological complexity were important from the start. So, too, were continuing streams of new products to match those of competitors, and wave after wave of new manufacturing technology to support the new products. Changes were also seen in product applications, in markets, in channels of distribution. In many ways, electronics exemplifies the need for mastery of a broad range of factors, and above all for mastery of innovation. It is not enough to be good at product design, at manufacturing, at marketing, or even at all of these separately. Instead, in electronics a firm must excel at all – and excel, too, at balancing all of them, and at innovating within these areas and across them, often simultaneously.

Electronics: The New Engine of Industry

Electronics is important for another reason: it is fundamental both to the world we live in, and to the future of commerce and industry.

The electronics industry, broadly defined, shapes modern life, profoundly affecting every aspect of our culture and society. Predictions suggest that its influence will continue to grow and deepen: ours is truly an electronic age. Indeed, it is difficult to think of any aspect of life not affected by the pervasive influence of electronics. Electronics now accounts for over $300 billion of US industrial output, about 15 percent of the total. Electronics adds capabilities undreamed-of to formerly non-electronic items from talking stuffed bears to washing machines to industrial equipment to bombs. The electronics industry is both central to our lives and characteristic of our era. We shall argue that it is characteristic, too, of competitive environments for most businesses in times to come.

Companies that succeed in electronics do so in a remarkably demanding atmosphere. Roughly speaking, real prices drop by 25 percent per year – and have done so for decades. There is no indication of slowdown in this pace of change. Repeated technological shifts drive firms to maintain heavy research expenditures. In the semiconductor industry, R&D has hovered near 10 percent of sales for decades. In 1987, the all-industry average in the US was only 3.1 percent.

Electronics firms seem not only to tolerate change, but to thrive on it. New products continue to pour out, as do new processes to make them. While other, more mature industries complain of "resistance to change," the electronics firms live with 18-month product life cycles. They have a great deal to teach us about the persistent self-renewal that is crucial to their success.

It would be easy to believe that electronics firms are unique in their experience. Instead, we believe they have been ahead of the times in terms of technical and economic challenge. Electronics has always been in tune with realities only now coming to bear widely on the rest of US industries. Thus they may offer useful guidance to others. Today, some 80 percent of the US economy is under challenge from foreign competitors, up from 25 percent only a decade previously, according to the Commerce Department. So today, virtually every industry must adapt to faster, more demanding rates of change. If we have done our research well and can learn from electronics, perhaps firms in mature industries can avoid bureaucratic stagnation, and learn how to adapt productively to change.

Nor is this all. The same penetration that makes electronic products central to our daily lives makes the technology of electronics central to businesses of all sorts. Semiconductor components are increasingly important for automobiles, automatic tellers and toys, as well as for industrial controls, portable sales terminals, medical instruments, and inspection devices. Micro-electronics expertise is essential to industrial competition worldwide, because computers and electronic controls play an ever greater part in virtually every industry, from basic to service to leisure. Examples abound: computer reservation networks for airlines, laptop computers carried by accountants, insurance sales people, and engineers, or automatic controls on steel mills and microwave ovens.

The so-called electronic "future" also seems to have arrived in older industries long considered mature, like automobiles, machine tools, shoes, and textiles, as well as among the glamorous "high techs." Even where *products* are not electronic, often manufacturing, logistics, distribution, or key information *processes* needed to manage the business effectively are dependent on electronics. Running-shoe manufacturers use the latest Computer Aided Design (CAD) systems and elaborate solid-modelling software to design products, for instance. Most industries will be significantly "electronic" soon, if they are not so already.

What this means is that most industries will necessarily change in pace with electronics changes – not at the slower pace of their older technologies. Because their basic technologies are becoming electronic, more firms will begin to "look" more electronic in their competitive spirit, if for no other reason than that competitors who understand electronics-based competition will drive all firms toward exploiting new, electronic capabilities – or drive them out of business.

These realities – including vastly increased productivity requirements, demands for far higher quality, and a continuing need for innovation – have already swept over such industries as computers, or consumer products based upon electronics, to say nothing of steel, automobiles, machine tools, or even service businesses like banking. In each, the new order is far more like electronics industry competition than like the traditional consumer products, steel, automobile, machine tool, or banking industries of the past. Comprehending competition in electronics consequently offers important insights into the future of many businesses. The electronics industry's experience forecasts the competitive future for others.

Constant Challenge, Constant Change

The problems of the electronics industries also seem to forecast the changing competitive future. The electronics industry is highly volatile, and markets change as swiftly as the technology. After record profits in 1984, the industry saw a deep recession and major losses for most US participants in 1985, continued difficulties in 1986, and slow recovery in 1987. Like most US industries, electronics is experiencing great competitive pressures, especially from Far Eastern producers. As recently as 1982, Japanese share in world electronics markets was only about 23 percent. Throughout the recession of the early 1980s, Japanese firms enjoyed substantially lower capital costs and less pressure to show quarterly profits. As a result, they maintained investment in capacity expansion far in excess of US firms – and far in excess of then-current world semiconductor demand. The US merchant semiconductor makers' world market share fell to 40 percent in 1986, while Japan's climbed to nearly 50 percent.

In consumer electronics, no video cassette recorders are made in the US – although a US firm holds the basic VCR patents. Sony leads the world in compact disk players, although the product was developed by Philips NV, and many new competitors have entered the market. Casio drove US makers out of low-end calculators, while Seiko and Citizen pre-empted the watch business. The successes of such tough, competent players as Sony, Casio, or Hitachi – or Goldstar, the Korean challenger – underline the pressures facing electronics companies today.

Semiconductor components offer an even starker picture. World-wide, the Japanese are widely reported to hold overwhelming market shares – up to 90 percent – in some key market segments; vastly more than just a few years ago. DRAMs are one such market. DRAMs, or dynamic random access memories, are an essential component in most electronics applications, and their manufacturing technology a basic building block for all semiconductor manufacture. Mastery here is mastery of the basics of the semiconductor industry. This demands competitive strength in basic design and manufacturing, not just in the assembly of others' products. Japanese manufacturers have been significant competitors since entering the US DRAM

Table 1.2 US comparison firms

Company	Products/type of business	Employees	Structure	1988 Sales $ billion
International Business Machines	Information-handling systems; data processing machines and systems; program products; telecommunications systems, office systems, typewriters, copiers, educational and testing materials and related suppliers and services	403,508	3 groups 17 divisions 5 independent business units 18 subsidiary divisions	54.2
General Motors	Automobiles, buses, trucks, diesel locomotives and engines, engine electrical equipment, missile components	734,000	47 divisions 9 associated companies	101.8

market in 1978. They seized about 40 percent of the market by 1980, and had grasped market leadership in 64K DRAMS in 1982. Numerous explanations have been offered for this success, among them an unanticipated surge in demand in the US market that domestic manufacturers were unable to meet, MITI support and protective tariffs in Japan, and dumping. But no explanations can detract from the accomplishment, or its competitive consequences.

There are widespread assertions of Japanese market mastery. A telling statistic concerns changes in Japanese share of the worldwide DRAM market during the decade following 1974. In 1974, Intel held 82.9 per cent of the world DRAM market, and TI 13 per cent; by 1980, Intel's share had fallen to 2.9 per cent and TI's to 11 per cent; by 1986, Intel's share was 0.1 per cent, and TI's only 6.5 per cent. Meanwhile, the share held collectively by Japanese companies was about 78 per cent (Dataquest, April 1987). Intel, widely credited as initiating the dynamic RAM (DRAM) market, ceased that activity in 1984, accompanied by most other US firms, except for Texas Instruments and Micron, Inc. (Several US firms have announced their intentions to re-enter the DRAM market, with anti-dumping regulations offering some protection from the Japanese, and worldwide demand again increasing.)

The competitive threat is fundamental. It cannot be dismissed as simple copying or assembly, despite documented Japanese or Korean reliance on copying in the past, and despite US successes in new product design. Instead, the foreign competitors possess broad expertise in manufacture and design of both components and products, and also in semiconductor manufacturing equipment. They are worthy adversaries and tough, competent challengers. To succeed against opponents like these is to succeed in very real terms. There are no easy victories – and the battles demonstrate the competitive realities with which most US industries must now contend.

This degree of expertise on the part of foreign competitors creates many repercussions for US firms, especially given volatile market conditions and a worldwide, albeit temporary, glut of semiconductor capacity. During the world electronics recession of 1985 and 1986, for instance, major components maker Texas Instruments reported 1985 Fourth Quarter net losses of $41.2 million, and a loss for the year of $118.7 million, compared to a record profit the previous year of $316 million on 1984 sales of about $5 billion (1985 sales were down about 20 percent). This loss, only the second for TI since it went public in 1953, is largely attributed to semiconductor problems, including challenges in basic components such as memories and integrated circuits.

Yet while pundits lament TI's problems, it is worth noting as well that the company has also succeeded, surviving and growing amidst persistently volatile markets, the most complex mass manufacturing process ever invented, and turbulent technological change. TI and the other US electronics firms of our study endure, innovate, and even prosper, while delivering a constant stream of marvels at ever lower prices, all in the teeth of continued challenge. No industry, even one so highly innovative, intensely driven, and hitherto successful as electronics, is protected by past achievements from voracious foreign rivals. The competitive pressure is constant. "High technology" by itself, even highly innovative high technology, is not enough – not even in industries like semiconductors, computers, and electronics. These industries face incursions by highly skilled, determined adversaries in a global market. All competitors face not only technical demands, but marketing demands and, above all, managerial demands centering on the need for innovation.

Firms like Hewlett-Packard, Intel, Motorola, National Semiconductor, and Texas Instruments are at the forefront in coupling technological innovation with global competitive requirements. They innovate repeatedly; they remain competitive, technologically, in a very demanding race. How have these firms accomplished all this?

Table 1.3 Japanese comparison firms

Company	Products/type of business	Employees	Structure	1984 Sales $ [a]
Casio Computer Co. Ltd.	Manufactures electronic calculators, computers, electronic typewriters, terminal devices, electronic wrist watches, electronic cash registers and multitone electronic musical instruments	3,259	17 subsidiaries	884 million
Matsushita	Operates as a worldwide trading company through 44 manufacturing companies, 22 representative offices, 34 sales companies and about 100 distributors. Company exports consumer electronic goods such as video tape recorders, televisions, radios, tape recorders and hi-fi equipment, and domestic appliances such as washing machines, refrigerators and cooking appliances, industrial products, electrical and electronic components, and communications equipment. Exports under the brand names "National," "Panasonic," "Technics," and "Quasar"	not given	67 subsidiaries and affiliates	6.9 billion
Sony Corporation	Development, manufacture and sale of various kinds of electronic equipment, instruments and devices	42,654	14 subsidiaries	4.8 billion
Toshiba Machine Co. Ltd.	Engaged in the machine tool market, plastic molding industry, office automation equipment, hydraulic equipment, construction products, numerical controls, sequence controllers, etc.	5.519	6 subsidiaries	405 million

[a] For Japanese comparison firms, sales are restated in US dollars at the 1984 exchange rate of Y226 = $1; at July 1988, the exchange rate was Y134 = $1.

By understanding how they compete, we can outline a new American method for success in the future. By understanding their difficulties, we can more clearly define appropriate responses.

Lessons in Innovation

One lesson from electronics is that while technical excellence is crucial, it is not enough. Many competitors have access to similar technology, so new developments are almost always quickly matched. What is required is constant improvement, and constant balance and interaction among the varied elements of design, manufacturing, distribution, and marketing. Performing each function well constitutes the entry fee and perhaps the monthly dues permitting a firm to play. To succeed in the game, balanced excellence in all these elements must service constant innovation. Nothing else will succeed in the long run.

Another lesson is that innovation must be matched by bedrock mastery of the business. Any legislative protection scheme will ultimately fail if protected US firms cease to innovate. If they do so, they will fall behind technologically, and the US economy will stagnate as others surpass it. Any free-market ideology that fails to support innovation by providing the necessary infrastructure to sustain it will also fail. What is needed is not a simple barrier against competition, but a more effective way to compete, based on innovation. Although markets cannot be legislatively protected, they can be competitively commanded: innovation works. Accordingly, the focus of this book is innovation management inside the firm.

The impact of more effective competition applies around the world, and in many industries, underlining the innovation imperative. The Japanese themselves now face serious competitors in Singapore, Hong Kong, and Korea, as these nations move into high-technology manufacturing (both in "high-technology" industries and in more traditional mature ones as well) with systematic government support. Growing Korean successes against the Japanese in US consumer markets for products like microwave ovens and televisions, and their recent entry into the US personal computer market, point up the threat. Similarly, Japanese auto-makers face competitors from Korea and Yugoslavia, both in US markets and abroad. Only continued innovation offers real protection from competitive challenge for any firm in any industry. Here the electronics firms provide a model for the management of innovation inside the firm.

How have the electronics firms managed the balance among elements to achieve innovation so successfully and so often? The lessons from the electronics firms we have studied are not obvious to the uninitiated, but they can be worked out. From the manager's point of view, we found five key elements that stand out along the developmental track of any innovative idea. These are: the roots of innovation; its supports; structures; the managed transfer of innovations through a complex development process; and an overall strategy of innovation visible in these firms. All are necessary to successful innovation. The electronics firms we studied manage them in ways different from those of past traditional industry practices. Each factor offers an important leverage point for successful management of continued innovation. For success, however, the factors must be interactively managed.

Where do innovative ideas come from? In our sample of electronics firms, innovations do not spring solely from some "Department of Innovation" or R&D laboratory. Rather, ideas come from many sources, broadly scattered throughout the organizations we studied, and even outside it. Engineers, marketing people, senior executives, customers, sales reps, and many others provide innovative ideas. Much care is devoted to ensuring a constant free flow of creative ideas.

How do innovators get support for their ideas? The initial creative idea is merely the beginning; much more is required before an idea becomes successful reality. Good technical ideas often come from lower organizational levels, where detailed, specific technical expertise resides. However, a lower-level originator is highly unlikely to possess organizational clout or discretion, control of funds, broad managerial experience, or business perspectives. And, typically, even a good idea must be joined with many other insights if it is to succeed. Yet all of these are necessary, and must be carefully blended to produce an innovation that will succeed in the marketplace.

Innovative ideas that translate into marketplace success demand careful nurturing and many varied resources. Marketing skills as well as design, manufacturing as well as finance, dollars as well as backing play important roles. Both innovators and others must know how to access these resources, and how to tap into the decision-making authority that unlocks funds. Innovators also need access to marketplace opportunities, problems, and challenges as catalysts for their ideas. The successful firms we studied do not leave these vital resources to chance. Instead, they structure the organization itself as a map for locating resources, talent, and authority, and for directing attention. Structure can help or hinder innovation, depending on whether or not it effectively guides innovators toward needed resources and challenges.

Structure also fuels (or impedes) the transfer of innovative ideas, products, and processes from originator to developmental resources, from R&D to operational units and ultimately to the market. Every innovation must move along this path, and the transitions are difficult. Without an effective structure to guide it, the complex transfer of innovative ideas to volume production can grind to a halt. Our successful firms exhibited keen awareness of structure and forthright willingness to change it at need. Whatever shape it took, their structure was deliberate, clear, and definitive; they changed from one clear structure to another clear structure.

Above all, the successful firms we studied built their practice and aimed their activities at continued innovation. Their systems were constantly tested against the criterion of successful innovation; if systems impeded innovation, the systems were changed. Support for innovation was a key management task, and a central focus of discussion, attention, and effort in our sample firms. Management style and organizational culture were judged and changed according to how well they facilitated innovation. In addition, both the transfer of new product ideas, and developmental efforts in manufacturing, whether directly tied to a specific product or more generally focused, targeted improved innovation capabilities in our successful firms.

Management in High-Technology Firms

Electronic Diversity

A closer look at who our firms are is in order here. We construe "electronics" broadly, to include not only semiconductor components, but also micro-electronic equipment and computers, systems, and peripherals. This implies substantial diversity, which is both our aim in this study and the norm in the micro-electronics industry around the world. Amidst this diversity, the core technology, semiconductors, provides both an underlying logic and a central character within our sample. As electronics comes to play an increasing role in other industries, both diversity and the central role of electronics are becoming visible elsewhere.

Two of our sample (Motorola and Texas Instruments) are broadly diversified electronics-based firms; the others (Intel, National Semiconductor, and Hewlett Packard) are more tightly focused. All are technologically dependent on developments in electronics in general, and semiconductors in particular, despite growing diversification. Texas Instruments and Motorola, for example, each derive only about one third of their revenues directly from semiconductor components. Motorola's remaining two thirds is predominantly in communications. The remainder of Texas Instruments' business emphasizes defense electronics and systems. Hewlett-Packard has a long history in instruments. National Semiconductor has been active in several special computer markets, like point-of-sale registers, but focuses primarily on semiconductors. Intel has more recently begun to market some computers and peripheral devices. All these firms provide micro-electronic components to computer-makers, and find their sales responsive to trends in computer sales; all have shifted the emphasis of their businesses over time.

This diversity is typical, around the world: there are few "pure" semiconductor components manufacturers today. Most are diversified, both in the US and abroad. Our research reflects this reality, including merchant semiconductor firms and broader, more diversified companies as well. The industry cannot be understood without including more than semiconductor manufacture. Looking beyond semiconductors also highlights the impact of change in a broader range of industries while underlining the importance of electronics. Yet our companies' activities are still related closely to developments in micro-electronics, as we believe much industrial activity will be, increasingly, in the future.

We noted earlier that developments in the semiconductor industry carry implications for the growing areas where electronics is transforming older industries. Our sample firms illustrate this microelectronic penetration. Motorola grew from a base in automobile radios, short-wave and other portable communications gear – areas all radically transformed by electronics. Hewlett-Packard (HP) has its roots in instrumentation, in the pre-electronics days. Today, HP's activities in instrumentation and computers are also plowing new ground in factory automation, its instrumentation business having been already utterly changed by the advent of electronics. The sample firms' experiences provide an illustration of conditions and changes that apply, broadly, to many industries.

Tracking Innovation

Our focus has been on tracking innovation in these firms to address the question of how these companies succeed at significant, complicated and, above all, *repeated* innovations. The story of electronics is not of a one-shot or a two-shot battle, but of an on-going barrage of change that shows every sign of continuing indefinitely. Success lies not in pulling it off once, but in creating a self-sustaining organizational system that will replicate technological innovation repeatedly over the long run. Nor is success simple, for these firms manage complex businesses that cannot be run by small, simple, ad hoc organizations. Instead, they require carefully constructed, elaborated, and managed organizational entities with very deep pockets. That organizational focus is a key aspect of this study.

"Bureaucracy" and Innovation

Continued innovation in large firms is especially important today because that is where the resources essential for complex industry reside. A common excuse for failure in organizations, especially large ones, is "bureaucracy." We often assume that "bureaucracy" is inescapable in large organizations, and that "bureaucracy" undercuts creative thinking. Yet this begs the question. Modern societies accepting "bureaucracy" as inevitable face an important paradox: large, complex tasks require prodigious resources, carefully arrayed in large, complex organizations – yet they must continually innovate. Our data show the paradox to be more apparent than real, for our sample firms are large, complex organizations that do innovate successfully, in a highly demanding environment. This book will explain how contemporary managers have resolved the paradox.

Repeating Innovation, Despite Mis-steps

A rather different facet of our work is its critical exploration of efforts toward innovation. No firms, not ours nor even the Japanese, are universally successful; nobody bats 1.000 over the long term. Yet even the failures and mis-steps offer important insights. The ability of a firm's managers to reconstitute their strategy, reconfigure their structure, and adapt to changing circumstances is ultimately more impressive than simple success. Retrieving the capability to innovate, even after failure, is as important as innovating in the first place. Managing innovation over the long run, again and again, means managing new people, new technologies, and new interaction patterns, dealing with different demands both in good times and after bad ones.

In the semiconductor industry, the only certainty is that tomorrow or the next day there will be new demands for innovation, as technological advances and competitive pressures create new product, process, or enhanced function requirements. Revolutionary change is almost the norm. Yet the changes are not all so revolutionary. Many known supports for innovation can be deliberately provided.

We looked for organizational methods to enable successfully repeated innovation, not simple accounts of heroic insight or lonely persistence. This is not a book about "skunkworks," either. Insight and persistence are here – but they must be multiplied, sustained, and woven into the organizational context to succeed. That context is most visible in the *process* used by these firms to ensure successful innovation. An organized process is essential for complex technologies requiring enormous capital commitments and widely varied specialist expertise. Persistent success, definitively distinguished from occasional blind luck, rests on organized process.

Our firms go farther still, in that the organizational processes they use are not fortuitous, not left to luck. Managers in these firms are constantly concerned with encouraging innovation. When the methods, procedures, and systems fail, they are re-examined and changed. When the systems and methods work well, they are shared and fostered. Managerial attention and effort are central to avoiding bureaucracy, mitigating the complications that size and elaborate technology impose, and keeping innovation flowing. These are managerial, organizational modes of innovating.

What We Found

Electronics Industry Change and Stability

Micro-electronics-based industries are not like older industries. Their management practices and cultures, while by no means homogeneous, are discernibly different from those characteristic of companies in many older industries. Electronics managers emphasize change, tolerate it, and indeed embrace it. More than one manager, when asked about "resistance to change," quipped that "resistance to stability" was a greater concern. Yet random, undirected change will not produce successful commercial innovation, nor are new products themselves a guarantee of success. Staying power – stability as well as change – is required. In case after case in our sample, founders, managers, engineers, research scientists, and manufacturing personnel alike commented that both change and stability were essential.

Change and stability in what? In products, in processes, in methods and markets, in the complex manufacturing activities, and even within the organizations, in their structure, systems, and personnel, and occasionally in their basic organizational identity and strategic mission. Dynamic tension between change and stability is a central characteristic of the companies we studied. We believe it will be increasingly characteristic of worldwide competition for the future. By contrast, companies in other industries seem to change rarely, painfully, and, often, unsuccessfully.

"Small Company Culture"

The firms we study are large and complex. Nevertheless, they seek to retain a "small company" flavour. Often, they devote substantial effort – through restructuring and a proliferation of small reporting units, and through deliberately fostered social cohesion – to keeping managers close to the action. Hewlett-Packard, for instance, is widely known for spinning off new units when a site's headcount rises above about 1,000. "Corporate culture" is now a widely recognized phenomenon. The micro-electronics firms we studied do more than recognize culture. They explicitly foster it, seeking to "remain small" in flavor and feel, even while they grow.

Another source of the "small company" flavor is giving significant responsibility early in the career path. People rise quickly in electronics firms. While many "rise" in formal terms, formal status is nevertheless not essential. Even lower-level technical experts carry tremendous weight in far-reaching decisions to commit the company and its resources. New people and people well down in the hierarchy are vital, acknowledged contributors in electronics firms.

Tapping this "local" knowledge – a "small company" approach to constant renewal – is a central factor in electronics management. The reality and importance of technical expertise and responsibility, even at the lowest levels, profoundly shapes the firms we studied. We believe it is another key insight for other managers, and that its implications are wide-ranging. Formal practices – promotion rules, decision responsibility, ability to commit funds, consultation of subordinates on important issues – can provide systematic consistency to strengthen cultural norms.

Culture serves as an important mechanism for guidance and control, and it is increasingly important where more cumbersome, more bureaucratic methods will not work, as seems to be the case in the highly competitive, changeable arenas of micro-electronics industries. Yet culture alone is clearly not enough – especially when highly complex and detailed activities must be meticulously controlled. The successful micro-electronics firms we studied have both strong cultures and well-developed organizational structures and processes to shepherd innovation. This duality responds to important needs created by the market and technological forces they face. Because other industries will face similar pressures, there too this duality will be increasingly important over time, as we shall suggest.

Technology Risk

The risk involved in staying at the edge of the state of the art in a changeable technology environment is high. Technology decisions in electronics are often big ticket items of the "you bet your company" magnitude: a wafer fabrication line costs tens of millions of dollars and equipment turnover is rapid. With such large investments, there is genuine urgency in achieving economies of scale, usage, and efficiency across product lines, minimizing needless duplication and increasing the productivity of these awesome capital commitments. Unlike prior industrial experience, the opportunity for micro-electronics and computer firms to spread these costs across a long productive life is sharply constrained by the pace of technological innovation.

These continued investments have to be made in new areas, too, often with inadequate information. Significant commitments to research, for instance, are essential just to keep informed enough to have the option of development later. There is real pressure to move quickly into new technologies, experimenting and trying them out. Experimentation can result in numerous small units, each with a slightly different technology. Proliferating small units can create major headaches for efforts toward reintegration, because the scope of technological expertise is so broad. Many diverse pockets of separated specialist expertise have somehow to be drawn together, so that essential tasks can be accomplished. Our sample companies (like many other large, diversified firms) have turned to regrouping activities as a means of keeping people in touch and integrated. Unlike firms in older industries, however, the sample firms regroup frequently, not just at the project level, but throughout their corporate structure. Here, too, change is the norm.

These successful firms seek to mitigate technology risks and the inefficiencies of numerous small groups by new ways of organizing. Not only do these firms change organizational structure frequently. They also utilize newer structures frequently. For instance, they make widespread and explicit use of cross-functional teams and multiple reporting relationships. Potential users of new technology within the company are involved early on in its development. Cross-functional and cross-divisional teams concerned with underlying technical or market issues are also convened at need. Effective team management, visible in our companies, can guide others.

The guidance is relevant. Technology risks will be pervasive in other industries too, as the full weight of scientific discovery in micro-electronics, computers, automated processes (in both factory and office), new materials and process knowledge, and materials handling becomes felt. Indeed, with over 90 percent of all scientists ever educated in the history of the world alive and practising today (Merryfield, 1983), it would be extraordinary if the majority of industries did not experience massive change.

More directly to the point, perhaps, other industries besides micro-electronics and computers are increasingly making use of new materials, exotic techniques and processes, and computers. They, too, are experiencing global competition, shorter product life cycles, greater reliance on technical and scientific specialists. And they, too, are finding that new methods of managing team and project activities, technological risks, and capability developments are essential. It is not a question simply of investing in research that may fail, but one of new demands for managing complexity. Multiplying many small units that require reintegration if their investment is to be harvested is one of the issues at hand. Technology risks also include a growing, urgent need for frequent organizational reconfiguration in service of innovations in technology, products, processes and market insights. All are elements in an "electronic" pace of change, moving from electronics *per se* into many other industries and services.

Challenging Traditional Hierarchies

What organizational changes does an electronic pace bring about? Because the beat never stops, traditional hierarchy and management methods are simply swamped. Our sample firms need a high order of manufacturing expertise, along with good design ideas, co-operation among specialists and departments, and speedy reconfiguration to meet emerging new needs. Being right and contributing to project completion are more important than formal status as sources of power and authority, so both contribution and formal status are affected.

Technology moves so fast that managers "away from the bench" find their expertise decays rapidly. This means that junior members of the organization, especially in technical functions like manufacturing or engineering, are very important: they are often the source of all-important technological innovation, and they have the first-hand knowledge that must be integrated if innovation is to succeed. Yet because they are new to the organization and low in its ranks, they lack the credibility and wide business experience needed to make effective strategy. They also lack the legitimacy or power to commit the organization to major expenditures. The successful companies we studied transcend this paradox by cultural, managerial, and systems approaches in order to manage innovation. One important method used here is task-focused team management.

Teams of experts with diverse experience and training must be brought together: first, in the research team; next, to bridge the gaps between research and design, marketing and pilot production, and between pilot production and the large-scale manufacture typical of electronic products. Team management is different from traditional management where nominal hierarchy can be taken as an effective proxy for technical expertise. In the firms we studied, technical obsolescence dictates that rank may very well not coincide with technical expertise. Instead, very junior people hold key technical knowledge that must be effectively tapped. Yet juniors lack organizational clout. Team management, then, involves using juniors' expertise while also using seniors' organizational credibility.

Teams are also responsible for product support and updates. Because of turnover or transfer as new phases of development create new needs, teams change often. A different group of people from those originally responsible for developing the product may launch it, and then in turn hand the product over for full-scale production to a new group. Still others may be responsible for later updating and on-going product support. Yet while the memberships may change, the team itself must stay intact. There must also be much overlap to ensure continuity. Fragmenting the steps into separate fiefdoms has spelled disaster in traditional companies, causing visible slowdowns, errors, failures to co-operate and lost opportunities.

These challenges cannot be met by traditional hierarchical and functional organization, so our successful firms organize and operate in non-traditional ways. While boundaries exist and organization charts typically do include explicit manufacturing, design, marketing, and product responsibilities, for instance, these distinctions do not supersede overall responsibilities for fostering innovation. Our sample companies exhibit considerable variation in the newer management styles and organizational structures. For instance, Texas Instruments is widely reputed (by managers both in TI and elsewhere in our sample) to be far more intense and driven than Hewlett-Packard. Beyond the differences, however, all the companies are explicit about seeking to overcome the limits of traditional organization and hierarchy.

All the firms share some key characteristics. They place less emphasis on formal hierarchy. Micro-electronics, computer and semiconductor firms are far less hierarchical than many other industries. Their organization is more complex, and it changes more frequently. Junior people do have access to decision-makers, and to alternate funding. "Boot-legging" is a hallowed tradition, and all the firms tolerated or even encouraged people to innovate around existing arrangements, existing products, existing understandings. Status frequently has more to do with recognized technical expertise than with hierarchy.

Boundary Crossing and Temporary Teams

Boundaries, whether between the firm and its customers, between departments or among divisions, are also different in our sample. Boundaries are meant to be crossed in these firms. Temporary teams drawn from many different "organizational homes" are the rule, not the exception. The managers, scientists, and engineers we spoke with are all keenly aware of how different these practices are from those of traditional firms. Often, comparisons were made with other companies or past experience to underline the difference.

Nor are the boundaries themselves fixed. Reorganization is frequent, as we have mentioned, in response to changing market needs, new product design and development requirements, or changing perceptions. One manager commented that his firm had reorganized, on average, every six months during the 20 years of his employment there. This tends to blur boundaries, focusing people's attention instead on task needs. Nevertheless, as we shall show, managers are keenly aware of their responsibilities and reporting relationships – although they feel quite free to seek needed expertise wherever it may be, in the service of a current task.

Explicit Innovation

Innovation is an explicit activity in micro-electronics-based industries. Each firm has a more or less formal innovation framework or system, with identified people to go to for help, advice, funding, or support. Designated senior managers are responsible for watching over innovation, fostering it, and backing good ideas. And innovation is recognized and rewarded. The array of information systems, performance measurement arrangements, and alternative channels for funding and support make up an organizational infrastructure deliberately focused in support of innovation.

While these structures and systems are carefully managed and monitored, no one expects formal systems alone to do it. Above all, innovation is expected and anticipated, as part of "the way you survive in this business." Innovation is a strategic theme running through these firms, a continuous survival requirement – not merely "a nice idea." It is never left to chance. Systems are supported by management style and approach, restructuring and reward systems, culture and communication – all the elements interact, and are deliberately managed to foster innovation.

Beyond These Firms

Stability and Change

The semiconductor firms exist in an on-going tension between change and stability, technical innovation and operating efficiency. Both needs are fully conscious, and the means to satisfy them are conspicuously built into the systems and practices of our sample of successfully innovative firms. These practices and systems, aimed at maintaining a dynamic tension between stability and change, often contrast sharply with the more change-resistant norms of traditional companies in older industries.

In the companies we studied, new products and new manufacturing processes are continuing competitive realities. They force change as a way of life. But pressures for efficient operations, cost control, faster new product and new process cycle time, and higher yields are also imperative. Electronics is a "both/and" business, not "either/or:" both stability and change must be mastered. So it has been for decades, and so it continues today. And as micro-electronics and computers penetrate still further into mature products and factories, offices and processes, this tension will spread to other industries.

There are already signs of these characteristics in older industries, visible even in the popular press. *Fortune* (Saporito, 1987) and *Industry Week* (Thompson, 1987) both laud highly competitive and innovative steel mills – while noting that survival depends on adapting new approaches to quality. Meanwhile, *Iron Age* comments that a worldwide steel surplus widely predicted in October 1987, turned into a shortage by November (McManus, 1987), displaying volatility not considered normal in so mature an industry. In short, the world of industry looks a lot more like electronics than like our vision of "mature industry" even a short time ago.

The lessons of the electronics industry are not just "high-technology" lessons, of interest only to the high-technology businesses. Even the old "widows and orphans" stocks of the past, like AT&T or the steel companies – face urgent demands for change, new technology, and revolutionized management and organization practices. Mature businesses may face even greater vulnerability to change, precisely because they have been stable for so long, and have paid less attention to changes outside their industry that promise to radically shift their very context.

Certainly, businesses and firms other than those we survey have successfully innovated. The management practices we outline can be found in other organizations. We believe the demands of rapid, effective change amidst spiraling requirements for technical excellence, quality, and productivity are most clearly outlined in the experience of the electronics and semiconductor firms, but are by no means limited to them. The lessons are especially à propos because our sample firms are large, well established businesses, yet they continue to manage change successfully. High-technology businesses can learn from the electronics firms' successes – and so can astute mature businesses.

Testing This Work

Internal consistency is the first test of this research. Two other tests can be specified. One is to ask whether this analysis helps to make sense of innovation. Does it help to explain how these firms innovate, consistent with what we know of organizations? This is the theoreticians' test, yet our readers, practitioners and theoreticians alike, must apply it. We believe the book will help its readers to make sense of these companies' unique approaches to innovation.

The third test addresses practitioners more directly. It will be applied in two settings. One evaluation will come from the managers who generously contributed their time and thought. They will assess whether the perspectives generated here assist them in describing and understanding the processes they live with, and perhaps improving on them. Finally, managers outside the electronics industry can test these insights against their own current experience. If they help make better sense of what many presently describe as "chaos" from the perspective of their old assumptions, our work will be vindicated. We want to make sense of the successes (and failures) of innovation. If this work passes these tests, we will count it a success.

A Map of the Book

Our account begins in chapter 2 with a summary of electronics industry conditions. These conditions, so changed from the competitive environment facing US industry in the past, help to explain why US industry in general is experiencing such difficulty today. Conditions and constraints facing micro-electronics industry participants are outlined, with special attention to experiences we believe relevant for many industries beyond those represented here. These conditions are interesting in themselves, but they are far more important as forecasters pointing toward what appears to be the future for many mature industries, as computers and micro-electronics continue to spread into many, many other industries.

The basic technology of semiconductors, the heart of the electronics revolution, are briefly described in non-technical terms. The awesome complexity of electronics manufacturing processes is a central feature of the industry. But such complexity is not visible only in electronics. The increasing science base and technological changes in manufacturing, materials, and factory control in almost every business all promise that complexity, too, will become more common in mature industries. Under pressure from foreign competitors, many US manufacturers are paying much more attention to production complexity, and to how it affects (and is affected by) product design. Elsewhere, CAD systems are improving product quality by minding the details. Indeed, it is easier to think of examples of electronics applications in businesses than to think of exceptions to the trend. As electronic methods and products become more widely applied, we can anticipate continued increases in manufacturing complexity and, in service businesses, operations complexity.

Chapter 3 prepares the ground for the chapters that follow by describing how two very different electronics firms, Texas Instruments and Motorola, managed innovation. One firm seemed to emphasize an exhaustive, systematic approach, while the other firm appeared almost "chaotic" in its lack of systems at the division level. The special perspective offered by managers who moved from one firm to the other underlines common elements and key differences in the firms' approach to innovation.

Similarities and differences among the firms, and in the elements of their strategies of change, are visible in the first instance to the external observer in the account of their past actions, successes and failures. Chapter 4 describes externally visible elements of the electronics firms' strategies of change. While there are no "simple answers," the complex answers are comprehensible and useful. Innovation can be managed, and a good bit is known about the strategies firms employ to do so.

To understand innovation management, however, we must go "inside" the firms, to the pattern of practices and attitudes and commitments that people live with on a day-to-day basis. Here, the importance of innovation sources enters our story. Chapter 5 addresses the source of innovation in these firms: it is, in one sense, "from everywhere." Nevertheless, there are some positions that exert special influence and are particularly important in sparking innovation.

Continuing our "inside" story, chapter 6 looks at the implementation of informal management. A central paradox is visible in chapter 7, which describes how formal strategic systems produce adaptable strategies. Chapter 8 outlines the role of organizational structure in guiding strategic implementation and ensuring control on the one hand, and flexibility on the other.

Chapter 9 traces the cycle of innovation, the path an idea follows from its individual originator to its ultimate fate in the marketplace. Along the route, a whole panoply of resources, talents, funds, commitments, and investments – in time, dollars, effort, attention, and other foregone opportunity – must be mustered. This complex process shows high-technology managers engaged in the innovation process.

Chapter 10 addresses the "manufacturing end-game," the follow-on in stability, improvement, and persistent achievement that tells the tale after the glamour and excitement of initial innovation. The sample firms' growing commitment to success in the end-game may be one of the most important findings of our book: innovation must be followed up, if its potential is to be realized. Like our other results, these distinctively distinguish the practice of successful micro-electronics-based firms from that of traditional companies. This challenge is in some ways the most formidable. It involves translating innovation into a way of life in business, rather than simply a stream of products.

Chapter 11 turns to organizational culture, a persistent theme through our account. Strong culture is at once essential and potentially very costly, both to individuals and to the organization. This chapter describes the potential hazards of strong culture, and suggests both the costs of managing it, and potential remedies.

Chapter 12 contains our conclusions and the implications of this research for managers. We believe that the patterns of innovation outlined here have much to offer managers in a wide array of industries. We can learn much from the successes of these extraordinary firms. Equally, the difficulties that the high-technology firms have experienced offer valuable insights. What matters is not "Who is excellent now?", but "What can we learn from these firms?"

Electronics-based firms are exciting and diverse. They are the masters of change and innovative practices. They manage in non-traditional ways. Yet despite vast differences in culture among the firms, abiding similarities stand out. Let us turn now to the firms themselves.

2

Old Ways, New Days

If you don't know you're in a war, you're very apt to lose it.
                                        Wilf Corrigan, LSI Logic

NEC [Nippon Electric Corporation] is Motorola's number one
competitor, with $4 billion in sales. Over [1976–82] they grew
at 25% compounded, and $1\frac{1}{2}$% margin on sales. Motorola couldn't
do that, because we couldn't finance the growth on less than
6–7% profit, in the U.S. markets.
                                        John Welty, Motorola

Why the Old Ways Don't Work

For every complex problem, there is a simple, attractive answer –
which happens also to be wrong. Many of the simple diagnoses
offered to explain what has gone wrong with US competitiveness
have a certain plausibility. It is said that US managers have become
complacent; that US workers have lost the commitment to quality so
characteristic of the past. Other plausible explanations are that US
industry has systematically under-invested in plant and equipment in
comparison with its trading partners; and that US manufacturing has
been treated with contempt and lack of interest, as "a problem already
solved" and thus has been ignored for far too long. Yet others suggest
that the US suffers from a glut of MBAs, fixated on short-term
quarterly returns, overly rigid and unduly hierarchical in their
thinking, as well as ignorant of the technical realities of the businesses
they seek to run. Others still point to differential tariff and trade
practices, protected markets and subsidies that deny US manufacturers

Table 2.1   US R&D expenditures as a percentage of sales by industry, 1960–1982

	Average 1960–79	Average 1980–2	Difference
Total Manufacturing	4.23	3.10	−1.13
Food and products	0.43	0.40	−0.03
Paper and products	0.87	1.03	0.17
Chemicals	4.43	3.50	−0.93
Petroleum products	0.90	0.70	−0.20
Primary metals	0.77	0.60	−0.17
Fabricated metals	1.30	1.17	−0.13
Nonelectrical machinery	4.03	5.23	1.20
Electrical machinery	8.73	6.40	−2.33
Instruments	5.60	6.10	0.50
	1977–9[a]		
Semiconductors	5.76	7.20	1.44

[a] Prior to 1977, semiconductors were not separately identified in many listings; "electrical equipment and communications" was the category most frequently used.

Source: Adapted from: Eckstein et al. (1984), p. 67 and the *Business Week* R&D Scoreboard (for some data after 1977).

"a level playing field" and give competitors an unfair advantage. And others blame vastly lower wages in other countries, or burdensome US government regulations, or rigid American union work rules (see, for example, Buffa, 1984; Hayes and Wheelwright, 1984; Lawrence and Dyer, 1983; Prestowitz, 1988; Skinner, 1985; Thurow, 1985).

None of these explanations is really quite sufficient. Although each enjoys partial validity, each fails to account for other important facts. In specific instances, for specific industries or firms, evidence exists to support these claims. It is hard to deny the impact of direct labor wages one tenth of those in the US in some of the newly industrializing countries, for instance. American union work rules that insist upon separate job categories for dozens, or even hundreds, of tasks do inflate headcounts and inhibit practical changes in working procedures in industries unaccustomed to innovation and technical change.

Each of the simple explanations is an attractive candidate, too, because each apportions blame, often to some comfortably vague and distant "they." Like bureaucratic rules that encourage finding culprits, the explanations excite finger-pointing, while distracting attention from the problems to be solved. Each of the summary statements seized upon as "the" problem encourages us to ignore the difficult qualifications and complexities that must be understood if we are to act effectively. Interactions among factors may be far more important than single facts, and sifting through the data is difficult. Until recently, for instance, higher US labor costs were balanced by higher productivity, so "high labor costs" was not so powerful an explanation as it seemed at first sight.

Perhaps more important still, some of the "easy" explanations don't square with past facts. In the face of undeniable and sustained US manufacturing successes during the past century, and especially the last 40 years, blaming managers seems both inappropriate and unlikely to convince. How could they so suddenly have metamorphosed into incompetents? It is understandably difficult to persuade managers with a lifetime of success behind them that they are somehow the problem.

A survey of what has changed offers a more productive starting point. Key conditions have shifted – and the large-volume, stability-oriented, scale-economy practices and organizations of the past cannot cope well with the new conditions, for the older approaches to management fail to accommodate the dynamic shifts of contemporary competition. A closer look at the semiconductor experience will illuminate the situation.

The Challenges of a World-Class Industry

Electronics industries are nimble, science-based, and formidably complex. Firms exist only so long as they persist in innovating, adapting to constant change, and somehow balancing all the elements acceptably. Somewhat in contrast to other industries, semiconductors and micro-electronics have historically done "all the right things" for success. In contrast to the "one best way" approach so common elsewhere, electronics-based industries have thrived on change. They have persistently invested in R&D, when other US industries have not; and they have turned out a constant stream of new products and the processes to make them. (See table 2.1 for dramatic data on R&D investments as a percentage of sales in electronics, in contrast to more traditional manufacturing industries.) If technological obsolescence and lagging managerial attention seemed to characterize automobiles, steel, textiles, shoes, and machine tools, the electronics industry seemed to offer a different story, emphasizing innovation and continued technical improvement, not stagnation and defeat.

Yet though electronics firms continue to innovate despite their size and complexity, to do so has not been painless. A look at the industry's current difficulties, however, will illustrate a more subtle point: the merging of the high-change characteristics of electronics with some characteristics of older industries. Mature industries are coming to resemble electronics in their competitive characteristics, and electronics is becoming subject to some mature-industrial forms of competition. Yet the pace of technological change continues. This is a story of "no easy victories," but nevertheless of hope. Above all, the story highlights the need for careful management of innovation.

The consequences of this merger of growth industry and mature industry characteristics are important, both for the high-technology firms and for those in older industries. Because the new demands facing mature businesses are quite different from those of the past, experience in mature industry may seriously mislead managers now facing "electronic" competition. Understanding the new demands is crucial to mastering them, and the history of competition in micro-electronics offers a guide. Conversely, a comparison of electronics with traditional industry experience offers some important guides for understanding the nature of the challenge facing electronics managers today. For them, too, simple extrapolation of past experience can mislead.

We will turn first to the electronics success story, looking at industry results. Next, we will briefly examine some important electronics industry management patterns. These patterns are the main focus of this book, but to be properly understood, they must be seen in the context of electronics industry results. Finally, we will also note some of the challenges facing these firms. Industrial competence seems to us inseparable from economic security, and electronics competence is at the heart of the new industrial reality. Micro-electronics is so important to the US economy that understanding the threats it faces is at least as important as understanding its successes – the more so as the electronics experience seems to predict competitive conditions for all industries for the future.

The Electronics Story

Depending on your definition, the roots of electronics can be traced back to the turn of the century and Lee DeForest's grid vacuum tubes. But today's technologies spring most directly from the transistor, developed at Bell Laboratories in 1947. The transistor and all modern electronics are based on semiconductor materials – materials which are neither good conductors nor good insulators, but which can do either, depending on the circumstances. Silicon is the most widely used semiconductor material today, although others – such as gallium arsenide – are becoming increasingly important.

In the presence of carefully controlled, minute additions of other materials, semiconductor materials produce exactly designated electrical characteristics. Among other functions, semiconductors can switch, amplify, or rectify electrical current, as "solid-state" devices to be used in place of their much larger and more power-hungry predecessors, receiving tubes or vacuum tubes, mechanical relays, switches, or, in early computers, ferromagnetic cores. These varied functions, among many others, evolved from the transistors first developed at Bell Laboratories.

Because they are small, require very little power, and are highly reliable, semiconductor devices are at the heart of electronics today. And, while the original transistors were small and very low-powered for their time, they are far surpassed in the much smaller, much lower-powered yet more capable devices of today. Integrated circuits and microprocessors are essentially denser and more complex versions of the initial transistors. Today's devices are comprised of entire circuits or even miniature computers on a single minute chip of silicon, or, more recently, gallium arsenide. In general, semiconductor devices continue to become steadily smaller and less hungry for current, while simultaneously becoming cheaper and more powerful.

Semiconductor production has grown more demanding, and more expensive, as the requirements for control, precision, and complexity have grown. Increasingly, advanced scientific and technical training is the rule, rather than the exception. Even production line workers in micro-electronics, computer, or semiconductor firms are often highly-skilled technicians with extensive training to ensure that production processes are, in fact, operated as scientifically designed and intended. Operator knowledge is important, to be sure – but it is now more often scientific, calculated, and data-based, instead of merely happenstance or serendipity.

A related characteristic of the semiconductor industry is the complexity of its technology. Production technology for semiconductor products is easily the most complex process ever adapted to mass production. Production stages can run to weeks and require hundreds of steps, each of which is intricate. Each step is also highly dependent for success on the mastery of sub-micron precision, temperature controls within one or two degrees in a thousand, "clean room" conditions, and the presence or absence of parts-per-million quantities of carefully specified "dopants" in controlled atmospheres. Moreover, each sequential stage is crucial – failures cannot be retooled in a components line, and when something goes wrong at any step, all the previous work is wasted. The product is scrap. Nor do the processes show signs of slowing in the growth of complexity.

Complexity in Using Science

Another facet of semiconductor complexity is the extremely broad spectrum of its underlying knowledge base. Specialists in crystallography, metallurgy, ceramics, physics, chemistry, electronic engineering, mechanical engineering, and other areas all contribute to the semiconductor knowledge base. This, too, is a source of distinction between science-based semiconductor production and design and the less systematic, more empirical knowledge bases of industries in the past.

One reason for the increasing complexity of the semiconductor industry is the vast array of its applications and derivative technologies. Circuits differ, depending on the characteristics desired in them. Some offer speed, some offer extreme sensitivity, others offer resistance to X-rays. Components may have to withstand the stresses of operating in an automobile engine compartment, amidst noise, jolts, dirt, and oil, and at a wide range of temperatures – or in a space station, in zero gravity, high stress from rocket thrust, and temperature differentials of thousands of degrees. In short, the uses of semiconductors also add complexity to both the underlying designs and the manufacturing processes to support them.

Another contributor to complexity is the industry's intense competition. From its very beginnings, the industry has been highly competitive, with competition pushing simultaneously on two fronts, technological advance and price. Because the competition is fierce, the pace of technological change is torrid. New discoveries are quickly channeled into products and manufacturing processes. This high rate of technological innovation affects basic conditions for competition and success in the industry. Armies of ingenious physicists, engineers, designers, and manufacturing specialists conspire in finding ways to push the technology, expanding the envelope of the possible – with increasing complexity as the outcome.

Complexity is expensive. Necessarily, research and development (R&D) expenses are high. Necessarily, too, as the production technology gets more complex, it is increasingly important to capture precise knowledge about process and to ensure its exact replication by means of extensive training and automated processes. Both are expensive. Equipment costs are high, and training is essential to use the complicated, expensive equipment. Even shop floor operators in this industry must be highly trained and uncharacteristically familiar with the science behind their tasks, as well as skilled in debugging new processes and maintaining expensive equipment. Capital intensity is illustrated by the costs of Texas Instruments' two sister plants in Miho, Japan and Richardson, Texas. These plants are equipped with Class 1 clean rooms (containing no more than one particle larger than 0.2 microns per cubic foot of air); they cost $100 million each. The plants also illustrate the sort of control that semiconductor manufacture now requires: a micron is about 1/100 the thickness of a human hair. The result is an increasingly capital intensive industry, staffed by highly trained specialists, and characterized by a quite "scientific" approach to manufacturing.

Learning Curves

These conditions create a central economic dilemma for semiconductor firms. To gain the benefit from the huge capital investments involved, costs must be amortized across a large volume of production. But in electronics-based industries, because of the pace of change and its competitive importance, firms cannot simply produce large volumes of identical products, as their predecessors did in other industries in the past. Change will be essential long before the heavy expenses are recouped on any single product. Instead, the equipment must be capable of manufacturing many components, many products, many different designs. This is "economy of scope" (Goldhar and Jelinek, 1983), rather than the "economy of scale" of the past. The TI plant investment described above is expected to serve for production of three successive "generations" of dynamic random access memories (DRAMs): 256 kilo-bit (256K) devices, 1-million bit (1 Meg) and 4 Meg DRAMs.

More recently, application-specific products (ASICs) have pushed the trend toward variety still farther. ASICs are essentially custom products, and no single user will order enough of any product to cover the heavy investment in production equipment. Thus the equipment must produce a broad range of product designs. This push for economies across a broad scope of designs to attain volume production is the latest version of the industry's practice of "learning curve" pricing: as cumulative volume of production increases, costs decrease, permitting price reductions. Where volume formerly meant volume of a single product, it now means volume across a related product family.

The producer who first moves into volume production can in theory seize market share and create barriers to entry by lowering prices. Because the market leader has greater cumulative volume, that leader's costs will drop faster, permitting profits even though margins may decrease. However, lower prices, justified and feasible for the market share leader, are potentially disastrous for followers who have not yet attained the knowledge that comes with volume production, and who thus cannot lower costs without incurring losses.

Costs for individual devices often fall rapidly: on initial introduction, a particular circuit or memory device can cost hundreds of dollars – only to be offered for sale at a tenth of the price a few months later. Prices for EPROMs (electronically programmable read-only memories), an advanced memory device, fell from $30 to $4 in just eight months during 1981, for example. Leading-edge products had often experienced similar price declines as rivals ramped up production. As one manager commented,

> The experience curve says "You should be willing to forgo profits in the early days to achieve market share, to make it up in the long run." That works unless everybody's read the book. Then there's chaos – even without the Japanese.
>
> John Welty, Motorola

If everyone is making the same device, prices fall – and nobody makes profits, undercutting the financial resources required for investment in the next generation of products. The dangers of standard products and production rigidity are apparent. Where formerly volume accumulated in a single, standard configuration of some device, today more variety and faster changes require firms to accumulate volume and learning across families of related devices. Though high volume production is still important, it is beginning to look very different from the "high volume production" of the past.

"Learning curve" pricing would seem to inhibit innovation, for it lengthens the time-commitment of a firm to a given technology and product conformation. Lower introductory costs mean lower initial premiums. It takes longer to recoup costs and gain an adequate return on investment when products sell at lower prices. Since new technologies or products might render obsolete existing investments, manufacturers might be expected to delay their introduction. Yet the pace of competition is such that no one dares lag far behind in production technology or in product innovation. Such conditions reinforce the heavy spending on R&D, and the pressures for innovation: through extensive R&D, firms may be able to recover from a slow start in one product by moving to launch the next generation more quickly. However, this is both difficult and expensive, counting as it does upon continued state-of-the-art R&D and the ability to move quickly from the lab into the marketplace, perhaps without extensive experience in the previous product or process generation.

For this to happen, development of production capability must be closely linked with marketing strategy and design, among other activities. As we noted previously, innovation in electronics is not just technical virtuosity: rather, it rests upon balanced, linked development across all aspects of the firm.

Electronics-Style Competition

The nature of electronics competition, then, can be summarized:

- exceedingly complex, science-based production processes;
- technological obsolescence, and technical innovation at high rates;
- economies of volume production – but often achieved across a broad product family, on scope, not scale;
- "learning curve" pricing;
- intense, worldwide competition.

The net result of these factors is a highly demanding competitive environment that stresses both the benefits to be attained by stability – such as volume production economies and lower costs – and those to be gained by continuous innovation. It is not enough to attain effective, stable production once. These firms must attain stable production again and again, on new products and the new manufacturing technology required to make them. All of this takes place amidst highly complex manufacturing and product design, with new product applications continually requiring creative new insights.

The impact of the transistor itself seems to have been overshadowed in the public eye by the growth of the industries and companies formed to manufacture and use the devices it has made possible. The computer industry, widespread applications of micro-electronics control technology, and other uses of semiconductors are often labelled "revolutionary," a usage for once not overstated. Space technology, computers, telecommunications, televisions as we know them and a proliferating array of controls, memories, and conveniences, from factory controls to automatic teller machines to jogging shoes that track bone stress – all are electronic, and fundamentally descended from the transistor.

Many of these products would not exist without semiconductors and the advantages in power, cost, and performance they make possible. Electronics provides substitutes for older, more bulky and awkward mechanical methods, so that older functions can now be performed in new ways. Gasoline engine carburetors, electronically controlled for clean combustion of fuel, lessening pollution and increasing power, offer one example. Electronics and semiconductors also permit wholly new and different products and functions feasible only by virtue of the technical advantages of semiconductors, especially their small size, low power requirements and reliability, which permit "computer assisted almost anything." It is possible and even economical to control appliances or factory equipment automatically, to provide instant access banking or telephone service, or hundreds of other products and services, only because of cheap, reliable, available semiconductors.

Semiconductors have shaped our times in other ways as well. Beyond the proliferation of new products lies an approach to business fundamentally different from what went before. Both the companies that produce semiconductors and those in the derivative industries that spring from semiconductors are science-based, highly complex, capital intensive and exceedingly competitive. Semiconductor production is science-based to a degree unimagined in earlier times, when the "state of the art" industries could still be mastered or even radically changed by bootstrap industrialists. We now expect science in "high-technology" industries. But even older industries, driven or encouraged by the data-collection that semiconductors make possible, are becoming much more "scientific," another aspect of the "semiconductor revolution."

In industries as complex as steel or chemicals, until very recently "art" was as good as "science," and sometimes better. The uneducated but observant worker might easily know more about production processes and how to make them work than any engineer. In steelmaking, for instance, it was not long ago that a trained steelmaker's eye judged temperature, knowing from long experience just when the molten metal might be poured, or how much pressure a slab would need, and how many passes through the mills to be reduced safely to strong sheet steel.

These judgments are no longer made by experienced guess. Automatic sensors now read temperatures throughout the furnace and adjust it to maintain proper, economical, and even heat. The mills, too, are automatically adjusted to correct pressure. The proper temperature is a matter of fact and control, not judgment. Product quality, production reliability and economy are vastly improved. Trained specialists, who may have no idea of the difference between this particular shade of cherry red and that, know the numerical temperatures and pressures to roll at, and can count on their machines to maintain them.

Winemaking, revered for centuries as art, is now a carefully studied science. Each step of the process is controlled, from grapes to the bottle. The advent of better-controlled fermentation in refrigerated stainless steel tanks instead of at ambient air temperature (which can vary greatly from season to season, even in California) is widely credited with the spectacular success of California's wines in recent years. In France, adoption of similar methods is deemed "essential" for successful international competition, particularly for smaller vintners without the snob-appeal of long-established labels (Ricklefs, 1986).

Increasingly, businesses long believed mature, like winemaking, steel, or textiles use science, aided and abetted by computers, sensors, automatic data recording and automatic response. Increasingly, then, these businesses too begin to look more "electronic" in their competitive conditions, their survival characteristics, and the challenges their managers face. Like basic electronics producers, these businesses too must cope with vast complexity, increasing amounts of science, and burgeoning capital costs. They must also cope with increasing amounts of change and rapid technological obsolescence, just like semiconductor firms. For these industries, then, the semiconductor firms offer useful insights, for they have had long experience with electronic competition. Their practices highlight difficulties that are increasingly characteristic today.

Micro-electronics is prototypical of industry in the future. Increasing complexity, innovation, and pressure for economical operations formerly almost uniquely characteristic of electronics are now increasingly visible in many older industries as well. Automobiles again offer a ready example: Detroit is expending enormous energy on mastering the details of zero-defect operations, where formerly 10 percent or more was an acceptable defect level. Robots, Computer Aided Design, and laser trimming operations are also widely utilized in automobile manufacture today. GM alone has spent some $66 billion on efforts to update plant and equipment to deal with increasing complexity (some would argue, without nearly sufficient results). In October, 1987, GM Vice Chairman Donald J. Atwood commented,

> We have to recognize that, in this fiercely competitive market, we'd better be there with the most advanced technology in both our products and plants . . . High technology *is* the future of the automotive industry. To be competitive, any automobile manufacturer must incorporate the latest state-of-the-art technology . . .
>
> *High Technology*, Oct. 1987

Almost 18 months later, GM Chairman Roger Smith was also emphasizing the importance of advanced manufacturing technology – while ruefully acknowledging the difficult, complex, important management tasks of reorienting his organization. Investment, research, technology, and equipment are not enough, even when $66 billion is devoted to the effort.

Contemporary innovation, with its attendant complexity, is quite different from innovation in the past, when – in automobiles at least – it was often only skin deep. Then, the underlying technology inhibited change (Abernathy, 1978); now, programmable controls seem to encourage it (Goldhar and Jelinek, 1983). New, also, are the sort of cost pressures that have driven Chrysler to vow to reduce its manufacturing costs by fully one third by the early 1990s. Such competitive factors were undreamed-of even 10 years ago. Yet just such pressures, which are characteristic of electronics-based competition, seem the rule for all industry in the times to come. The pressures so apparent in electronics and long thought limited to the high-technology industries, are increasingly visible in mature industries such as steel or automobiles or machine tools, especially where electronics becomes important in production processes.

Some specific net results will help to illustrate the pace of change in electronics, and the elements of competition we have been describing. The elements of a "competitive environment" may be more visible to industry insiders than to others. In the case of micro-electronics, that competitive environment has driven firms to very specific responses in the service of innovation. Innovation, so visible in electronics-based industry results, has contributed to the industry's aura of success.

The Industry's Results

The outcomes – the delivered results – are perhaps the most effective way of judging an industry's performance over time. Here the electronics story is one of almost unparalleled success, by many different measures. The semiconductor, micro-electronics, and computer industries have poured forth a cornucopia of products that perform a dazzling array of functions. Much that was science fiction, or expensive and badly done for the very rich alone in the days of older controls and technologies, is a matter of routine today, thanks to semiconductor electronics.

At least as important as function *per se* is the price/performance tradeoff. Not only have the functions and product capabilities kept increasing; their price for performing any task has dropped steadily. Almost any example becomes quickly outdated, as the cost for a given capability falls, most typically in the face of fierce price competition and swift adoption of new, more capable designs or devices.

Comparison of price/performance ratios in electronics with almost any other area quickly becomes ludicrous. The orders-of-magnitude performance improvements, and the associated orders-of-magnitude price decreases, are difficult to comprehend both because no single measure seems to capture the change adequately, and because the target keeps moving. In 1978, IBM reported that the cost of performing 100,000 calculations on an IBM computer had declined from $1.26 in 1952 to less than $0.01 in 1976, noting that "If aviation had progressed at the same rate, the 747 would have been developed just six months after Wilbur and Orville Wright's historic flight at Kitty Hawk." Today, the figure is perhaps 100 times less – though it is difficult to calculate. The speed of computer calculation, too, has increased, so that the 2,000 calculations a second of 1952 had increased to more than 2,000,000 in 1976 (IBM Canada, 1978). Comparable figures for today routinely mention "MIPS" (millions of instructions per second) or "gigaflops" (billions of calculations) per second, even for desktop machines. The end is not yet in sight. Computer speeds are regularly cited in nanoseconds (thousand-millionths of a second) – speeds most of us can barely comprehend. Rear Admiral Grace Hopper of the US Navy tried to bring the example closer to home by noting that a nanosecond was 11.8 inches long, and a microsecond 984 feet long, these being the distance light travels during a nanosecond or a microsecond.

Computational improvements are matched by and indeed rooted in, the increasing density and decreasing size of semiconductor components, and the smaller distance electrons travel to perform their tasks. Today, integrated circuits rather routinely contain hundreds of thousands of devices within a single tiny silicon chip. Experimental chips today contain tens of millions of circuit elements. Experts suggest that a billion-device chip is certainly possible with

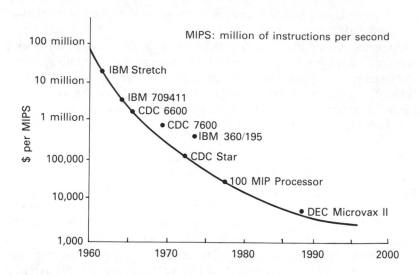

Figure 2.1 Price–Performance Improvements in Electronics
Source: adapted from published data and a curve originally developed
by the Rand Corporation in the 1960s. Prepared by the authors.

technology already in place today or anticipated shortly (Foster, 1986).

A common component, a Random Access Memory (or RAM) is now widely available in 256K bit size, containing 256,000 separate binary memory locations, generally organized as 256K × 1 or 64K × 4 bits. The next generation RAM, containing 1 Meg, or one million bits, is being shipped, while pilot production on a 4 Meg chip has begun at the time of writing – and will undoubtedly be well along by the time this sentence is read. Increases in device density over the 20-year period from about 1960 to 1980 occurred at a rate of about an order of magnitude – a power of 10 – about every five years. The first commercially available microprocessor, Intel's 4004, appeared in 1971, and contained 1600 transistors on a silicon chip of about one quarter centimeter square. As one manager commented,

> If you think back to 1959 or 1960, a "high performance" single transistor cost about twenty dollars. [Today's high performance device] sells for eight dollars and has 155,000 transistors on it –

you have a 310,000-fold reduction in the price of transistors. In fact, the thing also has a whole bunch of resistors and capacitors which we forget about – they come along for free.

Even newer products can see rapid price declines. The average selling price of a 64K RAM was about $30 in early 1981, but by the end of that year the average price had fallen to about $5. At the same time, older 16K RAMs – for which significant demand remained – fell in price from about $5.50 to $1 (Davidson, 1984). Retail prices to casual users are typically higher than those offered to original equipment manufacturers who purchase in volume. Even so, 256K RAMs were advertised in late 1987 for $3.55 each, or a set of nine for $26.00, while 64K RAM chips were offered at $15 for the set of nine. Although prices do occasionally jump, as they did while Japanese electronics devices were under quota restrictions, over the long term prices continue to fall, while performance continues to rise.

A New American Tragedy or Resurgence?

The US electronics industry is still locked in fierce competition with a wide array of adversaries, and the outcome of this struggle is not assured. Yet despite the intense challenge and substantial advantages enjoyed by its opponents, the US electronics industry has so far remained a formidable foe. Unlike many other industries, electronics has continued to develop new technology at a rapid pace. The global semiconductor marketplace has meant that a discovery anywhere in the world has an impact everywhere else very rapidly. Despite a lack of consistent US industrial policy or any systematic tariff structure, or even quotas to restrain competitors (who enjoy significant government support and have readily copied US designs) until very recently, US firms have continued to invest in research and plant, develop and produce new devices, and market new products.

Today, increasingly, the firms are finding that meticulous manufacturing mastery is essential to competitive success, even more so than in the past. The same interconnected global marketplace that rewards innovation also enables a firm with higher production yields to exploit its advantages widely. Innovation matters; but so too does production efficiency. And also important are carefully linked design and manufacturing engineering, and extraordinary research efforts in science, in product design, and in manufacturing processes and applications. The end-game, beyond the opening innovative salvos, has begun to attract much-needed attention.

It is not enough to be good at any single facet of the task, or even to be good at all facets individually. To succeed, the firms must marshal their resources to accomplish swift, efficient innovation again and again. The various facets must be kept in balance, carefully monitored, fostered, and integrated. Innovation in ideas must be matched with implementation in manufacturing and marketing, service and redesign. The firms we studied have resorted to practices emphasizing change, flexibility, and on-going innovation as well as stability. Innovation has been required in management methods and in organizational practices, in attitudes and expectations no less than in factory techniques.

Electronics firms have learned how to innovate, and how to innovate repeatedly. Now, they are learning how to maintain innovation while also fostering stability and control. This lesson is not a simple one to absorb, yet it is crucial to continued success in many businesses. The managerial practices required for both stability and change are discernibly different from the big business bureaucracy of the past, and also from the loose and freewheeling innovation practices well known in small businesses. These managerial and organizational practices are the focus of the remainder of this book.

Appendix
A Closer Look at the Technology

To understand the semiconductor industry, it is helpful to have a working knowledge of its technology. We will now turn to a brief discussion of semiconductor technology, addressing both semiconductor devices themselves and the processes by which they are produced. While this survey is necessarily brief, it should be sufficient to highlight the complexity, variety, and wealth of detailed expertise required for successful semiconductor manufacture.

Semiconductor Materials

These substances, usually crystalline, are neither good conductors nor good insulators, but, in the presence of carefully specified and controlled "impurities" of other materials can reliably produce precisely designated electrical characteristics. Among other functions, semiconductors can switch, amplify, and rectify electrical current. Thus they can be used in place of electron receiving tubes or vacuum tubes, mechanical relays, switches or, in computers, in place of older ferromagnetic cores.

Among their most important contributions is their ability to control electrical current at very low voltages. Thus components can be smaller and lighter, as they need withstand only 6 to 12 volts, typically; less for some devices. Power and heat dissipation requirements therefore decline, permitting savings in space and materials. Carrying these trends further along, componentry can be reduced to the so-called integrated circuit, enabling still greater savings by making possible even smaller circuits and lower voltage requirements.

Each decrease in the size of elements translates into a requirement for improved production control. Chips with sub-micron line widths are in production, requiring precision in the range of a tenth of a micron. The production processes required become very complex; the wave length of the light used to trace circuit line designs becomes an issue, with green or purple lasers offering differences, and some circuits drawn with X-rays for finer control.

As the architecture of circuitry becomes more minute, it decreases the distances that electrons must travel to activate devices, and thus the time they take to operate. An electron will travel 11.8 inches in a nanosecond; a microsecond will translate to 984 feet. Thus circuit design and timing are inextricably intertwined. The smaller the circuit, the faster it works (as well as requiring less material to manufacture, combined with greater production control precision). Smaller size also promises still lower power requirements (now down to 3.3 volts for some DRAM devices).

Ultimately, lessened power requirements permit operation of very complex miniaturized equipment with minimal power requirements. Battery-powered portable computers offer a ready example. Low power requirements and small size also make possible electronic wrist watches, sensors, and a vast array of other scientific, industrial, medical, and consumer products. These developments are at the heart of the electronics revolution of our times, and they rest firmly on semiconductors.

To attain precise electrical control, precisely determined electrical characteristics are required in the semiconductor material. These, in turn, are attained only by the most painstaking and minute control of elaborate production processes, based on thoroughgoing knowledge of the underlying characteristics of the materials employed. Commonly used semiconductor materials are relatively well understood, after much research effort drawing on fields as diverse as physics and electrical engineering, chemistry, metallurgy, and ceramics, among others. Newer materials that promise better operating characteristics, such as gallium arsenide (GaAs), are less well understood, either from the product design or the manufacturing process perspective.

While there are a large number of semiconductor materials, silicon is undoubtedly the most important. Silicon is widely available and therefore relatively cheap, it is well understood, and silicon devices operate reliably at higher temperatures than earlier germanium devices (giving them a desirable stability). Another important characteristic of silicon is its property of forming a tenacious, electrically insulating oxide (SiO_2, a form of glass) when exposed to oxygen. Once covered with the silicon dioxide layer, the underlying silicon is protected from external contamination.

These properties of silicon and silicon dioxide have had a tremendous impact on the manufacture of silicon semiconductors, and provide the basis of the most widely used production processes. As silicon is also for these reasons the most common semiconductor in use today, a closer look at silicon semiconductor technology will be useful here. Our focus will be on the planar process for manufacture of integrated circuits, the most widely used semiconductor manufacturing process.

Integrated circuits are essentially carefully specified regions of positive or negative or neutral electrical characteristics, precisely arranged so as to constitute an electrical device. Most typically, for our purposes, such a circuit is based upon a silicon surface. Electrical characteristics are attained by the minutely controlled introduction of "impurities" or dopants as delineated regions in extremely pure silicon. It is important to note that dopants are "impurities" only in the sense of being different from the silicon base; there is nothing fortuitous or uncontrolled involved.

Both silicon and dopants, and indeed all chemicals used in the various production processes, are themselves of extremely high purity to ensure that the desired electrical characteristics, and no others, are achieved. Impurity levels of one part per billion or less are routinely required in semiconductor silicon, in the aluminum and gold used for connections, and in the various chemicals used to clean, etch, or otherwise process semiconductors. Such purity was attainable only under laboratory conditions and at high prices only a few years ago; today, it is routinely attainable in tonnage quantities, off the shelf, from a large number of suppliers.

Typically, semiconductor manufacture starts with extremely high purity silicon (99.9 percent pure) in the form of long, slender bars. For semiconductor use, however, the silicon must be reconstituted as a single, continuous crystal. One end of the silicon bar is melted, and a seed crystal of silicon is introduced. Under carefully controlled temperature and atmospheric conditions, the liquid silicon will coalesce onto the seed crystal, continuing its crystalline structure without the intercrystalline boundaries characteristic of naturally occurring polycrystalline silicon. The atmosphere surrounding the process must be free of oxygen; depending on the process used, the atmosphere may be inert, or may contain a carefully controlled concentration of a desired dopant. Another method of introducing dopants utilizes neutron irradiation to induce transmutation of randomly distributed atoms of the highly purified, single-crystal silicon into phosphorus. This method achieves a more uniform dopant distribution, and thus more predictable and precisely controllable electrical characteristics (most particularly, resistivity).

The single-crystal silicon rods are ground to size – typically 10–20 cm in diameter – and sawed into thin slices or wafers, on the order of 0.25 to 0.8 mm thick. Wafers are etched and lapped on both sides, to remove damage to surface layers caused by sawing, and one side is polished to a mirror finish. Here, and at repeated stages in later operations, the wafers must be cleaned to remove grease, dust from mechanical operations, and any contaminants. This cleaning typically involves solvent degreasing, detergent cleaning, ultrasonic agitation, chemical and other processes. Throughout, the chemicals used here must be as pure as the chemical raw materials of the silicon and dopants.

The polished, cleaned wafer is now ready for further processing. Any of a number of steps can be employed in a variety of sequences to create the desired final device. While no device will necessarily require all of the steps, brief descriptions of a number of common steps will facilitate understanding of the production processes and their complexity.

Semiconductor Processing

Epitaxy With the single-crystal silicon as a substrate, a fresh layer of silicon can be "grown" to provide the specific, precisely tailored electrical characteristics desired. This is done by epitaxy, a process that grows a continuation of the substrate crystalline structure on the polished surface of the wafer. The wafer is introduced into a furnace containing both a silicon compound and any desired dopant of the required characteristics. Both compounds decompose on to the wafer's surface to continue the substrate crystal with the doped characteristics and without intercrystalline boundaries. Epitaxy is a useful means of employing a general-purpose wafer substrate as the basis for a multitude of tailored silicon layers. These layers are the locus of the semiconductor device, produced in subsequent steps. The unique advantage of the process is its ability to produce very thin regions of controlled purity.

Photolithography This is the principal method of producing circuitry on silicon. First, the wafer is exposed to an oxygen atmosphere to create a layer of the insulator silicon dioxide on its surface. Oxidation takes place in a controlled atmosphere containing oxygen at a carefully maintained temperature (usually between 900 and 1200 degrees Celsius). The same precise controls and painstaking accuracy as involved in other processes are visible here: half-degree precision at 1000 degrees is the norm.

A mask or master pattern is prepared on a glass plate. The pattern itself is first drawn at 100 to 200 times its final size, checked and rechecked, and finally reduced to final size using special cameras. Today, the lines of the final patterns are fairly routinely one micron (one hundredth the diameter of a human hair) or less in width. Several manufacturers are reported to be manufacturing circuits with line widths of less than half a micron. A typical circuit may contain many thousands of lines of this size. Absolute accuracy is essential, as any errors will be reproduced on the silicon as flaws in the resist, and thus in the pattern of the device. (Texas Instruments' new factories go so far as to isolate the production floor from the remainder of the building, rooting the surface to bedrock so that the amount of vibration is less than 0.01 microns.) The final master pattern is reproduced many times in a single mask, using step-and-repeat cameras, in order to mass produce copies of the pattern on wafers of silicon.

Next, the wafer is spread with a photosensitive material (called photoresist), which is dried and then exposed to ultraviolet light through the mask. The pattern is developed, and unexposed areas of resist removed. The silicon dioxide in unexposed areas of the wafer is then chemically etched away, and the remaining resist removed. What remains is a carefully defined pattern of insulating silicon dioxide and clear, single-crystal silicon areas. The insulated areas are protected; the uninsulated areas can be further processed, most typically by diffusion or ion implantation processes. The basic processes of resist, mask exposure, development, etching, and diffusion or ion implantation are typically repeated to obtain the final desired device. Needless to say, in any subsequent step, the masks for desired patterns must be perfectly aligned with earlier patterns.

Diffusion The patterned wafer can now be diffused with a dopant. This requires it to be introduced into a carefully controlled atmosphere at the appropriate temperature. The dopant will diffuse into the unprotected areas of the wafer in a predictable fashion, with the diffusion concentration determined by the atmospheric concentration of the dopant, and the diffusion depth determined by exposure time, both of which must be precisely controlled. The same impurities or dopants will be much slower to diffuse into silicon dioxide, so oxide-covered areas of the wafer are protected against diffusion. Moreover, since some diffusion will also occur sideways under the oxide layer, the edges of the junction area of diffused dopant with the silicon substrate are protected by the oxide, providing for high reliability.

Ion Implantation Dopants can also be introduced by directing a high energy stream of dopant atoms at the wafers in a vacuum. Both the number of atoms introduced and their depth of penetration can be carefully controlled.

Metalization Since silicon is not a good conductor, some other material must be used to electrically connect the semiconductor device to other components, or, in the case of integrated circuits, to connect various portions of the circuit to one another. The usual means of connection is metal. Aluminum and gold, which are easily available in the required purity, are the metals most commonly used. Typically, a thin layer of metal is evaporated on to the surface of the wafer in a vacuum. Unneeded portions of the metal film are etched away, leaving behind the pattern of metal required to establish the desired connections. Pure aluminum is subject to deterioration in reaction to electricity passing through it, so it is often supplemented with small amounts of copper. The metal pattern can also be used to isolate areas to be implanted with ions, since the metal will absorb the impinging ions.

Layering Repeated layers of silicon dioxide, metal, silicon, and various dopants can be constructed one atop another in an elaborate sandwich to create the memory chips, devices, and circuits desired.

Mechanical Protection Often a final step in the process is to add a layer of deposited glass or quartz, with appropriate openings for leads to connect the device to the outside world. This layer provides mechanical protection of the semiconductor surface.

Testing Every wafer is electrically tested. Each circuit or device can be automatically tested and any defective circuits discarded before further processing. Testing equipment containing an array of carefully positioned needle-like probes can make electrical connection with each device on the wafer. Typically, defective devices are identified by a dot of ink, so that they can easily be set aside after the wafer is separated into dice.

Scribing and Dicing The processes we have been describing all take place across the entire surface of a wafer, containing 100 or more chips, each an individual device or circuit. Once the layering, protection, and testing processes are complete, the wafer is scribed (either mechanically, with a diamond-pointed tool, or by a laser beam) and then broken apart into its individual components, known as chips, dice or pellets, which are identical copies of the master pattern. Defective chips are discarded, to avoid further handling in the labor-intensive processes of assembly.

Assembly Individual chips are next assembled into packages. Chips that have passed the electrical test are mounted on a header or lead frame, and very thin wires (approximately 1 mil – one thousandth of an inch – in diameter) are used to make connection between the device bonding pads and the frame or header. A gold wire can be melted on one end to form a ball. When pressed against the aluminum contact pad on the chip at an appropriate temperature (300 degrees Celsius) or against other metal contact points, the ball will form a permanent bond. Another method is to bond aluminum wire ultrasonically. After the wires are placed, the package is hermetically sealed and tested again.

Other Techniques The common production processes described here are widely known and used. One advanced technique for manufacturing DRAMs involves etching minute holes in the surface of the silicon layer to utilize the hole's side walls as insulators, while the hole itself is filled with an electrically conducting material. The retrieval time for stored information on such a device is only 65 nanoseconds. The device requires only 3.3 volts of power, in comparison with the 5 volts required by earlier memory chips. Further techniques exist for creating a range of elaborate miniaturized features on silicon or other materials.

Packaging As circuitry becomes denser, it becomes increasingly difficult to connect the circuits to the outside world. Older DIP (dual in-line pin) packages carried an array of protruding metal legs to be inserted into connection sockets to create the connections. While convenient, this package limited the number of potential connection leads that could be fitted to a package, and the potential speed of the circuit. Connection advances are now seen as a significant requirement for improving performance, since complex chips cannot function until they are connected to the outside world.

Surface mount techniques allow unpackaged devices to be mounted directly on a silicon wafer with a wiring pattern on its surface, replacing a conventional circuit board. This provides more potential connections, and also enables chips made from different materials to be positioned on the same wafer. Essentially, such developments are further elaborations of the miniaturization techniques that began with transistors. Such devices now routinely contain on a single chip more than the equivalent of entire computers from earlier times. There is no significant sign that such increases in complexity will slow down in the foreseeable future.

Design and Production Costs

The assembly and testing operations typically require human intervention and high skill, and are, therefore, highly expensive. Here, as elsewhere in the design and manufacturing process, much effort is devoted to lessening costs and increasing reliability by automation. Of the two reasons for automation, production reliability is the most important. Such reliability typically carries with it increased capacity to produce ever more complex circuits.

CAD (Computer Aided Design) is routinely used to design integrated circuits and memories. The complexity of current-state circuits is already so high that unaided human design is no longer feasible; it would take too long, and would be too unreliable. Instead, circuits are designed with computer assistance, and often tested and debugged electronically, using simulation capabilities, long before any commitment is made to production. Such CAD and Computer Aided Engineering (CAE) capabilities create a large demand for advanced computation equipment, complex software, and engineers trained to use it.

3

Patterns of Stability and Change

. . . A lot of bright, innovative people were all fired up to go do these things. But they never could quite seem to get themselves collectively organized well enough to make it happen.

I can't think of a single one of the [many required specialty] disciplines where we were just so inept that if somebody came in to straighten out that piece, then everything would have been OK. It was a matter of the combination not functioning as a larger team.

Everybody had to know that everybody else was going to do their part. [Before,] nobody ever trusted anybody else to do their part. Then, all of a sudden . . . all that discipline that Al [Stein] instilled, and the commitment and follow through and everything else – all of a sudden everybody started to believe that not only were they going to do their part, but everybody else was going to do theirs, too.

Anonymous Motorola Manager

New ideas are very delicate creatures and they are very easy to kill. I think one thing that's helped us is that the people running Intel really are R&D people by background. We have been on the other side of that long enough that we've seen some things that didn't work along the way. Just by our inclination and backgrounds, we are fairly receptive to new ideas. But even at a place like Intel, it was much easier when we were smaller to get new things done and out than it is now. We succeeded in putting in enough bureaucracy and red tape to stifle a good number of new ideas, I suspect.

Gordon Moore, Intel

The Innovation Dilemma

Managing innovation, especially in high-technology contexts, poses a dilemma. Organizations traditionally have been designed for stability and permanence; but high-technology companies must repeatedly and rapidly change. At the same time, although the firms we studied must stress innovation, they also require great precision and predictability to enable them to master complex design and production details. The implications of this dilemma must be worked out, in management style and systems, human interactions and organization structure, planning and control, and performance assessment. This chapter is about that dilemma, and about how our high-technology firms have addressed it.

The dilemma of stability versus change is repeatedly exacerbated by volatility in prices, market demand, and technology. Despite repeated suggestions that the electronics industry is "maturing," volatility remains a persistent problem. During 1984, the industry experienced a boom, with companies unable to keep up with demand. In 1985 and 1986, as capacity expansions undertaken earlier came on-line, the industry experienced worldwide overcapacity. Simultaneously, a general business downturn made that much more customer inventory superfluous. Prices fell precipitously, much as they had in the 1960s, in a similar situation, but even further and more swiftly. For some products, prices fell over 90 percent during the course of 9 to 12 months.

Today's competitive situations require a more sophisticated, less dichotomous approach to stability and change than in the past. This chapter focuses on a dynamic tension between change and practical stability maintained in the firms we studied. Semiconductor industry conditions underline this apparent paradox, for manufacturing processes are extraordinarily complex and sensitive (see appendix to chapter 2). Rigorous control and mastery of detail in manufacturing seem to demand stability. At the same time, global competition demands repeated innovation in markets, products, and processes, ensuring a constant stream of changes.

Successful innovation can translate into worldwide competitive advantage. Conversely, mere survival requires keeping up to global standards. Indeed, technology and competition conspire to create an exceedingly challenging environment. Managing in such a contemporary environment is quite different from managing in older, more predictable environments, where technology is less dynamic.

To keep up with the necessary pace of change, the firms we studied call upon extraordinary technological talent and creativity, which they must constantly update. Low-level newcomers must be granted substantial freedom to direct their own efforts, if they are to create successfully. Yet because so many divergent specialists must be co-ordinated, the freedom of the specialists must lead back to controlled effort. Freedom and control must be balanced, in a trade-off between "new and better ideas" and "what we originally planned." Unlike the traditional organizations of mature industries in the past, the firms we studied cannot choose the comfortably rational option of "plan your work, and work your plan." They cannot choose only innovation, either. Instead, they must both innovate and control, achieving both stability and repeated, often unpredictable change – and stability yet again, followed by still more change.

Complexity also means that the work of numerous specialists, each expert in a fraction of the needed knowledge, must be recombined and co-ordinated. This is not a problem unique to semiconductor firms, of course. Decades ago, Elting Morison spoke of this increasing specialization, and the interdependency among specialists as characteristic of modern industrial development (Morison, 1966). The trend has accelerated considerably in the semiconductor industry since that time, and shows no sign of slowing. The companies in our sample are large in part because they must be, to marshal the resources required. Even the smaller firms among them are "large" by most measures, and complex. High-technology innovation demands not only innovative product design, but also complex process design, and consummate skill in manufacturing, marketing, customer service, and product support.

Competitive pressures heighten these tensions, as we have noted. Global competitive standards are, quite simply, increasingly rigorous. More and better competitors have access to the published research of universities and laboratories, and to the talents of researchers – who are often trained at the same universities. Competitors around the world have access to the technology, standard production equipment, and a worldwide scientific community in which they, too, increasingly participate. Thus world-class standards are real. Intel, for example, already renowned as an effective innovator, doubled manufacturing productivity during 1984–6, and planned to double it again within three years. As one Intel manager put it, "There are two kinds of factories: those that are competitive and those that are closed." Such hard-nosed emphasis on cost and efficiency have not been typical from innovation leaders in the past, but it is increasingly common in the leaders of the electronics and electronics-based industries.

These conflicting demands must be ultimately reflected and resolved in management practices that maintain both control and innovation. The conflict can be summarized as an on-going tension between stability and change. Technological complexity requires systematic approaches. Without order, and very carefully controlled and specified order at that, it is simply not possible to manufacture devices with sub-micron architecture: there is little room for creativity or freedom from the constraint of prior plans within such dimensions. Nevertheless, these organizations must pour forth a stream of new products, and accommodate a stream of new processes as the technology continues to evolve.

With success, each of the companies in our study grew, and all have faced the danger of "creeping bureaucracy" as their size and complexity escalated. The need to co-ordinate the efforts of thousands of scientists, technicians, and workers suggests the need for firm boundaries, reliable arrangements, and stability. Their dilemma can again be restated in more general terms: how can large organizations provide systematic support and stability without suffocating innovation? How can they innovate without losing control? The need for innovation continually opposes the appeal of stability to the necessity of change. How can people gain the benefits of systems guidance without inhibiting innovation, which by definition means "something new" that upsets established procedures, products, and arrangements?

It is startling just how enduring some semiconductor industry characteristics are. In the discussion that follows, comments that date back well over a decade still clearly ring true – and are frequently reinforced by later comments. Perhaps more startling still is the relevance of semiconductor industry characteristics to contemporary conditions in an ever wider array of industries. The volatility, competitive pressures, and increasing pace of technological change so visible in semiconductors has become increasingly apparent in other industries, as they, too, dance to the pace of electronic change.

To explore these factors in depth, we will look at the dilemmas of control and creativity inside our firms. A contrasting "Tale of Two

Companies" illustrates alternative approaches, and thereby illuminates the problem.

A Tale of Two Companies: Texas Instruments and Motorola

Texas Instruments (TI) and Motorola are long-standing adversaries in the semiconductor business. Both are large (over $6 billion in sales with about 80,000 employees worldwide). Motorola's 1986 sales were $5.88 billion produced by 94,400 employees worldwide; by 1988, sales were about $8.2 billion. TI's 1986 sales were $5.6 billion, with 77,270 employees, and sales of about $6.3 billion projected for 1988 – growth in the range of 12 percent. Both have been successful over the years, and both have suffered reverses from time to time. In so volatile an industry, where prices can decline by 90 percent and volume increase by almost as much in a matter of months, nobody "lives happily ever after."

Both firms are diversified, although TI is more heavily dependent on semiconductor electronics components and computers, while Motorola's other main endeavors center on communications. Both firms compete in the global semiconductor market, and both must respond to its demands for simultaneous stability and change. Their arrangements – in systems, structure, style, and strategy – continue to evolve over time. While both do respond, their methods differ, and these differing responses to common problems illustrate some options in addressing the necessary tension between stability and change to manage innovation in this highly demanding environment.

Texas Instruments: A Highly Structured Approach

Texas Instruments, long the largest US merchant semiconductor manufacturer in the world and the industry leader, is widely famed as an innovative company. TI's initial success was in seismic oil exploration in the 1930s and 1940s, as Geophysical Services, Inc., the predecessor firm – a business TI finally sold in 1988. TI also successfully introduced large-scale commercial production of both reliable higher frequency germanium transistors in the mid-1950s, followed quickly by the higher performance silicon transistor. A TI researcher, Jack Kilby, is credited as simultaneous co-inventor of the integrated circuit with Robert Noyce of Intel. (Kilby conceived and demonstrated the integrated circuit in 1958; Noyce independently came up with the idea of a planar transistor, plus a method of interconnecting the layers of its elements.)

Many other original products, numerous technical advances and widely heralded manufacturing expertise all testify to the company's continuing strengths. Today, for example, TI is a recognized leader both in chip production and in artificial intelligence systems. A TI plant in Miho, Japan, not a joint venture, won the Demming Prize for manufacturing quality in 1985. In early 1988, TI was the last remaining major US supplier of DRAMs, successfully competing against much larger Japanese firms which, unlike TI, enjoyed substantial government support, as well as carefully protected home markets.

TI's structured approach to managing innovation is embodied in its famed OST system (see Jelinek, 1979 for a detailed discussion of the OST). The initials stand for Objectives, Strategies, and Tactics, the elements of a hierarchy of goals TI uses for structuring innovation. The longest-term Objectives describe major strategic thrusts for the company as a whole. Strategies are subsidiary strategic goals of a somewhat more limited scope (in markets, products, or processes) and time horizon. Objectives require the sustaining intermediate Strategies for their realization. In their turn, the Strategies are achieved by means of shorter-focus Tactics, which carry specific commitments of resources, immediate action time-tables, and explicit assignments of responsibility to named persons for concrete, immediate activities. When accomplished, the Tactics sum to the Strategies, which in turn lead ultimately to the farther term Objectives (see figure 3.1).

The OST: Focusing on the Future One key problem is how to plan for the future, encouraging innovation, while managing the present, which demands efficiency. As initially envisioned, TI's OST was intended to focus attention on the more important but less urgent activities that ensure an organization's future – long-term planning, new product development, and major new strategic thrusts. Patrick Haggerty, long-time head of Texas Instruments and the original

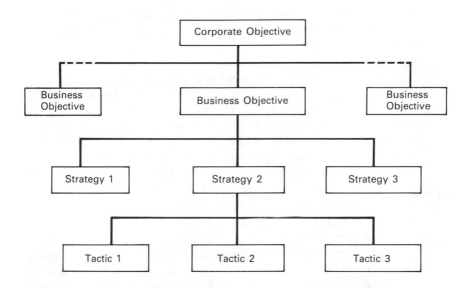

Figure 3.1 The OST's Hierarchy of Goals
Source: Texas Instruments Inc.

instigator of the OST, perceived early on that the intensity of the semiconductor business, even more than many older industries, would tend to drive out forward thinking and planning. As he put it in recounting his early reasoning, "The danger was that the urgent would drive out the important, and we would become victims of our own success."

Haggerty insisted on a systematic approach to activities that were, in the context of present business needs, discretionary, yet which were nevertheless essential over the long term. This need for systematic methods for innovation became clearly apparent to Haggerty and his associates, as TI successfully handled the difficulties of current business but seemed to falter in larger perspectives. From the early 1950s, TI prospered, grew, and became more complex, and successfully organized itself around close links between customers and products embodied in the basic organizational unit, called the Product–Customer Centers or PCC. Each PCC was intended to contain the fundamental elements of a fairly autonomous, stand-alone business: design capabilities, manufacturing capacity, and marketing. With a burgeoning product line and good market acceptance, TI's tight focus on "today's business" was essential to maintain management attention to and control over day-to-day activities of the business. However, it had limits.

The PCCs allowed managers to focus their attention narrowly on their particular products and markets, pushing essential decision making for a given product and market well down into the organization, in close proximity to the business basics of product creation, manufacture, marketing, and customer contact. A sophisticated and inclusive management information system provided precise performance data on a product-by-product basis to the PCC managers and their superiors. Since PCC managers had both resources and performance feedback along with decision responsibility, they could legitimately be held responsible for their unit's success or failure.

The PCC system – both in its structured arrangement of responsibility around an identified product–customer match, and in the associated information feedback on business results – was a carefully articulated, systematic response to the need for orderly management of current businesses. It allocated responsibility and provided budget, highlighted targets and funnelled performance data where they were needed for managing the discrete elements of TI's growing business activities. Despite these necessary strengths, however, the PCCs did not ensure effective response to change.

In a growth market, with strong demand for existing products, the PCCs' current business focus seemed quite appropriate. It certainly succeeded: by 1960, TI had attained the goal Haggerty set in 1949 of becoming "a good, big company." However, in 1960–1, growth hit a plateau just as recession struck. Prices plunged, despite continued shipments: the industry shipped twice as many *units* in 1962 as in 1960 – but for 3 percent *fewer dollars*. Such volatility at the time distinguished electronics from older industries' experience, highlighting its unusual demands. (Twenty-five years later, the far broader industry decline experienced in 1985 and 1986 seems quite similar.) While TI's survival was never in question, Haggerty and his managers in the 1960s were keenly aware of the need for effective co-ordination across the many PCCs. What the PCC system lacked were systematic guides and incentives to direct management attention to longer-term demands.

The year 1962 represented a special turning point for TI: the company deliberately moved to systematize its approach to strategic planning and innovation management. It was not that the company had undertaken no innovation before, nor that it had no strategic planning. On the contrary, TI had gained its pre-eminence in the industry by virtue of spectacular successes with transistors. TI was the first company to successfully manufacture large volumes of germanium transistors and the first to create a broad, non-military, consumer market for the component, through its Regency "shirt pocket" radio. Similarly, when TI announced commercial production of silicon transistors – a more technically sophisticated and capable product, produced by a far more demanding manufacturing process – no company matched the feat for two years.

While the firm had done well, though, its success before 1962 seemed to rely unduly on Haggerty's competence in directing the talents of others: "He almost became the project engineer" on several successful efforts, according to TI insiders. Haggerty himself felt that these successes had to be multiplied, and that competence in managing innovation had to be developed in many other individuals if the company were to successfully break through the 1960 plateau to continue its growth. It was not enough that Haggerty, as an individual TI employee, should possess those skills; instead, he felt, TI *as a company* needed to possess innovation skills and be able to retain, transmit, and improve upon them.

The need to develop *a system*, and through it to multiply the management perspectives Haggerty himself had used so successfully, gave rise to the OST. As Haggerty saw it, long-term goals and targets were crucial, but would be effective only when supported by intermediate allocations of resources and specific short-term responsibility assignments. The OST was designed as a purposeful system to link long-term goals with immediate efforts to attain them, guiding others in the methods that had proven successful in earlier strategic innovation efforts. While Haggerty described the OST as "nothing in the world but organized common sense," its insight was rare enough in the industry to set TI well apart from its competition. The systematic approach to innovation that TI developed and utilized is one effective method for organizing co-ordination, emphasizing the long term, and going beyond a single manager's skills in managing innovation. As we shall see, the OST has both strengths and weaknesses.

Aggressive Competition with a Long-Term View TI actively pursued significant innovation. By aggressively pricing to build market share and volume, TI in effect created many of the pressures still characteristic of the electronics industry to this day. Persistent innovation, learning curve pricing and fierce competition all rest on continued, effective mastery of product design and redesign, and of changing production details. The strategic commitment to innovation guarantees a stream of changes to be coped with. The need for ever lower prices creates strong pressures for stability and manufacturing mastery.

Having contributed to these pressures, TI was no less subject to them than its competition. Others, too, strove to extend the state of the art, in funded defense research, in OEM (original equipment manufacturer) sales, and in later consumer adaptations. Neither serendipity nor the one man band of some single innovation manager, even a highly successful one like Haggerty, was sufficient. Instead, as the company grew and the industry became still more competitive, the need for continuous innovation and continuous price and production improvement in existing products accelerated. Often, too, new products demanded new production technology, while increasing technical sophistication emphasized the need to bring in many specialists and develop many strategic managers.

Making Stability and Change Visible The OST separated out the discretionary, non-urgent but highly important activities of strategic development. These were accounted for separately, with an explicit set of goals and performance criteria enumerated quite deliberately apart from operating funds, operating criteria, and operating goals. Such separation permitted explicit management of strategic projects, rather than submerging them in the urgent details of day-to-day business. The OST's separation enabled TI managers to judge strategic activities by effectiveness standards, rather than the efficiency standards more appropriate for operational activities.

Managers in most firms are used to meeting budgets and production quotas, being assessed on day-to-day or quarter-to-quarter sales or manufacturing targets. The OST provided a system for targets, quotas, budgets, and goals applied to strategic projects – with a key difference. Targets and goals were set, deadlines agreed to and monies allocated – but instead of "efficiency," the criterion was "achievement." Strategic activities were specifically identified as different from operating activities, yet specific responsibilities for strategic matters were visible. Because these activities were separated out, and because different criteria were applied, senior management could focus explicitly on these activities as distinct from routine business – and could demand that operating management focus on them likewise.

Strategic activities, usually thought of in terms of longer time horizons, thus acquired a current-time operating dimension and greater visibility. They became action items, rather than deferrable or discretionary matters. Because milestones, dates, budgeted funds, and specific responsibilities were identified, it was easy for managers at all levels to readily see whether strategic activities were, in fact, being accomplished according to plan. This put a high premium on the targets set and the milestones agreed to: what a manager or engineer committed to, she or he would deliver. Properly set targets would permit go/no-go decisions on strategic activities by providing essential information (market response, test data, or pilot run results).

The OST focused managers' attention on the rather different needs of today's and tomorrow's businesses: stability, to master the details of today; change, to meet the challenges of tomorrow. Stability is fostered by the need to attend to details, and make continuous, incremental quality improvements in existing products and processes. Stability flourishes in an atmosphere of reliable commitments, budgets, and deadlines. Such activities take the current business as given, and build upon it. Focus on these activities, though, tends to drive out attention to the future. The OST prevented that by reasserting future needs.

In contrast to the incremental changes fostered by stability, significant change and innovation flourish in an atmosphere of definite long-term targets. Significant gaps between the present and its reasonable extrapolation must be identified, TI managers felt. Challenging targets were required, to highlight the importance of innovation, and those targets must be backed by the serious commitment of funds, attention, and time throughout the organization.

These future-oriented activities required a different sort of thinking from the incremental improvements emphasized by current business needs. Significant risk is acceptable, even desirable: some projects will fail, but others will produce superior returns. Change and innovation aim to subvert the current order – existing products must be superseded, existing processes rendered obsolete by newer, better ones. Senior management attention to these activities legitimates them and creates credible responsibilities for the future for employees throughout the organization.

By using standards for innovation different from those used for operations, the OST allowed the different natures of these tasks to be appreciated. By making visible both the ultimate targets and the connections between current-time tactical programs and the goals to which they contributed, the OST helped managers develop a richer, more sophisticated view of business and strategy. Their vision of the future was articulated and shared through the OST, enabling many managers both to understand it and to contribute to it – crucial factors, as the number of specialists and sorts of needed technical expertise grew. In addition, by helping senior managers focus directly on strategic activities, the OST helped to encourage potential for overlap and synergy among divisions or projects or development teams.

Especially during the 1970s, the OST was "how we ran the company," according to Haggerty. That is, TI managed its strategic innovation activities by means of the OST, in concert with the routine operational management provided by the PCC system. New products continued to roll out, while continued emphasis on manufacturing allowed prices to fall at an average of 25 or 30 percent per year. As the largest US merchant semiconductor manufacturer, TI contributed substantially to industry norms. TI's success during this era is tangible. The company was persistently the number one merchant semiconductor manufacturer both in the United States and in the world from the 1960s – until overtaken by Motorola in the US in1984, and by NEC in 1986.

Chaos and Culture: Resource Realignment at Motorola

TI's highly structured approach is clearly not the only option, nor is it without difficulties, to which we shall later return. TI's arch-rival, Motorola, illustrates a very different alternative. Motorola and TI are alike in having entered the semiconductor business from successful operation in other areas, but they are very different companies. Neither was founded as a semiconductor company; but there the similarity ends.

While TI's roots were in oilfield exploration and seismic technology, Motorola's beginnings were in the radio industry, making car radios. Motorola is also still discernibly a "family" company in many respects, marked by its founder. Paul V. Galvin established the Galvin Manufacturing Company in 1928 from the ashes of his own previously failed company. At its bankruptcy auction, he purchased rights to a battery eliminator he had recently developed. The device allowed people to use their battery-powered crystal-set radios after the advent of alternating current in homes by providing a direct energy source to serve in place of the battery. True AC radios quickly made the product obsolete, and Galvin began producing AC home radios in 1929. The Depression almost put him out of business again, but he saved the company by developing the first commercial car radio, the Motorola, which gave the company its name.

This business expanded even during the 1930s. Galvin soon began modifying standard radios so that police could receive broadcasts from dispatchers, and a Police Radio Department was formed. Just before World War II, Galvin became interested in a new FM mobile communications system for police use, and recruited its developer, Daniel E. Noble. The Army too was in need of better, lighter communications equipment, and Motorola developed a transceiver called the "Handie-Walkie" in 1941, just before Pearl Harbor. A longer-range version was developed, and eventually Motorola built over 90,000 of them for the war effort.

Motorola's expertise in mobile communications has been an important mainstay for its contemporary business success. Motorola became the world's leading producer of two-way radios, pagers and similar equipment, a position it still maintains today, although it exited the commercial car radio business in May 1980. Today, Motorola's Communications Division manufactures pagers, cellular telephones, two-way radios, and portable radio/data systems. Motorola's products, like TI's, sell well, even in Japan – although opening the market was a long, difficult struggle, despite high quality and lower prices than competing Japanese products (Prestowitz, 1988). Communications Products provided roughly 41 percent of Motorola's 1986 sales; Information Systems (13 percent), Government Electronics (9 percent) and other products (6 percent) together provide another 28 percent. The remaining third of Motorola's sales come from semiconductors.

Motorola's Semiconductor Division dates back to 1955, just as the solid-state transistor was becoming commercially available. By 1968, Semiconductor Division revenues were rivalling those of the much older Communications Division, having risen from $5 million in 1958 to $230 million by 1968. Sales growth above the industry average continued even after the defection of many senior managers when the Semiconductor Division's head, C. Lester Hogan, was lured away to Fairchild by a record-breaking salary offer. Both high salaries and the mobility of "star talent" are continuing features of the industry today.

So, too, are volatility in sales and profits, which were clearly marked out in earlier times. A key factor in Motorola Semiconductor's early growth was the decision to maintain its product line in the older discrete devices technology, while many of its rivals, including TI, abandoned discretes to concentrate on newer integrated circuit (IC) technology. Virtually unopposed in discretes, Motorola prospered. This strategy proved a two-edged sword in the downturn of 1975. Motorola was hit especially hard because its older discrete product business lines did not signal the coming downturn as others' newer technology products did, so the company was caught by surprise. While many competitors suffered only small downturns, Motorola took a $25 million loss, a sizeable figure for the time (Forbes, 1979).

As two thirds of its 1974–5 semiconductor business was positioned in older devices, there was serious concern that Motorola might lag behind even after industry conditions improved. The company seemed to have been outpaced in the newer technology, integrated circuits. Consequently, amid other management changes, in June 1976 Motorola brought in Alfred J. Stein from Texas Instruments to head the wayward IC Division in an effort to update IC products. This move represented a significant change from Motorola's prior practice of internal promotion.

The challenge facing Stein was to marshall the resources in a large division seriously shaken by losses in the downturn, management changes, an aging product line – and concerns about Stein himself, the outsider from TI. Within three years, observers were marvelling at the turnaround. New-technology ICs were generating the major portion of the Semiconductor Group's sales, and Motorola was marketing two industry-leading products: a 64K memory chip and a state-of-the-art 16-bit microprocessor, the MC68000. In September 1979, Stein was promoted from IC division head to assistant general manager of the Semiconductor Group as a whole. (Stein has since left Motorola to head VLSI Technology, Inc.)

Realigning Culture Amid "Chaos" What happened at Motorola offers a fascinating comparison with the course of TI's development.

The insights are especially apposite because managers familiar with both companies tend to draw the comparisons beginning from a deep foundation of intimate experience with TI. Differences between the two companies are important; but differences in perceptions and context are even more significant.

Stein, for instance, had spent his entire working life at TI prior to joining Motorola. Upon arrival, his first realization was that things were different at Motorola. For one thing, he simply saw no counterparts to the OST and other TI management systems explicitly aimed at innovation:

> I didn't know any other kind of culture or any other kind of way of doing things. Quite honestly, I felt the business world revolved around such a system as TI had installed. I had no idea that other companies could be quite so different.
>
> Alfred J. Stein

Motorola had no visible system in place to manage forward planning or assess performance at the division level, according to Stein. Instead, although many discussions took place, there was little or no follow-up. Problems or ideas were raised, but implementation was spotty and haphazard. Senior management might have strategic directions in mind, but these were not apparent to division level personnel. Nor was needed information available in a usable form. Numbers, performance, and results figures were not clearly tied to division activities or specific plants, and no one seemed to know about them.

It would be misleading to say that Motorola "had no systems"; any sizeable firm does, of course, have information and management systems in place, and Motorola was no exception. Others at Motorola, including some former TI employees, pointed to the existing systems in Motorola. What is striking is that the systems Motorola had were not functioning effectively to put information into the hands of those who needed it. The systems did not provide the sort of feedback that permitted rigorous assessment. There is widespread agreement, from both ex-TIers and from Motorola people, that those existing systems did not work. The result, to managers used to the excruciatingly explicit and visible TI systems, looked like chaos.

Despite what might appear an irresistible temptation, Stein did not seek to recreate his TI experiences at Motorola. He was joined at Motorola by a few others from TI, but the cadre was slim. There was no attempt to overwhelm Motorola with TI veterans. "I only brought a half dozen people over a period of a couple of years at high levels with me," said Stein. Neither sheer numbers nor iron-fisted re-creation of the TI culture was the secret of the Motorola turnaround. Instead, the new managers acted as catalysts to energize and co-ordinate existing resources within Motorola. All the former TIers repeatedly emphasized the strengths they found at Motorola. These comments are typical:

> To make the kind of transition that we did, from the number five semiconductor supplier to a very solid number two – [in 1984], in fact, in the US we are sure that we outshipped TI for the first time ever. So we have accomplished another milestone. We are growing much faster – continuing to grow faster than they are.
> You don't do that kind of thing with the size of operation that Motorola is, unless you have a tremendous nucleus of good people and the potential is there.
>
> Jim Fiebiger, Motorola

Stein also stressed the existing technical competence he found at Motorola:

> There were a lot of good Motorola people there. We just really got a good team together, and they did a lot of things. It wasn't all me. There is a good team there today, and I think that team will do well.

Nevertheless, despite the good people at Motorola, Stein found it difficult to comprehend the structure of Motorola's semiconductor business, at first, for want of the kinds of information he had been accustomed to at TI:

> The first thing I looked at was the P&L, to understand what the business looked like. And I would go to some of these key managers and ask them what their billings were, and their profitability and so forth, but I could never get a clear picture of what was going on, or what I had. A million in sales? A 10 percent bottom line, or this kind of a margin? It was really not anything that I could get definitively from them.

The difficulty was not one of refusal to co-operate, resistance to an outsider, or of dull managers, but was rooted instead in chaotic systems, in Stein's view. The information was presented in a format Stein found impossible to comprehend, or to translate into business terms. In the first weeks, observed Stein,

> The major thing I saw was the P&L. I really didn't understand
> how the business was organized, who was responsible for specific
> portions of the business, or how his report card told him how
> he was doing.

Neither responsibility nor results were clearly communicated, Stein
felt. In fact, the systems seemed to hide information, rather than
provide it, share it, or work for its integration:

> The three different P&L documents that came out were
> voluminous. One looked at the business on a worldwide basis,
> one looked at it on a US factory basis, and one looked at it on
> a market basis. The world basis took every product, like
> microprocessors, and consolidated microprocessors businesses
> around the world and came up with one P&L. . . . In that one
> report you had people all around the world, responsible for
> different portions of the business.

Nor was cost data provided in any comprehensible form:

> The guys didn't really know what the cost of actual manufacturing
> was. [Work in process] was transferred at inventory value. The
> manager didn't really know, even if he had the data, whether he
> had made money or not, because he got the incoming inventory
> at a very low cost. He didn't know what the variances were in
> making it, between the inventory policy and what the factor cost
> was.

Most particularly, at TI, Stein had been provided with clear bottom
line figures for operations and strategic projects. At TI, the operating
information was clearly linked to individual PCC performance.
Strategic information, for new product development for instance, was
also clearly identified. At Motorola, the information was fragmented
and reaggregated in a manner Stein felt was not useful to operating
line management:

> It was quite complex and very overlapping in responsibilities.
> Costs were all allocated, and really nobody understood how the
> costs were allocated. That was all done by computer. So it was
> a difficult thing to understand, plus it was secret. . . .
>   Very few people knew whether they were making profits or
> not. If they did, it was from a very complex set of data. Nobody
> really understood their P&L.

The figures available constituted a sort of "funny money," insufficient
for realistically assessing operating unit performance, or for assessing
plans, in Stein's view. Thus managers really had no idea how they

were doing, except for gross comparisons with last year's figures. The consensus among the ex-TIers was that Motorola had good people, but lacked the systems and information needed to provide co-ordination, organization, and concerted follow-up. It was not technical expertise, resources, or people *per se* that was missing, but rather the systematic approach to organize them all.

Others at Motorola testified that the needed information existed, but that Stein's approach brought it into prominence:

> All the data was there, in the old system and the new, but Al didn't understand it [in the old system]. His real contribution was in forcing follow-through. The division or group had operated semi-detached from the operating level. [Stein and his managers] got involved in the operating level – they were hands-on managers. The encouragement, the involvement, and the absolute insistence on results were the real contributions.
>
> William Howard, Motorola

Of course, by contrast with TI's highly structured approach to management, almost any other company would seem far looser and less organized. But what TI veterans found seemed to them more like chaos by contrast. Stein and others from TI quickly agreed on a diagnosis:

> I think the thing that was lacking, frankly, was discipline, in that people had programs that didn't necessarily always tie together to where things were in synch.
>
> Alfred J. Stein

"Discipline" is a relative notion. What appears to be "lack of discipline" or "anarchy" to one group is merely "healthy autonomy" to another. Nevertheless, what we have here is the considered opinion of managers with experience in two very different organizations, looking back after successful experiences in both. They articulate a clear need for more structured information sharing and more systematic follow-up than Motorola had when they arrived – a diagnosis corroborated by others inside the Motorola organization who did not have TI experience.

Equally compelling, at the same time, all of them preferred less formal control and more flexibility than they had experienced at TI. They wanted systems to effectively provide for both control and change, stability and innovation. There is no question of an exclusive dichotomy, embracing either rigid control or diffuse and indeterminant responsibilities. Instead, there is a clear vision of the dual need for exhaustive but directly useful information, methods of allocating responsibilities clearly, organizational supports for decision-making, and consistent follow-up, along with encouragement for innovation and initiative. Without the systematic supports, even "good, innovative, competent people" cannot function effectively.

Systematic management of innovation is not "adhocracy" – a point to which we shall return in later chapters. It is not undirected "freedom," nor random experimentation. Rather, successful innovation management includes insistent follow-up, push, attention, and "absolute insistence on results." It is an organized format for raising issues in a forum – here, the operating review meetings – in which decisions can be made and difficulties resolved.

Systematizing Motorola Stein and his ex-TIers approached the problem by recognizing in advance that reproducing TI methods was not what they wanted, although they did believe more orderly procedure was required. The newcomers, seeing things in the perspective of another system, could readily see what was needed. In contrast to what Stein saw as secrecy and lack of information, the TI newcomers opened up enormously more detailed and forthright discussion of operational details, as we shall see.

Before we embark on the following discussion, the terms "book" and "bill" need explanation. A "booked" order is one written up, which may, in fact, be eventually cancelled by the customer before it is shipped – semiconductor customers notoriously overbook during periods of product scarcity, when demand is high and the economy is booming, to assure supply – only to cancel their multiple bookings when their first shipment of components comes through or the downturn comes. This, of course, translates into precipitous drops in the "billing" rate, which is shipped product, invoiced to the final customer – "real" orders, if you will. As a consequence of the multiple booking phenomenon, the semiconductor industry has evolved a book-to-bill ratio to track actual demand for its product more accurately. The book-to-bill ratio allow managers to estimate the extent to which business is booming, as opposed to merely collecting orders which evaporate before shipment. Forecasting billings accurately remains a task requiring much experience and information, along with some luck. And, of course, it doesn't always work.

We have noted that existing systems and information in place when

Stein arrived at Motorola were not functioning to ensure effective operation, despite the company's acknowledged strengths. The TIers brought a context of past experience and expectation with them, to shape and affect much that was already in place, as well as to add a few key measures and bits of information they felt were essential. But above all, they brought a management style that put that information into the hands of those who had to make decisions. Their method had many affinities with the visibility that the OST had provided at TI.

A close look at an operating review meeting highlights the nature of the shift. In place of the dearth of directly useful operating information they had found originally, these meetings provided a forum for discussion and for continual negotiation of targets, and the disciplined follow-up that pushed people to deliver on promised goals. The reviews address not only what was promised and what was actually achieved, but what the specific shortfalls were, and what remedial action might help. Both insistent, demanding attention to performance and negotiation for what is realistically needed to accomplish targets are visible here. Jim Fiebiger described the sort of operations review the newcomers set up:

> One of the key things that we brought to the party was an organized format of operations-type reviews. Every month, religiously, in the operations we have an in-depth operations review. We do it at our sector level, and the guys that report to us also do it with their staff. It is the whole gamut of, "Here is what we've got in terms of orders. This is what we said we were going to get. Because we got this upside, this downside, or no change, we should be able to do XYZ as far as the billings are concerned, or shipments. We can do more because we got more orders; we're going to do less because we got less orders, or well, we're right on forecast – everything looks solid. We actually did this, in terms of profit. Our main problems were such-and-such. Had we done this better . . ."
>
> Throughout these operations reviews, there is a series of action items taken on things. "We didn't get the new orders because of the fact that we missed the billings." "OK, why did you miss the billing?" (And this would be talking to the marketing guys.) "Well, we didn't get such-and-such an order," or whatever. "Well, why didn't you get such-and-such an order?"Or, "Well, next time, let's make sure we do this." And "What potential orders do we have pending, that if in fact we pulled those in,

and got those, instead of a 50 percent probability, we brought it to 80 percent probability – would you be able to cover the bookings for the forecast?" And then the answer is, "Yeah, we think we might be able to."

"OK, then, you have the responsibility for getting this guy out of the operations to go up and interface with the technical people; and this guy out of strategic marketing to present it from a systems standpoint." And action follow-up things are decided *right there* as to who was going to do what, when.

For whatever problems there might be, or even if you didn't have any problem in relation to the forecast, how might you do better? Then, the next month, for all of those things as to what you were supposed to do, the individual stands up and talks about what he did against what he said he was going to do.

From one perspective, such systematic follow-up constitutes "holding people's feet to the fire." It is not loose or "democratic." And it depends upon a tough, committed manager. The persistent follow-up is very much carried by the manager running the meeting. If questions are not raised, the review could be toothless. Because questions are raised, it drives performance. As one manager commented,

> When you say you're going to do something, it better happen, you know. Or else you certainly would be at the receiving end of some of Al [Stein]'s disdain. And that is very important in these new product programs, because they're very complex. Various people have to do certain things by certain times. Whenever any one part of the puzzle is missing – because people are sloppy or undisciplined and don't think that meeting a certain due date is all that important, then the whole project – you know, with many, many people involved – [the whole thing] tends to slip. And if it happens over here, and then it happens over here, and then it happens over here . . . pretty soon, you're out there still trying to do something that your competition introduced a year and a half ago. In the IC business, a year and a half is the whole ballgame: you've lost the war.

This comment is very reminiscent of a famous comment by the legendary software manager Frederick Brooks: "How does a software project get months overdue? One day at a time!" To avoid being months overdue, or losing the war, operating reviews had to be insistent. People had to be counted on, and they had to be committed to doing what they had promised, when they promised to do it.

From another very important perspective, however, this system made available for the first time the information and the resources to do the job. By recognizing the necessity of co-operation across functions and departments, and by making the negotiations for necessary assistance visible, the reviews enormously expedited effective action. They also helped create a shared view of why a particular action is important, and how others depend upon its completion:

> The marketing guy probably can't do it all himself. So the question is asked, "Well, what do you need to do it?" Well, he needs this engineer out of this group, he needs this engineer out of this other group. He needs this systems guy to go in together with him, and then they'll do it. So it's decided right then and there that the team will do it. He gets what he needs from the standpoint of the support needs, and then they go off and make it happen.
>
> Jim Fiebiger, Motorola

Systematically marshalling the resources and the decision authority required to produce operational results was at the heart of what the former TI people provided so that Motorola could realize the potential that was already in place. Yet what was put in place also recognized fundamental differences between the two firms:

> The general philosophy at Motorola in terms of how motivation works is trying to give the manager more flexibilities to make his own decisions, and weave quite a creative-type atmosphere. We'd probably tend to foster that kind of thing. What we needed to do was to not stymie that, but at the same time bring enough of the . . . "discipline" is probably not the right word . . . more of the follow-up. Getting the right people together to make a decision, and give whatever.
>
> Very seldom does one guy have all the horsepower to do everything. But getting the key people together who can address the problems, collectively decide that "This is an important thing. We probably could fix it such-and-such." And saying, "You, you, and you are going to do it, because collectively you guys have the right responsibility." And then follow up on it the next month to see what was done. And, "Do we need to modify that?" Or did it work so super – that, "See how it worked there, we better apply it to these other 15 different places."
>
> Jim Fiebiger, Motorola

This lengthy series of quotations again and again strikes a tone of problem solving. Practicality, support, and resource networking, along with managerial attention, insistence on results, and specific responsibility are explicit aims. Above all, the approach to operations is one of orderly co-ordination across specialty areas, responsibilities, or levels, as needed. According to Fiebiger, this was accomplished by bringing the needed expertise and the responsible decision makers together in the same room at the same time, and insisting:

> It is all the key people that can make all the decisions, together in one room and *doing* it. You know, you can't remember; if you don't get a set of action items that has your name on 'em, chances are, if you've got a lot of things to do, you might forget about them. And then, with the more "let's-let-people-be-creative" and "let's-not-let-them-get-tied-up-with-too-many-hours-in-meetings" type philosophy, the problem was you really didn't tend to get enough of the people together at one time to get the consensus of the right guys to make something happen, and all agree, "Hey, yeah, let's go ahead and do it."
>
> Jim Fiebiger, Motorola

Others corroborated this insight, noting that before Stein's demands for systematic information and decision making, Motorola had had many bright people, much technology development in the lab that never made it to market, and many good ideas that somehow did not come to fruition.

Motorola managers since Stein have repeatedly emphasized the need to co-ordinate, to bring together information, resources, and responsible parties so that matters might effectively proceed: "We try to let more decisions be made at the level they need to be," according to one. This practice is informal, in that its essence is problems and solutions, rather than forms, paper statements, or formal presentations. Especially in comparison to TI's OST system, Motorola's approach seems relaxed. Motorola's version is highly systematic, however, in comparison to the company's former practice. Regular, specific meetings, prompt decisions based upon data in a common format, and action-oriented problem solving all provide necessary discipline. They also produce the required follow-up. Above all, they bring continuity, information, and conviction to development and operations activities.

Both up and down in the Motorola Semiconductor organization, the changes involved greater information sharing in the service of better shared assessment of performance; better co-ordination; and, through the information, a more realistic perspective on the business. This trend continued at Motorola, to the top of the organization and through the years to the present:

> Our Chairman of the Board and Vice Chairman of the Board come down on a regular, routine basis to see what is happening from the standpoint of technology; a couple of times a year for each one of the major operations. So that means they spend a lot of time. For us, that would mean they would make those reviews for four operations, twice a year. That material is not scrubbed. In general, nobody will have looked at that material. It will be the presenters showing that to everybody at the same time. It's their view, their outlook, how they are doing, what the constraints are.
>
> Jim Fiebiger, Motorola

At the opposite end of the scheme, down to the first level of supervision, monthly action items with specifics of date, detail, responsible party and follow-on, rigorously reviewed at operations meetings, characterized the business long after Stein had left.

There are, of course, risks in such practices. Shifts from a loose, unstructured way of working to such a systematic discipline require intense effort. They succeed best with a charismatic, forceful manager to guide the change. And, like all "hands-on" management, insistent operations reviews run the risk of centralizing decisions – in the meetings, in the hands of the insistent, forceful manager, or both. The Achilles' heel of relying on operational reviews is that people can become reluctant to make decisions outside the meetings. The meetings themselves, and the senior managers running them, can displace the very responsibility and commitment they are designed to create.

How Motorola Was Moved Repeatedly, the ex-TI managers commented that they had not imported enormous amounts of TI practice and procedure, an assessment echoed by Motorola people. Instead, they utilized much that they found, previously developed or nascent, in Motorola's practice: "They just needed somebody with a little different idea on how to do things," was the frequent comment. The newcomers catalyzed, they precipitated, they drew on existing resources. They cast existing information into a different, common format that related activities directly to the operating units.

What changed was not so much the information, or even the

systems – although changes are clearly visible here – so much as the style with which it all was run. It is almost as if the former TI people infected the Motorola organization with a different view, enabling Motorola people to recast and redirect their efforts better. Motorola even had its own long-range planning system, according to Fiebiger:

> The whole Motorola way or equivalent of an OST type of thing, that was basically in place, and we didn't really change that. We still use that. Maybe we attend those meetings, and hold those meetings more faithfully than in the past, but I'm not even sure that's true. But then there's a lot of other changes and innovations that we've done, that long since are not really holdovers or carryovers from TI, but are really new things that [Motorola people] thought of.

Yet systematics are undeniably important, especially systematics with a discernible purpose. Without a systematic approach, meetings can be wasteful or useless. Without directly accessible information, decisions cannot be made. Another manager who worked closely with Stein underlined the nature of the contribution that Stein made, in catalyzing talent at Motorola:

> [Before Stein arrived] it was pretty hard for anybody in [a management position] to keep track of what was going on because you'd hold operations reviews or something, and everybody had everything in a different format. You spent 90 percent of your time trying to figure out what you were looking at. Al came in and immediately rejected all of that and said, "That's baloney. Everybody is going to do it exactly the same way because that's the only way I am going to be able to absorb this enormous amount of data that I want to personally see." So, you know, he came up with a form for this, and a form for that . . .
>
> What evolved over time was that all these forms and reviews became literally the way we ran the business. It became the tools with which all the management actually ran the business here. The business was being managed in the past with very little discipline, and in a very disorganized manner. So these tools, while they made everybody do it the same, also made everybody do a better job of managing their business. It was very, very useful from that standpoint.

The Limits of Systems: Choice and Balance in Systematizing

What is not visible at Motorola is also significant. While Stein made insistent, "outrageous" demands for explicit information and follow-up, his team made no attempt to simply replicate the TI experience, the TI culture, or the TI approach. While TI's culture suited TI, it had, in their view, decided limits. Indeed, these managers felt they represented individual TI failures: each had left the company after a long career and much achievement, on account of his personal dissatisfaction with the TI system, as it had evolved over time. These managers' critiques of TI, like their comments on Motorola, illuminate the special needs of innovation management in high-tech firms: systematic approaches, but not bureaucratic rigidity, authoritarian management, or overemphasis on "the forms." Open tolerance of individuality and initiative are crucial, but not at the price of lack of system, failure to follow up, or unclear responsibilities.

Their critiques also highlight some of the risks that any system faces. These managers can be said to have left TI because they felt that the OST and PCC approaches had turned into "too much control." Because of the high level of visibility that the TI systems gave to strategic activities, managers operating within it were highly vulnerable to senior management, highly dependent on how the system was used. Any such system, because of the exposure it produces, can thus be used to "catch the perpetrators" as easily as it can be used to guide strategic activity. Where the system's use is perceived to shift from strategic planning to punitive control, rational managers will duck the system, cease to take the risks that make innovation possible, and ensure that any goal they commit to is easily attainable.

The vision that emerges is of the need for simultaneous organization and innovation, simultaneous stability and change. Its validity is only underlined by reports of how Texas Instruments has responded to its difficulties of the past few years, difficulties widely described as "too much bureaucracy" by sources both inside and outside the firm. *Business Week* (1983) noted that TI had "tripped on its own red tape," and needed to "clean up its act." Insiders concurred:

> You cannot be an entrepreneur and make great things happen
> while doing review after review after review with Bucy and
> Shepherd. They've created a paperwork mill that makes it
> absolutely impossible to respond to anything that moves quickly.
>
> Anonymous TI manager, quoted in *Business Week*

TI's failures were not failures to produce creative, innovative ideas.
Indeed, TI's reputation for design creativity has remained strong. Its
engineering computers, for instance, were initially designed with a
proprietary system, and delivered better performance than competing
IBM models. TI's home computer product was praised by engineers
initially as an excellent machine, but it was slow to market. Even
with substantial consumer advertising, it failed to gain much consumer
acceptance. In this era too, TI's long-standing reputation for
manufacturing control was also praised – but somehow, success never
came together in the marketplace.

TI's computer failure was serious. In 1983, the firm lost $145 million
on revenues of $4.6 billion, a result in large measure of difficulties
in the home computer market, which TI ultimately abandoned.
Among other difficulties, although production successfully produced
a flood of machines, enabling the company to reduce prices
substantially, TI had difficulty with retail distribution, consumer
recognition and competition from other entrants in a crowded, fast-
changing field.

Perhaps most importantly, production continued as the firm seemed
not to recognize its difficulties. A "captive of its own success" at
producing, TI ran on with home computers until large losses were
accumulated. In short, far from providing exhaustive and detailed
information to monitor and control the business, TI's systems
somehow failed to communicate market realities. The very sort of
thorough and exhaustive "report card" on actual results that Stein
was imposing at Motorola seems to have been missing back at TI.

One source of this difficulty appears to have been managers' feelings
that bad news was not welcomed by top executives, most notably
President Fred Bucy and Chairman Mark Shepherd. According to
one report,

> Bucy and Shepherd tended to hear what subordinates perceived
> they wanted to hear, says one senior manager, because both were
> such intimidating personalities.
>
> *Business Week*, 1986

Other sources also commented on the difficulty and risk of

communicating problems or poor results. Perhaps most tellingly, sources commented on the lack of motivation they experienced in reaction to the tightly controlled managerial style increasingly in evidence at TI during this era:

> It's a weakness [at TI] to tell a guy that he did a good job. You can find out something he did wrong, no matter what he did, and make sure that you remind him that he could have done ABC better. [Also] tending to make decisions – more decisions – at the executive level and higher, and one guy making the decisions on his own, saying, "Hey, this is what we are going to do."
>
> Anonymous former TI manager

Similarly, a knowledgeable outsider who knew them commented that "TI lost a lot of humanity under Bucy; he didn't share Haggerty's philosophy." More than one manager described the difficulties TI had fallen into as an "accounting mentality." This was the bureaucratic result of too much control, where control rather than results or useful information was the focus, a problem identified by a number of TI insiders as well. As a result, information was increasingly filtered:

> That [information] would have been through three levels of review prior to Bucy or any of those guys seeing it. And in general, with a little modification at each level, what started in and what comes out are not necessarily the same. There [was] too much filtering, and it tends to go more towards everything being hunky-dory, instead of surfacing problems.
>
> Anonymous TI manager

TI's results became sufficiently troublesome for the company to provoke a reaction. In early 1985, Bucy was replaced by a new CEO, Jerry Junkins, a long-term TIer who nevertheless moved quickly to loosen apparent rigidities, encouraging much freer exchange of ideas and even disagreement from his subordinates.

Junkins's style is frequently described in terms of contrast with his predecessors' personalities. A more useful perspective is to focus on the shift Junkins's style represents in terms of stability and change: to allow disagreement also encourages commitment, the freer flow of information, and thus the possibility of genuine alternatives emerging. Change and flexibility, rather than rigid control, seem the aim. At the same time, however, Junkins also closed nonproductive facilities, including two computer plants, trimmed the corporate workforce by

10 percent, and froze salaries through mid-1986. There is little sign here of lack of control, or abandonment of demanding financial standards.

A Move Toward Simultaneous Stability and Change

At both Motorola and TI, then, managers can be seen evolving a middle-ground organizational response, characterized by both meticulous control and flexibility. In a global marketplace of intense competition, this seems essential. The competition has become no less intense in recent years, as Japanese imports and, increasingly, those from Korea and Singapore too, contest markets in fundamental products like DRAMs. US semiconductor makers have experienced continued Japanese success and continued pressure. Prices for common DRAMs dropped by almost 80 percent in 1985. On 9 October that year, in response to this unrelenting pressure from Japan, Intel exited from the DRAM market that the firm had pioneered. For a time, only two other US firms, TI and tiny Micron, Inc., remained in the market. TI moved to improve operating margins, cut costs, and improve production yields.

By early 1988, TI's efforts were beginning to show results. Coupled with the fall of the dollar against the yen, strenuous cost-cutting and manufacturing emphasis enabled TI to beat its Japanese rivals on costs for the 256K RAM. As we have already commented, however, continued success will require balance. TI must continue to match both the required pace of innovation and the manufacturing efficiencies of its rivals. These tasks are especially difficult in the face of much higher capital costs in the US than abroad, and foreign governments' concerted support for their semiconductor industries. Of course, these challenges also face Motorola, Intel, Hewlett-Packard and our other study companies.

DRAMs are important as a widely used product in themselves, reflecting the continued penetration of computer controls into equipment, appliances, and products of all sorts. Further, however, they represent a testing-ground for new design and manufacturing technology, as TI has long recognized. Their regular, repetitive structure makes them exemplary products for testing new techniques to be used in other, more complex and difficult products such as custom and semicustom chips. Application-specific integrated circuits (ASICs) are seen as important by both TI and Motorola, and by some market experts as a potential new boom product. The simultaneous push by many makers toward ASICs promises another round of intense competition, however, not the refuge from competition that some seem to seek.

What is most interesting from our perspective is that here again the link between stability and change is apparent, this time in technological terms. ASICs represent new and innovative custom or semicustom products of high volatility. Nevertheless, ASIC development depends on expertise developed on a more stable, regular product: memory chips. The known and well-understood product, the DRAM, is seen as an entry into the far more uncertain (and potentially more lucrative) ASIC.

Electronics industry managers simply do not manage in dichotomous terms – old *or* new, stable *or* innovative. Instead, they must contend with a hybrid situation demanding both stability and change. This hybrid demand is well recognized, and explicitly managed. There is a quite conscious effort to lever the knowledge that stability and relatively predictable, routine products provide into the higher risk, higher return areas of custom products. Systems like the team-oriented operations meetings, and organizing arrangements like physical proximity of specialists who report through product teams, emphasize the carry-over of expertise on the one hand – a stability factor – with continuous new product, new process orientation – an innovation factor. Emphasis on efficiency in production, matched with the need for repeated innovation, both in products and in processes, underline the constant tension of stability with change.

The data from TI and Motorola show that rigid control, bureaucratic systems, and authoritarian patterns, formerly so often successful in other industries, do not work in the high change, high challenge environment of micro-electronics. It is equally clear that loosely structured, ad hoc "organic" approaches are not an option for the electronics industry either. What can be seen in these firms' responses, different as they are, is not ambiguity, uncertainty about responsibilities, or any lessening of the demands for performance. On the contrary, these companies illustrate the crucial necessity of "both/and," not "either/or." Disciplined, systematic management of innovation, however apparently paradoxical, is required.

At both Motorola and TI – and at our other companies as well – the detailed operational specifics of production yields, cost control, and budget planning, and explicit targets for design sign-offs, sales goals, and costs are constantly revisited. Where the discipline works well, the focus is on solving problems, putting together the resources of decision makers and information to co-ordinate essential tasks and decisions. What makes it finally work is the discipline and insistence and trust that each will do what he or she commits to. These controls are visibly useful in that they link activities and results in a direct, unmistakable way.

Equally important, these tools work best when they are in the hands of those operationally responsible – not just senior management. Where seniors take charge, they risk excessive centralization, silencing not only dissent but important information or perspectives that do not coincide with their own. Also, the tools must be properly directed. Their use is for problem solving, fueled by an abundant flow of specific information, presented in a common format and widely shared. Skilful senior managers recognize the importance of keeping the systems honest by directing them at problems, not punishment.

Because they are useful, such controls are accepted. Because responsibility for results is pushed down, success can be shared and ownership is possible. In contrast, where the focus is on finding fault – as it often has been in traditional organizations in the past – the result of such control is resentment and filtered information. Where the focus is on problem solving and providing the resources to make achievement possible, the results are energetic motivation. Where the focus is on control and discovering failures, by contrast, risk taking, openness, and with it innovation dry up. Good ideas cannot come to fruition in a complex business without the concerted co-ordination, cross-disciplinary teamwork, and disciplined follow-up we have been describing. Finally, however, even good systems can be subverted if trust and commitment to innovation and flexibility are seen to be lacking.

Our argument, that both technology and environment contribute to apparently opposing needs for simultaneous stability and change in the semiconductor industry, is neither one of "technological determinism" nor one of homogenization. While these firms' technologies and competitive environments are quite similar, their approaches to management differ notably. Despite a common goal of simultaneous control and innovation, stability and change are achieved by different methods, different "cultures," different organizational structures. The firms' differences in culture, style, and structure have already been suggested in quotations from their managers' words. There are differences, too, in the way these firms seek to skilfully apply systematic management of innovation. These differences and commonalities, and the skills required, are the subject of the remainder of this book. Further substantive differences are to be seen in their strategic approaches, to which we shall turn in the next chapter.

4

Does Strategy Exist? Does it Work?

> I think the biggest thing that I can do is to set strategy, such
> that the innovative efforts are being expended in the right
> direction . . . It's creating an effective effort, setting the
> directions, so we're applying those assets in an intelligent way.
>
> Charlie Sporck, National Semiconductor

Strategy in an Environment of Change

Despite MITI and dumping, volatile markets and technological
change, high capital costs and runaway complexity, extraordinary
turbulence and challenge, the US semiconductor industry has
demonstrated a remarkable talent for managing innovation successfully
over an extended period. How do semiconductor firms attain their
innovative results in such a challenging environment? Do these firms
really strategize? Or are changes so pervasive and unpredictable that
the firms simply respond ad hoc, regardless of what is said about
strategy?

If strategy is possible, there should be evidence of it both in the
firms' observable patterns of action, and in their internal processes.
Equally, if these firms really are adhocracies with no consistent plan
of action, then there will be no consistent patterns in their behavior,
and they will either spend no significant effort on strategic management
or ignore the outcomes of that effort.

High change and turbulent conditions are the norms for companies
in the industries we have studied. The precipitous drop in sales and
profits during 1985 and 1986, following the boom year of 1984, is

only the most recent example of the peaks and troughs characteristic of electronics industries from their infancy. The semiconductor industry in particular has experienced repeated surges in demand throughout its existence as new technical achievements, new products, or new processes come on line to drop prices and boost performance, and new applications become technically or economically feasible.

Price levels at the peaks typically averaged roughly five times those of the troughs during downturns in the 1960s and 1970s. In the most recent swing, the prices of some products dropped by about 90 percent in a 9- to 12-month period, a drop similar to that experienced for 16K EPROMs over three years between 1979 and 1981. Still, after each drop, surging demand seems to promise opportunities for superior profits and market position. Peaks traditionally entice participants to invest in more capacity, boost production, and cut prices as worldwide capacity temporarily surpasses demand. Meanwhile, the industry must still cope with new products, with ever greater demands for circuit density, production finesse, and technical precision. All of this fuels a constant push for innovation.

Can firms really strategize under such conditions? Some industry experts and some academics argue that strategic planning does not work for high-technology companies, because of high rates of change in both technology and highly competitive markets. They argue that survival requires swift response, so managers must maintain flexibility by not constraining themselves with long-term commitments. Digital Equipment's founder and President, Kenneth H. Olsen, typifies this stance, or so it seems: "We never make predictions in the future. We set short-term goals of a year or eighteen months" (cited in Patz, 1981). Some scholars agree, arguing that strategic planning undermines flexibility in high technology industries. Mintzberg, for example, asserts that the concept of strategy loses its meaning for firms in dynamic, complex environments where sophisticated innovations are required for survival:

> When the central purpose of an organization is to innovate, the results of its efforts can never be predetermined.
>
> Mintzberg, 1979, pp. 442–4

According to this reasoning, the firms will not be able to specify strategy in advance.

If these assertions are true, it ought to be difficult to detect strategic patterns in the decisions of innovative, high-technology firms. The argument that strategy makes no sense in high change environments presumes that change is random and unpredictable, and thus that the firms' responses to change will also be random. Consequently, there should be no pattern to decisions, and no systematic, discernible impact from any persistent course of action on financial performance, because "strategies" would be as random as the changes with which they are supposed to cope.

This view suggests that managers and their firms are solely reactive, capable only of responding to changes as they occur. Yet others have argued that managers and firms do seek to proactively influence their environments. Numerous proactive commitments, from advertising, acquisitions, and lobbying to boundary spanning positions and vertical integration are widely documented and explicitly identified as intentional by managers (Galbraith, 1973; Thompson, 1967). Others have argued that firms seek to extend their control over external events to increasing their own dominance and decrease their reliance on other firms or constituencies in the environment (Child, 1972; Pfeffer and Salancik, 1978). Some limited data also suggest a more outward, proactive view among semiconductors executives as contrasted with food processing industry managers (Miles and Snow, 1978).

We can test these views from several perspectives. First, we can look at objective data on the commitment of semiconductor firms to externally verifiable strategies, and on the impact of those activities on financial performance results. An earlier study of the top ten US merchant semiconductor firms for the five-year period 1975 through 1979 (Schoonhoven, 1984) clearly illustrates the existence of discernibly different patterns of action that persist over time. The same study also shows that some patterns are more effective than others, and that consistency in the chosen pattern is a plus. This is scarcely surprising, since most managers and most strategy texts assert the rationality of consistent, mutually reinforcing actions in strategic management.

These external data can also be compared with managers' statements – in annual reports, for instance – to test whether their announced intentions are consistent with observable activities. Here too, classical strategy analysis argues that inconsistency is a flaw, and that unclear or inconsistent announced intentions can cause confusion and difficulty with implementation.

Another test of the adhocracy view requires a very different sort of data. We can seek persistence and change in established patterns since the data of the earlier study. For this, we must move "inside" the firms to examine their strategic intentions. For all the companies we examined, numerous published statements by managers describe their rationale for strategic actions, as well as visible commitments to the courses of action they identify.

Thus we offer two sorts of data: the external evidence of consistent, concerted past action that persists over time and has an impact on performance; and internal evidence of intention, effort, and response to external change. Taken together, these data create a powerful argument in favor of realized strategy that actually occurs over time, and of intention and deliberate actions to achieve it. In this chapter we will argue that strategy does matter, especially in times of change, and we will demonstrate the existence of consistent and persistent strategies over time in this industry. We will also illustrate different patterns of strategy among our sample firms.

Strategy Data in Semiconductors

A look at external data relating to semiconductor firms – such as R&D investments, sales, return on investment (ROI), and firms' market positionings – reveals visible evidence of consistent patterns of behavior which persist over time. Apparently, these firms do maintain a course of action, despite changes in environment and technology. However, their patterns of action are not identical strategically, despite common environments and technology. All face the urgent need to produce a continuing stream of complex product and process innovations while maintaining high quality, economical production, but their methods differ. Nor, as we shall later discuss, are their courses of action irrevocably fixed.

Turning first to the external evidence of persistent past commitments, several explicit strategies are to be found in the semiconductor industry. The top ten US merchant semiconductor firms offer a useful window into the industry and its strategic elements. Among this top ten, Schoonhoven (1984) identified a number of distinct patterns. The evidence argues for systematic, persistent efforts to address business in a consistent fashion, and for different fashions in ways of being in the semiconductor business. The evidence is most easily visible among merchant components makers – that is, firms whose main business is the manufacture of semiconductor components for sale to others. (Evidence for semiconductor strategy in other firms which manufacture substantial amounts of components for their own use – IBM, for instance – is less visible because these firms do not sell their semiconductors on the open market, and in any case, their main business is elsewhere.)

Various strategic elements coalesce into broad patterns.[1] Some firms engage in the business as broad-line suppliers of a wide range of products, while others pursue more limited business areas. Some firms pursue a leading-edge technology position, while others are content to follow. Some aggressively slash prices, stay with a product through its maturity stages, or seek dominant market share, while others follow contrary practices. These strategic elements address various facets of each firm's positioning vis-à-vis its markets, technology, and competitors. Strategy theory argues that a number of mutually reinforcing elements must be crafted together to support a strategy, and these elements should be rationally consistent. No single element alone really constitutes "a strategy."

The first elements listed in table 4.1 argue proactive and deliberate choices through which a firm seeks to select and influence its competitive arena. The choice of "what business to be in" is the classic description of strategy, but far more limited decisions on pricing, technology positioning, licensing, and product line maintenance also affect the strategic arena in the semiconductor industry. Firms seeking a broad-line position have defined for themselves a different business from that pursued by narrow-line specialists. The first two elements in table 4.1 are alternatives regarding the breadth of product line: firms can choose a narrow niche strategy (as Intel, Analog Devices, and Mostek traditionally have in the past) or a broad spectrum approach (as TI, Motorola, National Semiconductor and Fairchild traditionally have).

This corporate level choice carries powerful consequences in terms of the skills and resource allocations needed to support it. Such a choice could be made by default, with a firm blundering into various products and markets with little or no relationship among them, but this is unlikely to lead to survival in so tough and demanding an environment. A more effective approach is explicit choice, with periodic assessments of product line breadth to ensure complete coverage, on the one hand, or to prune the product line and maintain focus, on the other.

Table 4.1 Realized strategic action by firm

Strategies	Intel	National	Analog Devices	TI	Intersil	Siliconix	Motorola	AMD	MOStek	Fairchild
1 Broad-line supplier	✓	✓	✓	✓	✓	✓	✓			✓
2 High-tech high-growth niche	✓	✓	✓		✓	✓		✓	✓	
3 Technical dominance	✓									
4 R&D as % revenues, five-year average	10.0	8.7	6.2	4.3	8.1	9.1	6.3	7.5	7.2	5.1
5 Protects technology	✓									
6 High-end pricing: gross margins, five-year average	50.3	31.3	48.8	32.4	37.1	48.2	40.2	37.6	35.7	33.6
7 Early abandonment of product in life cycle	✓		✓			✓			✓	
8 Patents sought, licences granted		✓		✓			✓	✓		✓
9 Maturity and decline support		✓		✓			✓			✓
10 Aggressive price slashing		✓		✓						

11 Dominant market share or market abandonment				∨						
12 Aggressive manufacturing cost-cutting: fixed asset productivity	4.5	6.1	4.6	5.4	9.5	3.0	4.4	4.6	3.1	3.6
13 Second sourcing–high growth		∨					∨			
14 Second sourcing–general policy		∨		∨	∨		∨			∨
15 Marketing–merchandising					∨					
16 Vertical integration backwards				∨						∨
17 Vertical integration forwards	∨	∨		∨	∨		∨	∨	∨	∨
18 Capital expenditures as % revenues	16.9	9.3	11.3	10.6	4.5	10.9	7.3	11.8	17.2	7.7
19 Off-shore plant: low labor cost	∨	∨	∨		∨	∨	∨	∨	∨	∨
20 Off-shore plant: market penetration				∨			∨			
21 SIA Charter Member	∨	∨					∨	∨	∨	∨
22 SIA Member	∨	∨	∨			∨	∨	∨	∨	∨

Source: adapted from Schoonhoven (1984).

Product line focus can be founded on technology (MOS technology memory, for Mostek, for instance, or microprocessors, for Intel), or it can be based on market coverage (especially as in the case of broad-line suppliers).

One test of whether the patterns are deliberate is consistency. The elements and their logical coherence will be discussed at length later; for the moment, our point is that the elements do coalesce into broadly discernible patterns. Another test is stated intention. Executives in micro-electronics do assert that such choices are deliberate. Two quotes will suggest their views:

> We certainly try to define overall corporate strategy, the kinds of things we want to do, the kinds of things we don't want to do . . .
>
> Gordon Moore, Intel

> We [initially] designed a group of instruments around that audio oscillator . . . we built up a complementary group of instruments in that field. Then we decided that we would concentrate on the field of electronic instrumentation. . . . This made a logical package to go together.
>
> David Packard, Hewlett-Packard

A closer look also argues for deliberate choice among these firms, on account of the consistency and relatively persistently maintained commitments visible in their actions.

Niche Elements

Technical dominance, strategy element three in table 4.1, refers to the explicit choice to establish and maintain technical leadership. The firm choosing such a strategy would logically be expected to offer the most advanced products, to enter the market first with these products, and to be at the forefront of manufacturing technology, at least for its leading-edge products. Intel is the acknowledged industry leader among US corporations, both by reputation and on the basis of repeated market "firsts." Intel is also thought to be the world leader in microprocessors, and the firm continues to assert its intention to remain dominant, and to do so by continued investment in R&D for new products and new processes. (Some maintain, however, that Intel's deficient manufacturing has enabled its competitors to drive it out of the markets for DRAMs, SRAMs, and more recently EPROMs – now all commodity products. We shall return to a discussion of the manufacturing end-game in a later chapter.)

Technical dominance in a rapidly changing scientific domain must be maintained by sustained research and development expenditure. Strategic element four measures R&D expenditures as a percentage of sales. The five-year average used reflects the realities of research: R&D expenditures cannot be expected to yield fruit immediately, and time is required to move a product from the lab into the marketplace. Intel's R&D expenditures as a percentage of sales, consistent with the firm's technical reputation, lead the US top ten. Siliconix and National ranked closely behind in 1975–9 data; Siliconix, like Intel, is a narrow-niche producer. Dollars alone will not guarantee success, of course, but it is difficult to imagine a firm successfully maintaining technical leadership without consistent, persistent, sustained investment in R&D.

Strategy element five refers to a firm's choice to deny competitors access to technology that it develops. Here the dynamics of the semiconductor industry and the practice of "second sourcing" play a role. Traditionally, customers like General Motors and the US military have demanded that some "second source" be available to produce any crucial element. Such demands are most likely to face a smaller firm – but all firms in the US industry at least face intense user pressures to permit second sourcing. Thus, in order to sell a new product, the developing firm must license others to produce it, sharing with them both product design and any associated manufacturing technology, in some cases at least.

Second sourcing has two components: first, the "seller" or inventor of a device may license its design to others; second, "buyers" may license designs originated by inventors. The first instance is a strategy to spread availability of a device, often in hopes of making it the industry standard. This is strategy element five: a firm may choose to make its designs widely available, or not. The second approach is a means of upgrading product designs by using research done by others, either as a means of penetrating high-growth markets (strategy element 13), or as a general practice (strategy element 14). Among our sample firms, National Semiconductor, Texas Instruments, and Motorola pursued general policies of second sourcing others' designs, and National also second-sourced in high-growth areas.

The purchase of second sourcing rights requires "sellers" of technology licences. Of the top ten firms, Intel was the only firm consistently mentioned as only selectively second sourcing its cutting-edge products. In choosing to deny others access to its leading-edge technology, Intel limited these products' availability – and also limited the spread to others of its discoveries. (In a parallel fashion, user–manufacturer firms IBM and DEC have also sought to protect their proprietary technology by manufacturing key components or retaining key technologies in-house.) Some years after the period analysed in the Schoonhoven study, Gordon Moore of Intel commented on the company's need to permit second sourcing:

> We have to do some of that. Well, tactically at least. Some of the things we get into become so much a part of our customer's business, they get very uncomfortable with a single source. We have had to reluctantly set up alternative sources for products along the way. Increasingly, we're going to have to be less reluctant; otherwise, people gang up on us – other companies. If we're competing from a position where we're sole source and there are three others who have agreed to make the same product [a competing version] at roughly the same point in the customer's decision cycle, that puts us at a distinct disadvantage.

These firms face tough choices between protecting proprietary technology and sharing it in order to expand the potential market. The interplay between second sourcing and competitive advantage is explicit, and so, too is the trade-off involved in revealing proprietary information. This is not a minor matter. In dealing with the substantially closed markets of Japan, the US semiconductor makers' market share has remained constant at about 9 percent since 1973, through repeated dollar devaluations and "open market" agreements (Prestowitz, 1988). Here, second sourcing acquires added importance, because of Japanese firms' preference for dealing with other Japanese firms. Second sourcing may open opportunities – and may help strong competitors upgrade their capability.

Where a firm can deny competitors access to proprietary technology or component designs, its cutting-edge advantage can be more easily sustained, supporting the next strategy element: premium pricing. Electronics customers will pay premium prices for top-end items offering superior performance, or items for which there is no viable substitute. In the early days of electronics, the military was often a customer for high-end items, although military contracts often require second sources to assure supply. Today the potential for technologically based competition makes many consumer goods OEMs or industrial goods manufacturers active premium customers. Computers offer examples in a dazzling array of applications, including business machines like the MacIntosh II or Compacq 386 machines, engineering workstations and CAD systems.

By contrast, entering into second sourcing arrangements can enfranchise competitors, as Moore and Andrew S. Grove, Intel President and Chief Operating Officer, observed in the firm's 1986 annual report, commenting on why 1986 had been such a difficult year:

> In 1983, demand for semiconductors exploded, fueled in large part by the rapid expansion of the personal computer business. No one could get enough semiconductors, especially Intel microprocessors, which had emerged as the standard for personal computers . . . We licensed other semiconductor manufacturers to produce Intel microprocessors, peripherals, and microcontrollers. We met our customers' needs and helped expand the total market for our products, but we also lost control over a generation of our products and created our own competition.

High-end pricing is typically of very limited duration: it holds up until alternative sources can provide the same component, through second sourcing requirements, for instance; or until others seeking to gain market share force prices down with comparable products. In semiconductor markets, substantial price slashing is routine, as new competitors enter the market. These price cuts also take place when some new device becomes available to substitute for an older product, providing all its capabilities and perhaps others as well, or providing existing capabilities at notably greater speed, in a smaller space, or for a significantly lower price. All these substitution effects regularly take place as electronics manufacturing capability and product designs advance, and have done so predictably through the history of the electronics industry. Product uniqueness is quite ephemeral, putting a short time limit on the possibilities for premium pricing.

Table 4.1 uses five-year average gross margin data as an indicator of high-end pricing. Intel's average gross margin of 50.3 percent during 1975–9 leads the top ten, followed by Analog Devices and Siliconix, both, like Intel, narrow-niche, leading-edge technology producers. Such data depend in large measure on industry-wide conditions (such as worldwide overcapacity, or a general economic downturn), and are most sensibly interpreted in comparison with industry averages rather than in isolation.

Strategy element seven, abandonment of the product early in its life cycle, deals with the choice to manufacture only small volumes of unique products. By abandoning products when other competitors enter the market, a firm would presumably be following a "creaming" strategy – remaining active only so long as premium pricing could be maintained, and avoiding the larger capital expenditures required to ramp production up into high volumes as broader markets (and more intense competition) developed. From 1975 to 1979, Intel was a consistent practitioner of this strategy element, again along with other niche players Analog Devices, Siliconix, and Mostek. However, in 1985 Intel reassessed this strategy, and has since elected to remain in contested markets, seeking to maintain share through aggressive improvements in manufacturing cost to support competitive pricing for older products.

Pursuit of strategy elements three through seven (technical dominance, high percentage level R&D expenditures, selective licensing to protect technology, premium pricing, and abandonment of products early in the life cycle) suggests a consistent pattern. All these elements make sense as aspects of a choice to limit market participation to a selected niche, where leadership is the hoped-for outcome of heavy R&D expenditures. Without heavy R&D expenditures, a special niche might be gained temporarily by acquisition or good fortune, but it would be difficult or impossible to maintain in this industry without significant on-going R&D commitment. Intel was the only one of the top ten to consistently pursue all of these elements as a concerted niche strategy in Schoonhoven's (1984) study.

Broad Market Strategy Elements

A different set of elements seems more consistent with a broader strategy. Patenting discoveries, and licensing patents or proprietary technology (strategy element eight) represent the converse of the selective second sourcing noted above. In licensing, the firm seeks revenues more widely by permitting others to use its technology. With widespread mobility among firms of managers, technicians, and scientists, and with the broadly shared scientific basis of semiconductor technology, licensing represents a bet in favor of gaining assured advantage from technical developments quickly, before others can duplicate the achievement.

Quicker marketplace acceptance of the firm's product as the standard can also result, if for no other reason than that it becomes widely and quickly available from multiple sources. Product availability in some markets – computers, for instance – has often turned on market share size: thus IBM is the *de facto* standard in personal computers because it holds the largest market share; and MAP (Manufacturing Automation Protocol) is the *de facto* standard for manufacturing automation interfaces because General Motors demanded it. The tradition of second sourcing in semiconductors has amended the product availability question so that wide licensing can create such a standard product for the small firm as well. Nevertheless, large firms also stand to lose least by second sourcing: their larger capacity will enable them to occupy substantial market share, while at the same time licensing others satisfies customers' demands for a second source. As might be expected, broad-line suppliers TI, Motorola, Fairchild, and National Semiconductor are all prominent practitioners of the licensing strategy, in 1975–9.

Learning Curve Elements

The next four strategy elements relate to the product life cycle "end-game" and to the learning curve popularized by the Boston Consulting Group (1972). Learning curve effects are widely observable in both high-technology and low-technology products, in emerging and growth industries, in services as well as in manufacturing industries, including automobiles, turbines, petrochemicals, and crushed limestone, among others (Abell and Hammond, 1979). Under learning curve conditions, as cumulative output rises, the cost per unit declines. Average per unit costs may decline because employees learn how to manufacture the items or provide the service more efficiently, or because improvements in design, manufacturing engineering, or production technology lower costs, sometimes radically.

Cumulative volume learning and its associated benefits can sustain lengthy competitive advantages. Where costs do decline in this fashion, and in semiconductors they often do, the firm with the greatest accumulated base of manufacturing experience will have the lowest costs and thus be able to offer lower prices while still maintaining its margins. This, in turn, should allow the firm to prosper and gain market share while competitors struggle. The firm with the largest accumulated experience gains advantage by staying with the product through its life cycle: it should continue to lead its competitors in costs, prices, and margins. Strategy element nine in table 4.1 is staying with a product into its maturity and decline stages, in contrast to element seven, early abandonment of the product (as soon as other competitors appear, for instance). Broad-line suppliers Motorola, TI, National Semiconductor, and Fairchild typically stick with a product, thus accumulating more experience.

Occasionally, the firm that stays with a product gains a marked advantage when others elect to abandon an older product that is not completely displaced by newer substitutes: the survivor gains vast market share in a virtually uncontested niche, as Motorola did in the market for discrete devices when its chief competitors moved to integrated circuits. Discrete devices are separate transistors, rectifiers, diodes and so on, in contrast to integrated circuits, which incorporate various components on to a single chip. Motorola's niche position in discrete devices, maintained since others exited the market in the early 1970s, has continued to offer excellent returns. In contrast to more hotly contested markets with many competitors, Motorola is the only supplier of many older discrete devices today.

The cost advantage of the supplier with greatest accumulated experience suggests a trade-off, according to the Boston Consulting Group (BCG). The firm that aggressively lowers prices (strategy element ten in table 4.1) should gain market share and thus more experience and lower costs. According to BCG, lower prices, lower costs, and greater market share will together constitute a dominant position because the firm with the largest market share will be the firm with the greatest experience and therefore the lowest-cost, most efficient production. Such a firm should achieve better margins than its less experienced competitors, while its greater market share serves as a barrier to their catching up in accumulated volume.

Two firms best known for lowering prices are TI and National Semiconductor. Both consistently practise aggressive price cutting. TI, the initiator of this strategy in the semiconductor industry, characteristically holds a large market share. In contrast, Intel did not practice this strategy in 1975–9.

If the BCG reasoning holds, the firm that cannot establish a commanding market share should leave the market for that product:

it will be at a consistent disadvantage in accumulated experience and therefore in efficiency, cost, price, and profit in that market. Strategy element eleven, dominant market share or product abandonment, illustrates this choice; it is the opposite of staying with the product. Here, the firm abandons products in which it cannot sustain a dominant market share. According to industry observers, TI consistently abandons markets in which it cannot establish a leading market share, although it maintains its position in markets where it is well established.

Strategy element twelve also concerns the end-game. Aggressively cutting manufacturing costs is a way of forcing the learning curve. Instead of waiting for insight to come as experience develops, deliberately devoting resources, energy, and attention to the manufacturing process speeds up decline in cost. This permits earlier price cutting and thus earlier establishment of substantial market share with its associated benefits. Some firms are reputed to price to the learning curve even before the cost decreases are achieved, or to push very hard on manufacturing costs to support "early" price cuts. National Semiconductor and TI are again the best known for this strategy. TI regularly budgets for manufacturing cost decreases and provides incentives for their achievement. National has a reputation as a "no frills" company where low costs are emphasized.

Even in contested markets, approaches based on these strategy elements are visible. Recently, virtually all US makers of DRAMs left the market in favor of the Japanese, whose aggressive price-cutting and attention to manufacturing costs had rendered the product a commodity item. TI, in contrast, explicitly elected to remain in the DRAM market, and chose to do so by means of strenuous attention to manufacturing costs and efficiencies, traditional TI strengths. As of 1988, TI remains the only major US semiconductor maker in the 256K DRAM market, claiming to undercut Japanese costs and prices. In 1985 and in 1988, both before and after these results, TI executives asserted that the decision to remain was deliberate, and that it was related to existing TI manufacturing strengths and the desire to maintain them for longer-term, strategic advantage. TI chief executive Jerry Junkins observed:

> We decided making these high-volume memories would provide the best manufacturing disciplines.

Deliberate attention to manufacturing costs may indeed alter the older notion of learning as a simple function of experience, and not just in semiconductors. In automobiles, for instance, Toyota is widely regarded as having extremely low production costs, achieved by assiduous attention to the details of manufacturing. At Toyota, investment in engineering to achieve speedy changeovers from one model to another and to eliminate waste and down-time, and development of just-in-time methods, have contributed to productivity that was roughly six times that of comparable US plants in 1984, for instance (Schonberger, 1986). While Japanese makers did surpass GM as the largest manufacturer of automobiles, it seems that higher volume resulted from efficient production and lower costs, rather than vice versa. The learning curve notion must be re-examined in the context of attention to manufacturing costs and efficiencies, at very least.

Widely reported difficulties in the steel and automobile industries have provided a great incentive to electronics firms to cut costs lest electronics follow steel and automobiles into further loss of market share. The steel industry generally found foreign steel able to maintain a 30 percent market share for commodity items, primarily on the basis of cost advantages. Domestic automobile markets experienced similar penetration. In the electronics industry, the US merchant firms have repeatedly complained of Japanese dumping, and TI's suit was supported by the Federal Trade Commission. (TI has also sued a number of Far East producers for patent infringement.) Despite some apparent relief from the FTC and the courts, however, political answers do not produce chips. Manufacturing costs and product quality remain vital issues in the semiconductor industry. According to Mike Lockerd of Texas Instruments, speaking in early 1988,

> Manufacturing superiority is *the* issue, although time-to-market and design cycle time are also important. Today, you cannot compete without a world-class manufacturing base.

In a global market like semiconductors, aggressive cost cutting may be required by all participants because of competitors' successes. Relatively speaking, however, a firm may emphasize this cost cutting more than its competitors in an effort to maintain an extra advantage from manufacturing expertise, as TI and National are asserted to do.

Fixed asset productivity is the basis for strategy element twelve. It is frequently used as an indicator of modernization and level of automation in manufacturing activities. On 1975–9 data, TI and

National have high fixed asset productivity, exceeded only by Intersil. (Intersil's high figure is attributable to unusually high uncapitalized lease assets, however.) This strategy also relates to expert asset usage – usable output, even from new equipment, can vary substantially among firms. Differences in yield among semiconductor firms can rapidly translate into substantial cost differences.

The choice to maintain older equipment and seek to squeeze more production out of it is limited in high-tech firms, where often new products require new production facilities. The trend to ever smaller circuit architecture provides an example: it is typically not feasible to attain sub-micron IC widths with older equipment because of limitations in control, resolution or reliability, and higher contamination rates. A move from visible light to electron beam lithography, or a shift from green to purple lasers in order to improve mask resolution, offer similar examples.

The firm seeking a broad-line position should logically follow the sort of learning curve reasoning embodied in accumulating experience by staying with a product, aggressively utilizing its advantageous costs to cut prices, thereby gaining dominant market share, or, where this is not possible, abandoning the fight. The broad-line strategy would also argue for a degree of manufacturing expertise sufficient to maintain enough breadth of market position in enough products to mount a credibly broad line. Aggressive attention to manufacturing costs supports the broad-line position, as does consistent investment in advanced manufacturing equipment and engineering, to achieve high productivity with that equipment. Aggressive cost cutting can force production economies enough to match or better those of competitors based on established manufacturing experience. Whether by accumulated experience or aggressive attention to manufacturing details, those firms able to utilize equipment more effectively than their competitors can enjoy substantial cost advantages – as the Japanese were alleged to, in marketing the 64K RAM – enabling them to seize market share (Walleck, 1985).

In 1975–9, TI and National were the only consistent practitioners of aggressive manufacturing cost cutting. This fitted well with their generic strategy of overall cost leadership and market share goals. However, by 1986, both Intel and Hewlett-Packard in our sample of semiconductor firms were also aggressively seeking to cut manufacturing costs (by as much as 50 percent, in Intel's case). Between 1986 and 1988, TI continued to invest heavily in manufacturing cost cutting, and by early 1988 was able to underprice Japanese competitors on 256K DRAMs. These strategies are, of course, relative: in a global industry such as semiconductors, it is impossible for any firm to remain indifferent to manufacturing costs. Cost cutting acquired vast importance when Japanese firms penetrated US markets with Japanese government support while at the same time protecting their home markets as the base for covering fixed costs.

Integration Strategies

Elements sixteen and seventeen concern vertical integration. As the manufacture of semiconductors becomes increasingly complex, the value added rises and early detection of faulty product becomes more important. Thus testing and measurement occur frequently in the manufacturing process. Testing and measurement are the more important because profit margins are low while R&D expenses are high. Semiconductor manufacturers are keenly dependent upon outsiders for test and measuring equipment and for advanced manufacturing equipment. Backwards integration among the top ten components makers is relatively rare, despite the importance of test and measurement equipment and advanced manufacturing equipment. Among the top ten, only Fairchild integrated with these suppliers in 1974–9, by acquiring test equipment manufacturers Faultfinders and Testline.

As electronics components penetrate into other products, these, too, represent potential opportunities for integration. Early integration efforts in the industry centered on consumer products, because such products were uniquely dependent on semiconductor components and carried much higher margins than the components themselves. One National manager commented that his corporation was interested, in the early days, in

> . . . anything that was heavily IC dependent – calculators, watches, or games – essentially as forward integration from our existing IC expertise. The margins in consumer products were enormously larger than in semiconductor products, and it seemed so easy: we were sure we could make it, and make it cheaper and better.

Watches, calculators, games, and home computers are all examples of products where forward integration efforts were pursued by many of the top ten merchant semiconductor producers. Typically, these efforts were initially successful in a limited way, but ultimately failed – usually because, as components makers, the top ten had little or no skill or experience in consumer marketing or channels of distribution and service; and they seemed unable to develop these skills effectively. The firms' general emphasis on technology in contrast to marketing is notable in this regard. Only AMD was classified as "marketing oriented" by industry reputation (strategy element fifteen in table 4.1).

TI's experiences with calculators and watches offer excellent examples: with both products the company achieved early success, being relatively early in the market and managing impressive growth. Aggressive manufacturing cost cutting brought prices down for these consumer products, just as it did for components. However, market results were different: some retail customers felt cheated when a product for which they had paid substantially more 6 or 12 months earlier became available at the lower price. TI also experienced further difficulties in creating distribution channels. Many jewelers did not want to handle the lower-priced watch merchandise, feeling the lower profit per item not worth their time since they could not anticipate significant volume regardless of price. These small-volume distributors were substantially different in nature from the component wholesalers and distributors who handled TI's industrial products. Similarly, TI was unused to dealing with retail channels and their service requirements, nor was the firm skilled in fine jewellery design. In short, the techniques and approaches so successful in the OEM markets repeatedly failed here. After substantial participation and apparent initial success in these markets, TI failed to sustain its position and withdrew following losses.

Attempted forward integration is also highlighted in TI's withdrawal from the home computer market, despite what was widely recognized among engineers as a superior product initially, and the firm's success with scientific computers. The problem again was that TI's home computer could not be sold effectively, in part because TI lacked positive recognition among consumers. This recognition has proved a larger factor in consumer markets than the reputations for technical expertise and technological innovation these companies regularly rely upon in their dealings with OEMs. Delay occasioned by lack of recognition contributed to product obsolescence in a rapidly changing market.

TI's commitments in several consumer markets have been withdrawn when the company perceived that it could not establish and maintain commanding market share. In contrast, TI's engineering and scientific computers and other technical products still enjoy the benefits of the company's widespread recognition among specialists as a major component supplier. In artificial intelligence systems, sold to the same scientist and engineering customers as components, TI's approach again seems quite successful.

Unsuccessful consumer experience was by no means unique to TI. Many others, including Intel, Fairchild, and National, suffered great losses or withdrew from their attempts to penetrate widely diversified markets very different from those with which they had prior experience, despite the apparently close technological characteristics of the products. A National executive commented on the difficulties:

> We're perceived as *something* in the linear circuits business in National Semiconductor. When you're perceived as something, your ability to market a totally new concept is much greater. When you have no recognition in a marketplace, then you have to face that fact . . . If you want to innovate, and what you're innovating with is driving you into an area where you don't have [established] products, and you're not in that business, then you're kidding yourself. You either introduce products to your existing customer base, or you find new customers for your existing products.

The components makers experienced greater success with products aimed at industrial markets. National Semiconductor's point-of-sale computer cash registers are a highly successful product that took off after several years of development. In 1972, supermarket customers came to National asking for a point-of-sale product. Technical expertise in microprocessors, minicomputers, and software was available, and the product received top level support from Charles Sporck, National's Chairman and CEO. Equally important, a supermarket customer had initially approached National about a product. National's sustained success with this product stands in sharp contrast to the industry's experience with watches and calculators, where competitors used to consumer channels easily bested the components makers. Successful integration efforts at National include the company's acquisition, in late 1979, of the computer marketing and field service operations of Itel, a mainframe computer manufacturer and former customer for National's integrated circuits.

Integration strategies have received continuing attention in the semiconductor industry in part because of extensive integration (as well as substantial related-technology diversification) among major Japanese semiconductor companies. Matsushita, Toshiba, and NEC are all complex companies manufacturing a broad range of end-products among their affiliate companies, thus guaranteeing a certain baseline market for their components operations. The benefits of this linkage have been suggested as yet another source of competitive advantage for Japanese firms vis-à-vis their somewhat less diversified, somewhat smaller US counterparts.

Capacity Decisions

Other elements also carry implications for the position a firm takes in its environment, and thus for its strategic pattern. Capacity decisions acquire special importance in an industry so vulnerable to recession, so volatile in demand, and so subject to market share economics. Because semiconductor components are sold to OEMs, their market reflects and magnifies recessionary swings: such derivative markets are among the first to be hit, among those experiencing the steepest declines, and among the last to recover.

This pattern has been accentuated by significant foreign participation in US markets, sustained by "Japan, Inc.'s" advantageous home market base, capital costs, and government support, according to the US firms. It is particularly acute when global capacity – even "obsolete" capacity – exceeds demand. During economic slowdowns, just when income is reduced, important financial commitments to capacity expansion, continued R&D funding, facilities upgrading and the like must be made.

Should capacity be expanded during the downturn, in anticipation of good positioning when the recovery comes and competitors' capacity is constrained? This can be a deliberate and proactive strategy, or, especially since the Japanese successes of 1976, it can be a response to anticipated moves by competitors. Some observers have identified persistent downturn investments as a key to Japanese penetration of US markets during cyclical capacity shortages (Abegglen and Stalk, 1985).

Capital expenditures as a percentage of sales for the top ten US merchant semiconductor firms of the 1975–9 timeframe give some indication of this strategy (element eighteen in table 4.1). Intel, Mostek, and AMD rate as the heaviest investors, relative to sales: all were narrow-niche specialists during this time period. Broad-line suppliers TI, National, Fairchild, and Motorola trail the leaders. (Larger firms like TI and Motorola obviously enjoy advantages in that any single expensive facility will represent a smaller portion of their much larger sales base. Where they are substantially diversified, again, their reinvestment rate may be affected by businesses with lower rates of technological change.)

All the top ten US firms have substantially increased their capital expenditures as a percentage of sales since 1975; for example, they were up 50 percent for 1979. In total, capital expenditures for SIC code 3674, semiconductor and related devices, multiplied more than threefold from 1979 to 1984. This, too, contrasts with US industrial practice in general, which tends to invest a much smaller portion of sales, the cause of recent US manufacturing difficulties according to some (e.g. Eckstein et al., 1984; Hayes and Wheelwright, 1984).

A related capacity decision, that of plant location, also has special meaning in the semiconductor world. Like many manufacturers, the components makers have experienced competitive pressure on labor costs. All top ten have located facilities off-shore (strategy element nineteen), a strategy implemented virtually industry-wide about 1966–7. In 1967, wages represented 26.4 percent of total manufacturing costs for these firms; by 1972, this proportion had dropped to 14.8 percent, and 1976 data show wages at 11.7 percent of total manufacturing costs. Ten years later, while automated processes are beginning to affect costs in selected segments of the semiconductor manufacturing process, assembly is still often high cost and labor intensive. With per-hour labor costs in less developed countries of the Far East, South America and Southeast Asia at a half, a third, or even a tenth of the US rate, labor seems an important cost element. Presumably such an advantage is temporary, and labor costs can be expected to rise eventually, as they did in Japan. Nevertheless, the differentials may last for many years.

Other locations offer access to markets or information about local needs and preferences (element twenty). Facilities located in European countries like France, Germany, or the UK, or in Japan itself, while not offering substantially lower labor costs, are assumed to offer means of meeting local and foreign competition in the local markets. Thus, in contrast to the labor-cost basis of decisions to locate in Southeast Asia, the decision to locate in Europe or in Japan appears market-driven.

As table 4.1 indicates, in 1979 TI was the only firm to locate its entire manufacturing process, including product design and wafer fabrication (both relatively low in labor intensity) as well as assembly and testing (both relatively high in labor intensity) within an off-shore target market. TI was also the first US manufacturer to locate a complete plant in Japan, rather than turning to a joint venture or a local licensee. This is in part due to Japanese reluctance to have US firms' subsidiaries on-shore; TI declined to enter a joint venture, and used evidence of patent infringement to gain entry (Prestowitz, 1988). By contrast, National and Motorola have located highly technical, low-labor activities like wafer fabrication in Europe, while locating highly labor intensive assembly in lower-wage areas.

Plant locations abroad can carry very different strategic implications in the late 1980s, when Japanese or Korean factory workers are assumed to possess superior manufacturing skills. Particularly when combined with joint ventures, plants abroad may provide a means to access manufacturing expertise. This was the widely heralded reasoning behind GM's NUMI venture, and some have asserted that TI gained such skills from its plant in Miho, Japan – although TI sources assert that Miho and its Richardson, Texas sister plant are "very much on a par" in terms of yield and output results.

Affecting the Policy Environment

The next strategy elements represent deliberate attempts to change the environment, rather than to select portions of it or respond to it. Elements twenty-one and twenty-two concern the Semiconductor Industry Association (SIA), an industry trade group. About 1976, US components makers experienced the first significant market inroads by Japanese competitors, who seized noticeable market share when IBM's choice to purchase components rather than manufacture them internally created substantial unanticipated demand at a time when other customers' needs also increased. The US makers' capacity shortfall represented instant opportunity for the Japanese manufacturers, especially when combined with Japanese manufacturing expertise, knowledgeable marketing and willingness to accept lower profits in order to take market share.

The SIA was formed by a number of US firms in response to this unexpected Japanese success in taking and holding US market share. The SIA was chartered to influence US industrial policy in such areas as investment tax credits, R&D expensing, trade practices, and tariffs, where US semiconductor firms were perceived to operate at a disadvantage to their more protected Japanese competitors. Among the top ten US semiconductor makers, AMD, Fairchild, Intel, and National were charter SIA members and leading financial backers (strategy element twenty-one in table 4.1). All of the top ten except TI were members in 1979 (strategy element twenty-two).

Forming the SIA represented a new item in components makers' strategy, but it was not their only reaction to the tightening conditions of competition. Intel, a charter member and supporter of the SIA, devoted substantial resources to the effort to influence public policy in the person of Robert Noyce, a company founder and an accomplished technologist who, as mentioned earlier, shares honors for the conception of the integrated circuit with Jack Kilby of Texas Instruments. Noyce, widely regarded as a superb administrator and skilled technical manager, devoted increasing amounts of time after 1976 to public policy, speaking before Congress and granting numerous interviews in the public press. Robert Galvin, the Chairman of Motorola, devoted time to similar efforts, and Motorola also launched a nationwide advertising campaign to publicize its view that the practices of "Japan, Inc.", an informal coalition of Japanese government, banking, and industrial entities, prevented a "level playing field" in semiconductors.

Texas Instruments, although not an SIA charter member, has also actively moved to influence its competitive environment. TI brought suit before the Federal Trade Commission 1984 accusing Japanese firms of dumping components in the US markets at prices less than the Japanese firms' cost of manufacture, in order to take market share by driving US firms out of their own domestic markets. As one of the few US firms having located an entire semiconductor manufacturing process in Japan and as a widely acclaimed master of manufacturing practice, TI was especially well positioned to judge Japanese costs.

TI noted that US firms were systematically restricted in access to Japanese home markets, an observation also made by others (including several US trade representatives to Japan, the Secretary of Commerce, and the President). In 1986, the Federal Trade Commission found TI's suit had merit, and negotiated trade agreements with Japan included improved access for the US semiconductor firms. However, debate continues, as do negotiations, after the imposition of punitive duties on some Japanese electronic goods, and continued charges of dumping (Prestowitz, 1988).

TI also brought suit against several Far Eastern producers for patent infringement on some semiconductor items. One suit concerned DRAMs, a product for which TI holds roughly 20 percent of the US domestic market share, and Samsung, a competitor sued by TI, about 5 percent. Intel also brought suit, claiming infringement of microcode in its microprocessors by Japanese competitors. These and other suits are still going on, although some agreements on royalty payments have apparently been reached.

Specific attempts to change the environment, such as industry trade associations, lobbying, or law-suits, are neither new nor unique to the semiconductor industry. They do, however, represent a very different aspect of strategy than is typically discussed for manufacturing firms. Such proactive, "political" efforts may be of increasing importance in global markets.

Strategy Patterns and Performance

Our discussion suggests that certain strategy elements cluster logically and mutually support one another. Most particularly, two broadly different approaches can be readily identified among the top ten firms: a broad-line approach, aimed at supplying a wide array of devices to a range of markets; and a narrow-niche approach, emphasizing advanced technology products for a more limited market. Broad-line suppliers can be expected to emphasize manufacturing and cost cutting, seek to support their products through maturity, and aggressively slash prices to gain market share. High-technology niche firms can be expected to emphasize technical dominance, R&D, high-end pricing, and the abandonment of markets that come under attack by low-price rivals. The practice of Intel, a niche firm, can be contrasted with that of TI, a large broad-line firm, or National Semiconductor, a smaller broad-line firm, to highlight the patterns and illustrate how the strategic elements interact.

The High-Technology Niche Strategy: Intel

Intel is the outstanding electronics success story of the 1970s. Intel was the first firm to produce a microprocessor or a computer on a chip. Starting up in the mid-1960s, Intel grew from sales of $600,000 in 1969 to sales of $1.63 billion in 1984, despite a decline to $1.37 billion in 1985 (a year of industry-wide slump). The firm has consistently emphasized technical sophistication and continued investment.

Like many high-technology firms, Intel began as a spin-off from a larger firm, Fairchild Camera and Instrument. Robert Noyce, later a co-inventor of the integrated circuit, and Gordon Moore, who had been Fairchild's head of R&D, became disenchanted with the bureaucracy and lack of appreciation for the pace of technological change at Fairchild's Semiconductor Division. Fairchild had been a technological leader, important in the development of some early manufacturing techniques that made mass production of semiconductors possible. The technology continued to change, however, while Fairchild did not. Noyce and Moore left to found Intel, two of the many "Fairchildren" who started numerous semiconductor firms.

Moore and Noyce vowed that Intel would maintain its technological leadership, in contrast to Fairchild. Almost instantly, the new firm seized a commanding position in semiconductor memory chips. But soon a larger opportunity loomed. Intel received a contract from a Japanese manufacturer to produce a family of related calculator chips of complex design and interconnection – only a step away from a true computer, as Intel's project head, Dr Marcian E. "Ted" Hoff, realized.

Hoff combined processing circuitry with memory as a "computer on a chip," a more elegant solution than simply hooking together separate elements. Hoff saw his insight as "applying 'computerese' to a technology problem" in order to meet the customer's needs with the limited engineering and design resources of the small firm. Hoff's discovery would ultimately change the direction of the semiconductor industry, although at first this potential was not obvious.

Niche Strategy in a Growth Market The microprocessor made it possible to develop standard chips whose logic (and thus applications) could be determined by software, or programs. This permitted volume production and economies of scale on hardware, which could then be custom programmed for individual applications. The novelty of the advance was widely appreciated: "The microcomputer, in other words, is one of those rare innovations that at the same time reduces the cost of manufacture *and* enhances the capabilities and value of the product," as *Fortune* (1975) noted at the time referring to microprocessors as "microcomputers or computers-on-a-chip". While TI claims it was issued the patent for microprocessors, Intel did the major commercial innovation. Because competitors responded slowly, Intel established market dominance for the premium product which it has essentially maintained ever since, through generations of products.

For Intel, the decision to go ahead with the microprocessor entailed a decision to undertake educating its customers to microprocessor use, a departure from the firm's previous purely technological emphasis toward something more akin to market outreach, and toward system emphasis. Les Vadasz, Intel's Senior Vice President for Planning, noted that this concept grew from interaction with the original client, whose engineers had to be educated first. However, he also noted that "the most innovative stage of all was to decide to provide development support, software design aid to the customer, so that he could use the product and customize it for his own need." In short, Intel began to consider itself in the business of systems, not just the business of semiconductor component hardware. Between 1971 and 1974, Intel's sales grew at an average rate of 143 percent, an indication of its dominance during that period. By 1984, microprocessors constituted about 50 percent of Intel's $1.63 billion sales. In 1989, Intel remains the world's largest manufacturer of microprocessors.

Today Intel is a designer and producer of "electronic building blocks" for OEMs. Intel makes large-scale integrated circuits in two major market areas: memory chips and microprocessors (including associated hardware, software, and development systems). Since departing from the RAM market in October 1984, the firm has focused on more complex products. The firm's strategy is described in the 1985 Annual Report:

> Intel's strategy is to offer OEMs a wide range of solutions based
> on industry standards, and to offer these solutions at the
> component, board, and system levels.

Major product areas include microprocessors and microcontrollers, which contain a central processing unit, random access memory, program memory, and input/output circuitry. In essence, these devices are small computers specialized for control purposes, and embedded in a wide array of products. Intel also supplied advanced memory devices, like EPROMs, EEPROMs, fast static RAMs, non-volatile RAMs, and programmable logic devices, as well as software, development systems, microcomputer systems, and microcommunications products.

These products target premium priced, high growth markets. Growth in the microprocessor market worldwide for the 1980s was estimated at 32.4 percent; in microprocessor peripherals markets, at 30.5 percent; and in memories, at 17.8 percent (Dataquest, 1985). Older, slower growth markets do exist, for DRAMs, smaller components, and less complex microprocessors; Intel does not compete in these commodity markets, where price cutting often determines market share and many others offer essentially interchangeable products.

Intel continues to stress technological leadership, but as the technology becomes more widely used and understood, this position is becoming increasingly difficult to sustain, particularly across a broad spectrum. In many instances, leadership involves mastery of end-product details as well as component technology: microprocessors were used in more than 100,000 different products during the first decade of their existence.

At the same time, increasing competition has pressured even the technology leader to push hard to be the manufacturing technology leader in its industry as well, to reduce manufacturing lead-time, improve already high quality (currently measured in a few hundred defects per million parts), and lower manufacturing cost. Intel's productivity per manufacturing worker increased by 96 percent between 1985 and 1987, while manufacturing costs were halved.

In October, 1984, Intel exited from the market for DRAMs which the firm had initially created, citing as reasons the price and margin pressures in what had become a commodity marketplace. (Many other US components makers had also left the DRAM market.) In 1986, Intel ceased to make magnetic bubble memories. Both of these decisions sound like the strategy of exiting older markets so typical of Intel in the 1975–9 period. Even so, in the microprocessor market that Intel created in 1971 – today worth $1.9 billion – the company retains well over a third of the market. Intel has long dominated key

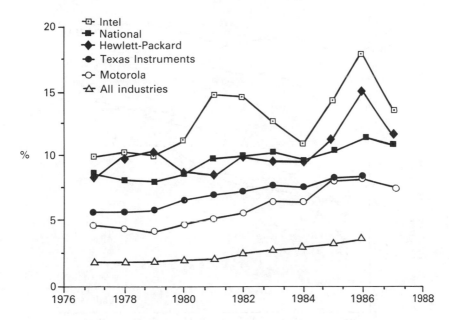

Figure 4.1 R&D as Percentage of Sales by Company and All Industries, 1977–1987

segments of the microprocessor business by its strategy of technological excellence. However, continuing technological change and technological competition are fundamental realities. Les Vadasz claims that "Two things drive this business, technology and paranoia."

To keep up, by explicit policy through thick and thin, Intel regularly spends over 10 percent of sales on R&D against an electronics industry average of about 6 percent. For comparison, the US all-industry average has risen recently to about 3 percent of sales and aerospace was about 8 percent (see figures 4.1 and 4.2). Intel's response to increasing competition and economic stringency has been increased technological emphasis: for instance, despite the 1980–1 downturn in the electronics market, its 1981 R&D expenses rose in both absolute and relative terms, to $116.5 million – about 15 percent of sales. In 1984, Value Line estimated Intel's R&D expenses as "about 13 percent" of sales in 1984, and "about 14 percent of sales" over the previous three years. In 1985, despite "a miserable year" for Intel and the industry, Intel spent $195 million (14.3 percent of

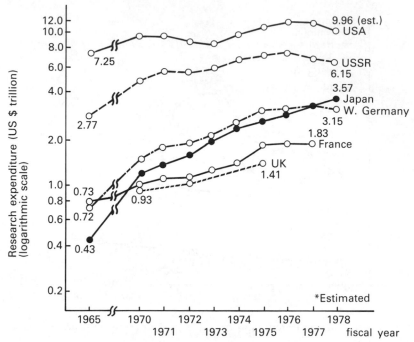

Figure 4.2 R&D Expenditure in Leading Countries
Source: Science and Technology Agency, 1979 White Paper, Tokyo: 1980. From: *Japanese Electronics Technology*. Gene Gregory. New York: John Wiley & Sons, 1985, p. 52.

sales) on R&D. The figures for 1986, when sales were even worse for the industry as a whole, are even more remarkable, since revenues dropped by 7.3 percent even against 1985's already low figures: yet Intel's 1986 R&D rose to 18 percent of sales. Such percentages document persistently high R&D commitments, through upswings and downturns alike.

Intel even sold about 12 percent of its stock to IBM in 1983, to fund continuing capital asset needs and R&D costs at a time of highly volatile sales and profits. IBM subsequently acquired another 7 percent, then sold it off in 1986, retaining its original holdings. Intel also cut salaries across the board and implemented a year-long pay freeze in 1983, to provide more funds for research. It is clear that the ante has gone up, and that R&D is considered essential to Intel's strategy by its managers.

In contrast to much of the industry, Intel continues to develop its own products, rather than acquiring technology through second sourcing. Intel is also the last remaining independent semiconductor maker of significant size to generate substantially all of its revenue from chip manufacture. In 1987, 70 percent of Intel's revenues were derived from the sale of semiconductor products. (However, National Semiconductor is close, with 60 percent of its revenues from semiconductor sales.)

Intel's stream of new products includes a 32-bit microprocessor, the 80386, which is finding wide use in the computer industry, and advanced EPROMS. Its newest offering in this family is the 80486 microprocessor, a more sophisticated and powerful computer architecture than the 80386. The 80486 was introduced in spring 1989. Described by *Electronics News* as "taking a back seat to no one in performance, the 80486 will carry a lucrative price tag . . . targeted as it is for high end systems." Products like these provide evidence of Intel's continued strategic commitment to developing state-of-the-art products with premium prices. Such products as this position Intel as both a driver and a beneficiary of the technological trends in electronic products toward increasing device density, lower power requirements, and, ultimately, lower prices per bit of storage. These characteristics of technological change are, of course, at the heart of the burgeoning application of electronic controls and memory to an ever-widening array of products.

Intel's reputation for niching and high-technology leadership is clearly reflected in its consistent practices. The 1975–9 data in table 4.1 show that the firm is reputed to be technically dominant; it invests heavily in R&D, and licenses only selectively, while not itself engaging in second sourcing. During 1975–9, Intel preferred to sell premium products, and to abandon markets when other competitors appeared: a "creaming" strategy. In a continuing pattern of consistent strategy elements over these years, Intel had not sought broad market dominance, had not manufactured in mass volume, and had not become known for aggressive cost-cutting.

There have been changes. Intel was and is often first to the marketplace with new devices. Nowadays, however, it does not always abandon products so quickly. Although the firm has consistently applied a niche strategy, coupled with leading-edge technology in product design, it is now adding to its strategy both aggressive cost cutting and strenuous attention to manufacturing details, to support continued market share and profitable harvesting of later product life cycle stages. Productivity has soared, along with output volume, cost per unit has declined, along with defective parts per million, and Intel has announced its intention to remain longer in key product markets.

Capital expenditures and R&D expenses have been key factors in Intel's business planning – but the company has also in recent years stressed manufacturing skills and innovation to fend off competitive pressure, especially from Japanese manufacturers of commodity electronics items who might seek to enter growth markets unopposed. Intel chooses not to be in commodity markets, and seeks to prevent its markets from becoming commodity-like by contesting possible entrants more than it did in the past.

Intel's extremely rapid rate of growth in 1978–9 in response to burgeoning demand was seen by industry analysts in part as a reaction to Japanese manufacturers' exploitation of US manufacturers' undercapacity after 1975, when the Japanese established a substantial beachhead in the US market for 16K memories. Reflecting this capacity shortage, Intel's capital expenditures jumped to 26.1 percent of sales in 1978, averaging 17.8 percent of sales for the decade 1976–86. Nevertheless, in 1983 and 1984, Intel again experienced capacity constraints when demand for its microprocessors exploded. The average age of Intel's plant was less than three years in 1987. A weighted average market growth rate would suggest that Intel would need to grow at roughly 30 percent per year – while maintaining technical leadership. These requirements underline not only the importance of technical excellence, but also the importance of excellence in managing both innovation and growth. Pressures such as these also carry continued heavy capital investment obligations when markets surge, and leave Intel especially vulnerable to the volatility of market demand when the industry slumps.

Intel's attitude toward second sourcing was somewhat altered in 1983 and 1984, but its original selectivity has been reinstated since that time. Explosive demand caused Intel to license more of its technology to others for a time, to ensure a ready supply for voracious customers. This also created new competitors for Intel. As a result, the company returned to a position of reluctance to license its proprietary products to competitors, resorting instead to manufacturing at multiple Intel sites, a stance that will continue, according to Andrew Grove:

> Our strategy on sole-sourced products is to manufacture them in multiple factories, which we are doing with the 80386s being manufactured in two, very soon three, and by early next year [1988] four factories. Our aim is to assure our customers of reliable and dependable supply of proprietary products. Whether or not we license someone to manufacture a given product depends on a variety of circumstances which we look at as they emerge.

The multiple-factory option is available only to a substantial company, given the cost of semiconductor facilities. Intel has licensed IBM to manufacture its 80386 for internal IBM use, another alternative to "creating competition" in the merchant market by licensing competitors, and one which also rests on a continued technology lead.

Innovation has continued to be a key focus, given rapid product and process obsolescence. As Moore noted,

> Every two years almost our entire product line turns over. We can almost go out of business in two years if we don't do it right. Maybe it's a much more vital part of our business than it is in other industries; perhaps, too, it's a different kind of planning. Our planning really tends to be the product, the technology, and the market opportunities, and only incidentally do we hang that together with the cost of capital.

Intel's dual emphasis on both growth and technological leadership is a shift from its "pure niche" strategy of the past. However, rapid innovation, technological leadership, and premium products continue to be central to the firm's strategy.

The Broadline Strategy

In contrast to Intel's focus, National Semiconductor and Texas Instruments follow a broad-line strategy of wide participation and sustained product support. The contrast between their practices and those of Intel highlight the different elements appropriate to the firms' initial fundamental choice of strategy.

Texas Instruments

TI can justly lay some claim to launching the first sustained growth of the electronics industry with its germanium transistor radio, the

Regency, and with the first commercially produced silicon transistors in the 1950s; and TI's Jack Kilby is credited as co-inventor of the integrated circuit with Robert Noyce of Intel. TI also contributed Forward-Looking Infrared Radar, voice synthesizer chips and a host of other important discoveries. Along the way, as one of the world's major component producers, TI has influenced the dynamics of the electronics and semiconductor markets by its devotion to learning curve pricing and aggressive selling.

TI has had many successes in technological achievement and in efficient, economical production. Its calculators, watches, and semiconductor components all shared a common pattern of continued engineering for improved manufacturability and lower price – the "learning curve" approach that is an enduring TI mark on the industry. The company's failures have largely resulted from apparent weaknesses in marketing, rather than from shortcomings in technology *per se*. Since experiencing difficulties with selling consumer products like watches and personal computers, TI's activities seem to have become more strongly focused on components, OEM markets, scientific and instrumentation-related computers, artificial intelligence (AI), and military products. In 1986, TI's consumer sales were only about 10 percent of total sales. In several areas – notably AI and some advanced semiconductor components like CMOS (complementary metal oxide silicon) and gallium arsenide integrated chips – TI seems especially strong.

The breadth of TI's activities is indicated by a glance at some of its major divisions. Although by early 1988 the company had sold 60 percent of its Geophysical Services business, the predecessor company from which its electronics activities sprang in the 1950s, TI remains an active participant in metals and controls, government (primarily military) products, and scientific computers, as well as semiconductor components. Within semiconductors, TI markets products in seven major areas comprising over 3600 products. Digital Logic Products, Processors and Controllers, Memory Products, Linear Products, Telecommunication and Speech Products, and Military Products, plus Application–Specific Integrated Circuits cover a vast array of semiconductor technology. TI offers a number of proprietary technology items in these categories, as well as a variety of product support and customer service activities, including workshops and technical seminars, technical literature and new product information through an on-line computer network.

Like Intel, TI's plant and equipment average only three years of age, an indicator of continuing innovation and updating – and heavy capital investment. TI also invests in research, but, reflecting its somewhat different businesses and strategies, its R&D as a percentage of sales is somewhat lower than Intel's. In the industry-wide slump of 1985–6, TI saw substantial losses, following a poor showing in 1983 as well (1983 losses were $145 million, 1985 losses $119 million, and 1986 was barely profitable, at $29 million). During 1975–9, TI's R&D as a percentage of sales was 4.3 percent, while in 1986 R&D was 8.2 percent of sales. For 1987, however, TI earned $309 million as its semiconductor markets recovered.

Some observers have suggested that TI's difficulties in consumer products distracted its managers from basic semiconductor activities during the 1980–5 period. The firm's withdrawal from computers and watches, and its renewed emphasis on components manufacturing, seem to suggest a return to the earlier strategies in place before TI's move into consumer products, focusing instead on military products and industrial markets.

The company's reorganization in 1985 and 1986 seems typical of the industry's response to performance problems, following as it does TI's retreat from the home computer industry where its technologically superior product was unable to compete in consumer markets not well understood by its managers. Rearrangements at TI do represent continued change – but not a retreat from the multidivisional links and cross-unit communications, or from the company's emphasis on highly strategic management to guide the firm.

Besides withdrawal from consumer products, TI's renewed emphasis on manufacturing is visible both in public statements and ads, on the one hand, and in specific quality and cost information revealed by the company on the other. For instance, TI cites consistent improvements from 16 FITs (failure rates per billion unit-hours) to just under 2 FITs in bipolar and digital products, an improvement rate that cuts failure rates about in half every two years.

The emphasis TI has placed on these details translates into a substantial push for market share and cost leadership. TI positions its products as being lowest in total cost of ownership, defined as the total cost to the customer to own a component or to employ it in a product expected to be in use for a specified period of time. This includes not only the purchase price, but additional amounts for incoming inspection and board rework; inventory cost for anticipated needed replacements; in-house reliability testing costs; warranty field failure repairs; and after-warranty failures through the expected life of the system. In 1986, TI had 49 customers who accepted TI shipments directly into stock or use without incoming inspection.

This complex background underlines a major competitive arena for the 1980s: quality assurance. The quality emphasis is not limited to so-called high-technology products, but its impact is especially visible there. In earlier times, when the US alone was the source of high technology, availability alone would make the sale. Now, with the entry of numerous other suppliers, customer service, quality, and reliability are becoming important selling points. In particular, the legendary and almost fanatical attention paid by the Japanese to production details has established an important position for them as suppliers, even though they may not have the very latest products.

In so complex a production process as semiconductors, meticulous attention to details translates into higher yields, lower-cost production, more reliable products – and thus loyal customers. The Japanese have also used testing as a way of controlling their production processes, typically testing every item in a production run in order to iron out details. Thus any product shipped, having been tested, is significantly less likely to fail than competitors' products. This quality emphasis has raised the level of quality required of all suppliers.

TI's current push on quality and manufacturing mastery is quite consistent with its broad-line supplier strategy, market share dominance, and licensing activities in 1975–9. Because quality is essential to market share, and because attention to quality improves manufacturing yields and thus costs, a broad-line supplier like TI must emphasize quality to survive. Indeed, it appears that TI has renewed its broad-line, cost-leadership, large market share goals, and systematically invested in the manufacturing technology necessary to sustain such a thrust in preference to the higher R&D expenses so visible at Intel. Such statements are relative, however; Intel also invests in manufacturing expertise, and TI in R&D, and both companies' commitment to these activities far exceeds the norm for all US manufacturing industry as a whole (see figure 4.2 above).

Another visible change since 1979 has been TI's shift into more active second sourcing arrangements to bolster its technical capabilities. By arranging to second source others' advanced products, TI can upgrade its knowledge. During 1987, TI made such arrangements with Intel and with a smaller company, Linear Technology, to expand its product lines by alliances, rather than "doing it all alone," as it had formerly. The Intel agreement provided for a joint library of common designs in ASIC products, a move that will facilitate further second sourcing between TI and Intel. Both companies gain by such arrangements, since TI gets access to Intel's advanced technology, while Intel gets a highly reliable manufacturing partner with substantial capacity for high-demand products. According to CEO Jerry Junkins,

> Ten years ago, you could have counted our alliances on one hand. But the environment has changed. We can't do everything ourselves.

In addition, TI also made a major acquisition in 1986, the first in almost 30 years, of Rexnord Automation's industrial systems and control business. Rexnord's expertise will help TI, already an accomplished manufacturer; Rexnord's customers will provide further markets for TI products. This acquisition also represents further vertical integration, into industrial control markets that seem a logical outgrowth of TI's continuing emphasis on manufacturing and automation in semiconductors, and its existing product lines in controls. Customers for the acquisition's products are anticipated to be food, specialty chemical, and pulp and paper companies. The acquisition provides an additional major market area in place of consumer electronics, one much closer to TI's traditional markets for components with industrial customers and OEMs.

National Semiconductor

National Semiconductor is a major manufacturer of semiconductor components and, through its subsidiaries, of IBM-compatible computers and point-of-sale systems. The company concentrates on high volume production of integrated circuits. Since 1974, sales have grown at an average annual rate of 28 percent, with some dips, like others in the volatile semiconductor business, while profits have grown annually by about 17 percent in recent years. Sales for 1987 were $1.87 billion, substantially up, along with the rest of the semiconductor industry, after the previous two years' recessionary results.

National has positioned itself as the low-cost, efficient producer of integrated circuits since about 1970. National's strategy includes a variety of second sourcing arrangements – most recently, with TI for National's 32-bit microprocessor. Despite its low-cost profile, however, National's performance has been problematic in recent years. To begin with, the firm is not quite so diversified as some of its chief competitors. It derives a larger percentage of its sales and income from semiconductor components, making the company more vulnerable to semiconductor volatility. In 1987, 60 percent of National's revenues came from semiconductor sales, almost as much as Intel's 70 percent, and considerably more than TI's 40 percent.

National's R&D is backed by a highly regarded engineering group and substantial investments. Like TI and Intel, National's plants average three years of age. National's 1983 R&D investment was 9.5 percent of sales, a figure which rose to 11 percent of sales in 1985 and 15 percent of sales in 1986 (however, National's sales were down by over 17 percent for 1986, reflecting the industry downturn). These figures, like those of other components makers, are also affected by the impact of the slump on profits: National experienced eight quarters of deficits from the last quarter of 1985 through the third quarter of 1987.

In August 1987, National acquired Fairchild Semiconductor from Schlumberger. This acquisition boosts National's semiconductor sales to sixth rank worldwide, and broadens its product lines. The acquisition also positions National ahead of TI as the biggest semiconductor supplier to the US military, while National also becomes a strong second behind TI in standard logic chips. Fairchild comes with substantial capital investments of $1.2 billion made by Schlumberger since it acquired Fairchild in 1979. The acquisition represents a substantial increase in capacity and capability for National, at a very low price (estimated at about a third of Fairchild's book value).

Like TI, National Semiconductor has also made a deliberate move into ASICs, semi-custom products that are increasingly important in the components industry, with some estimating that such devices will comprise almost 30 percent of the worldwide IC market by 1991. These products represent an important trend for the future, because they offer customers a closer match to their needs than do off-the-shelf products. Also, they are typically newer, higher-technology devices. National's 1986 annual report stated that over 75 percent of the firm's new products in that year were proprietary products or National designs.

In addition to proprietary designs, National continues to engage in a variety of alliances with its customers for new product development, technology exchange, cross-licensing and quality assurance programs. Like ASICs, these activities suggest a fundamental shift away from standard components and toward closer customer links and more specifically tailored products, even among broad-line suppliers like National and TI. Second sourcing remains a strong element of National's strategy too, allowing the company to gain access to advanced products quickly, to bolster its product line.

TI and National both seek to be active in a broad array of products. To support this intention, both firms have stressed development of products for a variety of markets, products which are offered in a complete range of standard configurations. Both firms have pushed their manufacturing capabilities to enable them to survive on lower margins, to maintain markets in which they are already positioned, and to fight off rivals. Both firms second source as a means of accessing advanced technology at less cost than would be required to mount the sort of aggressive R&D commitment that Intel has mounted. They have thus put in place a set of elements that might provide continuing, incremental improvements in costs and designs.

Strategic Patterns Compared

A comparison of these patterns and performances highlight a set of key observations about strategy. For all the firms listed in the table, including those we studied in greater depth, consistent and mutually supportive strategy elements pay dividends. Turning first to the merchant semiconductor firms, tables 4.2 and 4.3 present performance data for the top ten US components makers. In 1975–9, Texas Instruments and Motorola, both diversified broad-line suppliers, persistently held the largest market shares in semiconductors, a key strategic target for each (table 4.2). Their broad shares provide large dollar returns. As persistently, however, sales performance in terms of yearly growth rates has favored the niche performers – smaller companies, on the whole, but also much more tightly focused ones (see table 4.3).

These data require substantial updating and revision, however, to take account of the impact of off-shore competitors on worldwide

Table 4.2 Sales market share:
Five-year averages, 1975–1979

Texas Instruments:	37.4
Motorola:	33.3
Fairchild	8.3
National	7.5
Intel	5.9
Mostek	1.8
Advanced Micro Devices	1.3
Analog Devices	1.0
Siliconix	0.6

Source: Schoonhoven (1984).

Table 4.3 Sales performance: yearly growth (%).
Five-year averages, 1975–1979

1978		*1979*		*5-year averages*	
Mostek	56.6	Intel	65.6	AMD	54.8
AMD	48.6	AMD	60.6	Intel	48.4
Intel	41.8	Mostek	53.0[a]	Mostek	43.5
Siliconix	36.9	Analog Devices	52.6	Analog Devices	35.0
Analog Devices	31.0	National	45.6	National	32.2
National	27.6	Intersil	37.3	Intersil	24.9
Texas Instruments	24.6	Fairchild	26.7	Siliconix	24.0
Intersil	23.4	Texas Instruments	26.4	Texas Instruments	23.9
Motorola	19.7	Siliconix	25.8	Fairchild	23.4
Fairchild	16.0	Motorola	22.3	Motorola	12.9

[a] Estimate.
Source: Schoonhoven (1984).

market share. These figures are difficult to obtain, and more difficult to substantiate. Estimates vary substantially by product and by market, and figures from different sources are seldom truly comparable. What does seem apparent, however, is that foreign competitors, particularly the Japanese, but more recently the Koreans and other newly industrialized countries (NICs), have made significant headway both in US markets and worldwide. Japanese firms now hold the top positions as largest worldwide semiconductor components suppliers (although some argue that substantial portions of their sales are to affiliated firms, and to the protected Japanese domestic market, reportedly as large as the US domestic market).

A telling comparison is presented in figure 4.2, showing R&D expenses in leading countries, presented earlier. These data are at the level of national economies, not individual firms; nonetheless, they suggest that R&D benefits gross manufacturing expertise. The change in Japanese investment relative to that of the US, and the change in US investment over time, both suggest a more pointed reason – inadequate R&D investment – behind the common explanations for Japanese successes and US difficulties. If US firms systematically under-invest in R&D, they will be unable to compete because their technology, processes, and products will be obsolete.

The most consistently recognized criterion for success, however, is commercial success: products that sell at a profit, and profits reflected in return on equity, assets, and sales. Table 4.4 presents such data for the semiconductor firms. Here Intel's performance stands out notably in the 1975–9 data, not only among the niche strategists but among the top ten as a group. Intel, the most tightly focused and consistent of the producers, achieves the most consistent results. In terms of 1979 data, focusing on the five-year average figures for return on equity and assets, Intel's focused concentration on technological dominance has proven highly successful. Table 4.5 displays the relationship between performance and four key strategy elements, two representing technical dominance (R&D investment and premium pricing/gross margins) and two representing broad-line manufacturing emphasis (fixed asset productivity and capital expenditures as a percentage of sales).

Table 4.4 Comparative financial analysis of ten largest US semiconductor manufacturers

Firm	Return on equity		Return on assets		Return on sales	
	Five-year average	1979	Five-year average	1979	Five-year average	1979
1 Intel	26.7	30.6	17.6	18.2	11.4	11.7
2 National Semiconductor	20.9	22.9	10.3	10.3	5.0	4.8
3 Analog Devices, Inc.	19.8	24.7	7.9	9.9	5.6	7.1
4 Texas Instruments	16.1	19.5	9.2	10.2	5.4	5.4
5 Intersil	15.1	22.6	9.4	14.0	4.9	7.3
6 Siliconix	15.0	17.5	8.3	9.9	6.6	7.5
7 Motorola	13.2	16.3	7.4	8.7	5.3	5.7
8 Advanced Micro Devices	12.1	21.4	5.7	11.9	2.9	7.4
9 Mostek	11.6	20.4[a]	7.0	11.0[a]	4.4	8.2[a]
10 Fairchild	10.0	16.2[a]	5.3	8.4[a]	4.0	5.72[a]

[a] Estimate due to 1979 acquisition of Mostek by United Technologies and of Fairchild by Schlumberger.
Source: Schoonhoven (1984).

Table 4.5 Relationship between strategy and performance in the semiconductor industry

	Performance	
Strategies	*Return on equity*	*Return on assets*
R&D investment	0.53**	0.60**
High end pricing–gross margins	0.48*	0.40
Manufacturing cost cutting– fixed asset productivity	0.19	0.20
Capital expenditures (% of sales)	0.33	0.38
Pearson correlation coefficients	*p≤0.10	***p≤0.01
n = 10 semiconductor firms	**p≤0.05	

Source: Schoonhoven (1984).

Strategy Conclusions

The data suggest that there is no "one best way" to compete in semiconductors, nor even "one best broad-line strategy." Since niche strategies are more focused to begin with, they are less well represented in a survey of the top ten merchant semiconductor producers, although Intel is a good example, particularly in the 1975–9 data. Still more focused strategies abound, but these are practiced by far smaller firms. VLSI Technology, for instance, concentrates on very large scale integrated circuits. Other smaller companies have announced their intentions of specializing in gallium arsenide chips only; in chip design, or in the manufacture of others' designs as so-called silicon foundries. However, the consistent practice of mutually supportive strategic elements appears to pay dividends over less consistent approaches, in any strategy, as we should expect.

It is important that there is not "one best way" to compete. Since alternative approaches are available, firms need not simply mirror one another's methods and go head-to-head. In turn, this suggests that strategy plays an important role: the firm that can distinguish its strategy may evade a potential rival.

Not even the major firms are identical, even within such broad categories as high-technology niche versus broad-line supplier. While all firms face the urgent need to produce a continuing stream of product and process innovations, their methods differ for handling both R&D and the crucial interface between R&D and manufacturing in service of an overall corporate strategy. Notably, the corporate strategies differ substantially too, as do the firms' means of structuring appropriate participation in large organizations where the technological innovators with the most up-to-date engineering and science skills tend to reside at the most junior levels, while the strategic and marketing experience and perspectives are found at the top of the organization. These elements will become more apparent in the following chapters which draw on internal data.

5

The Roots of Innovation

What happens for [a major innovation breakthrough] is that somebody has the idea, has the creative inspiration or whatever . . . Corporate overall management then backs the ideas. For that, you really have to credit Gordon Moore. You see, Gordon really is the top management, and Gordon has a very good knack for picking out the bad and the good ideas. Once we pick an idea that we want to go with, we go with it. We tend not to falter with them. I think it is a combination of picking a direction and then sticking with it and making it work. Whereas a lot of companies will start in a direction, and when it doesn't work quite right, they sort of stop – then they never know whether they're really going or not.

Gerhardt Parker, Intel

Generating Innovative Ideas

At this point, we move back inside the companies to capture the perspectives of those who make innovation happen. Our aim is to understand how efforts at innovation looked to those responsible for them, how they are shaped over time, and how and why people chose to act as they did. Most especially, we are concerned with how people in these organizations experience the conflicting demands for stability and change that surround any persistent attempt to innovate repeatedly.

This chapter will describe where the innovative ideas come from and how innovators obtain the necessary resources to develop their ideas – a crucial linkage, if firms are to maintain a stream of innovative product and technology developments. We will also portray the technical ambiance and the context from which innovation springs within these companies. Because there are more innovative ideas than the firms can develop, choice becomes a central issue. Embedded in the choice process is a resource allocation question: how does material support for development flow from those who hold the resources to those who have the ideas?

The epigraph to this chapter, from Intel's Vice President for Technical Development, suggests a partial answer. While individual innovators provide the creative inspiration, top management plays an important role in selecting from the pool of innovative ideas and then backing those chosen for support during the long development process. Ideas spring from many quarters within these large organizations, and the time and attention of senior executives like Gordon Moore, Intel's Chairman of the Board, are limited. Somehow, ideas and resources, ideas and decision makers, must be brought together for selection and support to result.

Our findings about the roots of innovation can be summarized in three key themes. First, while innovative ideas in these companies come from "nearly everywhere," the best ideas are technological ideas, rooted in core competences. Next, generating innovative product and process ideas is not the issue for these companies. They have many more ideas available to them than they can ever hope to develop: for these companies, choosing among "too many" ideas is far more of a concern than stimulating innovation. (Nevertheless, these firms do pay constant attention to maintaining innovation.) Third, innovation cannot be walled off as the responsibility of a small, clearly defined group of formally designated innovators. Rather, innovation must pervade the firm, with roots and links in all key functional areas. This free flow of innovation is an important characteristic of the firms we studied.

Innovation in these firms is an integral part of on-going operations; it is the expected norm, rather than the exception. To maintain this innovative climate, much energy and thought are devoted to maintaining the organizational context that permits choice, yet keeps ideas flowing. This chapter will look more closely at the sources of innovation and the interplay between technological and other sorts of expertise. Chapter 6 will examine the process by which these companies choose among "too many" good ideas.

Multiple Sources, Technical Bases

Technical Literacy

The managers, executives, and engineers we spoke to in our companies were agreed that innovative ideas do come from "nearly everywhere." Jim Sherwin, an engineering manager at National Semiconductor responsible for engineering in six business units, described the multiple sources of new product ideas:

> The ideas can come from engineers, managers, people like myself, marketing – they can come in from anywhere.
>
> Jim Sherwin, National Semiconductor

Yet our sources also insisted that the best ideas, those that really made a difference in the marketplace, came from technical people. Gordon Moore of Intel emphasized this view:

> That's the way we like to have it. The best ideas come from technological people. The best ideas are technological ideas.
>
> Gordon Moore, Intel

Moore's assertion about "the best ideas" is consistent with other research. For example, in a study of internal corporate ventures, new business opportunities were found to originate in on-going research activities in the corporate R&D department (Burgelman and Sayles, 1986). Other studies of innovation also suggest the importance of technical expertise, and some speak of "technology first" as the dominant model of conceiving of a new innovation (Schon, 1967).

How does this observation that best ideas come from technical people square with the assertion that "ideas come from everywhere"? Does it imply that only technologists are listened to in the corporations we studied? That the origin of all worthwhile technical contributions resides in a formalized corporate R&D Department? Or that somehow these firms manage a "technological fix" to the innovations problem, simply "throwing technology" at it? The answers to this apparent paradox come from "inside" data: to understand, we must look more closely at the people in these companies, and how they interact.

To begin with, in these as in many other high-technology firms, employees at all levels are, in many senses, "technical." Some – the engineers and scientists – are more technical than others, of course, by virtue of their scientific training or job experience. But virtually everyone, including administrative assistants with whom we came in contact, seemed more comfortable with technology than their counterparts in other, less technically based firms. In education, their work experience, and their daily milieu, the emphasis throughout these companies is overwhelmingly technical. Electrical engineering, solid-state physics, computer sciences, mathematics, or chemistry are typical educational backgrounds of managers here. A manager is more likely to have had formal technical training than formal training as a manager. Although MBAs are not uncommon, the business degree is typically coupled with an undergraduate engineering degree, or advanced training in science. Very few managers come to these companies with only managerial, economics, or other non-technical backgrounds (although a few do).

Technical expertise is widely spread throughout the organizations we studied, in nominally non-technical as well as technical jobs: among managers and marketers, as well as design engineers and production staff. Technical background is especially visible among top management, who are uniformly well grounded in the technologies essential to their firms' competitive survival. It is extremely rare, in these companies, for a senior manager not to have a rather formidable technical background, coupled with extensive hands-on experience, frequently in the technical side of the business – in research or manufacturing.

Nor are the high-technology managers newcomers to their industry. There is no "generic manager" trend apparent. Instead, our senior managers typically have grown up in the semiconductor or computer businesses, experienced their vicissitudes over time, and internalized their lessons. Many are alumni of other firms; but often they have worked for extended periods of time in only one or two firms within the industry. It is rare for managers to come into the industry from outside. To our knowledge, only two of the more than one hundred executives, managers, and engineers we interviewed were not semiconductor or computer industry veterans.

Technical Ambiance

In these high-technology firms, widespread technical literacy was matched with a generally technical atmosphere: there was much talk about technical matters, and many reminders of the technical heart of the business in every office – computer print-outs, technical manuals, diagrams, and product posters, as well as computer terminals, printers, and the like. Even front office or executive suite decorations tended toward the technical. Beautifully abstract high-magnification photos of microprocessors were favorites, along with art photos of complex production processes. Technology never seemed very far from people's minds or concerns, regardless of their formal position. For these firms, technology is of quite central importance.

Broadly diffused technical familiarity produces a wide range of technically literate idea sources for innovation throughout the company, as well as many others who can encourage, serve as sounding boards, or simply cheer because they recognize the importance of technical ideas. Beyond the generalized technical familiarity apparent throughout these firms, some key positions are especially important as idea sources and supports. Many important ideas come from, or are initiated by, top level managers, division general managers, engineering managers, marketing and sales people, and customers, either individually or interactively. It is not just the design engineers who come up with ideas.

In our sample firms, each of these key managerial positions, even those that are nominally non-technical, is staffed by a "technical" person – someone whose education or work experience (or both) has provided a thorough grounding in the technology of the business. Technical grounding is normal for managers in these firms. Neophyte managers, MBAs perhaps, may have begun their careers by supervising a production line – not as a rotation exercise, but as *their job* for an extended period of time. Nor is this a new phenomenon; it has been characteristic of the industry essentially since its inception. The underlying message, which rings loud and clear throughout these organizations, is, "The technology matters."

New Roles for Top-Level Technical Expertise

Managers in the key positions, then, are technically grounded and extensively experienced in the business. They frequently supply the initial inspiration behind many important ideas for new products and processes. We might ask: why top managers or division general managers? In many US firms today, the consensus is often that technical details are best left to technical experts, and product design is best delegated to design engineers and those who specialize in designing new products. This might even seem reasonable, with top managers presumed to be too busy managing the business and making important decisions to be concerned with technical details. Also, since the technology is moving so fast, we might expect that top managers would find their technical knowledge becoming rapidly obsolete.

Where such responsibility is delegated, management tends not to concern itself with "technical details." This is perhaps to be expected of managers whose background is in business or law, rather than detailed, operational specifics of the firm's technology. It is typical of many US firms. The results of technical unfamiliarity at high levels of the firm have been outlined in a survey of executives from the 1000 largest US firms:

> A lack of involvement of top management in the technology process resulted in consistent underfunding of technology-related activities. Instead, they emphasized those areas that have a more immediate impact on profits . . . Three in five respondents said top management's role was limited to either reviewing major development programs above some dollar threshold, or singling out and following programs of key importance . . . This limited involvement of top management may be a major reason why technology functions are perceived to be significantly and chronically underfunded.
>
>   Harris, Shaw, and Sommers, 1983

Chief executive officers (CEOs) of top US companies have a predominant educational background in finance, law or marketing; they have little technical emphasis. As table 5.1 shows, the predominant career path for CEOs across industries is through administration, which is far and away the most common single route to the top. If finance is included, the managerial, non-technical route accounts for almost half of this sample of 1000 CEOs. Educational backgrounds show a similar picture. While banks and insurance companies are well represented among the 1000, the emphasis on business or legal education, rather than technical education, is striking.

Our sample of high-technology firms stands in sharp contrast to this picture: in these firms, technical familiarity is the norm. All of the executives and general division managers we spoke to had had a technical formal education, most typically in electrical engineering,

Table 5.1 CEO career paths from *Business Week* Top 1000

Background				Qualifications		Advanced	
		BA	BS	Engineer	LLB/JD	Science	MBA
Administration	314	141	98	52	37	29	9
Business development	1	1					
Engineering	97	3	18	65	1	30	2
Entrepreneurial	11	2	3			2	7
Finance/banking	163	88	60	5	9	2	1
Founder	78	22	25	12	7	8	
Insurance	14	8	4		3	1	
Journalism	3	3					
Legal	58	29	15		58		
Manufacturing	1		1		1		
Merchandizing	17	6	7		1		
Marketing	80	34	28	8			2
Operation	148	45	54	38	9	21	2
Personnel	1	1	1				
R&D	4	4	2	1		4	
Sales	3	1	1				
Technical	6		5	1		5	
TV Programming	1	1					
	1000	385	322	182	126	102	23

International management career path	22
Other advanced education (beyond secondary school)	16

Source: Drawn from *Business Week*'s survey of the top executives of *BW 1000* corporations, May 1988; table prepared by authors. Figures do not sum horizontally because of multiple degrees.

but solid-state physics, chemistry and other scientific fields were also represented. These managers had worked all or nearly all their careers in "the industry," although experience at several firms was not uncommon. Some had begun as individual contributors in engineering, others as research scientists, and still others had gone into management after an undergraduate technical degree topped off with an MBA. All had had personal, hands-on experience with the technology, usually over extended periods of time. Personal involvement with or supervision of product design, manufacture, and contact with customers using company products was routine. Thus they really understood the technology.

Despite the reality of technical obsolescence in a rapidly evolving technical field, despite the very real dependence of senior managers on the finely honed expertise of their more technically adept subordinates, senior managers in these firms maintain an active interest in and a fundamental appreciation for the current technology. They know what the cutting edge is, and why. These executives "speak technical," and they are conversant with the latest crop of technical problems in a fair degree of detail. They read widely about developments in the industry. They understand the technology broadly, and extraordinarily well, even though they themselves quickly insist that they are "a long way from the bench." Their technical grounding plays a key role in strategy, as we shall see.

Outside Contacts

Broad technical strength is not the only contribution managers make to innovation in these companies. Another is keeping their organizations in touch with the external environment around them. They have extensive contacts outside their own organizations, and spend time with customers' engineers and designers, not just with executives. They often travel worldwide to customer locations. This is not just "staying close to the customer" as some management prescriptions intone (e.g. Peters and Waterman, 1982). There is nothing pro forma in these contacts. In a swiftly evolving technical field, customers can be a key source of information (von Hippel, 1986).

Necessarily, some of these contacts are accessible only to senior-level executives, whose formal positions enable them to contact important customers, other high-level executives or scientists. This seems, at first glance, something like the figurehead, liaison, or symbolic representative roles managers are known to fill (Mintzberg, 1975). In these firms, however, managers actively take the lead in creating and maintaining constant contacts with technical information sources and, especially, with customers; and those we spoke with repeatedly noted that their most important customer contacts as regards ideas for innovations were contacts with the customers' technical people – the users or potential users of their products.

Top-level managers are not alone in such contact. In the firms we studied, we found employees many levels down who were also in touch with their customer base – well beyond the sales and marketing functions. Engineers, technical contributors, and scientists in these companies all have high market and customer awareness, derived from significant contact with customers, and often with the user-level technical personnel of the customers. An engineer at National commented that contacts with the outside world – with the marketplace and its customers – are essential for effective idea generation:

> Inspiration comes while working . . . If I had a group of people and put them in a room and closed the door and said, "Invent!", the company would go broke. Conversely, if you hire a group of people and put them in a bunch of rooms, and say "Invent!", but you cut a window in the room so they can look out at the world – to the customer, to the marketplace, to the competition – and give them a bunch of telephones . . . you will probably make some money. You need the [multiple] rooms, and you need the windows.
>
> Jim Williams, National Semiconductor

We will return to a more extensive investigation of the perspective of engineers in chapter 9 on the 'innovation cycle'. Here what is important is that throughout these innovative organizations, from top executives down to engineers in operating groups, access to customers and the external environment is routine. Such contact is not only taken for granted, it is widely identified as necessary.

What customers provide is not so much "the answer" as "the question," or "the problem" against which to blend, negotiate, and assess technical possibilities. This is an active process that goes well beyond extrapolation from existing customer needs. It is deeply rooted in technical familiarity both with existing products and processes, and with developing trends in relevant research sciences and applications. A broad general feel for the thrust and direction of technology and markets, continually fed into the organization, helps maintain an on-going relation to the environment, rather than a wholly internal technical focus.

The role of customers in advanced technology innovation is not simple, nor is the electronics industry the first instance of this complex relationship. Close links to customers – as strategists have pointed out for some time – can be a key source of competitive advantage (e.g. Andrews, 1971; Porter, 1980). Other industries, considered "high-technology" in their time, offer examples of close customer contact as essential to success – and as the source of enduring strategic advantage for the technical firm that builds such service into its repertoire. Classical examples come readily to mind, among them the experience of Allegheny Ludlum with stainless steel just after World War II. Stainless, with substantially different characteristics of use, chemistry, and interaction with other steels, could not be used as a simple substitute. Allegheny's expertise in helping customers to exploit the new product's potential was crucial in creating early markets. A substantial applications engineering effort was required. Once established, it provided Allegheny with a significant and enduring competitive advantage in the early days of the stainless steel market. Allegheny's applications engineers bridged the gap between customer needs and technical possibilities, utilizing their familiarity with the product's capabilities – and with the customers' problems.

The Allegheny experience shows that familiarity with both technical product characteristics and limits on the one hand, and with customer problems on the other, is required. These twin perspectives must be brought together in an advanced technology market. In Allegheny's case the union of those views provided for a non-obvious response quite different from contemporary norms of older steel sales and service, and one difficult for other competitors to appreciate or to duplicate. (The example is close to Intel's experience with microprocessors, to be recounted shortly.)

What seems different from traditional approaches in our sample is the degree of conscious attention paid by top managers to fostering and maintaining the technical familiarity and customer contacts. The active part top-level managers play in keeping these contacts "evergreen" is noteworthy. Top-level technical familiarity in these firms is consciously sharpened by extensive interaction with other specialists – at technical meetings, for instance, or by continued education, technical reading, involvement with research projects, and the like. It is also honed by frequent communication with customers' problems, needs, difficulties, and desires. Roving senior executives and technical specialists infuse fresh ideas and variety into the firm through their wide contacts with customers, other technical professionals, and diverse facets of the organization's external environment. The notion of "NIH" ("Not Invented Here" [and by implication thus to be ignored) is a recognized enemy. Wide arrays of outside contacts are an important method for hybridizing technical and market appreciation, thus helping to spark creativity.

Integrating Innovative Inputs

Diverse contacts provide the variety essential to successful innovation, and senior managers in these firms are a deliberate and central source of this variety. Two specific instances of semiconductor innovation, in two different firms, illustrate how these key factors of technical expertise and knowledge of practical needs interact. This sort of interaction, where the whole is greater than the sum of the parts, is illustrated by the impact of senior managers' familiarity with both technical facts and customer needs, and gives rise to synergy – a crucial concept in our discussion.

The development of the first widely successful semiconductor consumer product, the famed Regency Radio produced by Texas Instruments at the very beginning of the semiconductor era, is one milestone event: Intel's development of the microprocessor a decade later offers a second. Each event involved both technical expertise and a wide range of non-technical inputs and insights, and each event helped propel its founder company toward its current status as an industry leader.

Comparing the two events, which involved different people, different corporate cultures, and different technical insights 15 years apart, illuminates a persistent innovation process as it occurs in high-technology firms. The common factors in these two apparently different events are striking, and highlight important senior management roles in implementing innovation.

The Regency Radio

Texas Instruments was not the first company to manufacture transistors, nor was it their inventor: those honors belong to Bell Laboratories, where Shockley, Bardeen, and Brattain invented transistors in 1948; and to Western Electric, the manufacturing arm of AT&T (as Bell Labs was the research arm, before the break-up of the AT&T system). Nor was TI the only company to undertake commercial development of transistors. Along with some 35 other firms, TI sent executives and researchers to attend a seminar on transistors offered by Western Electric as part of a licensing agreement for a $25,000 fee. The then small Texas company learned what was known about transistors in the company of such giants of the electrical industry as RCA, Sylvania, and GE in 1952, as soon as licensing was made available.

Even before this time, however, Patrick E. Haggerty, then in charge of TI's manufacturing activities, was already aware of the transistor from his readings about electronics research, and was fascinated by its technical possibilities. He described his views of the time:

> It was clear, if one looked at it, that the heart of electronics was the valve that controlled the flow of electrons. I began to imagine what might be there, as compared with vacuum tubes, and what might be *inherently* there in terms of reliability, low cost, and all the rest. Of course, it was highly speculative.

Nevertheless, Haggerty was convinced that the transistor was worthy of pursuit, and he convinced other senior TI officers. Western Electric was not at first impressed:

> Beginning early in 1950, Bob Olsen and I, Erik Jonsson and I, Erik and Bob, all called on Western Electric with respect to patent licensing in the semiconductor field. I suppose at first they were just amused at us: we hadn't done a thing, and here we were . . . and we were certainly being persistent about it.
>
> Patrick Haggerty, Texas Instruments

Haggerty and TI persisted, however. Commercial licensing was eventually made available to all comers for a fee, beginning in 1952, as part of the unique antitrust arrangements that permitted AT&T to operate as a regulated monopoly prior to the 1984 divestiture decree. With the others, TI acquired initial detailed laboratory knowledge. No one knew much about manufacturing the device.

Commercialization of the new idea required substantial further development. Early point-contact germanium transistors had been used by other companies in hearing aids, where they developed an unfortunate reputation for failure, temperature and moisture sensitivity, and erratic performance. Early transistors were also expensive. Haggerty was certain that manufacturing expertise and volume production held the answers to these problems. He was also certain that transistors had to be a volume product, if they were to be successful. That meant applications research on the manufacturing process, going far beyond the Bell Labs seminar.

Gordon Teal, a pioneering Bell Labs transistor researcher who just happened to be homesick for Texas, was hired in 1953 to direct TI's newly established research laboratory. Teal's earlier work at Bell Laboratories had included growing monocrystalline germanium, a feat that made transistor manufacture possible (Bernstein, 1984; TI interviews). Teal undertook to assist TI's engineers in developing volume manufacturing processes.

To justify volume production, some sort of "market pull" was required, but there were few existing commercial applications, and most possibilities were seriously limited by transistors' high cost and reliability problems. Haggerty and his marketing manager, Buddy Harris, hit upon a new idea: a "shirt pocket" transistor radio, aimed at the 1954 Christmas market. They determined that the new radio could be sold at a price of $50, well above the $10 or $12 typical of tube sets, because of its novelty – but that was the highest possible price, they concluded. Thus the semiconductors to go into the set had to be produced for around $10, to allow a distributor's price of $30. Haggerty described the key technical link:

> The people working on the germanium transistor were in the laboratory, for all practical purposes alongside the ones working on the circuits. And yet it was amazing, if you walked from one to the other . . . how sometimes they were so involved in what they were doing, they weren't talking to one another. And so somebody had to say, "Now, what are the problems, and what directions are you going?" One of the important . . . reasons why people weren't able to make a successful pocket radio was because the germanium transistors weren't quite high frequency enough . . . The logical question was, "Why not make [the

circuit at a] lower [frequency]?" It worked. It wasn't the best [circuit design for a radio] – the higher frequencies were better. But it worked, and that's why we had the first radio. Why we could do it, and why we did it for $50.

The Regency radio was the first broad-appeal consumer product of the transistor revolution. It launched a whole array of industries concerned with transistor-based, miniature personal consumer products, a trend that continues today. The Regency seems to be the direct ancestor of the Walkman and Watchman, too: senior Sony executives, impressed by the Regency on a 1954 US trip, copied it quickly with their own version of a "shirt pocket" radio in Japan.

It was Haggerty himself who asked the essential questions, and sparked off the answers necessary to make the product work. Haggerty's role underlines what he saw as the key management task, integrating skills and expertise from various fields – here, circuit design and semiconductor product design characteristics, but also design and manufacturing – to ensure success. Managers didn't perform the tasks; instead, they oversaw them, instigated, induced, and encouraged their technical subordinates in useful directions. Getting the experts close enough together to generate novel combinations, and paying attention to the linkage in order to solve bottlenecks, were central. This was what Haggerty called being "tightly coupled," a major strength of TI's early operations that distinguished them from competitors:

> The fact is, it was being close enough, and talking, and saying, "Well, what can't you do?" and then saying, "Well, why does the frequency have to be so high? Why can't we stay below 300 [megahertz]?" It was true that the higher frequency was better, but it wasn't essential for a pocket radio.
>
> We were small, and we were *appreciably* better organized. Our emphasis then was on coupling the design and the production together very, very tightly.

The key point here is not the pure technical details of how the radio was made to work, but that a technically knowledgeable senior manager was able to intervene, breaking the conceptual log-jam of diverse specialists who could not see past their own expertise to the design's need. Haggerty provided an essential linkage that made the pocket radio succeed, by overcoming the limits of the specialists' individual viewpoints.

TI got into the transistor business because of management's familiarity with research developments outside the firm. Senior management – not some anonymous researcher – initiated TI's involvement in transistors, although the key technical work was necessarily done by researchers. Technical expertise and familiarity with the product at hand (here germanium transistors), with the specific technical difficulties encountered, and with the hoped-for application (here, the radio circuit design) resulted in the necessary breakthrough, again assisted by roving management. These managers are not abstracted from the realities of their business, but deeply engaged with it.

These broad perspectives on technology, market possibilities, product characteristics, and project needs are not generic, although they can be described in generic terms (such as "technical familiarity," "awareness of market needs," and "project management skills," for instance). Instead, broad perspectives are linked to very specific, elemental appreciation, within a particular industry, of the specific, relevant technologies that must be brought to bear, and the details of where fruitful union of insights might be brought about. All of this melds together under a broad, yet clearly articulated strategic aim: a specific, high volume potential consumer product aimed at a particular market window, with specified price and manufacturing characteristics.

TI was able to get the transistor out of the laboratory, into the marketplace, and into volume production for consumer products faster than the competition because TI had a strategy, and managed the requisite technical links to accomplish it, according to Haggerty. TI's senior managers deliberately fostered specific connections, specific research achievements and directions. As they had foreseen, increased customer demand justified further efforts and expense in production, which in turn lowered the price to create still more demand: an early example of the learning curve pricing still typical of the electronics industry today, almost four decades later.

Intel's Microprocessor

Some 15 years after the Regency radio, another invention launched another extraordinary era in semiconductors. The microprocessor forcefully advanced the miniaturization that transistors had begun, making possible a vast array of new devices. Yet what is important about this account is not the technical development so much as the means by which it was achieved. Again, we shall see the central role played by senior managers who can commit their firm to significant endeavors, can appreciate the technical possibilities, and can link the insights of diverse specialists.

The microprocessor was invented at Intel in 1969 by Marcian "Ted" Hoff, a noted electronics inventor, an Intel Fellow and an early member of the Intel team (he has since retired from Intel to pursue private interests). Hoff, at the time a researcher at Stanford, was invited to join a new venture set up by Robert Noyce, Gordon Moore, Les Vadasz, and Andrew Grove. Noyce himself is a recognized technical superstar, credited with TI's Jack Kilby as independent co-inventor of the integrated circuit. The Intel founders sought Hoff out for his state-of-the-art technical expertise. According to Les Vadasz:

> [Because they were] all technical people, they drew good technical people to the company. They knew the complexity of integrated circuits was going to grow, and sought out Ted, whom they knew to be a good systems-oriented person.

Hoff was recruited because the Intel founders anticipated the need for someone capable of handling the future complexities of integrated circuits, and most especially, of the systems such devices promised. Initially, Intel had set out to exploit the newly developed large scale integration (LSI) technology, which made it possible to place thousands of miniature electronic devices on a single silicon chip. Intel targeted the computer market, but customers with other needs also sought out the firm's LSI capabilities.

Work on what eventually became the first microprocessor began as a typical custom design job. The customer was a Japanese calculator company, Busicom, seeking a custom calculator chip. Les Vadasz, who was then working as the metal oxide semiconductor (MOS) engineering manager (and thus as one of Hoff's bosses) described the project's evolution. It began with Busicom's need for a set of custom chips:

> Before we progressed too far, [Busicom] realized that they really didn't want one calculator, they wanted a number of different calculators – one for scientific, one for business, and one for a variety of applications. A few chips suddenly grew to a very

large number of products to be developed. We suddenly realized that there was no way in hell that at our stage of development as a company, we would be able to handle the job.

As Ted Hoff got into the picture, he realized that the problem could be solved if there was a different way of putting in the system architecture.

Les Vadasz, Intel

In Busicom's original design, each calculator required at least five chips. When Hoff was assigned to the project, he realized that the initial design was too complex to be cost effective. Furthermore, as Vadasz intimated, Intel's small MOS engineering staff was fully occupied with other tasks. Extensive design resources were simply not available, since Intel was at this time a small start-up company.

Busicom's engineers had designed a brute-force solution – an overly complicated device – that Hoff realized was inefficient. Hoff himself came up with a design that was still complex:

> [The original solution required] too many chips – about nine to twelve – which had to communicate with one another. I thought they could reduce the number of chips by implementing the more complicated steps as programs in memory, not as hardware logic. They weren't very interested. They said they knew how to design calculators. In other words, "Don't bother us with that thing – we know what we're doing!"

Ted Hoff, Intel

Hoff himself, commenting on the inspiration that led to the microprocessor, noted that although his initial design was still too complex, the underlying idea was intriguing. Hoff was encouraged to go forward with trying to simplify his design and improve the idea. This encouragement came from Noyce and Moore as senior managers, and from Vadasz as the head of MOS design engineering. Hoff's improvement was a revolutionary simplification: instead of a large number of custom chips, each a discrete component, the new version used only a few common chips and one programmable memory. Eventually, Hoff outlined the concept and developed the basic architecture of the microprocessor. His unique idea was to combine supporting memory devices to contain special-purpose instructions, enabling the core of the device to function with less complex instructions in a far more general way. In essence, the general-purpose processor's functioning was modified by programs stored in memory.

The product moved through several conceptual stages, overcoming various difficulties en route. Hoff's original idea for a systems-level chip was a response to the constraints posed by too few personnel for the job facing Intel: the simultaneous design of multiple custom chip sets for the scientific calculator, the business calculator, and the general-purpose equipment desired by the client as well, was simply impossible.

With two other engineers, Frederico Faggin and Stan Mazor, Hoff eventually came up with a design involving four chips: the central processing unit chip (CPU), a read-only memory (ROM) chip for the custom application programs, a random access memory (RAM) chip for processing data, and a shift register chip for input–output (I/O). The CPU chip, although originally without a name, eventually became known as a microprocessor. The first microprocessor was the 4004.

After work began in earnest, the team labored furiously for nine months to complete the design. Masatoshi Shima, who represented Busicom and later joined Intel, designed the 4004's logic. The chip measured one eighth of an inch wide by one sixth of an inch long, and was made up of 2300 MOS transistors. Intel's first microprocessor was equal in computing power to the first electronic computer, the ENIAC, which had filled some 3000 cubic feet with 18,000 vacuum tubes. The 4004, which could execute 60,000 operations a second, seems primitive by today's standards, but was revolutionary at the time.

Broader Applications, Other Markets Intel's approach prevailed, and Busicom eventually sold 100,000 calculators. It took some time for the microprocessor's potential to be appreciated, however. Hoff's systems solution was first viewed as a useful alternative for the Busicom design project, but little else, according to Vadasz:

> At first, we did not really use it for anything else but for the Busicom product line. It was later when we really decided, "Here we have a set of general-purpose products which could be applied to a variety of other problems, other than just these three or four different calculators."

Vadasz observed that the microprocessor both was and was not extraordinary:

Instead of a number of different custom chips, we would have only three or four different chips, but one of those four would contain a program memory which could be reprogrammed for the different types of machine configuration.

By doing certain clever things, you could also package more compactly, and suddenly there was a general-purpose function [chip], useful for a number of end products, just by different programs. In a way, it was very much analogous to some of the early computers: you had a computer there, and a peg board in the back, and you just wired it up differently. That's how you gave instructions to the computer. It was not a new revelation in computer architecture. It was not an earth-shaking computer science idea. It was simply applying "computerese" to a technology problem. That was the birth of the microcomputer.

Like many great ideas, the microprocessor's design was reasonably simple in retrospect, and in some ways almost obvious, with the benefit of hindsight. Nevertheless, at the time its potential was cause for much debate within Intel. The debate centered on three issues: what it was good for, whether there was a long-term market for it in more general applications, and therefore whether Intel should negotiate for return of the rights to the new chip, which had gone to Busicom in the original contract.

Some within Intel had little concept of what the new product was. Ed Gelbach, then the Director of Marketing, recalled the initial perspective:

> Originally, I think we saw it as a way to sell more memories, and we were willing to make the investment on that basis.

Others, including Mazor and Hoff, were certain that the chips had broad general-purpose product potential. They generated lists of possible product applications: cash registers, coin changers, traffic light controllers, and so on and so on. They lobbied loudly, acting as product champions. They even argued that Intel should return Busicom's $60,000 fee in exchange for the original design rights.

Intel's founders and top managers eventually made the critical decision to offer Busicom a lower price for its chips in return for rights to the microprocessor design, and the right to market the design for non-calculator applications. With this decision, Intel's senior management acknowledged that the microprocessor represented a whole new type of computer with substantial commercial potential. The device also offered the company an opportunity to further its position in memories. Gordon Moore observed:

> As soon as the microprocessor was a reality, we recognized that
> this was the next thing we wanted to do after semiconductor
> memory – a new direction in LSI [large scale integration]. By
> programming, we could make a standard LSI circuit perform in
> a wide variety of applications. We seized it as another step in
> the direction we wanted to go.

The Intel people became more excited as the potential of the new
approach began to dawn on them. What at first seemed a purely
technical issue – reduction of multiple designs into a single set of
chips combined with a programmable memory – translated into a
major strategic move, enabling Intel to tap a vast and hitherto
inaccessible market for the new product.

The product needed assistance to reach the marketplace, however,
and again senior management provided backing. Organizationally,
still further innovation was required, as Vadasz noted:

> The next phase was probably the most innovative phase of them
> all. Once you recognize that you have this sort of product, this
> new sort of chip, what do you do to it? If you look at the
> traditional logic world – the hardware world – they don't know
> how to program this. Just having it doesn't mean you can use
> it. So really, the most innovative decision of them all, in my
> mind, was to decide to allow development support – design aids
> for the customer, so that he could use the product and customize
> it for his own need . . . He understands logic [hardware] design;
> he doesn't understand programming. So the idea of giving him
> programming tools as a way to sell the product and allow him
> to utilize it, I think, was one of the key elements in the innovative
> process, and one of the key elements in the success of the
> microprocessor product.

Creating Markets with Design Tools At this point, top management again became central to further evolution of the microprocessor.
While the product was in place and had enthusiastic management
support, and even development tools, the customers remained to be
convinced. Customers in this case were relatively sophisticated people
who nevertheless still did not understand the concept of programming
what they conceived of as a hardware product – an LSI circuit.
Vadasz views the vision and business acumen of the founders as very
important to the microprocessor's eventual spectacular success:

> I think probably the strongest proponents for the idea [of development support] were Gordon [Moore] and Bob [Noyce], who really saw it as an opportunity to amortize the very high design costs associated with this type of product over a large number of applications. Perhaps the volume in each application was small, but the number of applications were very large, thus amortizing the development costs. We believed that the development support idea really was the key to capitalize on it.

Development support, to convince and assist customers, was a new hurdle for Intel to surmount. Just how to accomplish this generated much internal debate, as Vadasz commented, but eventually customer contact provided a solution:

> We had lots of debates about what to do and how to do it. The marketing people had absolutely no idea what a development tool was. The customers started to play with it, and one fed on another. So, before we knew it, the idea got legitimized that, "Yes, you need to provide development support for microprocessors." Marketing suddenly had product development responsibility.
>
> Les Vadasz, Intel

The initial market research was unsophisticated and informal, as is often the case with truly new products. Gelbach and his people had to convince customers' logic designers to use the new technology. Potential customers were actually asked by Gelbach and his staff, and by Moore, Noyce, and other key executives, why they didn't program their own logic functions into the new circuits. Invariably, the answer was, "Too expensive." Noyce recalled that he would ask, "What if it cost $5? Would you do it?" The answer to this question was equally invariable: "Sure!" As Noyce commented,

> We had to create the need, and [we had to] get the price right.

It had become apparent that to create the need, Intel had to help its customers use the new technology and exploit its potential in their own products. Gelbach and his group then developed one of Intel's most significant marketing innovations: they produced the first generation of software development aids. Essentially elementary programming tools, these aids made it easier for customers' engineers to use Intel's first microprocessors.

For a few years, the design aids actually produced more revenue than the microprocessors themselves. Intel's marketing strategy was to sell a $5000 development aid in hopes of producing orders for $50,000 worth of components within a year or two. The plan would eventually pay off, but initially it generated more curiosity than cash. The company found itself spending more on printing and mailing operating manuals – to enable customers to research this new option – than it generated in microprocessor sales.

The 4004 was revolutionary, and the development aids were nearly as innovative, but Intel's doors still were not being beaten down by customers. The first turning point came with the Intel 8008. The 8-bit 8008 microprocessor had been developed in tandem with the 4004, exemplifying one of Intel's long-standing practices: developing two new products for each new concept or technology, to demonstrate its wider utility. (This also meant that manufacturing development expenses could be spread across two products.) The 8008 was introduced in April 1972, targeted initially as a custom chip for Computer Terminals Corporation of Texas, later known as Datapoint. The 8008's ability to manipulate data or characters, in comparison to the 4004's arithmetic orientation, caught the attention of a new group of users. With their response, Intel basically turned the corner in developing the market for the microprocessor.

Another big advance came in 1974 when Intel's 8080 chip, the first true general-purpose microprocessor, was introduced. The 8080 was conceived as a project to speed up the 8008. The new device was introduced in April 1974 with an original price of $360 apiece. Said Dave House, who joined Intel at that time, and has served in a number of senior positions since,

> The figure had a nice ring to it. Besides, it was a computer, and they usually cost thousands of dollars, so we felt it was a reasonable price. I think we paid for the R&D in the first five months of shipment.

Market response to the 8080 was enormous, and it soon became the industry standard. Its vast array of new uses far surpassed the lists that Hoff and Mazor had drawn up four years earlier in their efforts to proselytize in their product's favor. Motorola introduced its 6800 microprocessor about a year later, and it had the advantage of an architecture more familiar to programmers. However, as House observed, Intel enjoyed the first mover's advantage:

> We were ahead of Motorola [in our design] and faster to produce and deliver. Furthermore, we did a more effective job of selling,

using the "solutions" approach to our customers: We've got the support systems and peripherals to make your product more effective." It was a domino effect after that. Within six months, Intel walked away with the 8-bit market.

Product Strategy Shift

The microprocessor and its applications are so pervasive and so widely appreciated today that it is difficult to realize how significant a departure the product represented at the time for Intel, then a small components house. In undertaking so large a shift from its established product base, Intel had to develop much more than "a new product," or even "a new manufacturing process," although both of those were required. While many innovations demand these two phases, breakthrough discoveries like the microprocessor require a third phase of development to bridge the gap between the new product and its potential users. As with Allegheny Ludlum in stainless steel, Intel had to create a new way to sell the product that enabled users to access its benefits.

The role of management here is substantial: not only must an organizational ambiance favorable to technical innovation be created and sustained. In addition, a new aspect of organization must be conceived to get the product across to its intended market. The leaders must be capable of envisioning both technical outcomes and the organizational wherewithal to bring them to market. What is more, they must enable others to share this view, thus creating an amended organizational mission, shifted in response to the new needs engendered by the breakthrough product.

Intel's decision to pursue the microprocessor fully committed the company to a major shift in strategy, from hardware and component emphasis into integrated systems support: it was no longer simply in the business of making components, but making components *and* providing the wherewithal to enable the customer to effectively make use of a new class of product. Only after this understanding was well entrenched could Intel proceed with the hardware design effort – itself a significant breakthrough – that generalized the microprocessor idea beyond the initial, limited Busicom application.

A variety of good ideas, superb insights, and creative breakthroughs – in design, in manufacturing technology, in fundamental approach, in market positioning, and other factors – had to come together to realize Hoff's initial, brilliant concept. The consequences and implications had to be understood, and the necessary resources provided. New kinds of expertise, and new sorts of management skills, had to be marshalled and co-ordinated in service of a vision implicit in Hoff's concept, but carrying consequences far beyond product facts or potentials.

This sort of collaboration, around issues of design, fundamental manufacturing processes, and other technical elements as well as marketplace insight, blending a variety of expertise and viewpoints, is increasingly characteristic of innovation in electronics: a broad range of technical skills are involved, and teams, rather than isolated individuals, are essential to success. No one individual, even among contributors as highly talented as these, is capable of single-handedly accomplishing the complex innovation required to bring such a breakthrough into being.

Equally important, even brilliant product design must be coupled with strategic vision to achieve significant breakthroughs. The strategic character or impact of the technical accomplishment must be appreciated, if it is to be properly exploited. This vision is especially important because the initial idea, while certainly crucial, is not enough by itself. A whole infrastructure of support and development, well beyond the purely technical, will be required to move the idea into actuality. The resources required for success are enormous, and must be skillfully deployed in persistent effort over time.

Without the vision, the resources will not be forthcoming; a technical achievement viewed as trivial or limited does not justify such substantial expenditures of time, talent, and resources. From this perspective, it is obvious why top-level support is required. Such support, and the strategic vision upon which it depends, rest on top-level technical insight, broad literacy about the issues of technology, and an informed appreciation of marketplace needs. Strategic vision, in its turn, is supported by the combination of technical familiarity and diverse contacts we have been describing.

Intel's microprocessor development effort illustrates quite well the importance of synergistic interaction between multiple sources of innovative ideas. The innovative technical idea itself is by no means sufficient to produce a commercial hit in the marketplace. Interaction occurred among a large number of variables – an externally generated need, a customer's requirement, combined with bold technical insight; encouragement by top management, and willingness to support risky development; interaction among a team of talented engineers, not simply the original innovator; manufacturing acumen; marketing and top management links to potential customers, and willingness to develop new ways to market a product. All of these elements were supported by a growing band of product champions, and by top management, to produce the success that the microprocessor eventually became.

Strategic Top-Level Support

Strategic vision requires long-term support. From 1969 to as late as April 1972, when the 8008 was publicly announced, Intel had ideas, prototypes, test data and significant expenses, but as yet no identifiable external market: the product was simply too new. The microprocessor represented a significant departure from older technology, in substituting programmable instructions for some of the hardware logic previously employed. It is at times like these, when no ready market exists, that executive foresight and imagination are most crucial – along with executive tolerance for risk. Senior executives must be able to envision uses for the new product without the assurances of market surveys.

Executive judgment is not analytical, nor even wholly rational – certainly it is not the result of any quick or linear calculation. We have argued that technical familiarity fuels this strategic imagination; so, too, does familiarity with what is going on elsewhere in the marketplace, and above all with customers and their needs. Carefully selected "leading edge" customers (von Hippel, 1986) can provide important market insights. But just as clearly, the idea of a predefined "right" customer can mislead, as Burgelman and Sayles (1986) noted:

> . . . There is a tendency to address the needs of atypical users and to invoke their acceptance of the new product, process or system as evidence for the existence of a new business "opportunity." The scientist–entrepreneur has a knack for coming up with convincing evidence to demonstrate the "interest" of prospective users. As one scientist-turned-business manager put it, "If you address yourself to the 'right' people in any market, you will hear them say: 'Wow! This is what we have been waiting for'."
>
> Burgelman and Sayles, 1986

There are no easy answers, nor any clear source of insight for the future. The manager's dilemma is that "the right" customer will sing a product's praises even if, in truth, the product is one that "only the lunatic fringe of the customer base would appreciate" (Burgelman and Sayles, 1986). Yet the true breakthrough product, the one that initially seems likely to attract only such a "lunatic fringe," is the one that ultimately becomes the new industry standard, displacing its predecessors precisely because it is different and better, because nobody thought of it, or because nobody believed it could be done. In the case of the microprocessor, a few devoted Intel insiders perceived widespread applications that others initially failed to recognize.

Strategic vision must somehow identify possibilities that are truly ahead of their time, and not merely heading into a blind alley. In the case of Intel's microprocessor, as in the case of the transistor at TI, senior management understood both the nature of the innovation and its needs for different sorts of skills and supports. They appreciated the benefits of a product with advanced capabilities while not being captured by isolated, "lunatic fringe" ideas. They backed applications with staying power and potential – they viewed product possibilities in wide, strategic terms.

Similar examples come readily to mind. The first estimate of the market potential for mainframe computers was that a few large users like the US Census Bureau might require perhaps a dozen. Apple's personal computer was an outrageous idea – a computer for individual home use! Who on earth would want one? Hewlett-Packard's hand-held calculator was a similarly conspicuous departure: the best estimates at the time, from the makers of slide-rules (remember slide-rules?) was that perhaps 15,000 calculators a year might be sold to engineers and technicians. Today, Casio turns out more calculators than that in a day, and the devices are routinely offered as premiums for business magazine subscriptions. And Hewlett-Packard is still in the calculator business, still at the high end.

In each case, the rational market estimates were completely wrong. Apple was a start-up, so perhaps in a different category. But at IBM and Hewlett-Packard, both established firms, senior management had to commit substantial resources to what appeared to be simply a wild-eyed idea. Top management saw far enough beyond the very conservative market research to commit their firms to major expenditures and changes, major risks and potentials. Those commitments constitute tangible bets on market possibilities, firmly rooted in technical familiarity with the business.

Resources and Funding: Tangible Backing

At Intel, significant design and development funding was provided over a period of almost four years. A development support group was created, people were hired, equipment and space were allocated. At TI, senior managers persistently pursued licensing options, hired expensive new talent, established a research laboratory to further their new endeavor, and incurred substantial manufacturing start-up expenditures. Haggerty backed the transistor, while at Intel Moore and Noyce were especially strong supporters of the idea of the microprocessor. Neither company's confidence was founded on market projections; Noyce and Moore commented that they had only "very naive" numbers to go on, while Haggerty confessed that he and Jonsson were both consciously operating more on gut feel and personal conviction than on any available data, either technical or market.

In strategic situations created by breakthrough innovations, linear analysis is unlikely to provide the necessary vision, and may seriously mislead. IBM elected to go ahead with its computers, as did Apple, and Hewlett-Packard with its calculators, despite contradictory market research. This is typically the case, according to Intel's Les Vadasz, for significant departures:

> You tend to be over-optimistic on the front end, and because you don't see all the applications, more pessimistic on the tail end. Once we really got convinced ourselves about how to go about it, we created a group specially in the marketing organization that had responsibility for developing support and providing it to customers. That was the seed of the Microcomputer System Group.

Recognizing the possibility of undue optimism, senior managers nevertheless did commit their companies to these landmark projects. Their commitments were not based on analysis, but upon judgment, strategic vision, and technical insight rooted in broad familiarity with current technical issues.

Ultimately, both Intel and TI were changed fundamentally by their innovations, which also in turn changed the semiconductor industry. TI moved definitively from oilfield service and minor amounts of military work into the new semiconductor components industry, diversifying broadly into a range of electronics-based products. It acquired its present identity as a merchant semiconductor supplier as a result of this commitment. At Intel, the change was from components towards a systems approach. Instead of selling stand-alone components, pure hardware, Intel expanded its mission to the design, manufacture, and sale of "solutions" composed of interactive hardware and software. In both firms, wholly new strategies emerged, springing initially from technical insights, but requiring vastly more sophisticated managerial judgment and vision for their completion.

The strategic options in turn led to pervasive organizational changes. At Intel, as we have seen, staff with special skills in verification and testing were recruited, to broaden the company's approach beyond individual devices. New software expertise was acquired, and systems background became central. The microprocessor also demanded new sorts of marketing, and Intel managers promoted it, both at technical and corporate levels, whenever the occasion arose. These efforts provided the necessary push to bring the product to the marketplace, but constituted major changes within Intel itself:

> Just the creation of this group in marketing was a major change. Marketing suddenly had product development responsibility – it wasn't just in manufacturing [any more]. That was a major change. The addition of more and more systems people – people with systems background – was a major change. We were a component company, and in 1968 or '69, we had one or two systems people. Today, over half of our R&D staff has some systems background, and probably half of those have software background. So there was a definite shift in the makeup, the mentality of the development organization. It's now much broader. Our marketing staff, our sales staff, our technical support – all of those activities went through major change. We all had to adapt to a new language; also, we had to learn new disciplines to manage.
>
> Les Vadasz, Intel

A new department, a revised recruitment focus, personal investment of credibility, new interdepartmental relationships, and a complete redirection of the firm's thinking about the nature of its business were all required, above and beyond the dollars. Such major changes represent tremendous investments for the organization, in time, money, human resources, energy, and in their potential for lost opportunities. They also require individual managers' putting their own credibility on the line, backing the new venture. Thus they constitute substantial personal risk, not just firm risk.

At TI, strategic options led to a move from the firm's initial area of endeavor into completely new markets and technologies. For Intel, the character of the firm shifted from LSI hardware toward systems and software, its current focus. Such shifts fundamentally redirect the firm – and they are central to the sorts of major innovation that open new horizons. These investments cannot be proven out over night, nor can they occur without top-level support. Indeed, if they are to succeed at all, they must occur over extended periods of time, accompanied by persistent efforts in the face of inevitable and numerous difficulties.

Integrating Innovation Activities

Interactive (Re)Sources for Innovation

Major innovations such as the microprocessor constitute "order breaking" technological changes, not "order maintaining" innovations (Tushman and Anderson, 1986). Though top management support is important, it is by no means sufficient. Support must be woven into organizational arrangements, so that interactive resources can support and sustain the innovation. If innovation is to succeed, many different resources must be brought to bear from around the organization. These wide resources are the essential seedbed required to complete the initial innovative idea. Intel Chairman Gordon Moore's contention that the most innovative ideas are technical ones holds up – but non-technical insights, support, vision, and innovation are all required to bring the technical idea to fruition.

As noted earlier, all the support necessary to teach the customer how to use the product had to be provided. That support was essential to commercial success. So, too, was high-level management commitment to providing this new array of resources. Then, the resources from around the organization had to be marshalled in service of the innovation. Management had to understand that the new strategy encompassed this new task of education. Because this was a different way of pursuing Intel's business of selling semiconductors than that hitherto practiced, it represented an internal reconfiguration, not just a product or technology shift. To succeed, many varied resources and many innovations had to come together around a vision for the future.

Top management's ability to see the revolutionary potential justified plans to amortize heavy custom design costs across multiple applications. Flexible programming of the microprocessor has helped create its markets. Without the expertise to accurately assess the technical risk, management could not have reasonably committed the company to this effort. Without technical familiarity with both the product and the markets into which it might be placed, management could not have judged the risk. Without substantial breadth of technical sophistication, Intel managers would have been unable to understand what resources might be required, or how they needed to be integrated, or how they might ultimately be applied in the marketplace.

Such managers as we have been describing keep up on scientific developments that might possibly be relevant to their organizations. They "graze" on technical information, often reading widely outside their nominal charters – as Haggerty did. They maintain contacts with users and clients as well, deliberately keeping in touch with a variety of stimuli. They are consciously alert to potential innovations that may come their way.

In addition, they are "tightly coupled" into the research, development, and product proposal activities of their firms. They are intimately acquainted with innovation activities throughout the firm, and make themselves accessible to those who have ideas. Technical ideas *per se* are fostered, but so too are innovative insights affecting any functional area. These are welcomed because they are so often necessary to commercial success. These firms envision innovation broadly, and readily entertain appeals for the wider support, organizational, and management activities that translate technical ideas into commercial realities.

Management's involvement – cheerleading, idea generation, brainstorming, sharing, connecting, and integrating – creates not just the crucial connections on individual landmark efforts such as the Regency Radio or the microprocessor, but a milieu or ambiance within which innovation can self-consciously mature and flourish. Each succeeding example is like another individual born into a functioning society that, growing and changing over time, nevertheless remains true to its basic character. Innovation is the key characteristic that is maintained, expanded, reinforced, and fostered.

Hybridizing Innovation

While innovative ideas come from people in many different positions within these organizations, often sparked off by customers from outside the firms, the ideas ultimately develop through close, integrated interaction with others. Early interaction of ideas across functional areas is important for successful innovation. What looks great from a design perspective will also have to be manufactured, marketed, and built into customers' products. What seems wonderful from a manufacturing perspective may impose crucial design limitations. Compromises and creative hints from one technology to another are as important here as they were in TI's Regency Radio, when a slightly different circuit design made the product technically feasible.

The sorts of interaction we are describing, drawing upon insights from a variety of technical and non-technical areas across virtually all business functions, create a class of innovation that can truly be called "hybrid." Such innovations are fundamentally dependent upon diverse expertise for success. Far from coincidentally, as scientific knowledge proliferates and as markets fragment, the possibilities for such hybrid innovation expand. While the high-technology industries of semiconductor devices and computers offer archetypes, Ford's "Team Taurus" experience with the benefits of integrated, hybrid innovation suggest much broader application of such concepts.

All this strongly suggests why "departments of innovation" are unlikely to exist in these organizations. Where centralized R&D activities do exist, they are never expected to provide all, or even most innovative ideas. Instead, innovation is deliberately decentralized and diversified, with responsibility pushed well down into each organization's operating activities. Nevertheless, innovation is seen as at least potentially fragile. There are, of course, explicitly designated research departments, development groups, and project management engineering teams in each of the companies we studied. However, as our accounts so far have shown, responsibility for innovation does not reside in any one single place. Innovation is expected from "just about everybody," not just from formally constituted leading edge groups. Les Vadasz of Intel underlined the point:

> You cannot have a "Department of Innovation." If all innovative, new things were decided under my organization only, this company would come to a screeching halt. We have to have the ability to have innovation within operating entities and outside of the [routine] business operations – operating under different time frames. We have to be able to create a mechanism to ensure that innovation goes on. Innovation has to be broad based, and it has to be protected.

Protecting Innovation

"Protection of innovation" is a phrase we encountered repeatedly in the companies we studied. It was widely described as a key to maintaining a sort of innovation root stock or "seed corn." Business cycle fluctuations, recessions, unexpected competition, or other revenue downturns hit all businesses occasionally – and volatile businesses like those based in electronics with surprising frequency. What responses are available to managers? Often, in bureaucratic firms, the coping mechanism is a cost cutting program, "fairly" applied across the board, to all activities. Equal cuts eliminate the potential political infighting, and above all avoid making tough decisions and enemies. But equal cuts have serious longer-term costs for innovation: their message that innovation is no better than "just like any other activity," seems ultimately fatal for continued innovation.

In traditional businesses, activities such as R&D or new product development are most typically among the first to go in across-the-board cuts. They make no swift contributions to the bottom line – except, perhaps, when expenses are deferred or eliminated. Because these activities are "discretionary," in the sense that they do not affect this year's revenues or sales, they seem especially vulnerable to cutbacks, especially deferrable as expenditures until income becomes more stable.

In the high-technology companies we studied, executives and engineers told us that innovation is so crucial to continued existence that new, innovative projects absolutely must be protected from cutbacks. Indeed, such projects acquire special urgency when established businesses and product lines are under attack. When severe belt-tightening measures are called for throughout the company, innovative projects in our sample were often fed. Their funding was maintained or even increased while salaries and hiring were frozen, layoffs incurred in established lines of business, and less profitable lines cut out entirely. Intel offers one example in a recent downturn: the founders agreed to a company-wide wage freeze (including management), layoffs, time off without pay, and plant closings to cut back established businesses – at the same time that 14.3 percent of revenues were expended to maintain critical programs and enhance some innovative efforts.

When we recall that high-technology product lines typically turn over within a two-year time span, and that in some companies the majority of product dollars come from products introduced within two to five years, the logic of maintaining innovation becomes clear. Because of short product life cycles, innovation is correctly seen as crucial to survival. Even, or perhaps especially when current business is threatened, the high-technology companies must maintain their investments in innovation. They cannot afford to undermine their future. The utility of their development projects is too immediate, too essential to near-term revenues. Not all new products will be hits, and it is notoriously difficult to distinguish those products likely to be most commercially successful, especially where significant innovation is involved. For these very reasons, high levels of R&D support are maintained to ensure that continuous innovation is protected in these firms.

The difficulties involved in protecting innovation in these firms can be guessed from the depth of the industry's most recent crisis, the worst recession in its history during all of 1985 and extending through 1986. Only moderate turnarounds for some companies were forecast for 1987. Despite these very difficult times, a look back at figure 4.1 shows that the firms have maintained, and in some cases even increased their R&D expenditures as a percentage of sales. (For comparison purposes, R&D as a percentage of sales is also given for some other industries.)

The bite of recession was deep: Intel, AMD, Motorola, and TI all announced layoffs during 1985–6, despite longstanding policies and substantial efforts to avoid this drastic measure. In the face of enormous financial pressures, and despite the widely heralded pressure for short-term profits facing these firms just like others in the US, here is evidence of long-term commitment and long-term perspective. These people manage in the conscious realization that corporate survival is related to continuous innovation. They do not just say that survival is dependent on innovation. They actively commit resources, laying their personal careers and their companies on the line in the conviction that strategic decisions must reflect the importance of innovation, and must in their turn be backed with real-time actions.

Of course, innovative activities are not completely immune to cuts; that would be unrealistically rigid. Budget shaving can, indeed, occur. What is important is that the budget cuts are made deliberately, with attention to the potential strategic contribution and anticipated timing of projects. Some longer-term activities can be allowed to slip in time, tolerating a slower, lower budget. Others cannot. Those less likely to survive slowdown, or most likely to ready the firm for the next upturn, or crucial to immediate improvements in yield or cost – or perhaps those expected to reposition the firm for the future – those can be strategically protected, often by cutbacks in current operations, as well as budget shaving in other innovation activities. All things are not considered equal, and tough choices must be made.

The consistency of these firms' behavior is quite evident on this issue, as was the reasoning managers outlined. Persistent commitments, despite pressures and numerous opportunities and inducements to do otherwise, underlines their conviction: the dominant issue in this industry is innovation. Without persistence, the roots of innovation will wither. Innovation is not to be abandoned summarily, ignored, or momentarily forgotten during times of adversity. More, it must be managed sometimes by means of very difficult decisions and major, risky commitments. Innovation is a permanent reality, the outcome of much conscious effort. So, too, is the resulting necessity of choice among innovation opportunities. Our next chapter deals with managing that choice.

6

Managing Choices, Maintaining Innovation

We have too many ideas. It is hard to decide which ones to develop.

Gordon Moore, Intel

All of the time, we have more ideas than we can use. We select innovative ideas . . . through an on-going discussion.

Peter Rosenbladt, Hewlett-Packard

We get product ideas all of the time. If you look at the ratio of product ideas to the components that get built around here, it's a very big number.

Jim Williams, National Semiconductor

Of Choice and Innovation Stages

The previous chapter illustrated the multiple sources of innovation in our sample companies. Certainly there was an element of luck in Busicom's coming to Intel with its calculator chip request. Yet it was not luck, but rather technical expertise and creative thinking that led to Hoff's initial conception of the microprocessor as the solution to the Busicom problem. While there was no meticulous planning in this initial insight, however, the choice to pursue it had to be made. Further, as time went on, the strategic implications of the choice became increasingly clear, and called forth a myriad of significant decisions that committed the company and its fortunes to this endeavor, as we have shown.

The present chapter delves beneath the apparent contradiction between choice and the free flow of innovation we have been describing. In companies as complex as those we studied, many choices must be made, and some of them occur well before any formal planning systems come into play. Without these "pre-formal" choices, the formal system would have nothing to work upon, or too much to work on. In either case, innovation would falter.

How can organizations manage this paradox? The secret lies in a middle ground, where the successful high-technology firms develop alternatives to the extremes of innovation by pure chance or innovation by meticulously planned, controlled effort alone. Our sample firms made use of both planning and chance. Although the specific *content* of any innovation cannot be foretold, nevertheless we argue that the *process* of innovation is much more predictable than is currently recognized in either theory or management practice. This process of innovation, rather than any innovation's specific content, is the center of attention, in these firms and in our chapter.

The key to the dilemma of managing an innovation strategy is to be found by focusing on innovation processes. Given the fostering context and top management vision described earlier, two innovation aspects may be pinpointed: the informal interplay between plans and reality that allows a strategy of innovation to emerge in a complex, unpredictable world; and the individual exercise of expertise in choosing what project to spend time on, what effort to back. There are other tensions as well – between change and stability, between management perspectives and technical perspectives, between formal rules or commitments and the spirit of the organization. All of these ultimately rest upon individuals' exercise of choice as a front-end filter to the formal processes of innovation management.

Here, too, there is tension: between choosing to develop some innovative ideas, and choosing *not* to develop others. Motivation must be kept high enough to ensure a continued flow of ideas and genuine choice. Too much direction or constraint on what innovators may work on, and their willingness to produce new ideas or commit their efforts will dry up. Not enough direction or constraint, and the organization "go off in all directions," fail to follow through, spread its efforts too thinly, and do a poor job on everything.

Shared judgment, widely dispersed, is the solution we found in our research. Care and maintenance of this judgment is woven into the fabric of our sample firms, and characterizes them in terms of strategy making and innovation choice, which are closely interwoven for these firms. Yet choices are not always shared. Many of our sample firms were themselves founded as spin-offs from earlier companies, when the founders' ideas were not selected for development. Intel was founded to exploit integrated circuit advances Fairchild Semiconductor was unable to develop to the satisfaction of Noyce and Moore. Our firms, too, give rise to new firms: MOStek, a Texas Instruments spin-off, was founded by innovators who lost patience with TI's slow move into MOS technology. Similar stories abound in the industry.

Equally, while managers and many others speak of "stages," the innovation processes we describe here are far less cut-and-dried, and far less distinct from one another than that word might suggest. Instead, a characteristic context makes for simultaneity, overlapping activities, and much mutual interplay. It is messy – but it works, and it helps innovators in these firms to wring more benefit out of what might otherwise be considered discrete ideas.

Many of this chapter's illustrations will be drawn from two companies, Hewlett-Packard and Intel. As in other chapters, the specifics of names, labels, and procedural details do refer to an individual company. In each case, however, the underlying pattern could be easily illustrated from our other companies. While the names and some details differ from company to company, the pattern holds true across our sample. As with earlier examples, the specifics are illustrations of practices widely visible in our innovative firms.

"Too Many" Ideas: Chosen Contests for Innovation

"More Innovative Ideas Than We Can Use"

Maintaining innovation, as we have shown, means creating a context within which it readily occurs. The general culture of these firms taps deep wells of innovation, at a variety of sources. Senior executives have an expanded role in instigating innovation, and of course many specialists of all sorts must also contribute to the complex development process. The outcome is that these firms have far more innovative ideas available at any one time than they can possibly implement. Intel's Gordon Moore put it succinctly in the first epigraph to this chapter: "We have too many ideas. It is hard to decide which ones to develop." As all our introductory quotes suggest, this situation is echoed well down in other organizations we studied. The pressing problem in these firms thus shifts from one of finding ideas to that of selecting among ideas – meanwhile, of course, keeping the ideas freely flowing, so that choice continues to be possible. Choices must be made, and the method of choice must not inhibit later ideas.

The importance of this situation, and its difference from traditional management views, is noteworthy: many managers assume that any reasonably good idea that comes along must be seized, lest opportunity be lost for ever. This mentality, which might be called an internal "economy of scarcity," may well be an accurate reflection of firms in which innovation is not a central focus. (It may be an unconscious analog to the "scarcity mentality" enshrined in business lore and accounting systems that emphasize cost-cutting.) The "innovation scarcity" view is however diametrically opposed to the "economy of surplus" visible in these high-technology firms. In our sample firms, issues of innovation management, protection, and nurturing come to the fore, led by the issue of innovation choice.

The difficulties are far more complex than merely dollars and cents, although they matter too. Innovation opportunities are not wholly independent – engaging to do one project means at minimum electing not to do something else. Mutual interactions of other sorts among projects are also important. In short, a decision is not merely a yes or no; instead it reflects and interacts with many other decisions that steer the company into a chosen strategic path. Thus such decisions require a broad overview and strategic perspective on the business. Les Vadasz of Intel described the importance of intellectual resource limits:

> I think that one of the most important elements of innovation is to nurture it, to be able to give it critical mass. There's a tremendous effort and a tremendous investment [in any single innovation], and you can only do a selected number of projects if you want to succeed. So you have to make choices. Sometimes you have to let go of a perfectly good idea, because you cannot afford it. Not necessarily because you can't afford it financially, but because you just don't have the intellectual energy to do it all.

Our sample company executives and their managers and engineers recognize that they are simply not capable of effectively developing every exciting new idea that comes up. Nor can they address every customer need identified by marketing, or launch every possible product conjured up by designers – even those proposed by the exceptionally talented. While selection is difficult, it is essential. The managers, engineers, and executives in these firms scrupulously seek to avoid too many projects at one time, lest they starve all their efforts of the necessary nutrients of talent, managerial attention, physical resources and funds.

Uncertainty and Choice

Technical Focus, Shared Business Sensitivities Choices must be made, but how? In each of these innovative companies, we asked: "How do the people with the innovative ideas obtain support from the resource-controllers to develop their ideas?" In each company, the answer was far more complex than either "follow the rules, get the check-offs" or "do what you please". These companies are neither engineering nirvanas with unlimited resources, nor rigidly plan-driven automatons. Nor were these firms "organic," uncontrolled adhocracies without control or hierarchy. On the contrary, we discovered instead a genuine management of the innovation selection process which is broadly based, decentralized, and also strategically guided. The broad roots of innovation in these companies are cultivated by broadly shared choice.

Choice is readily visible in formal resource allocation processes, but is perhaps even more important at lower levels and earlier phases, before an idea enters into the formal allocation procedure as an acknowledged, selected project. A central factor in how pre-formal planning works is the sophisticated *business* judgment of innovators, which was widespread in the highly technical companies we studied. These pre-formal processes serve to fuel the subsequent formal allocation and strategic planning activities with ideas that emerge, are tested and shaped, developed and then – often with some degree of informality at first – passed along to the formal systems as proposals.

Sensitivity to business needs is not limited to "non-technical" or "managerial" employees; indeed, it cannot be. Just as ideas must spring from widespread roots, selection must also be a widespread responsibility. Choice among potential innovation projects is the essence of successful innovation, according to those we spoke with. It cannot be mechanized or automated, nor even centralized very effectively. Instead, like the ambiance of innovation, it must be broadly fostered and created over time. Choice must be shared.

Since knowledge of where to innovate cannot be centralized, it must develop in individual experts, whose choices are essential to an effective strategy of innovation for the firm. Without this ability to judge what is technically feasible – and judgment is crucial here – planning would rapidly degenerate into mechanistic formalism. At the heart of such judgment is awareness of how business factors interact with technical realities. Major market or business uncertainties can completely invalidate a line of research, or render a formerly promising project obsolete. Equally, a great business prospect rests ultimately on technical feasibility.

Specific examples will illustrate this, but the process is broadly similar across our sample firms. As Peter Rosenbladt of Hewlett-Packard noted, managers – and most especially those responsible for technical development and innovation – must choose to adopt each new discovery or to ignore it, knowing that either choice will carry consequences:

> Here we are developing a product. In some cases, building something like a computer, for instance, may take five years. But during this period, events occur in the industry which have a substantive effect on the world, so far as we're concerned. Something comes up that will change the structure of these products, and who competes where. And then we face decisions to either ignore it or to adopt it. If we ignore it, we have no impact on our approach, but we may end up producing something that is a ho-hum product that nobody wants – and we may have put millions of dollars in to it.
>
> Peter Rosenbladt, Hewlett-Packard

A Strategic–Technical Perspective The "rightness" of a choice is measured on several dimensions, and explicitly includes a *business orientation*, over and above the purely technical considerations we might expect from an engineer or scientist. As an R&D manager, Rosenbladt is concerned not simply with technical excellence and currency, but with market timing and competitive response. In this business new projects often affect the strategic positioning of the firm, because technical details have strategic business implications:

> Or we may decide to adopt [the change], which then again has
> multiple decisions that follow from that. (a) It may not be mature
> enough that it's really worth looking at yet; or (b) it may be
> necessary to have because it *is* there, and everybody else is going
> to have it. But if we do so, it's a major impact on our project.
> It may delay the product that we're working on by a substantial
> amount [of time], which again has negative effects [on our
> business goals].
>
> Peter Rosenbladt, Hewlett-Packard

Rosenbladt, whose title was R&D Laboratory Manager at the time
of this interview, is quite articulate about just what those "negative
effects" would be – in competitive terms, not just technical terms:

> It's a constant battle we face. We assume, and I think that's an
> assumption borne out in the last few years, that for a particular
> product, there is a finite life. If you eat into that lifetime, and
> you don't just push [the product] out, you can eat enough [time]
> that there's nothing left.

Or again, describing his vision of the job of the R&D Lab:

> Our role is to produce products that we put into manufacturing
> and that we sell for profit. So we are not doing any basic research
> – although we do work on new things, including things that may
> lead to patentable inventions. But they're always done from a
> point of view of producing product, or developing products that
> can be produced by the company somewhere in the manufacturing
> department.

Rosenbladt is a lab manager, not formally responsible for "strategy"
– yet deeply involved, time after time, with choices that amount to
enormous strategic consequences for the business. He serves as an
example of the union of business and technical perspectives we found
widespread in our sample firms. Educated, expert choices like
Rosenbladt's constitute an essential first-stage filter to innovation
choices, and are duplicated by others in our innovative companies.
Nor is Rosenbladt, as lab manager, the most junior element of the
filter. His subordinates also exercise innovation choices of a similar
sort.

Managing Business Sensitivities In these firms there is a clear
expectation that managers and technical experts will have this
joint business–technical perspective. Business sensitivity is neither

incidental nor accidental. Technical specialists in our sample make the "business" decisions, contribute to them, and understand the logic of those insisted upon by others. It isn't enough to be a technical whiz; business, market, and product sophistication are also required, even – perhaps especially – at lower levels, where initial judgments are made. In traditional firms, very different standards can prevail. One R&D manager in a more traditional firm asserted that he did not want his R&D people to be "contaminated" by business considerations when making technical decisions.

Business sensitivity is very deliberately fostered at Hewlett-Packard, for instance, as a result of peer pressure and shared criteria. At HP, the "next bench" syndrome is much revered. If an innovator cannot interest someone "at the next bench," a product is unlikely to succeed in the larger marketplace. The "next bench" criterion is also very consistent with what David Packard described as HP's initial orientation toward development, focusing on identified customer needs:

> It's fundamental that you've got to know what the customer needs, and the kinds of things he wants to have. If you can figure out how to do that, you've got an automatically developed market, right when you start [with a new product] . . . Almost all of the new products we brought out into the market were successful because we already knew ahead of time that was what people would like to have. We knew enough about the measurement business to know that if we could do something, there would be no question about being able to sell it.

In much the same fashion, Charles Sporck commented that even his junior engineers were familiar with competitive details and "knew their business," at National, much better than he as CEO possibly could. Elsewhere in National, others made reference to peer recognition for innovative success as an important reward. Yet surely these are not fortuitous circumstances. At National, for instance, Sporck encouraged such awareness simply by virtue of his attention to the innovative programs. For example, Jim Solomon described with admiration the command and reach his CEO, Sporck, had with respect to the many programs under development at any one time at National:

> When we were a $50 million company, Charlie [Sporck] sat there when I selected a product. He would ask sometime later, "How's that going?" He would remember that silly thing. Even today,

he knows all of my key products, every one of them. He's right
on top of them, and we discuss them from time to time.

Jim Solomon, National Semiconductor

Sporck's tracking of projects at National was informal, as Solomon
commented a moment later, but his attention was certainly noticed:

> There is a formal tracking which in fact Charlie isn't involved
> in. The formal tracking is at P&L [profit and loss] meetings
> monthly . . . and designers aren't usually a part of that . . .
> Those are probably good, because they give a consciousness of
> the money flow so that we are better money managers. But
> money management is not my job. My job is research. [My
> manager] tracks me by bottom line: the only thing he can
> measure, and we know it's the only thing he can measure. The
> bottom line is a very hard thing to track when it takes three
> years for this idea to prove.

At HP and at National, at TI and at Intel and Motorola, a similar
context and widely shared judgment are discernible. This interlocking
of formal and informal is both essential and quite representative of
practice in our firms: senior managers are interested – and they pay
attention to decisions made by subordinates, upon whose expert
choice they rely. Because they pay attention, they shape the attention
and judgment of subordinates, who in turn shape the decision
processes that guide innovation choices. The dual focus on both
technology and business is also characteristic of these high-technology
firms: the attitude is not left to chance, but is underlined by structure,
focused by formal systems, and counterpoised by informal interactions
in all of these companies, a subject we shall deal with at length in
later chapters.

At HP, divisions are responsible for particular technologies as they
are captured in products or product lines. Technical considerations
provide the focus for the division lab sections, the basic working
units responsible for maintaining a product line or product family
that shares some technical core. (This is a structural arrangement,
with strategic responsibility and an action orientation attached.)
Common technology provides an important technical focus around
which to co-ordinate, but carefully fostered attitudes and norms
concerning innovation choice go far beyond technology. Beyond
the technical focus, people are concerned with the market, the

environment, and trade-offs in plan versus change, among other factors:

> R&D managers are responsible for developing our products. What goes on day-to-day is a function of where we are with the product program. I think the R&D community at HP probably has the prime responsibility for making product proposals, but they work closely with the marketing management and the general management to measure those against market needs, investment, ability to do it, and then start a good overall business plan. [That's all] to make sure that we end up with an R&D program that's square with what we're trying to accomplish.
>
> Dave Sanders, Hewlett-Packard

Prime responsibility for formal technical proposals must rest with R&D people – who must also be sensitive to market needs, and must exercise an almost invisible choice, before any proposals are made. Criteria spring from expectations explicitly recognized as bridging common departmental lines. The cross-functional, business as well as technology flavor of HP is encouraged because, as Sanders commented,

> The way we look at things is that everybody in our organization is supposed to be creative. [President] John Young's supposed to be creative, I'm supposed to be creative. I'm not supposed to wait for my engineers to get ideas and then come and tell me about them. We kind of work together on the problem. So if you've got somebody that's got a good idea, and it's in our charter, well then he's got to sell some people on it . . . form an informal team and get some things rolling.

The strategy of innovation is quite explicit at HP, mirroring David Packard's assertion that "innovation is the name of the game," requiring a constant stream of new products. Those product proposals represent the outcome of a prior stream of possibilities and choices that never saw the light of day – filtered by choices that rest on technical specialists' expertise and understanding of the business needs of the company.

The outcome of these arrangements is an explicit charter. Each HP business unit is responsible for maintaining itself at the edge of the state of the art in its area of responsibility. Its charter is a product area, defined to an extent but loosely interpreted – allowing for choice and opportunism within the charter by the technical specialists, engineers, and scientists who alone are in a position to develop the charter's specifics as technologies and markets change. The interplay of formal organizational bases in products and markets, and informal judgments, beliefs, and attitudes here is typical of the high-technology management methods of planning amidst uncertainty. The richly configured interaction of structure with formal charters, procedures for funding, and judgment, within a broader context of innovative responsibility, encourages judgment and sensitivity with both technical and market roots.

A Predictable Innovation Process

Stages of Innovation?

A famous Roman motto had it that "*Fortuna favet fortibus*" – Fortune favors the bold. Our managers would add, "and also the best prepared." It is not so much that planning, analysis, and preparation guarantee success as that lack of planning, lack of analysis, and lack of preparation will quite likely prevent it. Planning, analysis, and preparation position the firm to take advantage of opportunities, or respond to changes. As a result, planning processes are anything but cut-and-dried, computational, or pro forma in our sample companies. It cannot be just planning; it has to be good and flexible planning.

Good planning supports choice, and also change. Choice is what was initially intended, but change is always a possibility, and planning should help poise the organization in case of need to change. Indeed, where the strategy process becomes static or mechanical, planning loses its verve and vitality, and quickly declines to futility. This above all must be grasped if we are to understand the role and process of strategic planning in an innovative, ever-changing environment.

The process of a strategy of innovation, in contrast to its content, is predictable. In essence, the organization must be readied to move in a new direction, whatever it might be. This requirement creates its own demands. The need for new directions must be recognized; ideas or opportunities for new orientations must be available; people must be prepared to judge the need for change, and ready to embrace the selected new direction when chosen. Also required is some method for reallocating attention and resources by actually selecting the new direction, and then shifting targets and monitoring criteria to reflect the shift.

This outline of the process suggests a linear, sequential set of steps to follow. It is useful as a tool for understanding – but any manager who has been through the process will instantly recognize it as a vast oversimplification. In fact and practice, such changes of direction occur sometimes hesitantly, sometimes quickly, but often with recursive and repeated retracing of prior steps, one step backward for every two forward. Still, for purposes of discussion, we will start with the linear outline, simply to capture the many elements of such changes. Choice, reconsidered, is at the heart of change.

The Selection Filters in Action

Recognition of the need for change is at the start of innovation. It is pervasively reinforced in these firms by commitment to a strategy of innovation. With ideas coming from "just about everywhere," in our firms the recognition springs from the richly elaborated context described earlier. The process of choosing among innovations is equally pervasive and sophisticated. One deliberate characteristic of this approach to innovation stands out especially: it is shared. With it, since innovation is at the heart of strategy in these firms, strategy making is also widely shared.

The decision making we have been describing in this most central aspect of strategy, choosing new directions even prior to any "decision's" surfacing in the formal planning system, incorporates substantial amounts of shared input and open decision making. This is substantive collaboration around major decisions rife with "futurity" and "irreversibility," to use Peter Drucker's evocative terms. It is a good deal more far-reaching than "participation" as that is typically understood (Litterer and Jelinek, 1988).

How does this work? "Selection" here embraces both continued generation of new options, and the self-selection and peer review processes that develop and test "buy in" by the idea generators and their managers. Thus it depends on the technical and managerial expertise of the innovators mentioned above. It also includes the more deliberate formal and informal networks that actually result in a "yes" to this project and a "no" to that, as well as the back-door methods that permit a committed innovator to gain *de facto* continuance in the face of an initial "no."

Thus "selection" is not an instantaneous decision, but rather a drawn-out, multiplex process. Selection and the generation of new options interact, back and forth, over time. Such elaboration is the key to a sophisticated, broadly shared decision process that both motivates and chooses, "de-selecting" some projects but generally keeping would-be innovators motivated even so. Within it, a delicate balance must be maintained, between direction and autonomy, guidance and choice. This balance is an essential element in the continued innovation of our sample companies. It is also iteratively established and re-established, by repeated choices and stimuli "from all over."

Early-Stage Filters: Encouragement as well as Choice

Selection operates through the innovators themselves, at the level of the individual managers, scientists, and engineers. It occurs through several mechanisms, some decidedly informal and cultural, others more deliberative, managerial, and formal. Engineers and R&D managers, themselves "technical" and most typically promoted in recognition of their abilities to successfully innovate, describe initial innovation, including initial funding, as a purposely informal process.

Preliminary innovation activities are regularly "bootlegged," by shoehorning the activity in around regularly assigned duties. People are kept fairly busy, with relatively little slack. Yet the norm of being "110 percent busy" creates a clear invitation to fill the "extra" 10 percent with explorations of one's own choosing. Both the inducement of freedom to choose, and the opportunity to fill one's time with a potentially major innovation operate here. So, too, do expectations that people will be "110 percent busy." Projects seek people, and people seek projects.

This first aspect of choice, like the "stages" of innovation, is not a "step" so much as an on-going, continuous process. Repeated and iterative choice constitutes an initial screening, applied quite informally by the researchers or idea generators themselves. They decide what to work on. In the aggregate, their choices select and de-select. Such initiation and selection takes place among research scientists and engineers, but was also described in administrative projects and departments.

Time is widely identified as *the* scarce resource, for specialists and technicians, managers and executives, operators and support staff as well. The filter, then, is the level of excitement generated in the innovator by an idea. If it is exciting enough, she or he will find or make time to work on it. The nature of this early, informal hurdle is really no "decision making process," but more like osmosis, according to Fred Schroeder of Hewlett-Packard (now retired). Nevertheless, the hurdle is important, and individuals' time constraints drive the process. Ideas must clear the hurdle early:

> . . . before they're even born. [A new product idea] has got to be a major contribution, in the technological sense, and in the economic sense. It's got to be something *useful* for the customer. We don't want to make something that's just a toy.
>
> Fred Schroeder, Hewlett-Packard

The same time constraint operates again, when others choose to sign on to support a project idea, or not. Access to more than one's personal resources occurs when, as these innovators put it, "you get others to buy into your idea." The shift from an individual to several others, involving the hurdle of outsiders' judgment, is another important step. The judgment of outsiders is as constrained and difficult as the initial self-selection, because it is as time-constrained. Every company used this filter, often informally enacted but always explicitly noted. These two early steps, self-selection and buy-in by others, operate together, rather than as wholly discrete stages. Schroeder, for instance, described it in terms of having to "find a potential home" for ideas:

> [Lab people with an idea] have no manufacturing facilities, so they can't put anything in the market. So unless a product survives all those internal tests [it won't go]. All these engineers have the "next bench" syndrome, in other words saying, "What's good for me must be good for customers" – that gives us an instant test we can do right here. By and large, the majority of our new products must be useful in our own corporation. That's a good test: if we'd buy that, for that money, and throw out everything that we have, then other people are likely to do the same thing, right?

While the example here concerns lab equipment, the same principles apply in general. In our companies, initial support by an individual must quickly translate into support by others if an idea is to proceed. Unless others are excited by the idea, they won't support it.

Personal credibility is also involved in signing on, so both potential "adopters" and proposers judge carefully where they commit this valued resource, as well as their scarce time. Schroeder underlined ready comparisons and others' judgments, from the backer's point of view. Unless a project is perceived as worthy, it won't go:

> That's right: otherwise it's a no-no, and through mere peer pressure, you would never succeed – because there are so many good things, and we have to be able to do them.
>
> Fred Schroeder, Hewlett-Packard

Individuals put their own time into projects they are excited by. They expose to others (and therefore persist in) projects and efforts of their own that they believe others will buy into, thus adding to (and risking) their own credibility in turn. Another HP manager, Paul Stoft, corroborated by stressing credibility:

> I think that innovation comes from the incessant need for asking, "What's the contribution of what you're doing? Where will it make a difference?" And so even on our [formal] planning [documents] for the future, we have a column there that says "Contribution." If it's a me-too item, something somebody else is doing, and you can't find a unique contribution, we tend not to do it – [we tend] to de-emphasize it.
>
> Paul Stoft, Hewlett-Packard

The stakes go up as the project proceeds. Personal credibility is on the line because to get an idea beyond its origin, the innovator must go public. Stoft again describes this process:

> Just because I was talking to people I have an idea. Now that idea is not going to go anywhere unless I really push. So the strategy for doing that is, of course, to get it through the filter, to get it through the system. To get it accepted all the way up and down the line is to try to sell that idea. So I've gone to my boss, I've gone to my previous boss, I've gone to all the heads of the labs around here to explain the idea to them. I said, "Hey, wouldn't it be great if we could do this?" They all say, "Yes, interesting; but what will really happen? Will it really change the course of the industry?" I don't know yet. But I know that in order for that to happen, I have to keep pushing . . . It's going to take half a million dollars to even find out the feasibility of it. So, you know, you go demonstrate.

The interplay of conviction and public "push" are visible enactments of the filter system. Stoft's conviction that his idea is worth pursuit is clear – thus he pushes, and puts his own credibility on the line, because, in his words,

> I know now that it will eventually happen. Somebody will figure out how to do that, and suddenly we are going to have another breakthrough in VLSI [Very Large Scale Integration – packing more circuitry, more densely, on a single chip] that we haven't seen before. That's exciting because no one else knows that but me, and that idea isn't going to go anywhere unless I really push it.

In these preliminary stages, self-selection and idea-sharing are quite informal. As projects become more articulated and require greater resources, the selection and sharing also become more formal, as we shall see.

Balancing Risk and Cost

Innovation is costly both to the organization and to the individual. The further an infeasible project is carried, the greater the wasted investment, and the heavier the cost in lost alternatives not pursued. Those best positioned to judge the progress of an innovation, its initiators and his or her peers, must be alert to spotting problems early on. To encourage this judgment, our sample of innovative organizations strive to create common interest, where personal individual cost coincides with organizational cost. Risking one's personal credibility and time put important elements of personal cost into the innovation process, as HP's Rosenbladt noted:

> If you are associated with a failure, probably the most important thing is that you lose credibility, and it will be harder to convince someone that what you want to do is going to be a success the next time.
>
> Peter Rosenbladt, Hewlett-Packard

Risk to personal credibility is not new; it has been recognized for years. Our sample of high-technology firms goes farther, in paying explicit attention to risk management, both for individuals and for the firm. The risk must not be insurmountable, or the costs of potential failure unduly burdensome, according to Rosenbladt. The costs of failure must not be too severe, or even minimal checks and balances will stifle innovation. If the consequences to the individual of any single failure are too severe, risk-taking, and thus innovation, will die. This, indeed, is where many bureaucracies recede into mediocrity – because "following the rules" is without cost to the individual, while doing something else entails substantial punishment. "Following the rules" can be fatal to the organization, especially in an environment of change. When goals are subverted to "following the rules," any deviation – and thus any innovation – becomes suspect; change and innovation become exceedingly difficult (March and Simon, 1958).

Our companies balance the costs of failure by creating informal opportunities for "little failures" that are relatively costless, through the early sharing and thus the early assessment of ideas. But organizations too incur costs associated with any change, any course of action. To commit to an innovation project is to incur costs of investment, time, and foregone opportunities. Early assessment also protects the company.

Broadly shared assessment and multiple resource pools also permit ideas to have several chances. Because "ideas come from everywhere," lots of choice and many opportunities for resources must be maintained. There is no single, central hurdle to clear; the availability of slack resources, bootleg opportunities and exploration options, monitored and controlled by individual, professional assessments, helps to ensure that good ideas get a fair hearing – and that people feel their ideas get that hearing.

Another important part of managing innovation in high-technology firms involves achieving a balance or necessary coincidence between organizational and personal costs. It is important that the individual's benefits are not achieved at the organization's costs, or the organization's benefits at the individual's cost. It is by far preferable to have organizational and individual costs and benefits coincide.

The balance is most effectively achieved by means of informal, shared and sympathetic judgment – by others who buy in (or do not), having themselves experienced innovative failure as well as success. The individual costs are real, although not unbearable; they keep the choice process honest. "Everybody loses once in a while," and "This happens all the time – you lick your wounds or give up and do something else," commented HP's Rosenbladt. Many others echoed his view. Above all, however, balance is achieved by individuals' interactions, where their judgment comes into play, not by top-level fiat:

> There is no single, top-down structure in this company that determines what we do. We depend very much, first, strongly, on ideas we create at many levels.
>
> Peter Rosenbladt, Hewlett-Packard

These firms also depend upon the judgment of peers, freely sought and given informally, as the first-stage filter for innovative ideas. In this process, expertise, insight and creativity are more important than seniority or position.

Trust and autonomy, and genuine sharing of the decisions about projects thus carry the risk that some things will fail. As a normal cost of doing business, even failure can be tolerated, both by the individual and the firm. A key point is that the innovators in these firms are outspokenly critical of new ideas, and this is a strength of the innovation process. These innovative companies operate much like an ideal academic community: new ideas must be scrutinized by peers, and they will be carefully examined for flaws or weaknesses in logic and substance. Not all ideas pass muster. Some do, receive funding, and face continued scrutiny until the ultimate outcome is determined in the marketplace.

This process of critique is an essential element of innovation in the companies we studied. So, too, is occasional failure. The problem is to handle the failures productively:

> It has happened to me. It depends on how the failure occurs. It is not uncommon in this company that people get rewarded for something that they did and how they did it, despite the fact that it is a failure. Usually the reward then has a corporate flavor, despite the failure.
>
> Peter Rosenbladt, Hewlett-Packard

Failures themselves can have value for the firm, beyond their intended target. For example, Rosenbladt described a project on which he and others labored for many months. The project was viewed as important by management, yet the technical goals were not met for reasons that were not predictable when the project was initiated. In the technical sense, then, the project did not meet its goals and was thus a formal failure – but it produced useful insights: the months of work produced valuable technical knowledge, not attainable except by the laborious development effort. Thus the corporation derived value from the work, and the development people were rewarded for producing knowledge usable in other projects later on.

This view is akin to risk management in lending: the banker who makes money on every loan is likely to earn lower returns by taking on only certain successes. Risk and reward tend to increase together

– in the banking world as in the innovation business. The high-technology corporation that succeeds with every research project is likely taking on only projects that are minor extensions of existing knowledge and application, readily achieved and readily duplicable by competitors.

To keep the ideas and interactions going, and to manage risks effectively, projects sometimes go on despite criticism. Committed proposers and project champions are entitled, in the view of these companies, to their day in court – the court of definitive proof:

> It's very normal in HP that a project be carried out with outspoken critics for a long time. And sometimes that may result in a cancellation of a project close to its maturity. Sometimes it goes through, and it is a success, and the critics were wrong. Sometimes it goes through and is a failure, and the critics were right.
>
> Peter Rosenbladt, Hewlett-Packard

Success and failure, risk and reward, choice and allocation are all intertwined, interactive factors contributing to success at innovation. Managed properly, they contribute to generating a constant stream of innovative options. Once these options surface, however, choice becomes inevitable, because the organization cannot fund every project or pursue every good idea. Innovation in our sample companies exists in an economy of abundance, and therefore an economy of choice. We found that after self-governed choice, the next form of choice is buy-in by others, a key feature for companies operating in complex environments. Buy-in activity constitutes both a filter and an on-going encouragement to continued innovation.

Buy-In, Holes and Semi-No

We can summarize the early stage filters in terms of buy-in, holes, and semi-nos. As we have described, Hewlett-Packard people express buy-in in terms of the "next bench syndrome," a very practical and concrete criterion. Each company has its version of this first hurdle a new idea has to scale early on, as we have noted. In HP's original instrumentation business, this was literally the ability of the innovator to get the interest of the engineer at the next bench. If that person could be interested enough in the new instrument's potential to find space for it on a crowded workbench, then the project was deemed to have some promise as a commercial product. In a parallel fashion, if others can be persuaded to find room in their busy schedules to support a project, it is likely to have further potential.

The early, informal sharing serves two purposes: it is low cost, because initially it is "just talk," and it encourages brainstorming and idea generation. It is also tentatively judgmental, allowing for working and reworking of nascent ideas. The early sharing has another purpose as well: keeping many partial ideas or solutions in search of problems in circulation. Because these ideas have not been exterminated, they exist in mid-air, as part of the operating repertoire – a primordial soup from which later innovation springs, much like Rosenbladt's "failed" development project. Ideas retained in the background keep innovation going both by priming the pump and by providing a "semi-no." Peter Rosenbladt of HP described the process, emphasizing its informality and its continual, evolutionary process:

> There's just an on-going discussion in the aisles. Those ideas evolve and they come and go and they die again. Some hang in there and grow. This process of an idea being "in the air" is very important to us. It usually *doesn't* work that someone has an idea, writes a proposal and makes a presentation and it's go. Usually that doesn't work.
>
> Usually what works is somebody has an idea, and talks to somebody else, and it sounds really good. Then it bounces back and forth and we chew holes in it. And if it holds up, it will continue to grow despite the holes.

Others, at TI and Motorola and Intel, also referred to old ideas or failed ideas from the past, that hung on "in every decent engineer's repertoire," as one source put it, to be pulled out and reconfigured and adapted. These ideas in the atmosphere are so important that "nothing is ever really thrown away." Old ideas – and new ones too – will be changed, however. The holes will be filled.

Ideas also get changed around non-technical aspects of ideas, even within technical departments. Rosenbladt's spontaneous self-correction is revealing. Did he mean holes in the technical argument, he was asked?

> Yes. Or not necessarily technical holes, maybe marketing type holes – this would be easily as important.

But, we asked, how do engineers and technical researchers acquire marketing information?

> They read. I mean, where do we all get most of our working information? We read articles, we read papers, we read newspapers – articles, books. We attend professional conferences and stuff like this.

The sheer matter-of-factness of his response is itself a telling commentary on the importance of being sensitive to information, to business and market news as well as technical news, as perceived by a *research* manager. The same wide net of attention visible in senior managers' contacts and thinking described earlier in chapter 5 is visible here, too, at lower levels. The ambiance of innovation springs from broadly encouraged sensitivity to a wide array of information in a wide array of people, not just those whose jobs are explicitly directed toward acquiring such information. Rosenbladt went on to describe just how important the internal marketplace for ideas was, and how important ideas about the marketplace were within it:

> It's the lifeline, really, of the firm, because everything is complex enough that you cannot take a hierarchy and say, "Okay, only the president knows what's going on, and so he determines what we all do." Totally unworkable. We work here, but we also are members of the outside world, and we see what's going on.
>
> Peter Rosenbladt, Hewlett-Packard

Quasi-Formal Filters

Choice eventually involves more formal processes, yet even these are not so absolute or definitive as the phrase "formal processes" would seem to imply. Managers do feel responsible for choice, recognizing that de-selection has consequences, as HP's Dave Sanders noted:

> My job is to decide what we're going to do . . . I have to set a priority order and figure out which ones we can afford. There are always some that don't make the cut. You always have more ideas to do than you have money to spend. If we ever didn't, we'd really start to worry. My job as manager is to try to make this decision on a rational basis, and make the best business decisions. [Then I] try to explain what the reasons for those decisions are, to the people involved in them, try to solicit their support for the things that we are going to do. My job is to do that.

Sanders has responsibility for deciding what his group will do – but any scientist or engineer has alternative sources for support, backing, and opportunity to pursue a project that Sanders may not back. Such was the situation at every firm we studied.

The more formal aspect of sharing ideas and seeking resources for innovation involves formal superiors – but not necessarily the person most directly over the innovator, and not necessarily programmed innovation. All our sample firms used some form of this semi-permeable formal decision filter – elaborated by alternative funding sources, bootlegging or "borrowing," horse-trading, shopping for support, and the like. Managers and technical staff at several of the firms commented on this deliberate fluidity, and on its selection aspects:

> Sometimes you go to your direct boss. If you think he doesn't listen to you, go to another boss – and maybe a boss's boss. But it could be anybody. Or, if you're really bold, you go to the president and say, 'I have this idea, and if you don't do it, you'll miss out.' It happens all the time, too. And very often, it ends in a 'no,' and people go off and pound at the computer.
>
> Peter Rosenbladt, Hewlett-Packard

Violating the chain of command, so serious a mis-step in bureaucratic organizations, flourishes in these firms. It is tolerated with amusement and cherished for its occasional successes. The successes are enshrined in company lore, as reminders that "what everybody thinks," or "what the bosses think" isn't always correct. The "formal" decision procedures are intended to "leak," and the committed project champion can continue, despite "noes," to follow his or her convictions for some time in these companies.

Such tolerance of deviant opinion, which seems to imply a lack of control, plays a crucial part in the commitment and conviction with which people in these firms carry out their day-to-day tasks. It most directly affects innovation, for it puts the individual's judgment on a high plane, with the organization officially taking that judgment very seriously. This tolerance rests upon a fundamental trust in the expertise and responsibility of the individual – to speak up, to pursue the truth of a technical matter, to champion what their perspectives tell them is right.

As such, tolerance also carries obligations, and thus exercises a highly professional sort of control. This is an important point, because this not-quite-formal, not-quite-final decision arrangement allows both control and necessary room for manoeuvre to committed project champions. If you care enough, you can push it: there are both accepted ways, and, in unusual circumstances, explicitly prohibited ways that are nonetheless accepted as well, as we shall see in a moment.

These arrangements, particularly in their quasi-formal, semi-permeable character, exercise a form of control and guidance amidst freedom that goes well beyond the traditional rigid hierarchy of large organizations. As we have been arguing throughout this book, however, this quasi-formal system is not ad hoc, not out of control, not purely fortuitous or wholly bottoms-up. The high-technology firms we studied are neither unguided nor out of control, as a closer look will demonstrate.

When a "Mistake" Isn't Wrong

Sometimes, a challenge persists and ultimately triumphs even though senior organizational managers resist. TI is widely regarded as a very controlled, tightly managed organization. Yet managers there recounted with great delight and some awe how one researcher persisted in an idea he believed in despite direct orders to desist:

> His manager had told him to stop. Even the senior managers in his business group were opposed to the project, as well as senior officers in the Air Force. But he kept saying, 'No, this is too important.' They even threatened to fire him – but he showed up for work to keep his project going. And when he got his results, he went down to the Department of Defense and *sold* them the concept of laser-guided ordnance, which is why Texas Instruments has been the major producer of this equipment ever since. He was right, and we were wrong.
>
> Charles H. Phipps, General Partner, Sevin Rosen,
> formerly of Texas Instruments

Phipps, formerly responsible for strategic development on TI corporate staff and at the Semiconductor Group, remarked that "people need some iconoclastic stories inside organizations." This story was alive and well at TI when we did our research. It was repeated to the researcher a number of times over a 10-year period by managers throughout the firm, often with embellishments: Pat Haggerty had turned the project off; or the researcher had actually been fired. A similar account described an individual who persisted and insisted upon the voice synthesizer chips that made possible the highly successful "Speak'n'Spell" toy, whose relatives now include a variety of military and commercial non-toy products. Other companies too had heroes enshrined in the rolls of honor for refusing to go along with what everybody thought.

While these incidents were not routine, they were clearly important moral stories within the organization, enthusiastically retold to illustrate "the way things really work around here." With each success, such tales enter the organization's body of myths and stories, to be repeated as examples of the highest traditions of innovation, where the committed innovator turned the mighty organization to his or her will, for its own good.

Reminders of the quirky, unpredictable nature of achieved innovation serve as correctives and adjustments to the formal process – managers, as well as engineers and scientists, tell these stories to remind themselves that sometimes managers are wrong. They also serve as constant encouragement for new ideas: scientists and engineers tell these stories to illustrate that individuals' ideas do make a real, discernible difference in the companies we studied.

Guidance is exercised in the more subtle "semi-no" of multiple, alternative sources for backing. These reflect healthy recognition of the potential for the formal organization procedures, or any single manager, to be wrong in the assessment of an idea's commercial potential or technical feasibility. Researchers and innovators seek support from a variety of sources, and this variety helps to ensure that more than one view of the future is in play at any given time. Subversion of the current direction is not only tolerated, but cherished and enshrined in formal "back-door" systems, as we shall see in the next chapter.

Informally, such subversion is especially important for maintaining an innovative atmosphere. The one sure thing is that tomorrow will be different from today. Thus "guidance" is *not* just top-down, but multifaceted and various and interactive. It depends crucially on deliberately diverse perspectives. If an innovator can sell an idea to a manager – not necessarily his or her own manager – with resources to support the proposed project, he or she gets that support. Rosenbladt again illustrates a process widely seen in our companies:

People in my lab know what my hot buttons are. This engineer comes up, gets me in the aisle and says, 'Let me show you something.' So he takes me into this checkout room and shows me something, and it excites me very much because it's exactly what I have been saying for a long time we should do. So I get very excited. But he has the project manager and the section manager between him and myself. He comes and shows me this, and I tell him, 'Go ahead, do more of this, and if you want money, I'll give it to you.'

Encouraging Cross-Functional Fertilization

Seed money is available from a variety of sources – both designated managers and, often, researchers recognized for their creativity (regardless of their formal management status). At TI, for instance, the "TI Fellows", employees recognized as successful innovators, are such a source of support. Typically, seed money is also available from other sources: it is in division budgets; it is created through formal annual budgeting for specific projects; and numerous lab and development and product managers have discretionary resources at their disposal. Multiple caches of seed funding enable an innovator to seek support outside his or her current reporting relationship.

Such seed money provides the opportunity to demonstrate, convince, explore and, indeed, subvert current directions. It also encourages the inherently hybrid nature of ideas, while calling into play the low-level filtering grounded in broadly diverse technical expertise required to separate good ideas from less good ones. Practices like these lie behind the constant upwelling of new ideas, potential products or processes or market directions. They ensure that the first hurdle is low, while keeping ideas "in the air" and thus subject to wide consideration, many stimuli from different perspectives, and many opportunities for support, development, or elaboration.

While small amounts of initial seed money may involve more than a single person, acquisition of more extensive developmental funds must involve additional individuals to excite support – the term is precisely descriptive – among people from different functional areas in our sample firms. When a project begins to look technically feasible or interesting, very early on, a team is assembled, and the innovator must test the idea against the very different perspectives of manufacturing and marketing personnel, for instance, as well as other technical specialists.

This step often constitutes the first formally recognized move in the complex path that ideas follow, from the initial insight through the many steps that lead ultimately to a finished product. The creation of this team may also be the first formal choice point of any sort in an innovation project, where forms and explicit criteria and management intentions impinge.

Some version of this cross-functional inquiry is visible in every company, in varying degrees of formality. At Texas Instruments, for instance, initial exploration can involve the innovator and "one or two" others with seed money provided by the IDEA program, or through the TI Fellows. These formally designated routes to funding are, as in every firm, supplemented by the informally "bootlegged" resources that people universally scrounge in these innovative organizations. At HP, the early team effort is designated as a "pre-project" stage – expected to be risky and exploratory, but important in keeping ideas flowing as well as for the development of any single idea on its own. At Intel, the process is seen as part of the charter of every unit to keep itself at the technological forefront of its designated product mission. While some development may take place within the confines of a lab group, development teams early on ensure cross-functional views.

Two points are important for our purposes. The first is that in these firms, many innovations find support, even those not popular with one's formal superior, or consistent with current thinking. The filter of current wisdom is deliberately permeable. This ensures that non-standard thinking will have a chance. Deliberate subversion of the current view is built into accepted procedure, because innovation is so central to continued success. To be captured by current success and blinded to its limitations is to unduly mortgage the future. Legitimated subversion, encouraged by keeping many ideas in the air, bootlegging, bypassing the chain of command, and seed funding for multiple options, helps prevent such grand failure, even if choice requires many little project failures along the way.

The second point is that innovation is conceived of as interdisciplinary and team-based even in its early stages, with clear managerial as well as technical criteria. The sheer complexity of technical issues requires widespread input, and the massive effort of moving a highly technical product to production and into the marketplace is seen *by the innovators* as legitimately cross-functional. The effort also can be multinational, as firms bring specialists from abroad to the US or send US specialists abroad to work with others. TI's showcase state-of-the-art sister plants in Miho, Japan and Richardson, Texas were brought on stream by essentially the same joint US–Japanese team.

Those whose work experience has been predominantly research-oriented, in the laboratory, are often joined with product, marketing, or manufacturing-oriented specialists. Engineers, managers, and researchers, marketing, finance, manufacturing, and design – all levels and functional specialties are required. All are regularly drawn upon for project participation, input, insight, and innovation.

Formal Systems, Informal Negotiations

The quasi-formal approval process operates through negotiations and informality in the multiple sources of funding. This negotiated resource net, because it is so often discretionary, draws upon the insights and perspectives of the funders – creating *de facto* priorities by weighting budget allocations, but allowing the persuasiveness of informal contacts to swing the results. An example of this is Hewlett-Packard's allocation of 1 percent of gross revenues to the centralized, more basic research of its corporate labs, and 10 percent to the more product-oriented divisional R&D labs.

Budget allocations are highly formal, yet the linkage between the two labs was described by Peter Rosenbladt as informal. The corporate labs served to explore the more distant technological horizons, even though in 1985 the division labs were closer in time horizon to the central labs than ever before:

> Five years ago, the standard sort of attitude was . . . "The [corporate] labs are esoteric, think tank, eggheads, and doing whatever they damned please, and it's never relevant for what we need." Now, it's more "Here's what we want to do, and two years from now we need to have this in our [division] labs, so why don't you work on this now and try it?"
>
> We need to look farther out through time, if you will, [through the corporate labs]. We use them more in a groundbreaking mode than we have before. We see things now, say, five to ten

> years ahead for what we need, and we get them to work on these
> things because we need them . . .
>
>   Peter Rosenbladt, Hewlett-Packard

Despite formal allocations and charters of responsibility, according
to Rosenbladt the relationship was informal because informality
worked better. The "better," we argue, springs from the exercise of
widely dispersed judgment, in place of centralized or top-down,
hierarchical decision modes:

> It's all very informal and it depends on individuals to get together
> and drive it. That is very much HP style. So if I choose not to
> use them, that's fine; nobody tells me to. But if I see that they
> can do something for me and I can convince them to do that,
> then that's even better.
>
>   Peter Rosenbladt, Hewlett-Packard

Numerous others at our sample firms made similar comments. Formal
procedures such as partial funding of central R&D that required lab
managers to "sell" research ideas or shop for research needed by
those in divisions with research funds to spend, is a widespread practice
that requires informal negotiation. As we frequently discovered, in
these firms formal and informal arrangements work together.

Using money to encourage needed research was deliberate, on
Rosenbladt's part, but it wasn't in any sense "an order." No one told
him that he had to fund the central lab; instead, his personal interests,
judgment, and departmental needs dictated his choice. His account
is very similar to accounts of events at TI, where the jesting definition
of The Golden Rule repeatedly offered was "he who has the gold,
makes the rules." That is, the person controlling discretionary funding
really does affect research direction. The interplay between formal
and informal systems is clear, with the formal system serving as the
means to achieve an end judged within a local context, against a
backdrop of what excites or seems pertinent to a particular manager:

> It was bilateral agreement, it was strictly nonformal, although
> when it was done it was very formal in that we actually moved
> funds around.
>
>   Peter Rosenbladt, Hewlett-Packard

Repeatedly, like others, Rosenbladt stressed the interplay between
formal and informal methods:

> I cannot overemphasize that as being a very normal trait of the HP company. We depend a lot on this kind of work. The informality is the only thing that allows us to do things like that. If it was formal, it would be rigid and it would never work.

The same informality of practice, amidst very effective control systems and resource monitoring methods, was embraced by virtually every company in our sample, although the methods and systems differed. The mixture of formal and informal provides the route for quasi-formal guidance – it can be monitored, through formal systems, but it is grounded in the specific informal familiarity with technical details, issues, and market needs essential for good decisions. The specifics seem to be transmissible only informally, because they change, and their locus changes, too fast for formal procedures. This informality was seen as essential by all our companies, for identical reasons. Formality, and structures, assume that projects and commitments and resource allocations or priorities are permanent, which is not true here:

> [Formality] presupposes how things should work. But that means somebody has to have thought about this, and then it only works that way. But in reality, it doesn't work that way at all, so we depend much more on an instantaneous, ad hoc type of relationship.
>
> Peter Rosenbladt, Hewlett-Packard

Informality mingled with formal systems arrangements demonstrates how these quasi-formal procedures work. The point is more than "there is informal interplay." It is that the informal interplay set amidst formal systems is an essential element in the flexibility of the control system, and in the early filtering process to which innovative ideas are subject. Without informal means to include individuals' "soft" judgments, the formal systems would be hopelessly rigid and unresponsive. Informality is especially important because it puts individuals' credibility and judgment into the loop very explicitly. They need not necessarily defend any decision, *a priori*; these are discretionary decisions. They will ultimately be judged on the basis of track record and outcomes – as they, themselves, know well – both on the basis of being right, and on the basis of how well they foster innovation over time.

Formal Hurdles and Approvals

The informal processes that work on ideas "in the air" are rather like the action of a virus, infecting others by enthusiasm. The formal choice process, in contrast, makes explicit a necessary contest between ideas. Approvals and filtering get more formal as a project progresses, yet a certain essential informality continues. A good idea must pass a communication hurdle, and be able to excite others:

> It's a battle – it's an internal selling battle. And it's fought, then, for funds. Whoever has the better arguments is somehow able to convince [others] who have the money to fund. That [idea] then gets funded. To be able to communicate those ideas has a lot to do with whether something gets funded or not.
>
> Peter Rosenbladt, Hewlett-Packard

The battle goes through fairly formally designated phases or checkpoints, although along the way there are informal choices and criteria at work, as well as switchbacks and alternative routes to funding. Rosenbladt describes the formal phases his lab recognizes, giving full weight to the importance of the informal era of development:

> We have a fairly well structured approach we call the project life cycle. The project life cycle involves several key phases of a project and transition between those phases . . . The first phase that any project goes through is the Investigation phase. Often, there is even a Pre-Investigation phase, which is what we talked about before – where people have ideas that nobody told them to investigate. They look at the feasibility of something – then they put something [written] together, and hopefully this results in opening a formal Investigation phase.
>
> Sometimes the Investigation phase will go on for two months. It ends in a transition point, a checkoff which is a very formal event that we call the "I to L" – an Investigation phase to a Lab phase transition. That typically involves a complete review of how this project is to be done in terms of what it will cost us to carry it out, what technologies we will use, what product will result from this, what are the risks, what are the external dependencies – other organizations within HP or often suppliers – and what will the resulting product do for us in terms of marketability and producability, and so on. What will it cost?

These steps are quite recognizable, and generally parallel to commonly identified project management stages. However, there are some key differences. Rosenbladt's account – typical of many others we heard – contains a high degree of awareness and articulacy about "links." He mentions internal, cross-functional links between marketing, production, finance, and technology development. He mentions external dependencies, especially HP's relationships with its suppliers. The risks, both internal and technological, and external and competitive, are clearly acknowledged and examined in the "I to L" review. The review process is most explicitly not limited strictly to the R&D Department, nor are the questions it raises solely technical:

> When we have successfully gone beyond this transition point, we are entering the Lab phase. The Lab phase is the main portion of the product development. The end of this Lab phase is when the product that is being developed *exists*, with full functionality, and does everything that it was supposed to do. [This can be] a single model, a single prototype.
>
> At that time, we again go to a major checkoff point, which is called the Lab Prototype Signoff. That already implies involvement from non-R&D functions such as Quality Assurance, Product Support, Marketing, and Production. In other words, even during the Lab phase, these non-R&D departments get involved in anticipation of the role that they will play in the transition of the product from R&D to production.
>
> Peter Rosenbladt, Hewlett-Packard

Even as early as the lab phase, that is, after the first serious formal commitment by the company to develop an idea, decisions begin concerning materials, processes and manufacturability, marketing approaches and positioning. These decisions and choices are made in concert, on the basis of non-technical considerations as well as technical. Our companies deliberately ensure that the non-technical elements are early entrants into the process. There is little of the heavily sequential, throw-it-over-the-wall mentality here. These non-technical considerations are essential, even in such highly technical companies as our sample, for the high rate of commercial success these companies enjoy. The constraints these factors may imply must be recognized early on, when designs and commitments are still fluid, and change or project cancellation are least expensive.

Initial commitment does not guarantee that production will be carried out no matter what. Instead, it is a commitment only to go the next step, to the next checkoff. Cancellation remains a real possibility along the route, should technical results or market conditions dictate, but as time goes on, the probability of moving into production increases:

> You can sort of assume that the Investigation phase may be equivalent to 30 percent of the total investment required to build the thing – to develop a product. Assume the next [phase], the Lab Prototype phase which results in the Lab Prototype Signoff, may be equivalent to having done 70 percent of the work to develop a product. From then on, it becomes increasingly assured that this product is going to fly.
>
> Peter Rosenbladt, Hewlett-Packard

At Intel, the process is conceptually similar; idea champions must push to clear hurdles and capture support as ideas proceed. After its initial informal successes, every project meets more formal and rigorous assessment. Ron Smith, a PhD in device physics at Intel, described one such assessment forum. At Intel, any engineer or individual contributor may propose a product or new technology to higher management. "Higher management," in this case, is the Technical Review Group (TRG) of the corporation. As Smith explained, the TRG review is typically preceded by more informal discussions. A contributor typically approaches his or her manager with the idea in embryonic form. Discussion and encouragement and informal assessment will often occur in a corridor, between cubicles, or over coffee. If the innovator is sufficiently articulate, the idea will be encouraged, and the innovator will begin to tie the idea down more tightly – preparing mathematical formulae or proofs, demonstrating feasibility in a preliminary way and the like.

"Encouragement" – a word used universally to describe how early-stage ideas are fostered in our companies – does not typically require a budget, nor any financial analysis. It is simply an oral green light for an innovator to spend time developing a concept. During an "encouraged" project, moreover, the innovator must keep up to date on his or her current assignment.

The more formal and rigorous assessment comes after the ideas have been "tied down," when they are capable of scrutiny by technically accomplished managers like Gordon Moore, himself a PhD. Moore and others similarly qualified sit on the Technical Review Group at Intel, where technical assessment is most definitively not a task delegated to underlings or segregated from business consequences. Smith described the experience of going before the TRG:

> It's like a stiff PhD defense. The idea of going before the TRG was initially intimidating, because its members are so good technically.
>
> Ron Smith, Intel

Besides technical assessment, the innovator also faces managers who represent a range of business concerns including marketing, finance, manufacturing, and technology development. The members of the TRG at Intel represent the company's best business and technical acumen. However intimidating a TRG presentation may initially appear, such a rigorous selection is essential: only ideas that have the full and enthusiastic support of their proposers will have a chance of survival and commercial success. Willingness to go before the TRG serves as a genuine test of an innovator's "innovative fortitude."

Only after an idea has passed the technical screen of the TRG does Intel require a financial analysis of the proposed innovation. Commercial viability must be demonstrated in the form of a sensible return on the investment required. Since few engineers are initially conversant with financial analysis techniques, the reasonably sophisticated investment analysis required is another surmountable obstacle. It is also a learning experience focused on the economics of innovation. Smith noted that corporate or division financial staff will assist, but that the aim is to enable the innovator to demonstrate for him or herself the commercial advantages of an idea. Acquiring elementary financial modeling skills is not an enormous challenge for mathematical sophisticates who design circuits or devices. The requirement does underline the importance of business considerations, while equipping the most capable judge, the innovator, to evaluate a proposal in real-world terms.

As a project continues further from the initial investigation and comes closer to the final product configuration, involvement by others outside R&D expands, as does their participation in decisions, and the formality of the decision process. We will discuss this multi-functional involvement as an important feature of the innovation cycle, described in chapter 9. For the moment, let it suffice that the formal process of project selection and funding ensures cross-functional, cross-departmental and cross-disciplinary input into decisions that can and often do affect these companies profoundly.

If the notion of project stages is old, the use of the formal system to ensure such deliberately fostered, rich networking links, and the wide sharing of decisions across functions are much newer. So, too, is the more complex view of stages as intentionally simultaneous, iterative, and overlapping, rather than clearly discrete. The joining of a formal decision process with the quasi-formal and semi-permeable processes we have been describing is newer yet. The essence of innovation is neither technology push nor market pull; instead, these companies seek to create a context which can contain both in variable balance. Equally, the essence of innovation management is neither formal systems nor complete informality: instead, these companies blend and merge and complement these apparently dichotomous elements to produce a responsive, flexibly controlled system that depends on individuals' judgment, while encouraging that judgment along organizationally useful paths.

Managing the Choice Process: "Innovation Elements"

In each of these innovative companies, we asked, "How do the people with the innovative ideas obtain support from the resource-controllers to develop their ideas?" The responses made it clear that these firms are not free-floating, "organic" organizations in which hierarchies and controls are non-existent. Nor are the firms uncontrolled, turbulent or, disorganized adhocracies. If for no other reasons than the demands for sheer technical mastery of manufacturing, of design details, and of co-ordination among diverse expertise and resources, innovation in these firms is very carefully managed to ensure early input from critical and diverse perspectives.

On the other hand, the nature of hierarchy and control here is vastly different from what those terms often convey elsewhere. Expertise, insight, and creativity are more important than seniority, and success at managing innovation is particularly admired. "Decisions" occur far more often in the form of successful (or unsuccessful) instances of convincing peers than by management fiat, and they may stretch over numerous decision points (or even refuse to die). Innovation is deliberately managed, genuinely co-ordinated and planned – but not in any rigid or mechanistic way. Instead, systems and practices encourage individuals to judge their own innovation opportunities.

By giving innovations every opportunity to succeed, realistic assessment is both fostered and more easily accepted. Sharing exposes ideas to critical assessment by more objective outsiders. And innovation managers assemble necessary contributors across functions and specialties, both to feed projects and to judge them. These firms organize to favor the innovative process, and to favor those managers whose expertise helps innovation to succeed. The management of the choice process can be summarized in what we call *innovation elements*.

The patterns of innovation in these firms revealed six major elements to the system by which innovative ideas were selected for resource support by the organization. While there were differences of degree or emphasis, often describable in terms of "management style" or "organizational culture" differences so apparent as to be almost tangible, the underlying common pattern was nevertheless visible, containing the six interrelated elements, apparent as attitudes or management practices, often articulated as management maxims.

The first element in this pattern is a directive: "Keep the technical contributors busy, and insist that they meet deadlines." Managers consciously sought to keep their good technical people busy, perhaps even just a little over-committed: "We operate at about 110 percent of capacity around here" was a frequently repeated comment, offered by managers and technical specialists alike with both good humor and pride. "We don't believe in slack," they frequently proclaimed – although their "extra" 10 percent is clearly slack, in the form of their personal investment. Because time is scarce, the investigators themselves choose.

This element addresses both the necessary pace of technical work in a highly competitive industry, the sense of urgency needed to push complicated projects through, and the personal challenge that motivates extraordinary performance (see Vail, 1978; Latham and Locke, 1979; Burgelman and Sayles, 1986). People in these organizations feel tremendous accomplishment in their company's success, a reaction encouraged by shared celebration as well as shared struggle. Hewlett-Packard's salary cutbacks and Intel's voluntary unpaid work are contextual examples. They are also aware of high standards and the expectation of others that they shall contribute. Non-contributors, and non-innovators, are less valued. Challenge and assessment, including self-assessment, provide essential interplay for both judgment and motivation, team spirit and innovation choice.

Explicit milestones, against which progress can be judged, are also frequent – but these are not so much fixed deadlines, rigidly applied, as concrete specifics that enable both managers and technical researchers to judge whether a project is going well and whether it is worthy of further pursuit. Most typically, the innovators themselves defined the milestones to begin with, and had a great deal to say about what would be "acceptable" results. Nascent, immature projects might have no formally articulated deadlines or milestones. Even here, however, experimenters typically had a sense of "go/no go" markoffs for themselves, if for nobody else.

It is widely believed in these companies that a project worth doing will "find" time. Conversely, if an engineer or designer does not believe in it enough to commit some personal time to it, the project is judged as less exciting, and not worth effort. This is not management fiat, but consensus among researchers, managers, technical specialists, and others. Practicing managers have long assessed their subordinates' personal commitment as a proxy for project quality (Dean, 1987). In technical projects where innovative insight is central, this is especially à propos. Similarly, personal investment of self guarantees at minimum that the project will not fail for want of the little bit of extra effort – so the proxy is a highly sensible one.

A second element is a deliberate and continuing effort to build up the organizational, business, and managerial skills of the technical staff experts. Much effort is expended to ensure that innovators can themselves judge whether an innovative idea has external commercial appeal, not so much on any individual project as over time. Milestones suggested by the investigators, the agreed criteria of success or failure, are often directly related to ultimate commercial use – whether stated in technical or financial, time or volume terms. At early stages a technical expert might not have a finished idea – but he or she will be quite clear about the importance of commercial success.

Equally, the process of innovation management is well defined and distinct, and the organizational skills essential for successful innovation readily articulated. Innovators are made aware early on that commercialization is a complex process, the management of which requires attention and skill. They are encouraged to develop the necessary skills, and those who do are systematically and observably more successful than those who do not. The visibility of innovation *management* skills is notable. So, too, is the interplay between choice and innovations management effort. As innovators become more skilled, they are encouraged to apply their insight in assisting with the selection process – for both their own ideas and others'.

A third element in the innovation process is the push provided by product champions, a role identified in previous research (e.g. Roberts, 1977; Schon, 1963). Because innovations in these firms are increasingly complex, drawing on widely varied expertise, a number of champions will ultimately be involved. Innovators must become champions of their own ideas, in order to engender the enthusiasm and support among others needed to garner necessary resources. Such push relates to superiors' assessment, of course, but it contains strong elements of judgment, leadership, and management as well.

The engineer or technical specialist who is most likely to succeed at HP (as at the other companies we studied) is a far cry from the stereotypic introverted engineer who doesn't get along well with others: "Those types don't have a very successful position in this company," commented Rosenbladt, echoing comments by others at our sample companies. Those who will not champion their own innovation can scarcely anticipate much support from others:

> We do put value on and we try to assess during the process [of innovation]: "Is this person willing to take initiative?" We have this classification of "implementers" – that has a very negative connotation: someone who does as [he or she is] told. Even if that person is fully competent, they don't rank highly at all. And we also assess their performance in the process badly. The kind of people that we want are not only intelligent and competent professionally, but willing to take initiative and pose ideas or approaches that can change the way we do things. We have this concept of "agent of change" which we strongly encourage. We want people to be agents of change, because we believe that change is absolutely fundamental to not only this company, but also this industry. We want people to be noncomplacent.
>
> Peter Rosenbladt, Hewlett-Packard

The outcome of successful product championship is the creation of a team: element four. Initiative, in innovation, goes past the mere conception of new ideas to creating enthusiasm in others, building upon their ideas, expertise, and contributions, and drawing them into the process. This requirement is not academic; rather, it recognizes the complex realities of semiconductor development. Others have to become champions in response to the initiator's own enthusiasm; a cadre of champions must be created. Without them, the project will not succeed. In a bureaucracy, "The job isn't done until the paperwork is finished." In these firms, "The job can't be done until the team comes together." An engineer or scientist must tap into manufacturing and marketing, product and process design and, often, fundamental technical support as well. The marketer or salesperson with an idea must capture the imagination of the technical resources, the manufacturing people, and so on. Thus push is required.

Teams also serve another purpose, however: they assess and test innovative ideas by a filter quite comparable to the initiator's own internal filter, but more objective. If the idea doesn't excite knowledgeable people enough to gain their support, it's probably not worthy of pursuit. These are sophisticated specialists, widely informed on problems and possibilities, and keen to improve performance, make profit, establish foundations, make a difference in the company. They are on the lookout for good ideas, and eager to co-operate. But, like initiators, they have only so much time to expend, and the free flow of ideas around them imposes the necessity of choice. Their choice constitutes an important and realistic means of vetting ideas to keep the innovation process working.

The fifth and sixth elements of the innovation process are interrelated. Each company we studied had a concrete and coherent strategic planning process in which innovation was viewed as a dominant competitive issue. Formal planning systems, the fifth element of innovation, will be addressed at length in chapter 7. For the moment, it is important to note that formal, deliberate planning of "innovative directions" does in fact occur, although not in the form of some immovable, unchangeable Procrustean bed upon which all new ideas are stretched.

The sixth element is the context of informal methods which completes the formal system and enables it to work. These managers are pragmatic, energetic, achievement-oriented, people who are quite willing to examine their commitments and, if required, change or abandon unsuccessful directions. They are typically alert to possibilities of learning as they go, and of incorporating their learning in revised plans. Informality also enables these firms to respond opportunistically to possibilities not included in plans.

Nevertheless, planning for innovation is important. Persistence and coherency of action over time are required. Adhocracy, opportunism, and individual action are all insufficient by themselves in new technology acquisition, for instance, where extended and consistent problem-solving is typically required for successful implementation. Although clearly formal plans can neither specify details nor guarantee success, explicit plans for technology innovation distinguish successfully innovative firms (Ettlie and Bridges, 1987).

Such planning as we found, characterized by the interplay of formal and informal methods, is far more than a group improvization, and yet far less than a detailed recipe. Managers draw upon their past experience, but in concert, not as individual soloists: this sort of strategic planning is, perhaps, more a symphonic interpretation of familiar themes and notes.

Summary and Conclusions

A strategy of innovation is contained not in "plans," but in the pattern of commitments, decisions, approaches, and persistent behaviors that facilitate doing new things. This view suggests that an innovation strategy is formulated or articulated only as it happens; thus managers do not make grand pronouncements of exquisite detail and meticulous precision. Instead, they behave, make decisions, and commit in ways that persistently foster innovation. Similarly, while there is no hard-and-fast umbrella statement outlining the technical specifics of innovations to be sought, a clear commitment to maintaining a flow of innovations, ensuring an effective, yet semi-permeable filtering system, and wide participation is visible in our study firms.

A persistent strategy of innovation is discernible in a pattern of commitments, and embodied in the choices and behaviors of these firms. The pattern is exemplified here by Hewlett-Packard, but each of the sample had its version of all the elements we have described. The semi-permeable filters and quasi-formal systems and arrangements described here all foster continued innovation. These persistent, carefully maintained patterns serve to keep innovation vital and to keep ideas flowing. Simultaneously they contribute to judgment, exercised by those in the best position to assess innovative ideas.

Judgment can be shared, but only if those judging have a dependable, shared set of criteria. In our firms, technical expertise, individual commitment to ideas, contribution, and potential for marketplace success are all fostered by the arrangements described here. Consequently, while the material in this chapter has little to do with formal plans or planning procedures, it has everything to do with enacting a strategy of innovation.

Formal plans (as we shall see in the next chapter) do powerfully affect the direction of innovation in the companies we have studied. Beyond the self-filters, the next-bench "seduce me with your ideas" filter, and the quasi-formal filters, formal procedures also play a role. The plans are not cast in concrete, however, and both before the fact and afterwards, they are conditioned and affected by informal interchange, the up-flowing ideas in currency at any point in time, and the incremental, evolutionary results of real-world implementation. The informal processes themselves, as we suggest here, are also managed.

7

The Paradox of Formal Systems and Adaptable Strategies

How could anybody believe that you could set up a central research laboratory on 1 January 1953, and have a successful silicon transistor only a few months and a year later, in February 1954? Who would believe that you could work on a pocket radio, using germanium transistors, in the early part of 1954, and actually have it in production in October 1954?

In both cases, it was what we set out to do. We set out to make a silicon transistor; we set out to make a pocket radio.

Patrick Haggerty, Texas Instruments

Many of these decisions are, really, intuitive. You know that ad that *Time* was running at that time, for Cutty Sark? "Here's to gut feel, and to people who practise that." That's really very à propos. You develop a certain feel about it. You talk to people and you listen to people who understand . . . who have certain problems. You develop a certain conviction, more than an opinion, about what's right and what's not right.

Les Vadasz, Intel

Planning and Strategy

Planning for the future, and planning explicitly for future innovation, are essential to high-technology companies facing a constantly changing environment. So, too, are intuitive and opportunistic exploitation of possibilities. Each of our firms deliberately planned for its future and structured its innovations. Informal arrangements were used both to foster an on-going flow of ideas and to make preliminary choices among them, as we have shown. Formal systems selected from among the opportunities that survived the informal, preliminary screens. However, no firm planned in a mechanical fashion.

The interplay between intention and formal systems, and the evolution of such formal systems over time, are continuing themes throughout this chapter, one crucial to understanding how strategy takes effect in modern organizations. Many modern businesses, like semiconductor electronics, are simply too complex to be the brainchildren of a single actor, however deeply immersed in his or her craft, however brilliant in his or her specialty. Nor is it enough to have a good general feel; the details must be mastered, and they are myriad beyond individual comprehension. A "Great Leader" may indeed provide important incentives, insights and charismatic energy – we have been privileged to meet several. But many, many others must contribute their essential resources, if significant strategic achievements are to happen.

Formal strategic systems offer managers important tools for systematizing their approach to the complicated business of strategy. Plans and systems must support, but not overly constrain; they must make resources and talents directly available to strategy makers – not just the CEO and top managers, but many others, well down in the ranks. Above all, since strategy is *not* a cut-and-dried, once-and-for-all matter, formal systems must help to initiate broad support, to monitor the strategic process, and to revise it as necessary. These systems do not just restrict strategic outcomes; they marshal inputs, maintain a perspective, involve, motivate, and shape people's thinking.

To understand these relationships, we must go well beyond simple stereotypes of strategic planning, formulation, and implementation. We must go beyond stereotypes of leadership as well, for the management of innovation is so central to these firms' futures that it is a key leader role. Leaders, especially those in certain senior and boundary-spanning roles, are important links between the organization and the outside world, as we have noted. Their detailed familiarity with technical possibilities and with market needs helps to shape strategic vision from a wide array of contributions by technical specialists, researchers, marketers, customers and others. That leader responsibility concerns strategic content.

A different responsibility centers on the strategic process: leaders throughout the organization also oversee the formal systems that assist the strategic process, assess their working, and adjust them. This chapter will describe formal systems used in our target companies. Such systems are essential devices for ordering and tracking the complicated endeavors of these firms, and their results in an equally complex external world. But no manager we talked to – including many from companies widely regarded as highly structured in their strategic management – regarded the current formal system as "complete" or the plans it produced as "final." Rather, both plans and systems were seen in process, evolving, to be improved upon as insights emerged and situations changed.

Such a situation is vastly more sophisticated than allowed for by the binary academic views pro or con, that "managers don't plan" or "good firms do plan," that strategy doesn't matter or that it does. In place of such simplifications, we found that our firms do plan, but flexibly. Our managers responded opportunistically and incrementally, but also used plans and the planning process. Thus this chapter must look both at and beyond the strategic planning systems and the "official" strategic plans.

Three key additions enrich formal strategy planning in these firms. First, the subsidiary systems and formal methods intended to bolster "regular" plans and planning are essential components of the way these firms avoid mechanistic responses. Next is the interplay between formal systems and informal practice described in the previous chapter in terms of front-end innovation filters. This vital interplay continues in the more formally structured later stages of innovation. Finally, the consequences of the planning process are fed back into adjustments of the planning system itself, not merely into revising any given plan. All three elements are consciously utilized by the managers and executives we studied at Intel, National, Motorola, Texas Instruments and Hewlett-Packard.

In short, this chapter will look both at formal strategic planning and at the non-plan activities that center on backstopping formal systems' limits – because, indeed, there are limits. We shall also discuss motivation, communication, and performance assessment in the strategic context, because they are closely related to effectively implementing strategy.

Strategic Planning

Formal Systems, Annual Calendars and Plans

All the firms we studied – and, indeed, most businesses of appreciable size of which we are aware – have some sort of formal planning system. Such systems may be simple or elaborate, purely financial or, as in our firms, also concerned with technical, product, marketing and other aspects. All of our firms explicitly addressed issues of technological innovation, as well as market positioning and new product strategy, in their formal systems.

The formal systems served a variety of common needs. They were used explicitly for identifying potential projects, for assessing them and bringing them to management attention in order to tap resources for further development and funding; and afterwards for tracking progress and deciding on either further development or ultimate termination. Formal planning systems also served for more immediate management of projects and programs selected for full-scale implementation. These innovations had to be integrated into on-going activities, and their results monitored. All the firms also fed back information on outcomes to enable adjustment of later action. Perhaps most importantly, however, the formal systems themselves evolved as new understandings emerged.

The structure of Texas Instruments, described earlier, offers a prototypical model for a strategic planning system, a useful model for comparison because it is so well articulated and so exhaustive. While TI's system has been variously praised and damned as the company's fortunes have risen or declined, there is much to learn from the OST system and its evolution.

TI uses a linked set of goals – at the corporate level, for the farthest time frame; at the group or strategic business unit level, for a somewhat shorter time frame; at the product or process level, for even shorter, action-oriented sort of planning. At the corporate level, a 10-year horizon is possible; such plans refer to "objectives." At the group or business unit level, "strategies" embrace a shorter horizon, and have predicted resource needs and estimated goals attached. At the product or process level, specific "tactics" address immediate time frames of 6 to 18 months, with explicit responsibilities outlined in milestones, named persons charged with tasks, and required budget commitments attached.

Performance assessment at TI rests quite firmly on the expectation that managers shall wear "two hats:" TI managers are expected to develop strength in both operational and strategic management. The two separate activities are accounted for with separate budgets (and assessed by separate criteria).

Similarities can be found in other firms' approaches. National Semiconductor also organizes planning around the budgeting calendar, but National's planning includes many factors beyond budgeting *per se*. When CEO Charlie Sporck describes strategic planning at National, he also mentions debates about direction, and strong endeavors to identify and respond to customer preferences. He comments also that planning focuses on the near term in greater detail, and on some years out in lesser detail:

> It's a yearly strategic planning [process]. It starts off with marketing at the corporate and division management levels defining what it is we want to do. That's starting out now [in January 1985] for fiscal '86; our year ends in May. We will have our plan done sometime in late April . . . The first step is for the management group to set out the various conditions that we want to assume – like the economic environment. What's the economic environment going to be? That sort of thing. Then we define what our priorities are going to be, and what modifications in our approach we might want to take.
>
> Then the next step is this strategic marketing function. They present their case for changes, necessary corrections to be made – "More emphasis" in what area? Less in which others? "Drop out of the business, we don't want that business any more, it's not important to our customer base." *We're entirely customer driven.* I say that recognizing that what I'm saying is not entirely the truth; we would *like* to be entirely customer driven.
>
> With that framework, we go to the product lines and tell them, "Okay, this is where we're going." This is not entirely single-sided; it represents a lot of debate. For example, when the marketing people present their positions, the product lines are there to argue about it. But in any case, at that issue, then, the product lines put together their strategic directions for the coming year.
>
> By the way, it's the coming year plus four more – a lot more attention in the short term.
>
> Charlie Sporck, National Semiconductor

The strongest emphasis in Sporck's comments falls on the one- to five-year time horizon. Being able to focus on the very near term without losing the longer perspective is imperative in a swiftly changing technology and marketplace. Going beyond the next quarterly return is essential for longer-term results, and clearly visible here.

The format described here is quite consistent with the traditional view of strategic planning; there is little here that is surprising, really. The approach is systematic; it links different time horizons and superordinate and subordinate goals. And it analytically breaks down the largest-scale and longest-term intentions into specific action steps intended to achieve intermediate goals. As Sporck's description suggests, these systems roll out in a pre-specified planning cycle tied to the firm's budgeting practices, and performance against plan is keyed to compensation.

Ubiquitous Plans – and Repeated Revision

Everybody plans in this industry. What is notable is that the managers and engineers we talked with use such systems, and more importantly, the structures of thought that underlie them. Every company we studied had a formalized strategic planning process, of course: these are multi-billion dollar corporations. Even the reputedly less structured firms such as Hewlett-Packard clearly operated with such a model not merely on paper, but in managers' minds:

> We spent most of our time in the last year clarifying the business strategy. How are we going to be in those businesses we select, to begin with? Derivative from that, you can have literally what we call tactical plans: sort of the annual approach to this thing. It gives you a vehicle at that time to identify the key tasks, who's going to do them, what kind of peripheral parts of the organization are essential in getting it done.
>
> John Young, Hewlett-Packard

Identifying key tasks and those responsible for them, earmarking necessary resources, and clarifying business strategy are widely recognized goals for any systematic strategic planning system.

National Semiconductor's initial approach to planning explicitly takes an outcomes focus, not a numbers focus. Target markets and customer segments and needs are identified. This preliminary plan is first put together by product groups after negotiation between centralized marketing personnel and decentralized product line personnel, according to Sporck:

> [The initial plan is] without any real numbers – this is not a numbers thing, it's a plan of action, as opposed to forecasts of sales and profits. When the product line personnel have that together, they bring that back to the division management staff and the corporate staff. The marketing representatives present how they're going to address these various targets they've set up. That plan gets exercised, modified, or whatever, and then it's done.
>
> Charlie Sporck, National Semiconductor

This plan of action for the year centers on negotiations and debates about product characteristics, above all, and how they will be fitted to market-segment opportunities:

> This effort . . . is an interlude effort between the design engineering organizations – each one of these product lines has an applications engineer who works with customers – between the strategic marketing group, say the telecommunications people, the telecommunications application group, and the design group, and the customer base that they're interfacing with.
>
> A basic outline of the product is defined. Then the design group goes to work with "How would we go about satisfying that – the functions that we've presented or described?" They come up with certain approaches, and maybe some very off-the-wall specifications as to what it would look like. Then they take that, and with the marketing guy, go out to the customers and the customers' engineering organizations, and say, "This is what we propose; what do you think about it?"
>
> It gets modified somewhat more, and then it gets back and you can start doing some real concrete design. The innovative portion of that is, "How would you go about establishing the function? Doing that function?" Because you've got a lot of options . . .
>
> Charlie Sporck, National Semiconductor

National, although widely regarded as tightly managed, has conspicuously inserted a "no numbers" negotiation period in the planning loop to ensure that concepts get dealt with. Quite similarly, although it is reputed to be more loosely managed, HP designated the budgetary specifics as concretely tactical, with true strategy as a lengthy, messy, and iterative front-end discussion needed to create shared perspectives on "how to be in the business." Customer contact, involving experts responsible for conceiving the devices and designing them, and the ultimate users, is visible here as an early input. Technical details, market details, and ideas in these companies take precedence over "the numbers" and financing considerations.

Once a strategy is determined, it is treated seriously. "Strategy" is a constant topic of attention in the companies we studied. It is simply too important to be treated as a casual, chance event. It is simply too complex to be treated loosely or incrementally or just opportunistically, when long-term, persistent innovation is a competitive requirement, as it is in this industry. Instead, strategy must be systematically thought about and planned for, funded and monitored and persisted in, over extended periods of time and in the face of difficulties.

Formal systems operate most explicitly after strategy has been developed, to monitor its achievement, assess its continued fit with reality, and signal major intentions. The formal systems serve to induce persistence, rather than abandonment, as the first reaction to difficulties. They help manage the details, and master the complexities of coordination. They force questions and guide thought, but they are not expected to substitute for creativity or management attention, which must come first.

Formal Systems as Attention Filters

A major advantage of formal strategic planning systems is that they permit managers to differentially manage routine and strategic activities. Some systems are very explicit about this distinction. The difference can be crucial, in so cyclic an environment as that faced by semiconductors. Across-the-board belt-tightening as a means to ride out downturns is insufficient: some activities have greater importance for survival than others. Systems that permit distinctions give better control. In difficult times, highly important strategic activities can be maintained or even increased, at the cost of less important, routine activities.

The firms of our sample do distinguish between routine and strategic activities. TI explicitly identifies strategic expenditures and endeavors as distinct from day-to-day business, so that both "today's business" and "tomorrow's business" can be monitored. TI maintains a separate budget and accounting record for strategic activities, with the explicit purpose of facilitating differential management of the two activities. Cutting back routine activities while sustaining or even increasing the strategic activities that ensure a place in the game for the future is a specific aim. The underlying distinction – between strategic and routine activities (and their budgets) – is universal among our companies, although the method to attain it may be more or less elaborated in formal systems.

Similarly, in 1986, Hewlett-Packard targeted three areas for continued funding despite company-wide cutbacks (including an across-the board 10 percent salary reduction in which managers participated), in the midst of an industry-wide recession. As John Young commented, strategic efforts were so important that "We just have to get them done." In like fashion, Intel chose to fund certain high priority projects even while sharing company-wide salary cuts and furloughs.

Continuity is needed in strategic activities, to position the firm for the eventual recovery. (Such continuity is both especially difficult and especially important amidst the emphatic short-term demands of a turbulent industry.) Formal systems and commitments help by ensuring persistence – persistence in a desired course of action for the future despite temporary and localized difficulties in current businesses and economic activity. For firms like ours, in highly volatile circumstances, any hope of long-term commitment must be founded on some means of transcending short-term dips and surges in revenues or profits or demand. Above all, formal systems institutionalize the understanding that "all activities are *not* equal."

In all the firms we studied, the basic strategic direction of the company is quite deliberately broadly communicated, by means of the strategic planning system and other mechanisms. Articulated strategy is seen as a key mechanism for attaining long-term goals and honing strategy over time, a key mechanism for ensuring stability of direction in the midst of volatile markets and technical change. Without communication, people do not know what to act upon. Without communication, plans cannot be revised. Without effective communication of strategy, in short, strategy cannot be managed.

Revising the Plan: Difficulties in Fact

Limits to Formal Planning

One difficulty with strategic plans is that they often do not work out as expected. One difficulty with strategic planning systems is that they can encourage a kind of tunnel vision, disenfranchising data that do not fit the agreed picture. A related problem is that projections and forecast outcomes can be like "vaporware" – software announced in advance but never actually delivered. Particularly where the existing planning process becomes sacrosanct, strategic plans can be filled with numbers as imaginary as the promised software, drawn from wishes and massaged into fitting the organization's hurdles for funding, or what people believe senior management wants to hear. Their spurious "accuracy" can delude people into accepting them without question, simply because "the numbers work."

The more innovative the endeavor, the less reliable the numbers and forecasts are likely to be. Lotus Development Corporation, which makes 1-2-3 (a spectacularly successful computer spreadsheet program that vastly speeds making numeric plans and projections) produced "perhaps the most wildly wrong forecast in modern business history:"

> Mitchell D. Kapor, the founder, wrote in his initial plan that he expected first-year sales of about $6 million. Ben Rosen [a well-known venture capitalist], who invested in the Cambridge, Mass. company, expected the business would take in $3 million. Lotus went right ahead and ignored the plan, posting first-year sales of $53 million.
>
> Larson, 1987

Lotus's error is unique only in the size of the wonderful surprise – many, many others have erred in forecasting, often by overestimating outcomes.

The rational outlook on strategic planning inherent in the structured approach described so far carries an implicit assumption: the plan will work out as anticipated. When it does not, the rational outlook may well encourage people to "try harder," to persist. The logic of the strategic plan is that when difficulties do arise, it provides a guide for increased efforts to overcome difficulties. Sometimes people should persist. At other times, people should *not* persist, for persistence will lead to disaster. In fact, they should be changing the plan.

Persisting in a badly flawed plan may prove catastrophic; yet even if the plan is working, sticking to it will entail opportunity costs. Indeed, while plans may work as intended, opportunities and shifts in markets, environments, technology, or a dozen other factors nevertheless render even a good plan obsolete or dysfunctional. Particularly in the fickle, mercurial environments of global high-technology competition, no plan can ever be followed blindly – however important a tool planning is.

These difficulties with strategic plans and planning spring from the inconvenient reality of a truly unknown strategic future. Any rational approach is, at best, a vast simplification of complicated reality intended to make action more efficient (or even just possible) despite uncertainties. Plans and planning are attempts to make rational and comprehensible what is fundamentally irrational and incomprehensible in practice. Reality frequently intrudes, to "keep managers humble."

Adapting Plans to Realities

These difficulties demand real response, not merely lip service, if planning is to be credible and legitimate. Plans and the planning system must be backed up by ways of dealing with these problems. Without response, as John Young noted, the new product innovation emphasis visible in these companies could translate into "many products, but no strategy:"

> We have had a lot more product strategies, as opposed to business strategies. They were consequently never as complete as they should have been, and therefore subject to change. We got them into a kind of rolling mode in which there's an elegant instability. I think that's cost us a lot over the last few years, particularly.
> John Young, Hewlett-Packard

Responses to these difficulties fall into two broad categories. The limitations of formal systems can be met with formal systems elaborations and alternatives. Or informal implementation approaches can be called on. Informal interplay between the plan and action steps can include, but is not limited to, changing the plan, elaborating it, trying alternative methods or reinterpreting the plan to suit a changing reality. At the other extreme, formal methods can be emphasized. TI, perhaps the most structured of our companies in terms of specific procedures for strategic planning, also had a full complement of "off-plan" alternative funding arrangements for strategic activities. We will deal in turn with a number of specific shortfalls in planning systems, and some of our firms' responses to them.

Adjusting Strategic Plans: Beyond Hierarchy and Calendar

Another inconvenient reality is the potential for misfit between the planning and budgeting calendar, and emerging strategic developments. No matter that the strategic plan was "put to bed" in May, for example; if a major technical breakthrough occurs in June, or a significant shift in the environment in October, these matters must be dealt with, not ignored. At National Semiconductor, new ideas could be proposed at any time of the year, regardless of where the planning cycle was, through the highly decentralized product lines. At National, Sporck noted,

> There are new projects starting all the time, but the only thing is, they have to fit into the budget that's been set up for the product line.

Central decisions are at a high level of abstraction, with general targets, while specifics are delegated, and can, within limits, be adjusted or changed: local management, close to the products, markets, and technical opportunities, must decide. This responsiveness is typical of our sample firms: plans can be changed, but this may entail tough choices. Tough choices, of course, are essential to maintain plan discipline and avoid simply drifting in response to every opportunity or threat that comes along.

As with committing time and personal credibility to innovation efforts, changes in the plan too are disciplined by personal judgment. Despite the genuine seriousness of the business plan, there is potential for appeal at National, even to Sporck, as he himself noted:

> Very often if there's a difference of opinion between an engineer and his product manager, he's liable to go to anybody to state his case. We would want him to, if he feels strongly about it, absolutely. And not just on engineering questions, on any questions.

As in many of the companies we studied, the discipline of the formal plan, its budget and requirements, is backstopped by alternative avenues for appeals – if the innovator "feels strongly about it, absolutely." Like the "110 percent busy" filter for initiating an innovation, pushing responsibility on to the change champion enables the first judgment to be made at the point of maximum local knowledge. Like the case of the laser-guided bomb at TI, where a product champion persisted despite orders to quit, the responsibility not to tacitly consent is taken seriously.

In short, the would-be innovator must judge whether he or she "feels strongly *enough* about it" to persist; but if so, persistence is both possible and legitimate. The appeal process is real, called upon, and honored in practice. Its very informality enables it to bypass and transcend formal plans. The visibility accorded to complaint ensures that people must feel fairly strongly to dissent. Ideas and innovation clearly matter more than some abstract commitment to "the plan," or to a hierarchy, in our sample companies.

Such corrections and complements to intended formal plans are as universal as formal planning itself in the high-technology companies we studied. The responses do not stop with a change of formal plan, however. At Hewlett-Packard, for instance, when three key areas were identified in 1985 for specific protection from company-wide cutbacks, much of the response was informal: those in the protected work-groups voluntarily scheduled an uncompensated extra workday when their cutback colleagues were furloughed for a day every two weeks. Informally, people budgeted their own time, providing an informal expansion of resources.

At TI, alternative formal systems were developed – perhaps because strategic planning itself had been the outgrowth of a purposeful, deliberate attempt to deal with shortcomings of previous practice: the OST (an acronym for "Objectives, Strategies, and Tactics") was originally developed to deal with the difficulties TI managers saw resulting from the PCC structure (based on numerous Product–Customer Centers: the basic operational organizing unit), and so specific systems were developed to deal with the shortcomings of the OST.

Alternative systems included the TI Fellows program, which enabled innovators to access corporate level funding outside of the formal budget. TI Fellows, specifically designated and respected senior researchers, can provide seed funding for others' exploratory efforts on their own say-so, with no further formal approvals. An innovator need not apply to the TI Fellow in his or her own division or area. Another effort, the Wild Hare program, provided that high risk programs could be specially designated and funded by senior managers.

Some of our sources, at TI and elsewhere, were nevertheless wary of formal systems. Alternative formal systems in particular were singled out for scorn by some, as "just attempts by insecure senior managers to get a handle on the bootlegging." Real innovators, one engineer commented, would deliberately evade any such system simply to prove that they could – and to preserve their autonomy. Informality, by virtue of its official invisibility, clearly provides essential protection for high risk innovation activities. Yet both informal methods and alternative formal systems were present in all our sample companies.

By reputation, Sporck of National is a "hands-on" manager, Young of Hewlett-Packard a master of delegation, and TI extremely tightly managed. By reputation, HP has a very relaxed company atmosphere, whereas National's is quite intense. Yet all three companies function within a broadly similar format. They all have formal plans, accompanied by numerous alternate routes and systems to adjust for possible limitations and rigidities of the central planning system. They work to keep the system from becoming an end in itself, although they do not always succeed. They recognize the difficulties inherent in formal planning, and struggle to adapt and adjust to fix its problems.

A Different Kind of Hierarchy

All these firms manage planning in such a way as to deliberately bring into the process people well down into the organization who will ultimately be responsible for execution. "Planning," in TI, National, and HP, is quite deliberately focused on generating necessary inputs, ensuring the debates that test ideas, and garnering the sort of familiarity and ownership down in the ranks that have far more to do with successful implementation than the production of a formal document.

Clearly visible in both Young's and Sporck's comments, no less than in TI's system, is an underlying view of strategy as hierarchical. This hierarchy has little or nothing to do with official organizational level, but everything to do with the locus of necessary knowledge and of power to commit the organization, and the need to bring these together. In these firms, broad business or market or technology segments are committed to at a very high level, while tactical plans are worked out in detail at lower levels. Tactics are much more than simply "carrying out orders" from above – they are essential avenues of local input. The firms of our sample all recognize the overriding importance of multi-level strategic management.

This shared realization of strategy is quite different from a traditional view of strategy as "top-down" – and equally different from a "bottom-up" description. It is not merely "participation," nor is strategy making limited to "decisions" (Litterer and Jelinek, 1988). Accurate large-scale vision depends on widely gathered specific local knowledge (Baba, 1988) and can provide powerful guidance and motivation throughout the organization. Implementation necessarily happens on the ground, however, and must deal with possibly inconvenient realities.

There is a deliberately general quality to the top-level thrusts – a direction is set, but details are left to be worked out by those closer to the action in all these firms. We found universally that working out the details is central to the re-interpretation necessary to fit top-level plans into action-level realities. In the high-technology companies we studied, re-interpretation and renegotiation do take place between the beginning of the planning process and its realization in action. In their turn, however, the impact of these iterations and detailings operates more on the basis of shared understanding than on the preparation of a document. Documents are almost trivial (though the firms differ on the degree to which this is so). Knowledgeable action is of far greater importance.

Changing the Planning System

Whether through a formal system or through more informal methods, or through some combination of both, all the firms did respond to the necessity for changing their plans in response to market realities, economic shifts, and technical developments. The common thread was that plans were seen as responsive guidelines, not straitjackets. Changes in plans can also raise questions about whether the planning system itself needs attention. Where methods to adjust formal plans were too cumbersome, or where they simply did not operate, firms fell into distress – or overly rigid methods were abandoned.

Constant vigilance is required, both to oversee plans, and to oversee the operation of planning systems. TI's difficulties in home computers, a major failure despite a product widely acclaimed as initially superior, were offered as one example of planning system difficulty. Some blamed the problems on persistence in an established plan while telling marketplace data indicating dramatic change were ignored. Others asserted that cumbersome and overly bureaucratic planning methods simply filtered out "bad news" as unacceptable, so that the corporation lumbered on with an obsolete plan. Eventually, TI withdrew from the home computer marketplace entirely, limiting its computers to professional and scientific products (including very high speed, complex computers).

TI's response was not limited to changing its strategy for computers, however. Ultimately, TI also adjusted its formal strategic system, restructured its organization, and changed its senior management as well. Hewlett-Packard's problems in co-ordinating software, peripherals, and computers, when each was the responsibility of a different division, provide another example. HP also restructured, and initiated a lengthy re-examination of its strategy and strategy making process.

Both firms utilized "structural" responses – formal re-alignments of responsibility and regroupings of activities into organizational entities – not just "plan" changes. We will address organizational structure at greater length in a later chapter. For the moment, we can note that formal responses to difficulties include structural responses, seen by managers in these firms as effective means for shifting people's strategic perspectives. The distinction often drawn between "structure" and "strategy" is somewhat less definite in these high-technology firms, where both strategy and structure must interact to cope with change.

Both HP and TI responded to difficulties by adjusting their strategic planning systems – making "planning" changes as well as "plan" changes. This willingness to re-examine the system for managing strategy is an important characteristic of the successfully innovative companies we studied. It is at the heart of how these organizations learn (Jelinek, 1979), how they capture insights and ensure that their best thinking is available for managing strategy. These are points to which we fill return later in this chapter.

Beyond Budgeting to Strategy

Budgeting always carries implicit an ultimate question: "Budgeting for what?" The danger is that the question may not be asked, or answered. In unwary companies, formal planning linked too tightly to budgeting, and to the budget cycle, can ill serve strategy by suggesting that "strategy" is reduceable to simple budgeting. Because budgeting and accounting are so often addressed in terms of cost cutting, those perspectives can pose inappropriate criteria for monitoring strategy. Measures more appropriate to cost cutting and strict control can undermine strategic activity, which is not necessarily improved by "efficient" approaches. In the 1960s, TI addressed this problem by specifying that strategic expenditures were to be judged against milestones and outcomes, rather than efficiency. As early as the 1950s, the OST idea had gone beyond budgeting:

> Something that was characteristic – and characteristic before the OST was recognized formally – was that this was planning the future. We started with our first formal planning conference in 1952. We had had informal ones in my office for a few years before that. It was *always* more than budgeting. Budgets are part of it, but it was *always* more than budgeting. Initially, it was only a year or two at a time, a year in detail, and then a couple of years past it in not very much detail. And it's true that it always ended up with the numbers and the budgets. But we were really much more concerned with products, services, customers, where were we going, growth rates, where was the third leg [of the stool] coming from.
>
> Patrick Haggerty, Texas Instruments

Haggerty was insistent that TI's strategic planning wasn't simply budgeting, even at the beginning, but rather planning the future of the business:

> I think it seemed obvious – that's what business was all about. After all, what were you trying to do? What did the business exist for? It didn't exist for a *budget*! It didn't really exist to make money . . . although clearly you were there to make money. It existed to *do* something.
>
> Patrick Haggerty, Texas Instruments

Haggerty's insistence on content rather than budget in strategic planning is quite consistent with Intel's multi-functional TRG assessments, National's "no-numbers" preliminary strategy, and HP's intense efforts to clarify how it would be in its selected businesses – all before financial analysis enters the picture.

These observations seem quite mundane – hardly new, even in the 1950s or 1960s. Yet in 1987, consultants at the Strategic Management Society's annual meeting noted that widespread use of inappropriate criteria still hindered investment in research and technology development in many US firms. These investments, constituting strategic expenditures, are not appropriately evaluated by "efficiency" criteria, most especially not against efficiency in terms of the products and markets of today. These investments either do or do not make sense in terms of the capabilities they deliver for the future.

Similarly, there has been much discussion among accountants and in widely read journals such as the *Harvard Business Review* of the need for new accounting concepts and measures to adequately account for the uncertainties and risks of investments in new manufacturing technology (for instance), without unduly biasing the decision by the conservatism inherent in traditional accounting measures. Faulty assumptions and undue conservatism are blamed by some for inhibiting investment in computer aided manufacture (e.g., Gold, 1982; Kaplan, 1986; Cooper and Kaplan, 1988).[1]

Such difficulties are a specific case of planning and measuring systems run amok, perhaps – but a more general warning on the limits of formal systems where they outrun the underlying informal spirit that interprets their vision to ask: "Does this make sense?"

Beyond the Plan to Responsive Action

Characteristics in the *use* of formal systems do give flexibility, by providing options to keep them from becoming dysfunctional. What is it that allows strategic planning to go "beyond the plan," in having value over and above the document itself? What methods-in-use allow the systematic, rational approach of strategic planning to transcend the limitations of logic and systematics? Several facets of the answer appear in different companies. The answers are not so clean and clear-cut, or so limited to what could be labeled "aspects of the formal planning system" as convenience might wish. They have an advantage far beyond simplicity or convenience, however: these complicated process elements work to guide effective strategy in a hellishly volatile, complex world.

Differential Time Horizons

One method is planning in different locations for different activities with different time horizons. At HP, for instance, corporate research and development activity concentrated on larger-scale, longer-term activity. Research in the divisions, in contrast, was more focused and more product-oriented. New products occur somewhat more rapidly than new processes, even in high-technology industries like electronics – although often enough, a new product's characteristics require significant process advances as well.

Ultimately, however, the process advances must be implemented in operating business units, even though such units rarely enjoy the leisure to investigate or develop process advances themselves. Segregation of research by its anticipated time-line is not new; it is a version of what corporate research labs have always been charged with. But the linkages here are more closely managed. At HP, for instance, corporate research and development activity is focused on larger-scale, longer-term activity than the more focused and often product-innovation oriented activities in HP's numerous divisions, but lab work is tied to divisions' anticipated needs. Motorola also tied exploratory development work to product divisions' forecasts of likely product developments and associated manufacturing needs. In other words, research is somewhat segregated by time-line – but not too strictly.

As with other such arrangements, adjusting the degree to which one side "needs" the other – by means of the percentage of central lab time that must be "sold" in divisions to fund activities, for instance – can allow managers to fine-tune response. R&D groups that become too isolated can be encouraged by funding needs to get closer to their users. Funding and specific charters can direct those that become too short-term toward more basic activities.

In a number of areas, the predictable path of development points to clearly mandated development work in support of coming division needs. Reducing the line width in an integrated circuit to well below one micron, for instance, is extremely difficult – but this is also quite obviously where product design is headed, even if operating units cannot make time to investigate how this might be done. Other specific technical areas can be identified for development. Refined photolithography, a skill closely related to line circuit width, is another requirement for increasingly dense circuit design. So, too, is surface mount technology.

What is important is not the specific technologies in question (except, of course, for these companies). The underlying idea is that longer-horizon development work may be difficult or impossible to carry out in operating divisions concerned with today's problems. Corporate labs' research in such areas can significantly improve divisions' competitiveness by enabling them to design to more exacting manufacturing requirements, confident of delivery capability.

This was a deliberate choice at HP: "We really opted to promote the coupling," noted Young. In contrast to the divisions, HP Laboratories, the corporate R&D facility, was the designated repository of "bigtime silicon knowhow to pull off lithography and all the process things, to make them function at a very high technical level," said Young. Structure and explicit charters distinguish different "clocks," of shorter- and longer-term activities – even within the innovation planning process.

Completing and Complementing Existing Plans

HP Labs is also the site of more exploratory efforts, outside the usual charter of existing divisions. This included targeted activities – "bringing to bear a concentrated set of resources to do some things that would solidify our competitive position in existing areas," as Young described it. The charter was to identify products to widen a market in which HP already had a sizeable share. This activity also bolstered the more focused innovations activity within the divisions, and operated in concert with it.

Internal contracting to fill out a division's line or expand an existing position links HP Labs to existing divisions. In this regard, it reinforces existing strategic commitments and revises them incrementally – fleshing out existing activities. HP Labs also took on less targeted activities, "doing things nobody else was doing," activities that simply did not have an obvious organizational home. This sort of activity in a corporate laboratory does not necessarily increase links or bolster existing activities, but instead creates alternatives. Depending upon how close or how distant the research is from existing commitments, such less focused activities can form the nucleus of significant strategic change.

Choices to fund activities through corporate programs that may stand more or less alone may develop strategic alternatives. Choices to run funding through divisions, in contrast, encourage links and collaboration. Our sample firms use funding in just such a fashion. Where more fundamental strengths are needed, corporate development teams – often enriched with division personnel – can be funded. Where incremental developments are needed, corporate labs can take on chartered research problems specified and evaluated by division management. Both corporate labs and division personnel take part in strategic management and assessment, so that problems and solutions, options and possibilities at both levels enter into strategic implementation in these firms.

What we see in these examples is how, even within a formal system, there are continual developments that keep strategy vital and options open. The key seems to be a context into which new pieces of data can enter and in which people can examine both new data and old plans in their light, asking whether the plan still continues to make sense as new developments emerge. Carefully maintained differences in viewpoint contribute by ensuring that no single view, time horizon, or commitment completely dominates strategic thinking.

Product Development Planning

New product development offers a case in point. All of our companies were keenly interested in maintaining momentum for innovation through context management. HP's fundamental response to a new product idea, once it has begun to coalesce – within the lab, for example – is to find an organization "to pick it up in some way, either an existing unit, or, in many cases, an entirely new unit." This response sits at the end of the planning process, as the outcome of a successful project that has demonstrated its potential. This demonstrated potential is a key goal of HP people:

> You can think about technical people as on some kind of continuum. There's a sort of model that you might hire at Bell Labs, before their breakup. This is a person who really is the

scientific mentality. They love investigating things, despite their practical irrelevance in the world. Their reward system is the recognition of their peers for the quality of their scientific work and the paper they present, and the scientific prestige. It is very much an academic forum.

At the other end are the kind of people that HP tends to appeal to. They are no less smart – they've got all the brain power, the analytical tools – but they wouldn't write a paper if their life depended on it. They are engineers – that's the other end of the continuum. Their value system says, "Gee, if it isn't worth something, if I don't get the rest of the organization or customers saying, 'Boy, that's a really good idea,' I don't want to spend any time on it. Why should I bother?"

John Young, Hewlett-Packard

"The kind of people that HP tends to appeal to" will propose ideas they believe will get customers and others in the organization excited. (This is the individual-level filter discussed in chapter 6.) These ideas are important aspects of forming, adjusting, and implementing strategy, and readjusting it as time goes on. They do not cease to function in the more formal strategy process. Instead, as innovations gain support and champions, they call existing views into question, and – marginally or substantially – adjust the consensus view of strategy. Intel's development of the microprocessor, described in chapter 5, illustrates such a radical adjustment. The microprocessor idea necessarily flowed through the formal approval process to acquire needed funding and senior-level commitment. Equally obviously, the hard choices mandated by the formal system redirected Intel's strategy in the most basic fashion, reconfiguring the firm's view of the business it was in.

HP and Intel are not the only firms that depend heavily on such a shared view – although others may generate the viewpoint differently. National Semiconductor, for instance, keeps development on track by marketing input, and by budget cycle monitoring:

> . . . The yearly review of what it is we're going to do, where we're going and what product effort is required. Secondly, the whole drive is heavily coming from the central marketing organization, which is inputting into the factory [organization], and monitoring – not from a responsibility standpoint, but from

an interest to satisfy customers standpoint – monitoring our progress and in fact pursuing those defined directions.

Charlie Sporck, National Semiconductor

Control of strategic direction, through new product development efforts and through identification of specific market areas, drives National's approach, as Sporck described it:

> This marketing effort is entirely driven by a segmentation of the marketplace approach. There are certain parts of the marketplace that we are interested in concentrating on, such as telecommunications, and we have a central marketing strategic effort in each one of these groups, like telecommunications. These people work closely with the customer base, understanding their requirements and what product is necessary for them to solve their systems problems. They, along with the appropriate product line and appropriate technologies, define these new product directions.

There is substantial difference between National and HP in the amount of perceived top-level supervision. HP's Young commented:

> Really, I don't have a list of the projects being worked on anyplace around here. I have to go out and ask them. So it's an editing at the lowest level: that division management team makes those decisions.

John Young, Hewlett-Packard

In contrast, National's Sporck is present at many of the new product planning sessions, focused around the strategic planning cycle:

> I spend most of my time dealing with marketing issues, so that I pretty well know all of the significant products: what's being developed – I am aware of what its purpose is and what the customer reception to it is.

Charlie Sporck, National Semiconductor

Despite these differences, however, Sporck was quite definite about his lack of control over the projects: "I don't decide anything," he asserted bluntly. At both firms, division-level managers, who bear responsibility for implementing product plans and taking them to the market, decide. Funding responsibility for the innovations they propose rests with the division managers, both at National and at HP. Such designations constitute formal recognition of just how important individuals' judgment and commitment is.

Keeping the Pump Primed

Pushing decisions down to operating levels, maintaining ease of access to the decision makers, and providing many opportunities for individual input are all important factors in keeping innovation going. People identify deeply with projects (as organizations encourage them to do): if funding is cut off, "your baby is dead," as one manager put it. So motivation here isn't as precisely, dichotomously "individual" or "organizational," as many discussions seem to suggest. Rather, the organizational and the individual are quite consciously brought together, so that individuals pursuing their own interests will also be supporting organizational needs.

Multiple ways and means to funding also demonstrate that alternative views are tolerated and that innovation is truly welcome. Because numerous individuals have input into the system, there is not a "single right answer." Because people subscribe to a common set of criteria, against which decisions are made, decisions are made "visibly." People believe they can control their own fate in the firms we studied, because they have recourse and alternatives.

This sense of personal input and control is quite central to the enthusiastic engagement of people in their work so characteristic of the firms we studied. (Not coincidentally, these characteristics are important also to feelings of power, energy and mental health; see Borysenko, 1987). The input and control are real, simply because the expertise required for good decisions is spread throughout these organizations. Innovation from everywhere is cultivated and pruned by choice that is as widely distributed.

The funding and decision responsibility aspects of the formal planning systems in these firms are biased toward pushing controls down to divisional levels and well below. Crucial specific information, both technical and business oriented, must be brought to bear through the participation of lower-level technical and managerial personnel. Because people are aware of the strategic directions and criteria, they are aware of how their knowledge can affect outcomes. Shared decisions translate into shared strategies, with the context and broader vision embedded in the planning process. Where systems took over, or decisions became too centralized, performance suffered, or people quickly responded for fear that it would.

Another important aspect of keeping the formal systems working responsively is explicit recognition of achievements and accomplishments – whether or not they have been specified in advance. People are measured in terms of their real results, within the context of what is happening out in the real world. Such realistic assessments are the ultimate measure of contribution or success in these companies. Not losing too much if the market experiences a massive downturn may be high accomplishment. "Making your plan" isn't all there is, and may be insufficient, if the market really takes off.

All of these firms offered financial rewards for achievers. The systems differed, however. At HP, there are no divisional or individual incentives, and co-operation is fostered by stock ownership and bonus systems tied to overall company results. At National, stock options are tied to the importance of the individual and his or her contribution to the company and to the product line, as determined by product line managers.

Moreover, among hard-nosed managers and pragmatic scientists and engineers, money is not the only reward. Other key marks of achievement include respect and recognition, accorded by colleagues who are themselves respected. At National, for instance:

> Beyond [salary and stock options] we have special recognition systems for patents or technical talks. I have a special internal recognition system for unusual items of service, not just in the technical area. But, in the technical area, if somebody or a group turns out a super product, we have a dinner. As a matter of fact, we do it up at my home. We have the guy or the girl and his wife or her husband, up for a dinner to recognize the fact that what they've done is important.
>
> Charlie Sporck, National Semiconductor

The criterion of "a super product" is defined by success in the marketplace. Texas Instruments designates "TI Fellows" who are acclaimed achievers. Motorola (and many others) puts achievers' pictures on display, awards plaques, and writes up accomplishments in the company newspaper. Recognition "from others in the hallways," deference to one's technical expertise in discussions, and other acknowledgements of success are also important. Like planning and innovation, recognition too has both formal and informal aspects.

Shared Strategic Control

Assuring appropriate push, performance, and persistence is one facet of strategic planning; correcting direction is another. Both address the issue of "control," which has a very different meaning in the companies we studied from that accorded in the traditional literature. There is little by way of order giving and taking. Instead, there are many more explicit criteria and performance measures, which assess outcomes, and which tend to operate over time – rather loosely in HP, apparently more tightly at National. Yet numbers do not rule the process, and finance staff do not run strategy in these firms. Even at National, according to Sporck,

> We have a strategic planning group in finance – but *they are not planning*, in the sense that we have talked about it. They don't do anything in terms of determining what product we deliver. All they do is accumulate inputs from the various organizations. They put something together, but *they do not input*.
> Charlie Sporck, National Semiconductor

Sporck's emphatic insistence on line managers as the authors of strategic planning is noteworthy. As TI people described it, "The doers plan, and the planners do." Finance expertise here acts as a resource for line managers and for marketing, handling the number crunching. Strategy, in contrast, is far more focused on products, market segments, and technologies. Its genesis lies in creativity, although control ultimately rests in explicit monitoring and criteria based upon the marketplace. Sporck's description is especially useful:

> Obviously all this has to be kept in balance, because the real strength of people is their ability to use their brains, their innovative capacity. At the same time, the company has to address the needs of its customers. So the way this would basically happen is this: by and large, the engineer understands that what he's going to develop has *got* to have a requirement out there. What the world doesn't need is a product to be invented that there's no demand for. Most engineers recognize that success, in terms of his design, represents a product that sells successfully. Not just a great product, but a product that sells successfully. That's what's successful. I think that's pretty universal that they see it that way. Nothing is more frustrating

for a designer than to design a product and have it bomb out – not sell.

Charlie Sporck, National Semiconductor

Sporck's comment was echoed by many others, not only at National, but also at the other sample companies. Since these companies continue to produce significant innovations, not merely line extensions, their market criterion seems to operate as a balance to internal creativity, rather than as a simple constraint.

Reliance on individual insight and creativity is visible also at HP. "The very best business plan you can have," according to John Young, is one that basically demarcated boundaries within which good people were turned loose:

> You make plans so that everybody can see what we're trying to achieve. Then you give each unit as much space as you can – "Here's what we need. I don't know how you'll do it. All I know is that you can tell as well as I can what needs to be done. Now you figure out how to do it the best way you can, and still preserve that innovation character within this space."
>
> With a plan, the R&D folks can tell themselves, "If I do things in here, I'm going to be all right. Nobody's going to come back in a year and say, "Forget that – we needed something else." That's the problem of having poor business plans – that the space moves. It drives people bananas. That's why I think there is a real premium on having a very clear strategic framework for people to be guided by, then engaged in.
>
> John Young, Hewlett-Packard

Young's notion of strategy is that it sets a long-term direction. It is not to be changed frequently:

> If you do [change it], you probably haven't thought enough about your strategic direction. It's too unstable if you have to keep coming back and redoing those things very frequently . . . You ought to have a pretty clear general direction that gets a constant tuning and a constant communication, but not leaps. If you're leaping around, I think you're in trouble. The tuning is to be expected and appreciated, since people know and see those changes themselves. But closing the loop to communicate and tune up and down is extremely important.
>
> John Young, Hewlett-Packard

Correction of action plans and control of people's behavior, in this atmosphere, are both dependent upon a shared perspective, Young noted.

Control of operating results and organizational outcomes are also explicit responsibilities throughout the organization at HP, not limited to senior officers. Responsibility is widely delegated, broadly shared, in order to increase HP's responsiveness. The firm's agility in responding to changes is described by Young as "real-time management," the ability of managers throughout the company to analyze events and decide "whether things are going right." If they are not, "that is the day you start doing something about it," according to Young.

Quick response, according to Young, translates into steady results: HP had never had a layoff, and Young commented that the 1985 downturn was "only the second time that we've ever had any unpaid time off from work" – although many in the industry experienced a 20 percent drop in shipments, after annual compound growth of about 18 percent from 1972 to 1984. "Making that system work really depends on a very tuned up set of people who do that kind of real-time management – and do make those reactions," said Young.

Central to HP's control of strategy is the question, "What is expected?" The expectation is "innovative behavior, to support strategy within a shared perspective." It is spelled out in the corporate objectives, talked about in the hallways, used as *the* touchstone for testing arrangements and procedures, and offered as a central reason for Young's own responsibilities in "beating back the bureaucracy," lest it stifle eagerness and creativity. It is also rewarded – while its absence is deliberately *not* rewarded:

> We expect things that lead the field, take a step ahead. We don't reward those who can't do that. Now this doesn't mean, "Don't miss that objective." But at least it's what you intend to do. I think that's extraordinarily important in bringing forth that kind of behavior: just because you talk about it. It's what we expect to do. In fact, everything we do is set up to make that kind of activity happen.
>
> John Young, Hewlett-Packard

HP's emphatic CEO sounds very much like TI's Pat Haggerty a decade earlier, insisting that systematic innovation was "what we set out to do." The account also bears some similarity to Al Stein's practices at Motorola, "absolutely insisting" on results. Similarly, at Intel, product line and divisional managers are highly visible participants in the planning process. Gordon Moore described a broad, general atmosphere of contribution and participation:

We just make it part of their job. There's actually a tremendous amount of interest in participating in the planning thing. We've gotten to the point where there's some prestige associated with it, and it's a source of information. They know what's going on by being in there.

Gordon Moore, Intel

The apparently rampant informality of HP and Intel, with so much dependent upon cultural norms and expectations and so seemingly relaxed an atmosphere, belies the intensity of employee involvement, and the tightness of control these systems permit. These firms are organized to produce commercially successful, innovative products. Despite what looks to some like a "country club" atmosphere, formal systems operate in concert with informal methods to insure tough-minded strategic management. What is often missed by outsiders is that tough-mindedness is diffused throughout these companies, and built into the informal norms as well.

Strong norms exist to define what constitutes the success of a new product or technological innovation. The norms specify commercial success, not merely engineering elegance, and they are quite explicit. "Does it sell well?" is a broadly accepted and recognized yardstick in all the companies we studied. While many popular press descriptions ascribe control to the senior managers, media accounts ignore the delegation of decision making well down into the organization. The very real feelings of control over their work that managers, engineers, and scientists in our study companies reported to us are rooted in the control these people exercise over their own work.

Formal controls and informal control systems at Intel and HP are ultimately very much like those at National Semiconductor, reputedly a very different company, operating under much tighter control. There, too, however, the CEO commented,

. . . Most engineers recognize that success represents a product that sells successfully. Not just a great product, but a product that sells successfully.

Charlie Sporck, National Semiconductor

HP's "loose" atmosphere is quite as definite about performance standards and strategic directions, and as deliberate about rewarding what is wanted, and not rewarding other activity, as National's, or TI's. Feedback, from objective market data, is readily accessible, and achievement is judged by well recognized standards in all of these companies.

"Control," in short, is very real and quite apparent in all our sample companies, but its methods are first and foremost internal, not external. "Self-control," participation and shared criteria produce persistent strategic directions and deep commitment to achievement. "People" and "the company" seem far more like partners in a strategic endeavor than the arm's length adversaries with differing goals many descriptions of strategic planning and control systems suggest. Chapter 11 will describe how strong culture contributes to this control. For the moment, we can simply observe that these are highly controlled organizations, as well as highly innovative ones, and that control is shared.

Formal Responses to Off-Plan Needs

Opportunities and insights for innovation are notoriously inconsiderate of calendars, as we have noted: they quite regularly appear in their own good time, rather than according to the corporate planning schedule. Since the good ideas don't show up on schedule, there has to be some way of capturing them, fostering them, and attending to them as they do come up. Such a need initially poses the requirement for some form of "off-plan budgeting" for strategic activity. Every firm that we studied had some method – ranging from formal systems for interim funds to widespread bootlegging – for transcending the calendar's limits; nor was the calendar the only stimulus for going beyond the formal system.

At TI, it seemed natural to evolve explicit programs to deal with the problems of off-calendar innovation. While the OST had been quite successful in funding, co-ordinating, and managing existing development efforts, it lacked any specific mechanism for initiating a program – especially a small one – despite much talk about the need for new development efforts. Moreover, as the company had grown, so, too, had the distance between potential innovators at the junior level and those who could commit resources to an innovation effort.

The IDEA program was created to provide recognition and funding for the embryonic projects TI considered its lifeblood by carrying an innovative idea through its initial feasibility demonstrations. "Step advances, rather than evolutionary improvements" were sought. To achieve preliminary demonstration, a four- to six-month span of limited funding was allowed. The IDEA originator could not charge his or her own time to the project; currently assigned tasks were still the originator's responsibility. To acquire funding, an IDEA originator wrote a memo proposal outlining the approach, impact, or application to be pursued. Expenses were estimated, and their uses (for a model, materials, testing) were outlined, along with the time required and anticipated outcome (demonstration model or paper analysis, for instance).

Funding requirements were stripped down to presentation of the memo to IDEA contact persons, themselves successful innovators. IDEA persons were designated for each division, but an IDEA originator need not work through his or her own division and could approach several contact persons for approval. The IDEA contact person checked by phone with Corporate Development to ensure, first, that the end result fell within the business interests of TI; and secondly, that there was not a similar project already under way. With contact approval, funds would be released, and the IDEA originator was free to pursue the project. Upon completion of the project or expiration of the time period, the originator was to review the project with the IDEA contact person, who would then arrange a demonstration meeting with Corporate Development to discuss results and explore recommendations for further action.

Simplified approval and funding, and quite unfettered exploratory activity were the deliberate intention of the IDEA system. Another very similar effort, the TI Fellows, was in place a few years later. Fellows, widely respected technical experts, were designated around the organization, and as described here, had decision control over allocations of up to $25,000 for off-plan development efforts. Such off-plan, out-of-cycle funding for innovation represents a conscious effort to expand the resources available to risky, exploratory, and more preliminary work, projects that don't fit into the regular development scheme quite yet. Beyond the system, in any organization, there's a need for messy, less controlled, and freer work, recognized early on by Patrick Haggerty:

> If you're not very careful, your top managers will forget that the other thing you better do is to have a certain amount of relatively free work going on. You control that by how much money you put into it. But because it is wasteful – and it *is* wasteful – in fact, the better managers you develop over here [in the day-to-

day management of on-going business] the more likely they are to keep looking at that and not being very happy with it, and trying to make this fit tightly.

Patrick Haggerty, Texas Instruments

Control can drive out innovation, and managers successful in routine management may stamp out the "messy" activities that give rise to genuine advances. Others agreed. Sizeable activities, once reduced to routine, tend toward an emphasis on control, according to Charles H. Phipps, a venture consultant and former TI manager:

> The characteristics and aspirations of the managers below the senior level are also very important [in determining] how innovation is pursued in their particular business activity. A business of any substance to the corporation breeds an atmosphere of conversion of assets and consistency of financial performance. Managers of these businesses are selected for these characteristics. If this criteria becomes dominant in the minds of senior executives over time, the innovative manager is essentially bred out of the organization.

Charles H. Phipps, Sevin Rosen

Haggerty's views were frequently quoted at TI almost a decade after his death, and managers at other companies continue to speak in terms very similar to Haggerty's, today. For instance, Haggerty's concerns were echoed more recently in our interviews by Gordon Moore, who worried about how bureaucracy might "kill innovation," and John Young, who insisted that tight supervision of projects was not effective, although realistic assessment was essential. Many other senior managers we spoke to repeatedly touched on issues that Haggerty, too, had mentioned, leading us to conclude that his insights remain important today.

Market Discipline and Innovation

Another TI effort to encourage risky activities was the "Wild Hare" program. Like the IDEA system, "Wild Hares" were designed to enable the OST to be more responsive to opportunity. Wild Hares were identified projects within the OST structure, with higher risk but also higher payoff, if successful. Typically, such projects might well be identified by lower-level managers, but de-emphasized because of their risk. In the quotes that follow, "below the line" projects are those that fall below the funding cut-off line. Readjusting the rankings can shift projects from "below the line" and thus unfunded, to above the line. OST review legitimated these riskier projects by corporate revision of the risk and rankings assessments:

> Very often you will find at the department level that these will be rather short-sighted programs – you know, the next year, year-and-a-half type of things, rather than the long term. And, sure enough, just below that line is your "wild hare," the thing that is a big risk, but if it succeeds, a big gain. That falls below the line. And it's part of the game they play between operations and corporate people, being candid.
>
> And so, lo and behold, usually you will find that . . . the OST committee are very forward thinking men – that's how they got where they were. And they're really awfully interested in, [fill in the blank], because of the thrust of the corporation. And here it is, below the line. So you go over there with that kind of a ranking, and very often they'll say, "No, your rankings are wrong. That one should be number one." Now it's your job to figure out how to achieve your results within these constraints. That's the reason you're a manager, that's your problem.
>
> Len Donohoe, Texas Instruments

Donohoe's description of the Wild Hare program points to a common, constant problem: trying to change a subordinate's direction in this highly involved, highly personally invested environment. Directed priorities meet corporate needs as senior managers see them, but can carry heavy costs, unrecognized at the senior level. The dilemma is to keep individual contributors engaged and autonomous, yet somehow have them actively involved in something the organization would like to benefit from. Those "ordered" to make a project top priority may disagree, withhold their real commitment, and, consciously or unconsciously, contribute to its failure. Contributors who are "turned off" a pet project of their own may leave, either physically or mentally. As we have noted, turnover of top engineering talent is a very real threat, with abundant opportunities for competent people up and down Silicon Valley, and beyond, elsewhere in the electronics industry.

Buy-in is important, personal investment is highly desirable, and individuality seems central – in North American culture at least – to such commitment of self. Yet shared direction is essential too, for the varied activities must ultimately mutually support a coherent strategy. There are no easy solutions, of course, although some formal review takes place in every firm.

Not everyone is enthusiastic about formal methods for encouraging innovation. Some engineers and managers insisted that systematic methods simply attempted to straitjacket the "creative crazies" who "really" produce innovations. "Overcontrol was the TI problem," according to one manager, who later left the company. The Wild Hare program, as administered during the 1980s, was a particular target of this manager's ire. Similar criticisms were voiced in the popular business press, and by a variety of observers. "The Wild Hare program was Fred Bucy's attempt," said another manager, "to ensure management control over potentially free-wheeling innovations." This accusation – whether true or not – points to another dilemma inherent in strategy planning, especially a strategy of innovation. When a plan is set, "freewheeling" can subvert it, distract attention, or squander essential resources in pursuit of unrelated or even contradictory aims.

Yet as Haggerty had observed so long ago, freewheeling activities are essential to genuine personal commitment. Management and, by extension, official plans, are necessarily limited and fallible. More than a decade after Haggerty's death, Sporck at National echoed Haggerty's sentiments, noting that innovators need lots of "wiggle-room," and that market realities could provide much of the needed discipline, if managers trusted it:

> You have to give them a lot of freedom. The contribution that they can make is very heavily dependent upon the interest that they have in that contribution. If you organize things such that there's no freedom – no delegation of authority to them in terms of making choices in their designs, etc., you're going to take the fun out of it. If you take the fun out of it, the guy is going to be in the mode of putting in his time, as opposed to enthusiastically doing whatever. So there *has* to be a lot of freedom.
>
> At the same time, the name of the game is getting the product out there before the competition does, so time is a real fact. It is an awesome fact. But they all recognize that, and that's part of the fun. It is a competitive situation; if you get the product out six months after the competition, even though it may be better, the market may be lost and so you've failed.
>
> Charlie Sporck, National Semiconductor

While formal systems have explicitly evolved over time at TI, at National they have not changed much recently, according to Sporck, except to become

> . . . more market driven. The process itself hasn't changed, but we do become more market driven. Also, we become less numbers involved. So much strategic planning is just strictly a matter of forecasting numbers, *which is not strategic planning at all*, in my opinion. We were that way, quite a few years ago. But each year, we do less and less of that. Now, we have no numbers at all until the very end. We just focus on what it is we're trying to do, from a conceptual standpoint.
>
> Charlie Sporck, National Semiconductor

Market-based control, "disciplines and consequences" from the marketplace itself in the form of customer acceptance or rejection, are far more acceptable than management fiat. But how to utilize them without risking marketplace disaster?

Dan Dooley, one of Charlie Sporck's Group Directors and responsible for six of National's product lines at the time of our interview, elaborated on market realities and the role they play in influencing strategic decisions at National:

> When you start capitalizing in equipment and so forth, you better have some pretty darned good reasoning, which is what brings marketing back into play. Frankly, if [our product innovation] is really all that super-duper, we generally have pretty good working relationships with key customers, and we interface with them. You know – "If you had such a thing as this, with these performance criteria, what would it be worth to you? How many would you buy? Where would you use them?" – that sort of thing. Generally . . . you're not running an R&D lab, *per se*. Obviously, the innovation is still on the side of engineering, but it's now more market driven.
>
> Dan Dooley, National Semiconductor

Dooley also reemphasized the decentralized nature of strategic planning at National, perhaps unwittingly:

> In the old days, back in the '60s in particular, the industry could do nothing wrong, because everything they came up with, the market was eager to have . . . In some cases today, one ends up having to sell senior management on the idea of funding [the innovation] long enough to where . . . they can get their arms around it. In other cases, it's strictly a business line decision

whether or not they want to fund it [i.e., not a staff decision or a corporate decision]. We have a great deal of latitude in that decision.

Dan Dooley, National Semiconductor

Systematic arrangements for decentralized responsibility institutionalize correctives for potential system faults and the human limits of senior managers. Guidance here is directed from below, toward senior levels: it is the lower-level scientists and engineers that have the technical expertise essential for good decisions. National's choice to decentralize the decision making formally acknowledges this reality, and corroborates Sporck's account of dispersed strategic inputs.

Time and Technology Perspectives in Planning

Formal planning necessarily includes financial aspects of planning for innovation – budgeting requirements, requests for resource allocations, expected results, and anticipated benefits – although, as Sporck indicated, these considerations are not the initial starting place or the key decision criterion. The anticipated technical outcomes are also part of the planning. These firms must plan to develop the firm's technical capabilities, not just its product lines. The annual plan offers an opportunity to step back and consider the whole picture. Hewlett-Packard's Young cited "technical plans and issues" as specific aspects of the annual plan clearly linked to long-term financial outcomes in his mind:

> We spend a lot of time over the course of a whole year working on strategic plans – but it culminates annually, in that you turn what you've done into an [explicit] annual plan for financial impacts and the micro-technical plans and issues we are going to worry about. We spend a lot of time doing that.
>
> John Young, Hewlett-Packard

In high-technology firms, as we might expect, the financial impacts are based upon technical realities, built into managers' thinking about the strategic planning process. The lead time for new technology development offers a case in point: major innovations typically require years of endeavor – yet the window of opportunity for introduction of a specific product, once the technology is shared by competitors, may be less than a year. Worse, integrating new technology into the fast-paced product life cycle is extremely difficult (a point we shall return to in chapter 9). Both technology and product planning are important.

The limited product opportunity window, and the product focus of much innovation, could act to narrow down innovation into primarily incremental, less risky activities. Much innovation indeed consists of incremental extensions or applications of ideas beyond the original insight. Major technical insights and product departures, though, while rare, are also extremely important. Constricting innovation only to incremental changes would be disastrous, when technology continues to develop as quickly as semiconductor technology does. And yet, of course, the demands of budgeting systems and current market urgencies tend in precisely this direction.

To overcome the short-term bias, significant development efforts are required, and CEOs see themselves as responsible for being aware of explicit technical developments outside their firms. Sporck offers one example, describing developments in process technology, such as pushing basic photolithography approaches into further miniaturization:

> From a research standpoint, probably the only true research work that is going on, is going on at the universities, and maybe at the very giant companies, like IBM and AT&T. If you talk interim, like "Who's developing one micron?", I think by and large all of us are – the significant companies – ourselves, Intel, Motorola, TI. But none of us are out there working at the half micron level, although the universities are doing it.
>
> Charlie Sporck, National Semiconductor

While the specifics may differ – one micron or one half micron or one tenth micron; 9 nanosecond response or 6; advanced silicon or gallium arsenide – the underlying concern for fundamental technology development is evident. Major technology shifts are important, and difficult, and of concern to top managers in these innovative firms.

Corporate level personnel may not be able to exercise much direct control, however. William Howard, Vice President for R&D at Motorola, commented on how much less control he felt he had at the corporate level, than when he had headed R&D for semiconductors, as an operating unit within the Motorola Semiconductor Group:

> Where the research and development organization is kind of half staff and half line, you get the ability to control very closely what goes on in a very small group of people, who are the corporate research and development labs. In our case, that's

about 100 people. In the bulk of the corporation, the remainder of the corporation, about all you can do is jump up and down and scream and shout. Depending upon whether people decide that they want to take your advice or not, something will get done or nothing will get done.

Bill Howard, Motorola

This is another side of the decentralization, equally as important in affecting innovation and strategic management. Corporate officers responsible for looking at more distant horizons and technical limitations, like Howard at Motorola and his counterparts, must somehow convince those in the divisions, who "live and die by the short term," to undertake, or perhaps to support, the more lengthy development efforts that are required for high impact results. For formal systems to work for long-term research, perspectives from corporate staff must be blended and integrated with those of operating division people.

Several difficulties intrude. Staff control is minimal in the firms we studied. Formal decentralization of product responsibilities and funding, combined with strong norms for market impetus, drive attention toward product development focus rather than process development or basic technology research. The product emphasis is strong enough for some sources in several firms to refer to manufacturing and process development as "step children," despite the rosy picture of integration and success we have painted in general.

Alternative funding – from corporate sources – seems an effective way to get results, but it carries potential hazards. TI's Wild Hare program was seen as overcontrolling by some, and loss of credibility and buy-in from innovators will be fatal to any centrally driven effort. Wholly funded corporate labs can be seen as quite useless. Even jointly funded efforts raise difficulties. As Motorola's Howard noted, if a division manager becomes "dependent upon your subsidy to make his business viable, then you're mismeasuring the business."

Marketplace criteria and individual commitment are essential, even in trying to guide longer-term efforts. Extensive decentralization can also cause problems, according to Howard:

> Decentralization encourages, if it's done right, entrepreneurship on the part of the people who are essentially running small businesses. But it gets you to the point where you have small enough business entities that they cannot afford to put sufficient resources into looking after their future. Let's say a microprocessor business: developing a new microprocessor is a long and expensive operation.

Bill Howard, Motorola

Thus decentralization is effective at motivating entrepreneurship and innovation, but it may mortgage the future by starving all of these myriad stand-alone efforts. Too many small shots offer an insufficient basis for maintaining a viable large business over the long term, especially where effort is fragmented into many unrelated markets or products.

Technology Road Maps and the Long Term

One response is a longer-term technology strategy developed by corporate research, in close consultation with operating units. Over and above the shorter-term product-development-based strategies that are more usually tied to specific market segments and identified customer needs, the larger-scale technology focus emphasizes expertise that will buttress a range of products and markets. HP deliberately developed "silicon knowhow" at its central labs. At Motorola, according to Howard, technology is forecast in a process that produces a technology road map. (Other firms used similar terminology, and similar processes.)

A sort of thinking different from their usual mode is required from operating managers to develop such a technology road map, so corporate guidance is extremely helpful. Divergent perspectives are of genuine use here; homogenized "medium-term" thinking would not do (Burgelman and Sayles, 1986). The new thinking must be called forth, despite the understandable intrusion of real-time action demands on the operating engineers, scientists, and managers. Howard's description bears lengthy quotation because it highlights the persistent, patient, informed prodding such a task demands. The account also emphasizes how productive respectful sharing of widely divergent viewpoints can be made to bridge conceptual gaps. The road map is:

> . . . an attempt to produce a forecast of where the technology is going in a scenario. Military people talk about scenarios where they think they will have to fight a war, or where they think they will have to conduct an operation of one type or another. We do the same kind of thing with technology. It's a four step operation. The process starts when the [corporate] people assembling the road map sit down with the marketing people. We have a group called strategic marketing whose job is to sit and think about what the customer wants in the future.
>
> The first reaction you get when you sit down and start this kind of discussion, which is ten-year scenario, is, "Don't bother

me with ten years out, I can't figure out what I'm going to do two weeks from now." And you go through a fair amount of, "Well, this customer says that. Customer A wants this kind of product. Customer B wants that kind of product."

[At first there is] a reluctance to make a decision of where they think things will go, because a lot of that is in the realm of opinion. But after about the third hour or third session of discussion, you find people get into saying, "Well, in 1995, the way I think it's going, we'll need memories of a certain size, microprocessors of a certain capability, various kinds of circuits, various kinds of communications capabilities. If our business is going to grow, this is the kind of thing we're going to have to be in a position to do."

So you develop what amounts to a kind of product road map. That product road map is nothing other than a stalking horse for the next phase of the exercise, which is to go to the people who design things and say, "If you're going to design, say, a 64 megabit dynamic RAM, what are you going to have to have?" The first thing you get is, "Well, the marketing people are crazy. They don't know what they are talking about. It can't be done." After sitting around and arguing for a while, they say, "Well, you know, what you really need is a better capacitor, and devices of a given size and a certain amount of voltage capability."

By the time you get everything all put together, they've got a list of things that they would need if they were going to design such an animal by year X. They may differ with what the marketing people say about the product future, because they may have technical ideas that aren't available to the marketing people and may have differences of opinion. We try to put all that into the equation.

Lastly, you go to the people who are the process people, people who provide the hardware technology or software technology, and say, "Okay, here's what the designers of the proposed product or the designers of the system say they're going to need. What kinds of processes are you going to need to go do that?" By the time you get done with this, there is a decision making process that you have to go through. Since a lot of capabilities are called for that are similar, you take the one that has to happen first, and name that "One."

You try to identify what are the critical paths of the whole thing. What you end up with is a series of "must do's." Those must do's, if they happen, and you've planned it right, [produce results] and then you'll have the technology to do all the stuff that follows after that critical point.

Bill Howard, Motorola

This lengthy description captures some of the flavor of protracted inquiry required for long-term technology thinking in the context of a market driven firm. Because of short-term pressures, many managers and engineers find it difficult to focus on long-term issues, especially those that necessarily contain substantial amounts of technical uncertainty. Of special note is the real urgency of the short term, the market, visible throughout our discussions.

Yet uncomfortable as they may be with looking so far ahead on technology issues, managers, engineers, and executives in the companies we studied repeatedly stressed the urgency and importance of long-term goals, long-term thinking, and advanced planning for innovation. Most specifically, these managers repeatedly stressed the need for innovation as a competitive weapon against highly competent global adversaries. Long-term technology planning was an indispensable requirement for long-term success, in their view.

Competitive Comparisons

Formal strategy in the longest term, based fundamentally upon innovation as we have argued throughout this book, demands repeated re-dedication to long-term programs and perspectives. In the midst of competitive pressures, this is difficult for operating units. While it is easier for corporate staff and corporate labs to engage in long-term thinking, ultimately they must validate their activities by generating acceptance in the operating units, if they are to succeed. The gap between short-term operations thinking and the long term must be bridged.

Nowhere was the issue more starkly drawn than in discussions of the Japanese threat. Many managers we interviewed professed admiration for Japanese achievements – both in getting their employees to work to meticulous standards in operations, with consequently exemplary yields; and in getting their people to believe in, and commit to, long-term goals and programs. By contrast, the managers suggested, American firms tend to talk very little about long-term goals, and to react only when the crisis is upon them. Bill Howard's description is typical of several we heard:

> When faced by a threat, the American businessman traditionally does what he's always done, which is to hunker down and prepare for a fight – which means that you forget about all the stuff that you don't have to do right now, and do the best you can with what you've got. The problem is, the Japanese didn't get there

by doing that. I get beset with questions all the time; it's been going on for probably five or six years now: "How do the Japanese develop products so quickly? Here are the Japanese on the market with the one megabit RAM. They're formidable in the 256K area. They've essentially turned the 64K RAM business into a rout, as far as a lot of US companies are concerned. How do they do it that quickly?"

Well, it turns out they don't do it quickly. In fact, they take a good deal longer to design products than American companies do. If you look at the details, the thing is, they started earlier.

Bill Howard, Motorola

Motorola found that Japanese designers had completed a design for the 64K RAM – albeit with some technical flaws – in the late 1970s, while the 16K RAM market was still in contest. The Japanese design process had begun five years earlier, well before the marketplace was contemplating anything so powerful as a 64K RAM. Managing innovation effectively requires long-term commitment, long-term perspective, and long-term persistence. Longer time horizons must be kept in view despite the short-term crises and urgencies of operational details, which must also be dealt with.

The semiconductor industry is not alone in its need for longer-term management. Other industries too face this issue – although more mature industries may recognize the need less readily, because significant change has occurred so rarely. When markets and technology have been fundamentally stable for years, it is difficult to maintain much interest in innovation management. Yet effective innovation in mature industries too relies on repeated integration of longer-term perspectives with current operating needs, and maintenance of the distinct viewpoints in between.

The account given here of semiconductor innovation is remarkably consistent with findings about innovation in the Japanese automobile industry. There, designs go through the same sort of steps and stages, from initial artistic design to marketing input, design engineering, product and process engineering and the like, all the way down to pilot production and volume manufacture – a process we shall describe for our high-technology firms in detail in the next chapter.

The US auto firms compartmentalized and segregated each step in the process, with little or no interaction between those responsible for early stages and those responsible for later stages. The predictable outcome was a crescendo of conflict as "Job One" approached, and the consequences for manufacturing of various design demands and decisions became more clear. Of course, changes late in this process are expensive and difficult; there are good reasons for people to resist change. Changes early on are much easier, because no firm commitments to tooling (for instance) have been made.

In contrast to US practice, Japanese auto firms overlapped the stages, intermingled the personnel responsible for them. They deliberately sought to bring difficulties and conflicts to the surface early on, when change was feasible and economical, and to solve the problems, rather than deferring them. The result: much more easily manufacturable designs, and a greater lead time for developing any needed special manufacturing expertise. They also explicitly developed underlying capabilities in manufacturing as a deliberate strategy (see Clark et al., 1988; Hayes et al., 1988; Wheelwright, 1985).

Linking long-term thinking and perspectives with operating realities is a core task for effective strategic management. Whether it is blending the abstract long vision of scientists and semiconductor engineers with the operating managers' needs, or linking new car development to manufacturing realities, innovative firms must bridge important gaps in understanding and perspective. Howard's technology road map provides one formal approach for doing so. Balancing funding ratios (how much assured corporate lab funding versus how much to be shopped from divisions) and dedicated corporate projects are among the other methods. Formal systems reviews of technology perspectives and operating needs provides yet another means.

The prime importance of all these methods, however, is that they typically entail discussion and interchange between divergent perspectives. The inquiry needed to create a technology road map creates links among and between those responsible for various aspects of technology development for product and process. So, too, does the process of selling lab research or contracting for specific project help. Given the enormous lead times necessary for major technology advances, or even significant increments in basic design or manufacturing technology, such efforts seem increasingly essential. Their importance is not limited only to high-technology firms.

Managing the Time Frame: Strategic Steering

Special interest groups can provide alternative methods for encouraging – and, especially, for funding – technology and innovation efforts, outside existing formal planning structures and existing programs. Off-plan routes to funding vary in formality. Where TI used the very systematic Wild Hare and TI Fellows programs, Motorola maintained much looser Technology Steering Committees. These groups coalesced, somewhat informally, around common technical problems, like voice processing, or photolithography, or sub-micron integrated circuit architecture. The groups were intended to bring together interested parties from various organizational units. The committees function as technical sounding boards and arenas for discussion, providing encouragement and some funding, rather than as filtering devices or decision makers. In 1985, Motorola had 13 such committees in operation.

At Hewlett-Packard, the time frame in forward operations thinking seemed longer, despite the simultaneous real-time focus that Young fostered for its sensitivity to downturns. Project choice at division level, a decentralized responsibility, nevertheless stressed state-of-the-art products that were seen to make a real contribution to their field. According to Young, success meant coming up successfully with genuine innovations:

> Since we work on a principle of management by objectives, we very much do evaluate people on quite a few years of growth and contributions, and some qualitative feel for "Do those products really advance the state of the art? Or are they just copies? Or are they always late, or do they not get the growth?" That division management team has every incentive to want to pick up the very best ideas they can get and work on them.
>
> John Young, Hewlett-Packard

HP divisions also have explicit responsibility for maintaining their premier status, enabling them to lead technology in their market segment. Yet all our firms, including HP, experienced the on-going tension between "today's business" and "tomorrow's business." The discipline and limited focus that "today" requires genuinely do contradict the new and different insights, longer-term approaches and exploration required to go beyond today's business into tomorrow's.

Necessarily, the firms of our sample do pay attention to the field, to the products and the customers of today – HP engineers are sometimes sent to sell products, in order to meet customers (including consumers) face to face. Similarly, National Semiconductor's applications and design engineers answer hotlines, to hear at first hand the customer's problems and needs. Other companies reported other activities aimed at maintaining touch with the real world of today.

However, attention does not remain focused on "today's business." Instead, the problems, difficulties, and concerns voiced by customers turn into grist for these technical experts' innovation efforts.

The firms must keep innovation bubbling up, and keep the important activities of today from undermining the genesis of tomorrow. The method of choice, in all our firms, was informal resource availability. In all of our firms, alternatives to the formal, planned strategic development activities existed – in the form of unrecognized, unmonitored, or very loosely monitored bootleg activities. They were endemic, and informal, even when recognized systematically, as at HP, TI, and Motorola. Their very informality is what keeps them "honest," and honestly different from officially designated activities.

These elaborations beyond planned commitments form an important component of strategic planning systems. Alternative funding and access methods, whether formal or informal, serve an essential function in fostering "legitimate organizational subversion." Such projects are subversive because they seek to provide an alternative view of the world, contrasting with that captured in current structure, market segmentation, and mission definitions. They are legitimated because these companies recognize that any system, formally designed to do some things, will necessarily leave out others – some of which may be crucial to later survival. "Legitimated subversion" in various forms is the response of our companies to this dilemma.

Formal Methods, Informal Outcomes

Nurturing Guidance, Not Punitive Control

The relationship between innovation and formal planning systems that emerges from this chapter is, we hope, far richer than that implied by the cut-and-dried versions so readily available in textbooks. In the real world of management, especially in the fast-paced electronics industry, plans do go astray and situations do change. Ideas occur to innovators in their own sweet time – although they can certainly be primed, facilitated, and encouraged (or, alternatively, stamped out). In the companies we studied, people and their reactions form an essential component universally recognized as far more important than any plan or system. High-technology managers' practices, in taking these realities into account, are richer in perspective than most descriptions of planning.

Planning in our companies is seen as a *process*, intended to produce a shared organizational state of mind, far more than merely "a plan." While guidelines, deadlines, targets, and goals do emerge from the process as well, it is noteworthy that these are with fair universality "bottom-up," rather than "top-down." Motivation, buy-in, morale, "fun," self-investment, and creativity seem at least as important as any other results. Revisions and iterations, shifts and corrections are the norm. As a result, the leader's task in a high-technology setting is not to set the goals alone, nor to detail the plan, nor even to hold people's feet to the fire. Instead, it is to "fight bureaucracy," to "let them know that what they've done is *important*," to get them to thinking beyond where they are, to provide an ear and a context within which innovation can flourish. These contextual leadership roles are crucial to successful innovation, in our view.

Visible in the innovative firms we studied are clear concepts of strategy that are elaborated at multiple levels of the organization. At most, broad statements of great generality are issued by the top level – and even those may well be the outcome of previous proposals, developments, and suggestions from below. Any meaningful details and action plans are quintessentially the work of those who must execute the strategy. "Planning" is nowhere a powerful separate function; there is rarely a planning department. Instead, "the doers plan, and the planners do": "doers" and "planners" are one and the same, from the top to the bottom of the firm as well as across departments or divisions.

Help may well be provided, whether through comprehensive computer programs available on-line or assistance from a central finance or marketing staff. But staff personnel do not plan, and do not control the planning process operating managers conduct. Iterations, trial balloons, proto-plans to be taken to the potential customer and the like are all likely to be part of the process, which has a decidedly incremental flavor.

Although each organization has a formal planning system and an explicit budget cycle into which the plan must fit, and although managers do spend significant amounts of time and effort in planning to meet cycle deadlines, *plans are not sacrosanct*. At Intel, Gordon Moore's comment was revealing:

> The overall thing – the strategic plan – I usually end up writing it. We do a fair amount of discussing; we do some cleaning up of it, and add some things. I should have a final [plan]. But

nobody ever reads them after they get to that point, but me. As Eisenhower once said: "The plan is nothing, the planning is everything." I absolutely believe that. By the time the thing is in the book, it's done with. Hardly anybody reads it again after that. But in the process of getting it there, everything that you want to accomplish gets done.

Realism and utility, real-time data and customer acceptance, long-term horizons and short-term urgencies all play important roles – but the *planning* is the thing, not the plan.

Beyond the cycle and the formal planning system, each of the companies we studied devoted resources to putting in place formal mechanisms for planning, as well as providing alternative routes for new ideas to reach those who controlled resources. Bootlegging was alive and well, too, and held in excellent repute. People well down in the organizations are highly visible participants in planning. Managers seemed to have both a high regard for plans, and also a healthy skepticism about their accuracy. They were knowledgeable users of planning systems.

Beyond the strategic action plans for the next year or years, longer term activities were difficult, yet nevertheless recognized as important. In the product-driven atmosphere of our companies, these long-term activities continue to offer an on-going challenge that will become clearer in later chapters dealing with product life cycles and continuous innovation. Now, we will turn to formal organizing for innovation. In our next chapter, the interplay between the formal and the informal will again be seen to play a central role in bringing flexible control and responsive stability to our innovative companies.

Note

1 For a discussion of the current debates on accounting measures and their problems, see, for example, Johnson and Kaplan (1987); Anthony (1987); Jelinek (1987); Cooper and Kaplan (1988).

8

Organizing for Innovation

People look at organizational change as, "Somebody did something wrong." That's nuts, because there's absolutely no reason why an organization that you created two years ago has any relevance to the organization that you need two years from now. The beauty of this business is that the technology will always change, [and thus] the organizations, the organizational interfaces, the customer interfaces, the vendor interfaces are always going to change, because of the technology. To assume that your organization makes sense today, just because it made sense five years ago, is really incorrect.

Les Vadasz, Intel

Organizing Innovation in Big Companies

How does Hewlett-Packard coordinate 87,000 employees, effectively directing their work to produce a constant stream of new, complex products? How does National Semiconductor keep track of the roughly 3,500 different types of integrated circuits it offers at any given time – products which account for less than half its overall revenues? How does any of these companies manage the innumerable and shifting products, activities and people, tasks and considerations, technologies and applications that are their world?

The companies we studied are large and complex by any standard. Yet they do not seem to succumb to what popular wisdom suggests is inevitable bureaucratic stagnation. Though managers and employees readily complain that their firms are not well enough run to suit them, innovation continues. The thousands of employees in multiple product groups and scattered research, manufacturing, and sales organizations continue to successfully create, develop, manufacture, and market a broad array of complicated microelectronic devices for a burgeoning range of uses. Somehow, these companies innovate, not once or twice, but repeatedly. How do they manage to pull off the incredibly complex sets of simultaneous activities required? For a company to continuously produce commercially successful innovations, product after product, technology after technology, year after year, suggests that an explicit organization of the innovation process takes place. This chapter addresses organizing for innovation.

Early in this research it became clear that creating the initial innovative idea is but a small part of the success enjoyed by the companies we have studied. No single idea, by itself – be it in product design or manufacturing technology – is sufficient. Good, even great ideas require carefully managed effort. They must be brought together with others' ideas and expertise. The funds and resources needed to move from idea to design to manufacturing to marketplace reality are vast and varied. At every step of the way, innovation involves complex activities, and a host of contributors whose participation must be effectively timed, co-ordinated, allocated, supported, directed, monitored, and redirected as needed. In short, these activities must be organized and managed effectively. Ad hoc approaches will not produce repeated long-term success. Explicit organization is the key to continued success amidst constant technological change.

It has also been clear from the beginning that the whole elaborate ritual must be repeatedly choreographed anew, to meet the changed needs of the next product, its technology and markets – which may be very different indeed from those of its predecessors. Wave after wave of new technology and new products succeed one another. New markets or applications emerge, and different dynamics of supply and demand, expertise and capability develop. Through it all, these firms must redeploy their resources to meet new circumstances:

> Every two years almost our entire product line turns over. We can almost go out of business in two years, if we don't do it right.
>
> Gordon Moore, Intel

Firms like Intel must not only organize, but repeatedly reorganize, knowing full well each time that yet another need will require yet another change soon afterwards. Thus these companies must develop simultaneous capabilities for both stability and change, held in a dynamic tension of control and innovation.

This chapter tells the paradoxical story of how complicated, sophisticated activities are co-ordinated through highly specific and well articulated formal structures which are deliberately temporary – yet anything but ad hoc. Formal organization structures are extremely important in these firms, which make full use of the guidance, authority, and power they delineate. Yet the structures, authority, power patterns, and information links created are not permanent. They are expected to pass away, to be succeeded in their turn by new structures more useful to the changing task at hand.

To cope with the torrid pace of technological development, we found four key aspects of structure in these companies, which interact to co-ordinate the many complex activities required in constant innovation : a dynamic tension between (1) clear structures and (2) frequent reorganization; (3) extensive use of what we call quasi-formal structures; and (4) informal structures of the organization. We will deal with each in turn. However, throughout this chapter, the underlying emphasis remains upon organizing for innovation, technical excellence, manufacturing efficiency, and marketplace success, and thus on producing predictability amidst virtually constant change. Mastery of those seemingly contradictory demands is central to success in the high-technology markets of today. We believe it will be increasingly important in many more industries in the future.

Old Recipes and New Realities

When we first began this project, we reviewed the existing literature as a guide to our research. While there are hundreds of studies on the organization and management of innovation, most advice to managers is derived from a groundbreaking study by British researchers Tom Burns and G. M. Stalker (1961). The best advice from the past was that innovation is best serviced by organizing according to principles of "organic management." Organic management is thought to enable fluid response to contingencies. In the original British study, the innovative high performers were organically managed to deal with the changing technical and environmental conditions they faced. Since high rates of technological innovation and environmental change have been well documented in the semiconductor, systems, and computer industries (see e.g., Webbink, 1977; Jelinek, 1979; Schoonhoven, 1984), organic systems appeared to be the structure of choice for the companies we were about to study.

What specifically are these "organic structures" and management systems? Burns and Stalker described organic systems as

> . . . adapted to unstable conditions, when . . . requirements for action arise which cannot be broken down and distributed among specialist roles within a clearly defined hierarchy. Jobs lose much formal definition . . . [and] . . . have to be redefined continually. Interaction runs laterally as much as vertically. Communication between people of different ranks tends to resemble lateral consultation, rather than vertical command.
>
> Burns and Stalker, 1961, pp. 5–6

This definition makes intuitive sense, and some parts of it fit. For example, we found a great deal of lateral communication. We also found that people do not seem to devote much time or attention to hierarchical status and its symbols. Shirt-sleeved informality and anti-status-symbol norms are widely evident in these firms, whether in California, Texas, Arizona, or Singapore. Though companies vary in how informal they are, all stress their own form of informality, and all de-emphasize hierarchy.

Yet a closer look at the definition proves it very unsatisfactory indeed. Burns and Stalker implicitly identify four separate aspects of organic structure: (1) ambiguous reporting relationships, with unclear hierarchy; (2) unclear job responsibilities; (3) consultative decision making based on task expertise; and (4) communications patterns that are as much lateral as vertical (Schoonhoven and Eisenhardt, 1985, 11–12). In short, according to the existing literature, we should have found what contemporary writers have called unstructured, loosely coupled, amorphous adhocracies (Mintzberg, 1979a; Toffler, 1970; Weick, 1976).

The Contemporary Structure of Innovation

Clear Organizations and Jobs

The contemporary semiconductor and computer firms we studied certainly do face unpredictable, unstable conditions, rife with problems that cannot be easily broken down. However, an organic structure is worse than useless for providing the precise and definitive co-ordination, tight controls, high efficiency and tough decision making needed in their fiercely competitive global marketplace. In contrast to loose, organic structures, we found that contemporary semiconductor and computer firms, embedded as they are in highly turbulent and changeable technical environments, display well articulated structures, definite reporting relationships, and clear job responsibilities.

Far from unstructured adhocracies, we found universally explicit reporting relationships and clear hierarchies. Executives, managers, and engineers knew and told us who their bosses were, who their bosses' bosses were, who their reporting subordinates were, and who their organizational peers were at equivalent hierarchical levels in relevant other units. There was simply no evidence of amorphous reporting, unclear hierarchy, or fuzzy job responsibilities. Quite the contrary: all of the firms we studied had explicit organization charts, readily available, and formalized from the top to the bottom of the company.

In a few of our 100-plus interviews, managers were cautious in sharing these data with us, because organization charts are regarded as serious competitive information which reveals how the company organizes its work. Organization charts also typically reveal valued key employees, whom some companies prefer to remain anonymous and obscured from competitors' knowledge. In these instances, the managers readily sketched a chart in our presence, and used it to describe structure, authority, and organizational arrangements. Not one chart "petered out into unresolved dilemmas," as with Burns and Stalker's managers. None had unclear reporting relationships. No managers gave the least sign of confusion, either about their own reporting relationships, or those of relevant others. The difference between our findings and earlier research and theory on the structuring of innovative companies is dramatic.

In addition to having clear structures of reporting relationships, the innovative companies we have studied also have clear job responsibilities. This too is in contrast to the earlier "organic management" studies. We found that employees' titles are clear. More importantly, they refer casually to one another's job responsibilities with certainty as to what others actually "do" for the company. Independent of their titles, this means that there is high predictability about what others' responsibilities in the organization are. There was no evidence in any of our interviews of Burns and Stalker's famous quote, " . . . nobody knows what his job is around here." Instead, we found highly predictable organizations with clear, explicit responsibilities and reporting relationships.

To illustrate how clearly structured these organizations are, Edward Boleky, a fourth-level manager at Intel, described his title, job responsibilities, and place in the organization during an interview, while sketching "his organization" on the chalkboard during the interview:

> I'm the California Site Fabrication Manager, responsible for three of Intel's wafer fabrication areas located in California. I'm one of four people reporting to Gerry Parker [a corporate Vice President at the time]. My organization right now is relatively simple . . . [sketching on the board] . . . So I have three fab managers reporting directly to me, and I have a fellow who is running a task force . . . that involves a 32-bit microcomputer, the 8386. The fellow that's heading that reports to me, also.
>
> Ed Boleky, Intel

Boleky continued by describing the remaining levels of reporting relationships in the organization for which he was responsible. He drew out the positions which reported directly to the four people who reported to him.

While one might predict clear structuring in a manufacturing sub-unit like Boleky's, what about the structure of technology development, the heart of the innovative activity at Intel? Surely uncertain research activities would be more ambiguous and less clearly organized? Among the several managers and engineers in technology development we interviewed at Intel, Kim Kokkonen was a project manager in Static Random Access Memory (SRAM) Development. Kokkonen supervised six engineers who were developing a semiconductor process technology, advanced complementary metal oxide semiconductor (CMOS) process, and the first two SRAM products to be produced using the new CMOS technology. The semiconductor process and the new products would be transferred into manufacturing – into Boleky's fabs, described above.

When Kokkonen was asked to explain the transfer process, he immediately picked up paper and pencil and began to sketch an organizational chart and a time line to express relationships over time. The organization Kokkonen drew started from the chief operating officer, Andrew Grove; it next went to a direct report of Grove's, Gene Flath; to Gerry Parker, the Vice President and Director of technology development; then down to the groups which reported to Gerry Parker, including Kokkonen's in Static RAM Development. This sketch exactly reproduced the set of relationships which Gerry Parker had drawn for us in a prior interview. The charts agreed on what the development organization was, who reported to whom, and what the separate positions and departments were. In Kokkonen's own department, SRAM Technology Development, there were 35 engineers and 6 program managers.

Having drawn that entire organization, Kokkonen began to describe what the various functions do. A brief example from his explanation will suffice.

> Okay, this is me down here [pointing to the organization chart], and this [other] group is working on an advanced CMOS process. There's another group that's very similar to mine that's working on a different definition of a product that attacks different market segments. There is yet another group doing something similar. There's a group which does nothing but circuit designs, which take advantage of technologies which have already been developed and designs new circuits using those technologies. Finally, there's a basic module development group that develops some of these basic capabilities that we need to have: equipment development – things that aren't product or market related at all. An example would be lithography.
>
> Kim Kokkonen, Intel

After describing his "own organization," Kokkonen continued to explain how new developments are transferred into manufacturing by again going to paper and pencil. He drew a three-year time line which he used to describe all of the various groups which come into play along the development cycle. In doing so, he described a clear set of relationships between eight separate development and manufacturing groups, each of which was bounded by time horizons and milestones along the path of development.

Kokkonen was precise about what each of these groups was called, when each came into play along the development path, what each group was responsible for, and how the entire picture went together. There is no fuzziness here, no failure to understand who is responsible for what, no ambiguity regarding who these groups are. Kokkonen's own words describe these groups with clarity: their responsibilities, the key interfaces, and the transition points. One example will again suffice:

> My technology in general has about the most complex set of relationships to other sub-units because we have a lot of internal ties. We also tie into all of the manufacturing arms of the company, in trying to transfer things. So the matrix of things that we tie into: first, the fab environment. There's a particular group set up in fab called "New Technology Engineering (NTE) whose *defined job* is to spend the last year of development with us and the year after transfer of the [new manufacturing] process in cleaning up bugs and in just getting it ready for a full manufacturing environment.
>
> Kim Kokkonen, Intel

As it developed, NTE was only the beginning of this complicated set of relationships. As Kokkonen continued, the entire diagram he had drawn came to life, with a heavy emphasis on desired outcomes: reliability for the process as well as for the new products. Kokkonen's descriptions highlighted extensive linkages between Intel's development and manufacturing activities, as well as the complexities of dealing with the multiple groups.

The project manager had fluently described the large number of people and groups with which he and his engineers had relationships, and the logic of the interfaces was quite clear. As to how he had developed this clear overview of the organizational complexities, Kokkonen cited necessity:

> I think it's forced on you. The first time I didn't know all of this, but to get to this transfer point [into manufacturing], you have to deal with all of these people. There's no way around it, so you just learn.
>
> Kim Kokkonen, Intel

Similarly, in each of the other interviews we conducted at the five companies, no executive, project manager, or engineer was unable to clearly describe his title, job responsibilities, or the organization's structure of reporting relationships and the myriad departments within the structure.

The clear structure of these firms is a deliberate artifact, not a bureaucratic mistake. John Young of Hewlett-Packard provided some insight to this unexpected finding. Young saw explicit structure as essential to managing change at Hewlett-Packard:

I just think it helps 87,000 people, particularly when you're having a lot of changes, to see what you've done, what we're trying to accomplish, to make it as clear as you can what are the central thrusts of the organization.

John Young, Hewlett-Packard

We believe that this is an important finding regarding the contemporary organization of innovation. Both as a product of prior successes and a requisite for future success, the companies we studied are highly complex organizations. They all produce multiple products in multiple divisions, using state-of-the-art equipment and processes. To survive among the most successful innovators requires keeping up with the pace of technology development, which is murderous and will continue to be so. As a consequence, employees must have high predictability within their internal organizational environments. Paradoxically, clear structures and job responsibilities provide the requisite predictability that enables these firms to manage change.

How then do these companies organize for repeated innovation? Very explicitly. These firms are characterized by highly effective, quite definitive organizations, with well understood and clearly articulated relationships.

Competition Forces Clear and Efficient Structures

In retrospect, it could scarcely be otherwise. The activities undertaken by these firms are complicated, and cannot be undertaken except by large, sophisticated arrays of multidisciplined talent, marshalling substantial resources of equipment, dollars, and information. Wafer fabrication lines run to the tens and often hundreds of millions of dollars: very large scale integrated circuit fabrication processes require hundreds of complicated steps. Without meticulous co-ordination and control, these processes simply will not be successful. The ad hoc organizations or loose, organic structures often recommended for innovation simply will not do, for the long run.

Even if ad hoc arrangements should, by chance, work once, repeated success would be impossible, given the complexity of relationships, technologies, and product changes. Innovation in these firms is simply too important to leave to chance. Moving an idea from concept to product design, through manufacturing process specification and into production is an incredibly intricate process. Indeed, because a wide array of expertise is brought to bear, the pre-manufacturing problem is more complex. It is too complicated to handle without explicit co-ordination. These companies need reliable, repeatable methods to bring good ideas from concept to product to market – not once, but again, and again, and again.

At the same time, because of the fiercely competitive environment, innovation must be executed efficiently. The stakes are very high: tens or hundreds of millions of dollars and the survival of these firms are at stake. "Good ideas" alone aren't enough; "good product designs" won't do it; even "fine manufacturing capabilities" or "superb market intelligence" are not enough, by themselves. Instead, what is needed is a wholesale integration of the flow from "aha!" to the customer, characterized by highly efficient movement, cost-effective methods, *and* innovation throughout.

The US semiconductor and computer industries are facing intense competition. As many analysts have pointed out, structural deficiencies in the US economy – such as the currently high federal deficit and a savings rate about one third that of Japan, with a consequently higher cost of capital – exacerbate the firms' dilemmas (see, for example, Dallmeyer, 1987; Defense Science Board, 1987; Prestowitz, 1988). One indicator of the competition is, of course, the success of Japan and other Pacific Rim countries in semiconductor manufacturing. Their successful penetration into world markets poses a real threat to US firms.

There is no option for survival other than effective organization. In our sample firms, people know who is responsible because they must. Tough decisions have to be made, and someone must make them, look after their implementation, and take responsibility for them. Resources must be allocated, attention directed, design time allocated, production facilities reserved, marketing effort assigned, and so on. Without structure, too many details simply cannot be managed at all; without effective structure and close control, the details cannot be managed efficiently.

While the competitive, turbulent environment forces efficient structures, a puzzle still remains. How can we account for high clarity of formal structure when Burns and Stalker and other theorists have argued that a fluid, ambiguous, ad hoc structure is adapted to high rates of external change? If these highly innovative firms do not have fluid, ambiguous structures, how do their organizations adapt to changes in their environments?

Frequent Reorganization and Dynamic Tension

When our data are compared with the work of Burns and Stalker and other contemporary writers, two major differences emerge. The first difference is that organizations we have studied *formally reorganize frequently*. As a consequence, responsibilities and reporting relationships change to meet modified external and technical circumstances. This finding illustrates one of the ways in which high-technology organizations adapt to technological and environmental change: they adapt by reorganizing. Changing the formal components of the organization offers much greater clarity than so-called organic structures where position responsibilities and reporting relationships are continuously ambiguous. This finding is also consistent with some earlier research on reorganization in high technology industries (Schoonhoven, 1980). Thus, while clarity of formal reporting relationships and of position responsibilities is a consistent pattern in the successfully innovative companies we have studied, they are far from structurally inert. We have discovered that these organizations adapt to change by reorganizing their formal structures.

The second important difference between our findings and the previous studies is that our firms exist in *dynamic tension*. Such tension seems inherent in semiconductor and computer firms faced with changing markets, technologies, and manufacturing processes. On the one hand continuity, control, and integration between functions and departments are required for the orderly development of new technology, new products, and reliable, high quality manufacturing. This is the efficiency push on the organization's design. That is why we have found clear reporting relationships and clear position responsibilities. On the other hand, constantly changing environments and technologies require organizational adaptability. Neither continuity nor change alone will do it: the firm must maintain a taut balance between the two. They *must* have stability; and they *must* be prepared to change when required. That is why we have found frequent reorganizations, to adapt to the changed circumstances. We refer to this dual ability as maintaining a *dynamic tension* between the ability to be flexible via reorganizations and retaining enough systematic order to be efficient.

Organic structures lack the dynamic tension we have found between clear structures and frequent reorganizations. Instead, organic organizations focus only on constant, free-form flexibility through amorphous organizational forms. Organic structures ignore the continuity and predictability of action that a clear structure provides for the organization and for its external constituencies. Success in the intensely competitive high-technology industries, where any feature or product will be swiftly matched by a competitor, and where no product- or process-based competitive advantage will be unchallenged for long, demands this constant tension between stability and change.

It is important to recognize that these companies do not move from one adhocracy to the next as some futurists have envisioned or as some have suggested that innovative, high-technology firms should (Toffler, 1970; Mintzberg, 1979). Adhocracies can be described as the "Structure du Jour" – the structure of "whatever works" for today's problems. However, if managers in an adhocracy were to perceive that their problems were changed tomorrow, so too would the structure. Literally "ad hoc," "for this," adhocracies have been described in the management literature as spur-of-the-moment, for-the-moment ways of arranging the formal elements of the organization. Adhocracies also carry a highly ephemeral, spurious connotation: "you had to be there to appreciate it." This is of little use to large organizations. In a large ad hoc organization others may not know how your sub-unit is structured, since they may not have checked recently. The lack of shared understanding and lack of predictability of behavior which characterize adhocracies are severe drawbacks in a fast-changing turbulent environment.

When innovation is technically specific and complex, when it requires massive resources and the exquisitely choreographed co-ordination so essential for innovation in microelectronics, ad hoc organizing is clearly wholly inadequate. So, rather than being organic adhocracies, the highly innovative companies we studied changed their structures when the problems for which the current structure was designed changed. They change from one existing, clear structure designed for a specific set of problems to another clear structure, designed for the new problems that have evolved over time.

Managing Structural Change

Changes in formal organization, then, are deliberate. Rather than signalling a major organizational error, reorganizing the company signals adaptation to a changing environment and technical circumstances for which the former organization is no longer appropriate. Changed structure signals adaptation, not organizational error.

Les Vadasz of Intel described the view of a typical, uninitiated outsider, unfamiliar with managing innovation. His comment, the epigraph to this chapter, bears repetition:

> People look at organizational change as, "Somebody did something wrong." That's nuts, because there's absolutely no reason why an organization that you created two years ago has any relevance to the organization that you need two years from now.

Vadasz went on to explain how Intel's environment and technology had indeed been modified:

> . . . The beauty of this business is that the technology will always change, [and thus] the organizations, the organizational interfaces, the customer interfaces, the vendor interfaces are always going to change, because of the technology. To assume that your organization makes sense today, just because it made sense five years ago, is really incorrect.

Change is both frequent and pervasive in these firms. Our first interviews began in the summer of 1981, our most recent in 1989. During the interim, all of the companies we studied made substantial and repeated changes in formal structure, both at the corporate level and at lower levels, within operating divisions. Obviously, corporate-level changes are more visible from the outside – and these may represent more significant realignments. Many more changes at operating levels do occur, however, with fewer external signs. Yet these, too, provide highly important reconfigurations. Some examples will illustrate.

National Semiconductor

In the spring of 1986, National Semiconductor reorganized into two basic operating groups: the Semiconductor Group and the Information

Systems Group. Throughout its prior history, National's key operating group had been its semiconductor business. The Semiconductor Group, composed of a growing number of divisions, manufactured a wide range of integrated circuits which eventually became components like metal oxide semiconductor devices (MOS), linear products, computer peripheral products, microprocessors, microcontrollers, and application-specific integrated circuits.

In 1979, a wholly-owned subsidiary, National Advanced Systems, was created as the first of a burgeoning set of businesses soon to develop around the information systems concept. By the end of fiscal 1987, National's information systems activities accounted for 48 percent of total sales, ranking National 14th in the United States among information systems companies. The significance of this business had clearly grown for National. Its technologies were important to the company in their own right, the more so as information systems were expected to play a significant role in National's strategy for future growth as a corporation. This 1986 reorganization formally recognized an explicit shift in business focus and strategy, no less than a major reorientation of business activities. Charlie Sporck observed:

> Our recent reorganization of the company into Semiconductor and Information Systems Groups not only gives us a structure more compatible with our customers' needs, but also gives us the opportunity to more quickly and effectively achieve many of our goals. Common management provides a more integrated and synergistic approach, strategic planning is more cohesive, and resources are used more efficiently.
>
> Charlie Sporck, National Semiconductor

Externally visible changes like the creation of National's consolidated Information Systems Group are one form of organizational change. Less dramatic but equally as important are other, less visible changes further down in the structure that take place with great frequency at National and at the other companies of our sample. We asked John Finch, a corporate Vice President and General Manager of National's Semiconductor Division, how frequently some part of his large, multidivisional Semiconductor Group might reorganize? Finch responded:

> Oh, there are things going on all the time. Small changes on a regular basis . . . There's always something happening [to change the structure]. A typical [example] . . . you've got three product

groups that are combined into one – or you had a central design group and you decided the product line managers have no design or new product responsibility and you want to develop these guys as businessmen, and so you call them product directors. They have a piece of a linear business, for example, and you spin off part of the [central] design group and give them part of it.

John Finch, National Semiconductor

Whether small or substantial, reorganization and structural change at National are constant shifts, "going on all of the time." This sort of change was a common event among the high-technology companies we studied.

Hewlett-Packard

Hewlett-Packard provides another example. During the several years of our research, numerous high-level changes were visible. In 1982, shortly after our study began, Hewlett-Packard commenced what John Young identified as the first of a set of organizational changes designed to address evolving technical and market conditions in HP's computer business. In December 1982, Hewlett-Packard reorganized: " . . . the Computer Group itself into more of a centralized marketing activity, as well as a product division." At the time, Young said, the group had had "a really big problem, which in 1985 we are still in the final throes of executing." The problem was the redesign of HP's entire computer line around a new underlying architecture, while simultaneously creating a new family of computers. The change in organization was substantial and carried important strategic and managerial implications.

Until 1982, HP's divisions had been highly autonomous, with diversified responsibility for marketing. HP's successes, to that point, were widely attributed to the autonomy of its divisions – as were its initial difficulties with marketing an interconnected line of computers, software, and peripherals. Critics claimed that autonomous divisions were simply unable to co-ordinate key technical details. By December 1982, when the reorganization took place, the long-term technical issues were still very much in the development stages. Nevertheless, HP clearly had innovative computer products to offer, as well as a recognized need to co-ordinate among its divisions.

Two key issues faced the company: a completely new architecture was in development, and the older organization had had some customers being called upon by two different sales groups. The field sales staffs were combined, so that customers were addressed in terms of their applications – manufacturing, engineering, or business applications, for instance – and a single, unified sales staff served the market. This ultimately necessitated a company-wide reorganization, to organize the firm "as the customers saw us," according to Katherine Nutter of HP.

Thus a separate Computer Products Group was created, joining together formerly autonomous divisions responsible for computer products into a unified structure. A more centralized marketing organization was created at the same time. Reflecting back on the 1982 changes almost three years later, Young described his rationale for the successive shifts:

> I really didn't want to disturb the product side of things until we had that really bolted down [technically]. Now [in 1985] that we have made more technical progress, I've made another change in the organization, and I think we feel we're in a position to deal with that. Again, that's a difference in the particular product, and how we've engineered things. We have one whole group that's doing nothing but engineering this one computer system: 800 professionals in it. This is quite a different [organizational] arrangement than we've ever had before.
>
> John Young, Hewlett-Packard

In July, 1984, Hewlett-Packard again reorganized, as its markets continued to converge. Traditional industrial computer users who needed test instruments also needed to link the instruments to personal computers. These uses were quite undreamed-of before the explosive growth and development of the personal computer market. Now, as personal computers became increasingly powerful, these new uses become increasingly central to HP's success in PC markets. Hewlett-Packard's former structure, composed of relatively autonomous divisions, had made it difficult to take advantage of these converging markets. Separate sales forces sold instruments and computers, even to the same customers. The result, according to one observer, was that "You had within HP an instrument company and a computer company treating each other at arm's length while trying to do battle with IBM" (*Business Week*, 1984). The 1984 reorganization dealt with these problems.

Technology development became more central, as a completely new architecture was being evolved. A central group was designated as responsible for providing core technology platforms to the applications-based field sales force. Hewlett-Packard rolled out three new products: a lap-sized computer, the Portable, and two new printers called Thinkjet and LaserJet. John Young remarked that "Creating the Personal Computer Group was an extremely good way of getting a focus on marketing. It was a way of communicating to everyone that this marketing was okay; that it's okay to eat quiche" (Saporito, 1984). Reorganization was also a way of signaling, both inside the organization and outside it, that Hewlett-Packard was formally addressing a hitherto disregarded or secondary activity.

The elevation of marketing to the Executive Vice Presidential level in 1984 was a major departure from Hewlett-Packard's prior methods of organizing. So, too was creation of the position Chief Operating Officer. But as Hewlett-Packard's products and markets were changing, so did its structure. Long renowned for engineering elegance sold to an appreciative and technically trained customer base, the company's focus now shifted to developing an equally elegant marketing capacity. Responding to implicit criticisms of HP's marketing expertise at the time, John Young observed:

> I don't think HP is bad at marketing. It's just that we needed
> to accelerate the marketing to complement the engineering.
>
> John Young, Hewlett-Packard
> (quoted in *Fortune*, 1 October 1984)

In 1985, Young described the changes in organization structure made in the late summer of that year. His comments are worth lengthy quotation because they lay out so clearly the relationships between marketplace changes, technical shifts, and the organizational means for dealing with them. Both formal structures and looser, quasi-formal and informal relations are apparent in Young's thinking:

> We see a lot of changes in the marketplace, over a period of years, I guess, both on the product as well as the customer side. The customers for our kinds of products used to be technically sophisticated people, buying things for them to work on, on their own. As we both changed the kinds of business to more information systems content, and even the technical side of that, customers have been growing less and less willing to do it themselves.
>
> Let's say the customers have been looking for more complete

answers to their business or technical problems. This is what put pressure on the factory side, to conceive and deliver and support and document solutions that were very sophisticated in nature. Of course, all of this means more teamwork, more things that have to work together, more interaction between pieces of the organization [within Hewlett-Packard], and less and less departmentalization, than is possible in traditional, division organizations.

So, we still believe in small work groups. We call those divisions at Hewlett-Packard, but we simply have to find ways of getting them to work more co-operatively, and to make sure that the system disciplines that are so essential, are put in place.

So basically what we did on the factory side is, we organized things more on market centers, as opposed to product centers. On the field side, we dissolved those product linkages and turned them around into more of a customer team organization. That's been going along for a year now, with a lot of work in reestablishing those informal communications back and forth.

Young's comments underline the importance of structure as a management tool. The interaction between formal organizational structure and the informal and quasi-formal activities of teams and individuals is also illustrated. Equally visible, however, is a shift from the prior focus of technical elegance as the selling point, to "solving customers' problems." In essence, this highly technical business has acquired a decidedly "service" tilt.

In late 1988, HP again reorganized, to re-emphasize technology distinctions. The new core technology of the HP computers was finished, so the central group was reintegrated into HP's businesses, its divisions. The new computer architecture, the RISC-based core system platform, was done. A new set of questions arose, regarding how to allocate responsibility for commercial, UNIX-based activities and DOS-based activities. Organizing according to operating system (DOS or UNIX) didn't seem sensible, according to Katherine Nutter. Instead, individual user applications versus network systems groupings seemed more useful to separate distinct market elements and the appropriate hardware and software to serve them. With this reorganization, business managers again were responsible for implementing the strategy under a reintegrated structure.

Like all of our sample firms, even Hewlett-Packard, reputedly "an engineer's company," is explicitly oriented toward marketplace success. Structure is deliberately used to emphasize this focus.

IBM

The companies in our research sample are not the only innovative firms to repeatedly restructure. One of the most repeatedly innovative of high-technology companies is IBM. IBM is also one of the longest lived of high-technology firms, having survived successive generations from mechanical technology through several subsequent generations of electronics. IBM is widely recognized for its ability to develop sophisticated, reliable products. Like the companies in our study, IBM also faces formidable challenges from its competitors: Digital Equipment, Data General, NEC, and Toshiba. IBM is also vast by any standard: some $51 billion in revenues, over 2000 product lines, and 400,000 employees. Nevertheless, the firm is widely regarded as exceptionally nimble.

It has been documented that IBM reorganized more than 20 times between 1968 and 1982. In 1982, it reorganized the entire company, fundamentally altering its basic structure. Since 1982, IBM has:

- dissolved its old Data Processing and General Business groups;
- changed the reporting relationships in virtually every major unit;
- formed 10 US Independent Business Units, but then merged or disbanded six of these, and formed seven more;
- moved from 12 major divisions reporting through three groups, to 13 major divisions reporting to five groups, and one reporting directly to the corporate level (of these 13 divisions, 5 have been changed from their forms in 1982, and 6 are new);
- formed Distribution Channels (later merged into the National Distribution Division), Entry Systems (which became a division), Industrial Systems Organization (later broken into two IBUs), IBM Information Services (which first reported to the Information Systems Group, but now reports to Corporate), Telecommunications Products Organization, and IBM Credit Corporations;
- changed its direct sales organization from two product-based divisions to two account-based divisions to two geographical divisions.

While IBM has restructured frequently throughout its history, its rate of reorganization appears to have increased as its markets and technologies have become more competitive and changeable. IBM also combines structural flexibility with tight reporting relationships

– carefully focused charters for groups, internal competitive "shoot-outs," tight management controls, and swift moves to address slippages or changes in the marketplace (Jeffrey, 1986).

Whether the case is Hewlett-Packard, National, or IBM, structure for all of these firms is a managerial tool. Clear organization and reorganization are used to fit resources to innovation problems and to marketing problems, and for preventing tunnel vision, bureaucracy, and stale thinking. Above all, rapid and effective structural rearrangement is central to responsive marketplace performance, for IBM as well as for the firms we have studied in depth.

Managing Transitions

Two sorts of transitions must be managed within these companies: the development of repeated new products or processes, with their transition from lab to factory to market; and the shift of organization structure itself. We will deal with both, because their interaction highlights the structural management of change. Both are of crucial importance, for new products and processes are the lifeblood of technological innovation. The ability to respond to industry demands with effective structure is at the heart of these firms' ability to marshall resources by means of repeated reorganization.

Expecting Structural Change

People in firms like HP, National, Intel, Motorola, and TI come to regard structural changes as a part of life in a company like theirs; and they anticipate more change in the future, too. Some of the anticipated changes are finer tunings of structure at lower levels; others are more general, more inclusive changes in response to marketplace or technology shifts. For example, in 1985, Doug Spreng, then Division General Manager of the Hewlett-Packard Computer Systems Division, showed us the most recent formal organizational chart. This chart reflected the changes in structure which John Young described in the paragraphs quoted above. Spreng offered the chart with a telling observation about structural change at HP:

Do you want a copy of the corporate organization chart? In fact, I've got a couple of slides I can give you that show the relationships, too. They're probably in transition; six to nine months from now, they will probably be changed.

Spreng's comment was neither flippant nor cynical. He was just reflecting matter-of-factly on the likely consequences of fairly predictable changes in the relevant technologies that affected current businesses, and important marketplace realities. For example, Spreng speculated on which changes in structure were likely to transpire in the businesses he was most familiar with:

My guess is what we'll finally end up seeing is three businesses separately managed. But we're still sorting that out, because the last year has been rather complex, and it's not as clearly definable as the other two sets of changes in the organization [made previously]. We're taking a little longer time, because we do not want to take false steps. It's really important I think for us, if we make a step, that we make it, it's firm, and we go from there. [We won't] . . . do any herky-jerky . . . as some of the things in the past [have been done].

Change in structure is not seen as cost-free, nor as always having been perfectly executed in the past. Nevertheless, reorganization is appreciated as important and useful. To be done well, it demands care and attention, but it may also deliver important improvements in organizational functioning. Done well, it will be explicitly and definitively related to competitive needs.

Spreng was among those division general managers whose formerly autonomous operations were somewhat centralized by the reorganization. Nonetheless, he felt the changes were both necessary and positive:

We're reorganizing the structure of the company, I think, in a much more solid way. The company is changing tremendously from the old days of what a Vice President calls the "futile abilities of the instrument divisions" to a vastly integrated, highly leveraged company. At the same time, we are growing at a very good clip, which is quite a challenge, but it is absolutely necessary for us to achieve that.

We don't want to become a centralized company like [others] – we're not going to become that. But we're moving toward a more co-ordinated, strategically oriented kind of a management balance, between the entrepreneurship of the divisional units and the strategic overview, the guiding hands, if you will. This computer business, which has basically overtaken the company, has dramatically changed the company at the same time.

Doug Spreng, Hewlett-Packard

Managing the Process of Structural Change

The process by which these companies reorganize is substantially participative. After clarifying changes in strategic directions which the company will take, the members of the top management team (the Management Committee, in Hewlett-Packard's case) sketch out the major skeletal changes in the structure. However, it is at the group and division levels of the company at which middle- to lower-tier executives determine structural changes in their own organizations.

Details of the reorganized structure must be worked out by lower-level managers, closer to the affected groups. Unless the company's top executives want to take forever to design the optimal structure, some interim approximations must be made, while refinements are left for later. Unless the redesigns are to be forever "management's problem," the lower-level implementers must be enlisted in designing the new arrangements to meet their needs. No top management team can be omniscient when reorganizing a large company. Consequently, they must discuss and consult, then place their best bets on what they believe the structure should be, implement it, and observe the results. The need for some elements of the new structure will only be recognized when it has been put into practice. For example, Doug Spreng remarked on the consequences of some changes which took place at Hewlett-Packard:

> You change things around . . . , and then the complexity of the interactions becomes awesome. You think that you've got this situation bounded, territories understood and so forth, and then you find out: "No, these three other organizations over there are intimately affected by what you just did here." You had no idea. Yet, you know unless you want to take forever in reorganizing you're going to have to make some of these decisions on the front end and hope that you haven't screwed something else up. Or hope that you can fix it.

Such "anticipated, unanticipated" errors and changes are the field of action for important lower-level input, to ensure that the efforts of top management really do produce the desired results. Spreng observed:

> Now, one of the neat things about Hewlett-Packard is that we're pretty resilient. Everybody realizes that the guys at the top are trying to do the best they can. What they do is they point out that we have this problem: "Here, we have this problem. Here, let's make this adjustment."

Detailed adjustments are the responsibility of managers farther down. When decisions regarding the reorganization result in problems, the lower-level managers refine the structural arrangements for better working relationships. Some of these changes indicate the clear links between informal interaction and formal structure at HP. Managers farther down, like Spreng, interact with one another to mutually adjust their organizations. Their organizations' capabilities are the focus of their negotiations. Spreng asserted:

> There's a lot of concessions going on . . . when you get down to some of the details. Like the guy across the mall, here [another division general manager]. I believe that at least one and maybe two of his lab groups ought to be within an organization that I've got . . . I've already broached the subject and asked him not to make any changes in his organization until we get it resolved, because I believe that we've got it wrong right now, and I don't want to keep it wrong.
>
> It's easy for us to do that because we both trust each other, and we know we're not trying to build an empire. We're just trying to do the right thing for the company and get these people to where they can make their best contributions . . . We're going to get together over lunch and talk about it some more. We're creating a document that shows what the recommendations are and why. I think the best thing about HP is that we can work these things out.

"Self-Designing" Organizations Know their Competition

The changes in formal structure at Hewlett-Packard and National described here amply illustrate the kinds of reorganization we saw taking place at each of the other companies that we studied. The timing of changes varied; so, too, did what each reorganization modified in its former structure. For each company, the changes in structure were customized to meet the modifications managers perceived in their company's localized task environments, markets, and technologies. In each of our companies, managers were constantly alert to the suitability and performance of current structure *vis-à-vis* markets, technology, and customers. In each, an on-going critique of structure was the norm. What is common is their ready and explicit use of structural change as a management tool, and the frequent shifts from one explicit structure to another that resulted.

Such attention to structure is said to produce "self-designing" organizations (Weick, 1977). These companies are able to be self-designing because of two factors. First, the people working within these organizations are highly self-critical regarding how they are operating and whether the current structure is facilitating goal accomplishment well enough. If an element of the organization is not functioning adequately, alternatives are considered. Change in major elements of structure is considered if more modest adjustments are deemed inadequate. Executives and managers in these firms openly evaluate the utility of the organizational status quo.

A second, related factor is that reorganization is seen as problem-solving to meet changed organizational needs and circumstances, not as proof of a past error. As we have previously noted, in these firms "it's not working" does not automatically translate into "somebody goofed". Consequently, we surmise, people seem far more able to let go of prior structures, both because they are not blamed, and because if a new structure doesn't work, it will be fixed.

Our data suggest that for organizations to be self-designing over time, widely shared agreements are essential regarding this activity. In our firms, such agreement is both part of the organizations' cultures and embedded in their managers' operating styles. Readiness for structural change is expected – and widely to be found – from top to bottom, down to the levels of the engineers and first-line managers. Founders and top-level leaders are very important in helping to shape such expectations and norms, of course, but mid-level and lower managers also play key roles.

We found that founders and members of the top management teams of these companies expressed great willingness to reorganize if it seemed appropriate. This was "no fault reorganization," where new needs, not anyone's "prior failure or bad decision," drove structural change. More importantly, however, this expressed readiness was acted upon: real changes discernibly took place, everyone knew of the changes, and the rationale for change was also broadly shared. All of this produced a high tolerance for change among the people at lower levels in the organization with whom we spoke.

Another reason why these companies can manage structural change so well is their close attention to environmental, market, scientific, and technical conditions external to their organizations. Effective organizational change must target for and adapt to major environmental and technological shifts. Structure is a deliberate artifact intended to suit explicit purpose; change is not merely random. Consequently, good knowledge of the external context must blend with a willingness to reorganize, as well as skill at structural arrangements. Anything less will have random effects on organizational performance – extremely dangerous in the intensely competitive environment these firms face.

These companies' managers systematically try to understand their businesses ever better. They pay much attention to measuring multiple indicators of performance. Performance results, efficiencies, ease of operation, and a myriad of operating details are constantly tracked. These are quite deliberately self-conscious organizations, with information shared and used in the process of structural modification. They also constantly monitor the competition, track technology and product shifts, and seek to understand both competitive moves and the strategic implications of external change.

For example, it is routine in these companies to rigorously measure manufacturing yields, the percentage of useable components or "chips" produced on a single wafer of silicon. Similarly, manufacturing cycle times and a host of detailed production data are also continuously recorded, analyzed, and examined for insights into potential changes in manufacturing equipment, organization, or people (either personnel, levels, procedures, or training) that might drive the yields up and cycle times farther and farther down.

Here, too, it is not simply a matter of getting it right once. Equipment changes frequently; new manufacturing processes are introduced frequently; existing technologies are constantly improved through process development; and new products are introduced on new and continuously improving technologies. Instead of getting it right once, it is a continuous battle to get it right, and then not just to keep it right, but to make it better and better under extraordinarily difficult technical circumstances.

Such extraordinary attention is driven by broad awareness of competitive hazards. "We've got to beat the Japanese through speed of development and consistently high quality," was one phrase we encountered frequently in our study companies. Variants of the phrase named other competitors – the Koreans, or other US firms – but no manager, and no engineer with whom we spoke, was not alert to competition and aware of competitive threat.

Awareness of the external market and competition extends throughout these companies. For example, the chief executive of National Semiconductor spoke of a newly graduated engineer, a circuit designer, who had joined National the preceding year:

> . . . His views of what the [semiconductor] business is all about are far fom perfect. But he knows where his product stands relative to everybody else's. Very clearly. He knows it better than I do.
>
> Charlie Sporck, National Semiconductor.

Such awareness enables the junior engineer to be both an effective contributor to the structural changes we have been describing, and an effective critic and consumer of them.

These self-designing organizations, attuned as they are to competitive realities, also illustrate the principle of dynamic tension around which the companies organize. Each time a reorganization took place, clear new reporting relationships were worked out. Clear new responsibilities were assigned to individuals and groups. And each time, these connections were refined to clarify any problems or ambiguities. Instead of loose structures, these firms shifted from one clear organization to another clear organization. People at all levels worked to make the organization clear and explicit. These companies can move so rapidly to introduce new products or technologies in pursuit of corporate goals, because people in the companies know what other people are doing. They know where to seek resources and decisions.

Quasi-Formal Structure

Teams, Task Forces, and Dotted-Line Organizations

While clarity of and changes in the formal structure are important features of the ways in which these companies have organized for innovation, formal elements of structure are only a part of the story. Organization theory seems to recognize only two dimensions of organizational structure: formal structure captured on the organization chart, and informal structure as the unsanctioned patterns of interaction devised around social and task requirements which the formal organization has failed to take into account. We believe that it is time to recognize an intermediate level of structure which pervades the companies we have studied.

This intermediate form of structure is not formally depicted on organization charts. Nor is it "informal," in the usual senses of covert, unsanctioned, purely social, or even adversarial, which the term traditionally takes (e.g. Blau, 1955; Connor, 1980; Gouldner, 1954; Leavitt, 1958; Roethlisberger and Dickson, 1939; Selznick, 1949). We have labelled it "quasi-formal structure," the term "quasi" referring to something that resembles, but is not, the thing in question.

In these organizations, quasi-structure involves extensive use of committees, task forces, teams, and dotted-line relationships. The quasi-formal structures we have observed resemble formal structures, because they are formally recognized and explicitly sanctioned by the organization as legitimate; but they are typically not designated in form, specified in defined charter, or delimited in terms of membership. They expand and contract at need. Nor do they take the place of formal authority and responsibility patterns. Instead, quasi-structure is used in combination with the formal structure, to support it and improve its operation.

Quasi-formal structure should not be confused with the "informal structure" of the organization; it is not unsanctioned, illegitimate, covert, or in any way outlawed or disapproved of. On the contrary, it is explicitly recognized, condoned, and encouraged by management at all levels, and accepted as a generally group-controlled mechanism for co-ordination. Managers themselves participate in the creation of this level of the companies' structures, but similar quasi-structures are the accepted mode for employee problem-solving groups as well, and may have entirely non-managerial roots. Thus this is *almost* a formalized element of these organizations.

Quasi-formal elements in these companies change even more frequently than the formal structure, as old problems are resolved and new problems appear on the horizon. Quasi-formal elements form, dissolve, or change at need. Also in contrast to formal structure, these groups and teams are relevance-based and problem-focused. Many transcend whatever formal structural boundaries might otherwise impede problem solution. Thus quasi-structure serves as an important organizational "lubricant" to enable explicit formal structures to work. Quasi-structure augments formal structure and bridges the gap between the skeleton of the organization and the informal, purely local and interpersonal mechanisms for doing things.

Quasi-structure also saves the companies from simply becoming adhocracies, paradoxically because it makes change so much easier. The organization need not move to a "Structure du Jour", and formal reorganization need not be a constant problem. Because structure can change at need, it need not lose clarity, and people need not face continuous change. Quasi-structure augments formal structure by creating a norm of interaction and relationship across boundaries that make the formal boundaries and their limitations less constraining. In short, it is quasi-structure that makes these organizations at once more precisely controlled, and more broadly participative than either "organic" organization structures or reliance on "culture" alone could permit.

In each of these companies we found extensive use of committees, teams, task forces, and dotted-line relationships to augment clear formal structures which were also present. Quasi-structural methods were used for both one-time or continuing problematic circumstances which required off-line, additional technical and managerial attention to devise solutions. Such quasi-formal approaches were diverse, broadly pervasive, and quite characteristic of the innovative organizations we studied.

These units of quasi-structure emerge in a variety of ways. Sometimes they arise spontaneously, as a self-forming response to shared problems: people across functions who share a problem, form a team to solve it. Sometimes management at some level will explicitly request that a task force or committee be convened to deal with a

designated problem or issue. A concrete example will illustrate the
ease with which elements of quasi-structure are created.

Richard Walleigh, a manufacturing engineering manager in the
Computer Systems Division at Hewlett-Packard, described a task
force that spontaneously formed around the concept of total quality
control (TQC). First, someone had to perceive the need for a joint
focus on a problem. In this case, Walleigh himself was the initiator.
He began with an observation to get people's attention:

> "Here's a great idea; we ought to do this." Then, once you have
> the light bulb turned on, the next thing you do in HP is get a
> group of people together and you start talking about it. It always
> requires a group of people to do practically anything. There's so
> few things that you can do in your own department without
> influencing other departments, that it seems everything we do is
> in groups.
>
> So . . . you get them charged up about it, and get them
> working on it in their departments through an informal
> mechanism. You just put together a team of the relevant players
> and say, "This is a great idea," and talk about it. We then say,
> "How can we implement it here?" Then everyone starts working
> on [implementation]. The team sort of meets, works on the
> project until the project's done, and it gets developed . . . It's
> our style here, and it's almost necessary. We do lots of things
> in teams, some formal and some informal.
>
> Rick Walleigh, Hewlett-Packard

Walleigh is not alone at HP in his enthusiasm for teams. His CEO,
John Young, fully understands and approves of the kind of teamwork
Walleigh describes, and corroborated the account with his own
examples:

> We have a million task forces around – particularly a lot of them
> on technical and marketing kinds of things. They really are very
> complex subsets of the organization – things that never show on
> this chart. It also happens in our administrative things: all the
> way from the Compensation Task Force, to you name it,
> to . . . just finding knowledgeable and respected people who
> want the chance to participate in this problem. [This] is probably
> the most frequent pattern we use for that kind of co-ordination
> and co-operative activity.
>
> John Young, Hewlett-Packard

Not Matrix Management

It is important to define quasi-structure in terms of what it is not, as well as what it actually is. It is not "matrix management." In the 1960s an organizational form called "the matrix structure" was created and experimented with in US aerospace companies, often under contract to the US Department of Defense and other federal agencies. In matrix management, either the entire structure or major segments of it are configured so that many people within functional departments of the organization have at least two bosses: a functional boss and a project boss. Both bosses in this "dual authority structure" have the traditional right of supervisors to assign tasks, evaluate work, and influence the rewards and promotions their matrix subordinates receive. We did not find such relationships in our sample firms. Indeed, when queried about matrix organization, managers repeatedly asserted that matrix structures were unsatisfactory because they did not give their firms the precise clarity of responsibility, reporting relationships, and decision-making responsibility they needed. Repeatedly, managers in our companies rejected the matrix structure as too equivocal and too ambiguous for their situation.

Matrix structures were regarded as a genuine structural innovation when they were originated, since they seemed well adapted to the vicissitudes of Congressional funding, long-term projects, and shifting organizational needs in the aerospace industry. Matrix forms were a clear departure from the rigidly hierarchical, vertical structures most often seen in large organizations up to that time. Because traditional organization charts do not show multiple bosses except in so-called "dotted-line" relationships (where a second boss has supplementary authority), some managers refer to dual relationships as "dotted-line" reporting, confusing matrix forms with other forms or organization.

Occasionally the managers and executives whom we interviewed did speak of "matrix" relationships. Invariably further conversation would reveal that the entire corporation was not structured as a matrix, nor were their divisions. The formalized dual authority structure was typically missing. Instead, project groups were created for technology or product development, drawing engineers from multiple organizations in the typical case. Other relationships initially described as "matrix" were later revealed as supplemental authority of the "dotted-line" form, rather than the multiple bosses in a dual authority structure indicative of a matrix. This is not a trivial or an academic distinction.

A dotted-line relationship in these companies typically designated a "for information only" relationship, where it was considered important that two positions on different levels, which existed diagonally across organizational lines, communicate regularly. In such cases, a dotted line was sometimes used to characterize the relationship on the chart. In another case, a project supervisor explained that he was "matrixed" to several other groups and divisions: this too was revealed to consist of information-sharing relationships characterized by committees or meetings to report about and solve problems with other disciplines and departments.

A structure of extensive dual reporting relationships was clearly not the way the term "matrix" was used in these companies. Rather, multiple organizational units were involved, in the usual case, in problem-solving, quasi-formal interfaces. More to the point, quasi-structures are both more formal, in their recognized status as problem-solving groups, and less formal, in their authority relationships, than matrix structures.

Quasi-structures are colleague-based, problem-focused entities which exist for the duration of the problem. They are also far more pervasive in our companies, more deliberate, and more explicitly utilized than "informal" relationships or purely "cultural" linkages. They address problems deemed too important to be left to chance, their results are attended to, and their contributions taken very much into account.

Many of the managers we interviewed were clear that they did not have a matrix structure and preferred it that way. Indeed, some believed that a formal matrix structure reduces the clarity of the organization and thereby reduces its effectiveness. Peter Rosenbladt, the R&D manager at Hewlett-Packard, had an organization of about 120 people who did research and development. According to Rosenbladt:

> Matrix management, wherever it's been tried [at HP], it's been very distasteful, because it is always resulting in undue complexity, unclear objectives, so we like to do it informally wherever we can. We have never successfully implemented a matrix of management that really does work, because it immediately means that everyone has at least two bosses, and that doesn't go well with things like who determines how well you did, what the priorities are, and those kinds of things.

Similarly, TI adopted a structure something like the matrix in the 1970s, but discarded the notion in the early 1980s for similar reasons: the matrix provided insufficient accountability, and relationships became excessively complex.

While investigating the matrix issue in our research, another point became apparent. These companies are organized according to their own unique needs. They do not import an organizational design merely because it is fashionable, nor do they have their structures determined for them by outside consultants. As Intel's former Vice President for Human Resources, Ann S. Bowers, explained, Intel uses consultants as efficient sources of information, for research. Invariably, such advice was nearly always reworked extensively by Intel people, to adapt it to "Intel's operating style".

> Intel does use consultants for research. Then we take what's useful for Intel and modify the heck out of it, to adapt it to suit our own needs – our unique Intel needs.
>
> Ann S. Bowers, (formerly) Intel

While the term matrix is certainly within the operating vocabulary of these well-read managers and executives, matrix structure is not what we found in the companies we have studied. These firms have organizational designs adapted to their special technological and competitive needs, not one imported from the slower-moving aerospace industry.

Managing Quasi-Structure: Costs as well as Benefits

At Intel, Les Vadasz described the prevalence of both task forces and dotted-line relationships:

> We have a lot of multiple reporting relationships, dotted-line reporting relationships and shifts in organizations, especially if you look at project organizations, as the project reaches different stages. People from multiple organizations participate . . .
>
> Les Vadasz, Intel

The function of dotted-line relationships for Intel's technical projects is to ensure efficient transfer of crucial information to where it is needed in multiple projects and departments, despite limited human resources. However, there are some complications associated with dotted-line relationships, according to Vadasz. Consistent with other research, dotted-line and multiple reporting relationships in technical projects and other organizational applications produce what Vadasz described as "some interim ambiguity:"

> There is a difference between knowing that you have ambiguity and knowing that "Hey, I want to work out of it." If you just ignore it, then you get chaos. What you have to struggle for is clear organization lines (knowing full well intellectually that you will not be able to accomplish it perfectly) because you want to do what's right for getting the project done. But if you always struggle to get the cleanest possible line [of organization], you have less chaos.
>
> Les Vadasz, Intel

In short, in a rapidly changing technical environment, constant vigilance is the price of clarity, even within a clear structure.

Another cost of maintaining innovation in corporations as large as these is time. Large amounts of time must be spent integrating across organizational boundaries. This is another aspect of quasi-structure: it simply takes a great deal of time, even if that time is at first glance "invisible." For example, Hewlett-Packard consciously strives to "keep it small" in divisions of approximately 1000 participants. Nevertheless, co-ordinating among some 50 such divisions is a far from trivial task. Task forces, dotted-line relationships, and other forms of quasi-structure are omnipresent among the Hewlett-Packard divisions – as, indeed, they are in all our firms. These quasi-formal elements of structure are absolutely essential mechanisms of organizing for innovation. Task forces and dotted-line relationships are part of the solution, with the time and attention demanded by them as part of their cost.

At each company, people acknowledged the essential role that committees and task forces played in problem-solving and co-ordination. Yet they were simultaneously critical of the time required for effective task force participation. At each company, managers were aware of the need to eliminate old elements of organization that were no longer essential. However, elimination was not always easily accomplished. Les Vadasz of Intel felt that this attention to quasi-structure was much like weeding one's garden:

Do we have too many dotted-line relationships? I would say "Yes, we do, because it is not easy to kill something." People get used to the fact that they are there, they have a committee of some sort . . . Although the committee has done its job and the problem is resolved, some committees nonetheless evolve into standing committees . . . We have to be able to prune them.

Les Vadasz, Intel

Vadasz was sharply aware of the need to eliminate non-essential functions, committees which survive beyond their functional utility, and meetings that simply take up time at Intel. But time *per se* was only one aspect of cutting back. Another was the impact of ineffective quasi-structural elements on thinking:

We are trying more consciously these days . . . [to address the longevity of multiple committees.] For example, we have a very extensive council system. About a year ago, one of the best council systems we've had from the beginning was our die production work. Because [we have] so many factories all around the world, we have to make sure the better processes are common enough in all the factories so that we have the flexibility to move [production] around. Well, those committees over the years [had] gotten a little bit stale. So we made a major change and pruned it dramatically. There were more people who felt that it was a breath of fresh air, and so it wasn't a big issue . . . to prune it.

Les Vadasz, Intel

Obsolete quasi-structure makes for stale thinking, because people expect it to map current conditions, and help identify current problems.

One latent value of task forces and committees is that they present opportunities for lower-level engineers and managers to begin developing their leadership and group skills – both essential components for future managerial success in an innovative company. This value also carries costs, however. Task forces will develop juniors only if their tasks are real and important; and if their tasks are to be real, the task forces must be managed. As Vadasz continued,

I think the biggest problem [with task forces] is that somebody has to do the supervising. Someone has to guide them. You don't just create [committees] and let them go. If you were to hire a manager and let the manager go without supervision, you generally end up with undesirable results.

This means additional managerial time must be allocated throughout the organization, since these teams and task forces meet throughout the organization. Similar complaints about the time required to manage these quasi-formal elements were as pervasive as the structures themselves, at all levels of these organizations. Thus although quasi-structure provides essential benefits, it also entails costs. Managing quasi-structure, for all its necessary openness and participation, is a demanding responsibility. Pruning old quasi-structures is as important as creating new ones. Despite the wide sharing of those responsibilities, throughout these organizations and at all levels, the burden is heavy.

The committees, task forces, project groups and dotted-line relationships are "absolutely not a freebie" according to Vadasz at Intel, because they require the scarcest of resources, time and attention, from participants as well as from managers. On balance, however, quasi-structure is an essential tool for accomplishing speedy, task-oriented, and complex interactions across disciplines, projects, departments, and divisions.

Just such interactions are required to effectively exploit the multi-disciplinary technologies of semiconductors and electronics. And, as technology, processes, markets, and products continue to shift, such interactions must be reconfigured, again and again, year after year. While not without costs, these organizational arrangements deliver tremendous benefits in the management of innovation, if monitored and attended, just like any other aspect of the organization which you expect to bear fruit.

Informal Structure

Collegial Interactions in a Team Environment

While we did not find "organic management" in these firms, we did find strong evidence of collegial interaction. Instead of the hierarchy-based interaction patterns typically found in traditional organizations, the firms in our study embody very strong norms and practices of non-hierarchical interaction based on problem-solving. (Some of these characteristics have already been described in terms of the roots of innovation, front-end idea filtering, and strategic planning.) Committees and teams which cross organizational boundaries and are composed of people from many levels create the possibility for such interaction. Norms of problem-focus and expertise-based authority also clearly facilitate non-hierarchical interaction. Informal interactions are what makes quasi-structure function so effectively in our sample companies, just as they assist in effective strategy making.

In innovative high-technology companies, multitudes of novel problems exist for which no established solutions are readily apparent. The sensible approach is to call on every available resource. These resources include anyone – regardless of formal position – with a useful perspective on the issue at hand. Insight, reflection, and substantive contributions, not hierarchy or status, seem more relevant in these companies.

John Young at Hewlett-Packard emphasized the part this phenomenon plays in maintaining an innovative organization:

> To make the structure as clear as you can is a long way from saying there are no ambiguities. There is a very big need for a collegial environment . . . to make it work. In fact, I think there is a fair amount of ambiguity. I think it's far more the style and the freedom of activity and association and communication back and forth that makes an innovative environment.

There are other contributors to collegial, non-hierarchical interactions. Consider that these companies deliberately hire the very best people they can. The range of required talent is broad. It includes young people with the most recent technical training and recent graduates from engineering and business schools; experienced engineers, executives, and managers; and the best people these companies can find or develop for a host of support functions. Even production workers, technicians, and equipment engineers – the present-day version of old fashioned maintenance people in factories – need to be the best, in an industry of Class 1 clean rooms that count contaminants to integrated circuit production in parts per million or less.

Now the cynical reader will remark "Well, surely there are some laggards, lower-quality, just plain zeroes in each of these companies." And undoubtedly there are. What distinguishes these companies, however, is the widely shared belief that they must use whatever human resources they can bring to bear on any given problem. Within these companies, we found a ubiquitous norm: virtually anyone who seems to have good ideas or is reflective will be consulted. They will be relied upon, regardless of hierarchy or official status, if their experience, expertise, or intellectual abilities appear relevant to the problem at hand. Meanwhile, the pace of change and the intensity of necessary contribution either speed up or de-select the least capable.

Accessing talent, and selecting among the thousands of people available in each of these companies is facilitated by the way the companies structure themselves. There are smaller working groups whenever possible, and the overall structure of each of the companies is clear. Any individual can determine without great difficulty where additional help might be found, if the people in his or her current organization do not have the requisite knowledge to help resolve current difficulties. People become known to those around them, and there are many opportunities to solve problems.

There is also a pervasive norm that people in the companies call "team mentality." Team mentality involves a broadly shared perception that "We are in this together, and it may take more than just me, myself, to solve a given problem." Indeed, if the team mentality were stated as a norm to guide the behavior of new recruits to these companies, it would read something like this:

> Given the complex technical solutions that we need, in addition to the complicated and uncertain market conditions we face, it is likely that more than just a single individual or a small group will be required to solve almost any given problem.

We asked a division general manager at Hewlett-Packard if the highly competitive computer market would change the willingness of HP employees to co-operate with one another internally. Is the pressure on HP as a company going to make it tougher for individual division general managers to survive and for their careers to prosper, and thus increase internal competition among such managers for future promotions? Might this perhaps reduce their willingness to collaborate, we asked? In contrast to what might be expected, the manager, Doug Spreng, responded:

> Oh, no, you have to be *more* teamwork oriented. Teamwork is the only way we can preserve our thrust into the markets as a company. The divisional structure will [continue to] exist, but [the reorganization] allows us to work at a much higher plane of co-operation as an organizational entity. So teamwork is our secret. We're finding measurement of teamwork coming up more and more in evaluations and in ranking sessions of managers. You just don't go off and do your own thing in this company any more.

Informal, collegial interaction was widely practiced at the technical levels of the organizations we studied, as well as among the managerial ranks. At National Semiconductor, for example,

> Sometimes [innovation] happens in the men's room. One guy's talking to another guy, and another guy's standing, eavesdropping on the conversation, scribbling on a napkin. If you dropped down right now to the cafeteria, you would see it going on. Most of [the innovation motivation] comes out of, let's say, frustration or irritation with the way something currently works. And a guy says, "You know, I really wish I had a fill-in-the-blank. What I had didn't do fill-in-the-blank." And the other guy says, "Well, you know, a few years ago, I had a problem like that and what I did was x, y, and z." And then the chemistry starts, and the result is a product that solves the problem..
>
> Barry Siegel, National Semiconductor

In the restrooms, in the cafeterias, and in the hallways, informal colleague-based interaction patterns permeate these companies.

Corporate Size: How Big is Too Big?

We cannot leave a discussion of structure in high-technology companies without mentioning organizational size. Large numbers of people pose significant problems for co-ordination in a fast-changing marketplace and technology. So, too, do geographically scattered operations, broad product lines, and global competition. Each of the companies we studied operates worldwide, in an increasingly global marketplace. These are large corporations. However, they have not always been large. Many within these organizations remember how much smaller and more manageable these corporations once were, perhaps 10 years ago. Although Texas Instruments, Motorola, and Hewlett-Packard, for example, were all founded over 30 years ago, they experienced their most explosive growth in the 1970s – just as the younger companies, Intel and National, were also experiencing rapid growth.

The founders or very early managers were unanimous in recalling how much simpler it was to communicate in a small company. It was easy to maintain close coupling between the organizational functions.

David Packard described how he and Bill Hewlett operated in the early days at HP, after World War II:

> When the company was small, [close coupling] was almost automatic, because we were all involved in everything. In fact, when we were small, I'd spend a lot of time in the laboratory, and I'd spend a lot of time in the factory, and I spent a lot of time in the field. And so you did all these things yourself.
>
> David Packard, Hewlett-Packard

The experiences of Hewlett and Packard are near duplicates of those described by Pat Haggerty of his early days at Texas Instruments:

> It was here that the setting of objectives, and being small and tightly coupled – without doing it with a system like OST – was so important . . . We put good people at the thing – and they were *very* tightly coupled. And tightly coupled? I was there most every day, Mark Shepherd in the semiconductor operation, Gordon Teal – and we were all talking to one another.
>
> Patrick Haggerty, Texas Instruments

Packard and Haggerty also agreed on the negative impact of boom-and-bust defense business dynamics, especially rapid growth followed by layoffs. Neither wanted to hire people only to lay them off. Both companies preferred building loyalty through a long-term commitment to the people who were hired. For both companies, as for others in our sample, more steady growth meant somewhat slower growth.

The benefits of steady growth included much clearer links among firm members and broadly shared views on management. However, any growth brought problems, even slow growth. Packard recalled how he had realized quickly:

> The first hurdle to get over is to recognize that you can't do all these things yourself. Then the name of the game is to try and get people to do things the way you'd do them, if you were doing it. So you try and develop people who would have the same ideas, the same approach, and the same philosophy, and so we developed a very close relationship.
>
> David Packard, Hewlett-Packard

As HP got bigger, the two founders and their close associates developed some methods to maintain this close relationship. Packard continued:

> As we got bigger, we decided that the way to manage this business was to break it down in small enough units so that

people could have expertise in a particular field. So the first thing we did, we built our engineering laboratories into two sections: one on low frequency instruments and one on high frequency instruments. That meant then that these people not only kept up with all of technology, but they knew what the market needed. It was their business to stay ahead of the game in their fields.

David Packard, Hewlett-Packard

A similar organizing philosophy prevails at Intel as well. Ted Jenkins, Intel's General Manager of the Microsystems Components Division, described how the relatively small size of his division allows him to readily communicate informally with a substantial number of people – to get them headed in a similar direction:

So, they're small organizations. My whole thing, including manufacturing and the whole ball of wax is probably about 450 people to 500 people. So by the time you divide these up, everybody knows everybody else, and so you can just run around and say, "Hey, guys, look at this. I just read this article, and we've got this technology, here's a neat idea. What do you think?" "Oh, that's good." "Well, let's do some work on this."

Ted Jenkins, Intel

The surprise is not that smaller divisions genuinely do facilitate communication. The lesson is the explicit attention which these managers give to structuring sub-units with smaller headcounts. HP's and Intel's small-unit focus breaks the company's size down into units small enough that people can comprehend their tasks. Not so coincidentally, this also enables individuals to exercise meaningful control over their tasks. This appears to be a fundamentally important organizing principle: in some form, all our study companies seek to maintain a "small company feel," although they differ substantially on how this is done. We conclude that, in complex businesses such as these, despite the increased time and attention required, it makes good sense to keep operating units small enough – within the cognitive limits of the human mind to grasp and manipulate them effectively.

Packard's successor, John Young, was among many in our sample companies who paid deliberate attention to this kind of size. He mentioned the importance of explicitly organizing people, of explicitly keeping the organizational units down to a smaller, more manageable size, and building the requisite linkages between divisions and groups to maintain innovation in a large organization:

> We are a six billion dollar company. That's one business [not a conglomerate]. We have 52 operating divisions, not because it's easy to have 52 operating divisions, but because we believe in those small work groups. That means about 1000 people per workgroup. It's more on the model of a small business . . . because of the interaction.
>
> I think it is extremely important for people to see who you need to co-operate with, and why co-operating is a growing, valued characteristic . . . The only excuse for having a big organization, it seems to me, is one where you generally have those linkages, that can build on each other. But linkage is a big problem. And it takes a lot of time. So, we have had to articulate [why it's worth time co-ordinating], and the organization form is one way to help do that.
>
> John Young, Hewlett-Packard

Size is literally linked to clarity of structure, in that clearer structure is more important in larger organizations. Both linkage and clarity derive from the communications, problem-solving and innovation-fostering quasi-structures that create "small company feel," and permit these large firms to operate as if they were much smaller.

Because they have learned how to manage large numbers of employees by grouping people into smaller units, the founders and executives of these companies do not appear to be overly concerned with becoming "too big" as corporations. We asked Gordon Moore, Chairman of the Board and a founder of Intel, if he saw any upper limit in size, an optimum number of employees beyond which Intel was not likely to grow, as a corporation? With a smile, he observed:

> We're in a business where you grow or you die. We'll grow as long as we can. We may start to worry when we get as big as IBM.
>
> Gordon Moore, Intel

Size, then, is not the issue. Instead, it is co-ordination, co-operation, information-sharing, maintaining a problem-solving focus, regrouping people into smaller work units, and maintaining collegial relationships via the quasi-structure of multiple teams and task forces.

Conclusions

In our judgment, the keys to the continued innovation success rates which these companies enjoy are to be found in their careful management of structure. This includes frequent, thoughtful re-examination of existing formal structures, in the light of changing technologies and markets. Enthusiasm for continual improvement of structure through reorganization provides a constant signal to employees that change is neither undesirable nor to be resisted. Willingness to change at need, and successful improvement of structure in response to employee concerns legitimate structural change. Managed effectively, structural change enables the firm to adapt to changed conditions.

This, in turn, requires a willingness to invest valuable time in structure *per se*. Formal reorganization costs time. So, too, do quasi-structural elements: cross-disciplinary, multi-level committees, task forces, and teams require fostering, attention, and support. Quasi-formal relationships to co-ordinate and exchange information are legitimated in these firms by widespread investment of time, including investment by senior managers who participate themselves as needed. Senior management commitment to the essential importance of quasi-structure is clearly not just lip-service. These executives vote by allocation of their own scarce personal time and attention, as well as the time and attention of others throughout the firm.

The interpersonal skills essential for working in organizations with extensive quasi-structural elements, like teamwork and co-operative ability, also underline the importance of quasi-formal structure. Those skills are increasingly used to assess managers' behavior. Hewlett-Packard now includes co-operation and team skills as variables by which employee performance is formally evaluated, for example, as do other firms. This recognition is among the most fundamental indicators of how important these issues are to the survival of the companies we have studied.

Our sample firms show a consistent pattern of structure – formal, quasi-formal, and informal – that encourages interchange and actively facilitates both innovative ideas and explicitly task-relevant co-operation. While they have thousands of employees, these companies organize clearly for innovation. They reorganize at need, and they retain the small company flavor by carefully fostering patterns of behavior usually associated with much smaller firms. These behaviors are encouraged by structure, but they are also an expected part of the culture, to which we shall turn in chapter 11.

Above all, it appears that effective, explicit, and deliberate management of structure to support innovation processes is a key to success in high-technology companies. This point is increasingly recognized by managers themselves, if not yet so widely in the organization theory literature as might be hoped. Contemporary innovation – particularly in research-intensive, high-technology industries – is a highly elaborate process, drawing on a wide array of technical specialties, as we have noted. Yet technology itself is by no means enough.

A dynamic tension between stability and change is required, providing enough clarity to operate these highly complex firms precisely, combined with sufficient flexibility to respond to constantly changing demands. Adept organizing for innovation is essential to continued success over time. Clear organizational structures, frequent reorganizations, and an extensive use of quasi-structure are significant contributors to the long-term innovative abilities of the high-technology companies we have studied: a dynamic tension between stability and change.

Notes

1 See, for example, three extensive reviews of the literature: Tornatzsky et al. (1983); Van de Ven (1986); and Van de Ven (1988). The Minnesota Innovation Research Program is an excellent example of contemporary research on innovation in organizations.

   In addition, a smattering of other works will illustrate the extensive literature on the management of innovation: see Hatch (1987); Jennings and Sexton (1985); Lundstedt and Colglazier (1982); Mintzberg and McHugh (1985); Prestowitz (1988); Tushman and Moore (1982); Tushman and Anderson (1986).

2 More extensive information on Texas Instruments in its earlier years, the 1940s through the mid-1970s, can be found in the book *Institutionalizing Innovation* (Jelinek, 1979). Haggerty was interviewed again, after publication of *Institutionalizing Innovation*, shortly before his death in 1980.

9

The Innovation Cycle

One thing we've done is we've tried to remove the barrier of transferring something from one group to another as much as we can. So we try to do the development close enough to the people that have to manufacture it – using the same equipment and the same people as far as we can – so that we avoid the "transfer" completely. We don't have a separate R&D laboratory. In our semiconductor area, for example, the development work is done right on the manufacturing floor, and anything we can get from manufacturing, we do. Theoretically, by the time the idea has been developed, it's already in manufacturing, and it doesn't have to go through this transfer at the time when it's not completely documented and nothing works except for the guy that believes it's going to work.

Gordon Moore, Intel

We really believed that one of the biggest problems in Fairchild's lack of success was the fact that one organization developed a technology or product, and then transferred it to another operating organization, in some other building five or ten miles away. So when Gordon Moore, Bob Noyce, and Andy Grove started the company, one of the absolute requirements in their opinion was that the product should be developed in a production facility, so that there was not a massive moving of the technology from one facility to another while it was in a fragile, relatively undeveloped state. So from our inception, we had that as a basic principle: that technologies would be developed right in a production facility.

Will Kauffman, Intel

The decision to design is really a joint decision. The decision must be agreed to by the engineering manager, because he judges feasibility of design. It's a decision made by the marketing manager, because he must make sure there's a place to sell it. It's a decision made by the product engineering manager, because he wants to view it as a manufacturable part, from his perspective. And then it's finally a decision by the product design manager, because he has to decide whether that's a reasonable place to invest his design efforts.

Karl Rapp, National Semiconductor

Into Development and Manufacturing

It is a long path from research, through development and into production for new products and technologies – from product idea initiation through prototype development to initial pilot line manufacturing and, for many products in this industry, on to high volume production. We refer to this as the innovation cycle.[1] To perpetuate a continuous cycle of innovation, we discovered that these companies simultaneously weave together several critical elements.

First, they maintain a dynamic tension between tightly scheduled R&D and innovation driven by serendipity and bootlegged resources, as we have described previously, but will see here again. Secondly, they are efficient facilitators of the movement of new knowledge into high volume production, and on into the marketplace. Commercialization, after all, provides the payoff for their innovation efforts. Yet again, dynamic tension operates here. These firms are efficient transmitters of new knowledge because each company strives to minimize barriers which otherwise impede sharing knowledge among groups. The firms are innovative because they cherish iconoclastic visions produced by highly disciplined engineers.

There are many nuances which contribute to efficient knowledge development and transfer into use. The paradox of discipline amidst serendipity and efficiency amidst innovation will be developed here. Throughout, it will be apparent that sheer complexity characterizes these firms and their activities – and that they have learned to manage it. They do not "complexify" unduly; they do cheerfully cope with what complexity seems essential.

Managing Transitions and Interfaces

Chapters 9 and 10 constitute the heart of what we have learned about the management of transitions and critical interfaces, with a special focus on the semiconductor industry. Since this industry leads all others in the US economy in its research and development intensity,[2] its managers have had extensive experience over time in learning how to deal with knowledge transitions across critical organizational boundaries: new products and technologies are constantly being introduced.

Fickle markets, global competition, and rapid scientific development (including some created by the semiconductor industry itself) now affect scores of other industries. These trends conspire to shorten product life cycles, just as they have for our firms. The trends argue powerfully that managing the conception, design, and delivery of new products will be at the heart of competition in the future. In short, constant innovation will be required across the board, in virtually all industries.

We will argue again in this chapter that a central issue in contemporary industrial competition is ensuring a free flow of innovative ideas amidst disciplined product/technology development, via the management of transitions and critical interfaces. We are tempted to say that these are tasks central to the successful management of innovation. Yet we have been tempted repeatedly in prior chapters to make similar claims – that cogent, persistent strategy, or effective organizing, or carefully balanced nurturance and filtering of a free flow of new ideas is central. None of these factors alone is sufficient. Rather, they mutually support one another in close interaction, a perspective this chapter will elaborate.

The successful practices we describe are all focused on deliberate innovation, persistent success, and repeated advances. In the highly complex environment faced by our firms, nothing less than carefully co-ordinated technical and managerial effort can possibly succeed: there are too many critical details that can go wrong. We believe other industries will become more like those we studied, partly because they, too, have begun to use electronics; or because they, too, have incorporated more science in an effort to counter increasing competition. Whatever the cause, they too face greater complexity and rates of change, and they too will discover the need to manage innovation effectively.

We begin this chapter's discussion by describing how these companies manage a classic dynamic tension between controls and innovative freedom – how these firms schedule planned new product and technology development, and simultaneously encourage innovation via serendipity and finagling of resources from supported projects.

From Concept to Volume Production

Every product was once simply an idea – a brilliant idea, an incomplete idea, half an idea, or several scattered pieces that combined to produce a winner. The original idea ultimately had to come together with the necessary wherewithal of other ideas, funding, technical know-how, others' assistance, manufacturing knowledge, marketing expertise, and commitment in order to get to the marketplace. Every industry that manufactures recognizes a set of roughly parallel steps and stages that new products go through, and many standard textbooks describe this process. Yet despite its commonality, this road from concept to production is problematical, lengthy, fraught with difficulty, and often poorly managed.

In the semiconductor industry, the path is still more difficult because of the sheer complexity of the manufacturing process, and the constant shifts and changes in product and process technology, no less than in markets. Success in semiconductor components has so far turned upon successful high volume production, and learning curve economies. It was not enough to be able to produce; the product had to be produceable at very high volume and with very high yields – cost control as well as excellence was demanded, in technologically advanced products.

In some other US industries, such as automobiles, for years quality was traded off against cost. Then global competition put more pressure on quality, proving that lower cost and higher quality went together in traditional manufacturing by providing consumers with high quality, low cost options. More recently, quality has become a central factor in competitive survival. The economics of semiconductor production have underscored the importance of quality in order to achieve viable production costs from early days. Simultaneous requirements for managing high complexity, low cost and high quality were initially met through high volume production and learning curve benefits. This strategy was particularly appropriate with commodity products, like general purpose DRAMs, or other widely applicable devices.

Today, the same demands for quality, economy, and technical mastery come into play even in specialized markets. Increasingly, in the future, custom or semi-custom products like ASICs (Application Specific Integrated Circuits) promise continued growth in complexity without high volume production of individual products on which to learn. In essence, this development turns the screw still tighter: low volume eliminates learning curve effects on any single product. To cope, electronics firms – and many others in traditional industries as well – must somehow master effective production even with increasing complexity and low volumes. To do so, they must utilize their knowledge across products, benefiting from economies of scope (Goldhar and Jelinek, 1983) to generate new products.

In many other industries – automobiles, running shoes, and even insurance offer examples – a similar push toward simultaneous requirements for high quality and cost control amidst increasing complexity have occurred. Increasingly too, those other industries are also seeing market fragmentation and growing demand for "custom" products. Capricious markets and repeated change have conspired to dramatically shorten product life cycles. In short, constant innovation will be required.

Interconnected "Stages" to Production

This chapter will describe the path from initial "aha!" through product concept, engineering, and on into volume production in our sample firms. There is much to be learned from their experience, both in its successes and in its difficulties. A framework of "early game" (distant forecasting and planning for technology); "transfer" from one innovator to another, through the necessary development "stages;" and "end-game" (manufacture and marketing) will guide our discussion.

The image of stages itself must be called into question, however, for whereas earlier thinking suggested a sequence of relatively independent stages that followed one another much like beads on a string, the view in electronics is different. As we shall argue, the steps and processes of constant innovation are far more interwoven, interdependent, and mutually involved. Rather than beads on a string, the interlaced fingers of clasped hands offer a more useful picture.

Different perspectives and managerial needs emerge along the way, yet in general in this business, the constant need for on-going innovation shapes the thinking of managers and technical people, engineers and executives. An overall, inclusive, general manager's perspective must link and guide the functional efforts of numerous specialists. These people must contribute to, blend with, and mutually reinforce one another. Different firms have developed different means to provide for the changing context of business needs along the innovation cycle. We shall describe some of the alternatives, focusing our account primarily on an individual firm's story at any one moment, but describing situations we found generally true. What is important is not any single firm or method, but the reality of a number of methods – and the underlying similarities of the linked transfer of an idea from concept to product to market, within a created context of on-going pressure for innovation and an overview of shared purpose.

Early Development Efforts: Exploration and Criteria for Finagling

It is old news that products are supposed to have life cycles. Indeed, product life cycles and the notion that products "are born," "grow," "mature," and ultimately "decline" are very much a part of popular wisdom. Similar ideas abound for technology life cycles, organizational life cycles, and industry life cycles. People talk of "sunrise" and "sunset" industries, for instance. The popular wisdom testifies to changing requirements and new challenges that arise over time. Research corroborates common sense, for some of the popular wisdom at least. Leaving aside the insidious ideas of definitive "life cycles," which suggest too certain a pattern, we will speak primarily of an innovation cycle.

On the front end of the innovation cycle, the process of innovation is primary. As we described in chapter 7, maintaining the free flow of ideas and creativity is essential. At the same time, not just "any" idea will do; there must be some connection with corporate needs (even with more local needs), and ultimately, with the market: the idea must translate eventually to a product that will make a profit. In our companies, there is a constant, visible, and explicitly maintained tension between liberty and control, freedom and responsibility. To keep things honest, the profit and results criteria must be explicit; to keep things free, these criteria must not be too tightly enforced, especially on the front end. There must be "wiggle-room," and tolerance for risk and even for occasional failure or fudging.

Engineers in these companies routinely "finagle" time to work on their own early ideas, which may or may not come to fruition, amidst the already tightly scheduled work they are assigned. Such finagling is expected and encouraged, within some loose limits, because it is seen as essential to continued motivation, continued creativity, continued participation by individuals. Jim Williams described his view of how finagling worked at National Semiconductor:

> This is a knuckle-slapping society. You go and you do what you want to until you get your knuckles slapped. If you really believe that you have the right to be doing what you want, you look up with fire in your eyes [when you get your knuckles slapped] . . . and say, "I'm going to work on this, because of this and that." He might say, "You know, that is the worst idea I've ever heard." I walk out of his office – and I just go off and I just do it.
>
> Jim Williams, National Semiconductor

National fosters creativity – as do all of our firms – by cherishing iconoclastic visions and polishing creative concepts. People who are only "competent," and not themselves deeply creative, can nevertheless make important contributions – if their efforts are guided, and brought to bear upon an idea that is creative. This phenomenon goes well beyond engineers, technical people, and product design as the sole sources of creativity, or even its most important parts. And it applies beyond National, to our other companies as well. Gordon Moore, Chairman of Intel, noted that non-technical expertise in defining the marketplace was an essential source of competitive advantage, even in his highly scientific, highly technical, leading-edge company:

> Engineering is a discipline. You can tell a guy to go design a product that has these characteristics, meanwhile letting him grind out the product. He can be a relatively non-creative

engineer and still do a very good job turning out the product that meets market demand, and so forth. And if we're far enough ahead, and have defined what the market needs, we come out pretty well.

Gordon Moore, Intel

Whether in defining a market and appreciating its potential, or seeing technical options, those who innovate are important; particularly at early stages, those who have the ideas themselves are the people best positioned to assess the potential of their efforts. Consequently, their alert attention to options and possibilities is an important resource. Another National engineer, Bob Pease, described this habit of mind, which he called his "serendipity hand:"

> Sometimes, [when you're] directing certain fractions of your effort in a scheduled product, then you have to keep your serendipity hand out. If something falls into it, you grab it quick and run like hell. You're a crook. That's your job.
>
> Bob Pease, National Semiconductor

Fortune favors the prepared mind, and an organizational context favoring innovation encourages people to be continually alert to new ideas that might shape, hone, or refine other ideas they are already working on. Relating ideas, inside an innovator's head, by virtue of their being worked on simultaneously, increases opportunism. "Stealing" good ideas and appropriating them to use in other projects isn't new. But the conscious attention to it, and specific management efforts to encourage such hybridization, are. Such efforts are pervasive among our sample of companies.

So, too, are the sorts of follow-up that spring from performance-based assessment criteria. It's OK to bend the rules a bit, for good reason and especially with good results. Finagling is sanctioned, recognized, and allowed – but employees are nevertheless held accountable for being productive. Indeed, they must be sufficiently productive to warrant the "off-time," "finagling," and resources (both time and others) "stolen" from official projects.

Boundaries and limits do exist, but seem to serve as guidelines, not absolute barriers. Rules exist to be bent, with appropriate attention. How is "appropriate" attention ensured? By yet another intermingling of formal systems and informal, individually internalized control methods. Rules are bent against a background of personal credibility and reputation. One need not be right, or on time, all the time; but one must be right much of the time – including on one's choice of when to bend a rule, reallocate one's time or efforts or resources – over the long haul.

Heroes and "Nudgey" Pressure

Having been given the freedom to bend the rule and "take ownership," did engineers still feel pressured or controlled in these companies? We wanted the perspective of the technical innovators, the engineers whom everyone wanted to schedule tightly, those who do not get much slack and yet are the essential resource for innovation. We asked several engineers whether they were under pressure to meet certain objectives, or whether high priority company objectives produced pressures for them. In response, Jim Williams, an engineer at National Semiconductor, described two kinds of pressure: that from inside the individual, because he or she enjoys the work, and "nudgey" pressure from "insidious" managers who convince engineers that they are doing what they want to be doing. Williams acknowledges being under constant pressure, but identifies his greatest source of pressure as himself:

> The pressure? Well, the most ultimately productive pressure in any situation is what comes from inside [you]. I'm under pressure constantly. There's a guy in the back of my head who's screaming. The driving force is ego: *I want it!* There's nothing wrong with ego if you channel it in the proper direction . . . If I were ever in a situation where I "worked for a living," where I found more pressure coming from outside than from inside, then it [would be] time to go.
>
> Jim Williams, National Semiconductor

"Nudging" from management certainly exists, according to Williams, but he regards nudging as an appropriate part of good management, an exercise in indirect control. Shared goals are important, and, since he and his managers want the same thing, achievement means that both he and his managers are pleased. Both want successful innovation:

> I'm not opposed to urging. To be nudgey is fine. In some cases, it's helpful . . . If you're a good manager, you always make sure that the way you exercise control is in a very indirect way. You

have to be very insidious about the whole thing . . . No one's
controlling me. But on the other hand, if I look at what [my
manager] is getting out of me, well, who's controlling whom?
By definition, that's a very successful situation, because, well,
gee: I don't know who's controlling whom, so we must all be
very happy.

Jim Williams, National Semiconductor

Williams's self-satirizing description as an engineer being managed
by nudging corresponds to Parker's description of the occasional
nudge given talented engineers at Intel. It appears that "running very
tightly," "scheduling people at 110 percent," but allowing engineers
to work on projects they ultimately find exhilarating are among the
secrets of continuous innovation at Intel, National, HP and other
companies of our sample. These people work hard, they are very
ambitious about what they can accomplish in a given period of time,
and they run on a fuel of intense motivation. Most appear to genuinely
enjoy what they do, even though time is "an awesome fact."

There is, necessarily, significant self-selection: those who cannot
thrive in such an environment will falter or leave. Engineers, scientists,
and managers who remain in highly demanding, high performance
companies like those in our sample are invigorated by the challenge.
These people live to make technical contributions. Bob Pease described
the privilege of doing his work his own way at National Semiconductor,
a privilege earned by "doing something financially rewarding for the
company:"

What do I get from this company for doing what I do? Well,
the most obvious thing is, I get money. Well, but I can get
money anywhere. I get the right and the privilege – it's only a
right after I've earned it – I get the privilege of doing what I've
been doing. You constantly have to earn your keep. There's no
free ride. If I want the freedom to define my work, then my
work damned well better do something for this company. That's
primarily what I get out of this company. You get the privilege
of trying to be a hero. If you're a hero one in three or one in
four times, or even one in five times, you will continue to be
allowed to attempt to be a hero. I get to run in my *modus operandi*
without too many questions as long as stuff comes out the other
end. That's the reward structure.

Bob Pease, National Semiconductor

Engineers at innovative companies like those we studied earn the opportunity to "do their own thing," within the broad arena of areas of interest to the firm. Earning the privilege of doing what they want to do, the freedom of defining their own work, and the opportunity to enjoy the esteem of technically capable peers motivates them far more than money. So, too, does the self-esteem that comes from working to "impossible" schedules, trying again and again to produce another winner. High performance in challenging tasks is itself rewarding and refreshing, despite and even because of what seems like pressure to an outside observer. High performance in one's own chosen endeavors, despite the pressure, is also motivating.

Of course, the official projects and deadlines are also still required. Jim Williams of National described the anticipated follow-up by a boss whose opinion he rejected:

> Now if he catches up with me four months later and says, "Oh, you went ahead and horsed around with that anyway," I'd better have some pretty good results: "Okay, *you've got to have some pretty good results.*" But more importantly, you better be fortified with the knowledge that, "Hey, my hunches have been good in the past, and I have the right to differ with you without being punished, without being intimidated on the spot." But I better have a good hunch!
>
> Jim Williams, National Semiconductor

Clearly, management at National (or at Intel, or any of our companies) does exercise indirect, perhaps even (as Pease and Williams have it) "insidious" and "intimidating" control over its employees' freewheeling ideas. However, these employees just as clearly have strong convictions of their own, and the support of management to maintain their views – a pattern widely observed among our firms. Individuals innovate vigorously, and defend their right to do so despite objections from others. The formal rules, systems, deadlines, and guidelines are corrected and held in tension by individual insight, expertise, and judgment.

People in our sample companies exhibit a recurrent pattern. They are expected to be good enough, enough of the time, to beneficially exploit bootleg ideas and material, equipment and space for "horsing around" – whether or not their managers initially agree with their ideas. Traditional bases for power like position in the organizational hierarchy, or "rules," seem balanced in our sample organizations by other forces: conviction that you're right, an encouraged willingness to resist "too much" control above, and a healthy appreciation by both managers and their subordinates that the aim is innovation, not today's status quo in products or markets or technology.

Track record, recognized expertise, persistence, and a convincing story also contribute to innovators' personal credibility and cumulative reputation for success. However, the innovators' efforts are far from chaotic, and certainly not ad hoc. The controls are often individual, internalized, and informal – but no less real.

The Front-End Filters: Domains of Inquiry

There is greatest room for independent action nearest to existing commitments – or for the most creatively successful innovators. This interplay is especially visible in the chosen domains of inquiry. The near-to innovations, closest to what is currently being done, can be important extensions of existing technology for product or process. The further-out innovations, more risky and probably more expensive, are undertaken more rarely.

Gordon Moore of Intel sees the company's basic domains as the first boundary, within which the technical specialists are encouraged to innovate. The boundaries guide innovation toward areas of established expertise, yet are permeable, enabling significant expansions of domain from time to time. But those boundaries are necessarily real; with the explosion of scientific knowledge, there are far too many options, not too few. These companies expressly renounce trying to be "all things to all people," and turn their efforts instead to a chosen field of inquiry:

> We focus our people. They are all working in a fairly narrow direction, and it's almost inconceivable that one of them is going to come up with an idea based on his work that's very far outside of the area we have him in . . .
>
> Fortunately, our plate's pretty full in the areas where we're already involved. There's a lot of room for them to roam within the technology and the general kind of products we're doing. But we're vulnerable in that we're not going to invent – well, we missed the revolution that's occurring in genetic engineering, for example. That is the other big high-technology field that's developing, and Intel didn't do anything in it. You know, we're five years too late, now. There's no way we're going to come up with something that's dramatically different [there].
>
> We happen to be in an area where there's lot of innovation in

the electronics area. There's plenty to do here, so we're just not letting people roam far afield. We don't encourage it a heck of a lot.

We occasionally try to do something to at least give some small group somewhat more freedom, so they can explore some outside ideas. But these are pretty small groups.

Gordon Moore, Intel

Underlying Intel's currently chosen domain at any time is a tension between two tests: a theoretical/technical test of what should be theoretically possible, based on science; and a real-time marketplace test, based on what customers want or can understand, what competitors are doing, and what can in fact be accomplished in the present, with existing resources, or near to existing resources (of talent, knowledge, funding and the like). Any firm's domain is bounded by the world of technical, theoretical limits on one side, and by marketplace realities on the other. Both choices and the consequences of past choices are real factors to be taken into account, although by no means absolutes.

Intel's basic focus rests upon the firm's commitment to underlying technologies and intentions, defined in a broad sense:

It's a very wide rut, I think, which saves us. We certainly try to define overall corporate strategy, the kinds of things we want to do, and the kinds of things we don't want to do.

Gordon Moore, Intel

Nevertheless, even ideas and technologies that might appear to others to be closely related may not be perceived as appropriate within the firm. Nor do the decision makers believe they always choose well. According to Moore, he, himself, has missed some opportunities that seemed obvious in retrospect:

Something like the personal computer – we really were presented with an opportunity to take a shot at it. It wasn't articulated to be what Apple has turned out to be. It was just, "Hey, you can make a nice little computer here, and the housewives are going to use them for recipes and such." I just couldn't imagine my wife sitting there poking buttons to get a recipe out of her computer. You know, I don't think these guys *have* wives!

No, the idea of a computer in the home was just ridiculous. Maybe a thousand engineers wanted that kind of capabil- ity . . . We never appreciated that that was just the way the idea of the personal computer got started – everybody wanted to control his own little computer resource . . . So there, we just didn't appreciate what the possibilities were.

Gordon Moore, Intel

Moore's self-satire about having failed to see the potential of the personal computer reveals another aspect of choice: recognition that mistakes will be made, upon occasion. It isn't expected that senior officers – or anyone else – will always make correct decisions.

For Intel, as for other large companies, new ideas at entry stages are often quite unclear; if not, they could scarcely be "new" ideas. Thus occasional failure is calmly anticipated, and accepted as inevitable, to be learned from. The issue is to be right often enough, not to be right every time. Above all, the firm's choice must rest on a balance between trusting the judgment of technical people, and somehow perceiving new potential:

> That's a typical big company problem, I think. At that stage of the formation of an idea, it was kind of a gut feeling on the part of these people that there was something useful there, and they couldn't articulate it in a way that we could understand it. You know, I'm a chemist by background. The technology, I'm comfortable with. But who wants a computer at home? In spite of the fact that we're reasonably receptive to new ideas, this one just bounced off us, as not being something that fit at all.

Gordon Moore, Intel

A constructive, dynamic tension is maintained between theoretical or technical possibilities and marketplace vision in our firms. Ideas conflict and compete, yet generally do so in a useful fashion, rather than in destructive contention. Recognizing the inevitability of occasional failure seems to translate into a far greater tolerance for differences of opinion, thus de-escalating contention. On-going innovation is not a purely rational process, but rather the outcome of *productive* tensions of the sorts we have been describing. Nowhere is this more evident than in the maintenance of the free flow of innovation we described earlier.

Since ideas do sometimes get turned down or fail, occasional "noes" or "failures" must be kept in perspective. Maintaining people's commitment, enthusiasm, and alertness, despite the limits and occasional failures, is a genuine issue. This is particularly so for technical people, according to Moore:

Technical people like to work. In fact, the better ones seem difficult to drive out, when they're working on any sort of project: that's where they are. Most of them would be perfectly happy if all you did was shut them in a room with all of the facilities they needed to do their technical work, and occasionally gave them something challenging to deal with. So the real problem in providing direction is, putting barriers in makes them unhappy . . . That's the biggest problem with technical people – you can frustrate them relatively easily.

Gordon Moore, Intel

Nevertheless, barriers and direction are important: innovation may flow freely, but the outcome is not free-form. Real guidance does exist, and it shapes innovative efforts. The clear criterion here – fit with the company's current strategic commitments – is not so much a precise directive as a starting point for discussion, according to Moore:

We talked about it. One of our guys, one of the engineers, was very strong that this was something useful. In fact, I think we talked about it at one of our long-range planning sessions, and decided that we had other things to do that were much more obviously good opportunities. We didn't encourage that at all. Also, that was at the time we were smarting under the watch business, and this just felt like a consumer product. That, maybe, didn't encourage us any either.

Gordon Moore, Intel

Having suffered along with other components makers in attempting to enter the consumer products markets with watches, Intel too retreated from its efforts in watches and the stillborn computer opportunity. Instead, the firm focused once again on broadly defined key areas of expertise, technology, product categories, and markets.

Similar major thrusts and refocusings are visible in each of our sample companies. Broadly defined "ruts" of product and process technology, market and customer needs emerge. These are the operational specifics of company strategies, maintained and evolved by relatively directed innovative efforts. These thrusts cohere, over time, and are rarely (although occasionally) changed. In short, strategy does enter, quite explicitly if in the very broadest terms, to guide innovation. Broadly construed strategic fit is not the only benchmark, however, nor the most emphatic.

In summary, domains are deliberately defined, most typically in terms of existing expertise. They are extended, elaborated, and evolved through a complex interplay of the possible and the "realistic" – itself an individual, creative vision that must be tested in balance between theory and the marketplace. The interplay of strategic intentions, at a fairly high level of generality as "limits," and informal, individual creativity shapes and guides innovation efforts. We turn next to marketplace limits.

Early Marketplace Criteria

Amidst the diversity of ideas and perspectives on different technologies, a single criterion emerged again and again as essential to success in the semiconductor industry, voiced by engineers and technical people as well as managers: marketplace success. The shared aim among all these companies, their managers and designers, is to create products that make money. Products that fail to meet customer needs, or focus unduly on "engineering elegance" without regard to manufacturing realities, or simply are not appropriately targeted, will fail.

How do these companies "guess" correctly frequently enough to gain an acceptable return for their innovative efforts? One secret is to keep their innovators tightly attuned to marketplace needs. Charles Sporck was very clear about this maxim among National Semiconductor's engineers:

> . . . Most engineers recognize that success represents a product that sells successfully. Not just "a great product," but "a product that sells successfully."

How do the engineers know this, we asked? Are they taught?

> They just know. Six months after a newly graduated engineer is hired, you're up to your ears with what the competition is all about. They pick that up. The thing that drives them is beating the competition, getting a product out there that sells, getting customer recognition. It's not something we do formally . . .
>
> Charles Sporck, National Semiconductor

The criterion is built into the culture at National, according to Jim Williams:

> Here [at National] the reward structure – and I don't mean just money, I'm talking about what peer group you establish yourself in, how many people smile at you when you walk down a hall,

and just how comfortable you feel when you walk in, in the morning – that's what I'm defining as the reward structure – the reward structure ultimately is defined in terms of "Does your stuff sell?"

Jim Williams, National Semiconductor

Others at National echoed this view. Barry Siegel, an engineering manager, referred to a measureable, management version of Williams's criterion. Siegel, like other managers, linked this marketplace criterion very directly to innovation:

> Our accountability as engineers is higher than in other industries. The amount a given engineer is supposed to produce, say in terms of investment in his salary and other related costs, is much higher than in other industries. The personal accountability is much higher. We must innovate in order to run the company.
>
> Barry Siegel, National Semiconductor

The marketplace focus goes hand in hand with our sample firms' highly elaborated science base – the specialists' accountability is both technical and economic. Ensuring appropriate marketplace awareness to temper the designers' and engineers' and technicians' creative ideas is an on-going effort. This is not "marketing's problem," and the technical people seem to take pride in their difficult task, and in the fact of competition. There are frequent reminders of the companies' adversaries. Barry Siegel explicitly linked his CEO's expectations with his view of competition:

> It's a no quarter shown, no quarter asked, no holds barred, free enterprise, all bare-fisted battle. Charlie [Sporck] will not be satisfied, for example, until we bury the Japanese – until we bury TI, Charlie is not going to bloody well rest. Or whoever else he sees in our way.
>
> Barry Siegel, National Semiconductor

Jim Williams spoke more directly of the impact of the outside world on creative efforts:

> You have to marinate engineering crazies in the fluid of the real world. That's what you have to do. We get product ideas all of the time. If you look at the ratio of product ideas to the stuff that gets built around here, it's a very big number. That's because of the marinating process that you have to go through.
>
> Jim Williams, National Semiconductor

This "marinating" process, at National, comes from repeated, on-going contact with customer problems. The result is a thought process focusing on problem-solving, and on real problems, not some arcane notion of "engineering excellence" abstracted from reality, as Siegel illustrated:

> What the hell *does* the customer want? What *are* his needs? What does he want to pay for it? What are his problems? And I'm looking. Here's a full pile of the customer's problems [waves a hand]. If we could do it for four bucks, we'd be heroes. He doesn't know how to do it for four dollars. In fact, he doesn't have a clue. In fact, he's a little naive. But how can we come up with a way of making the customer happy? If we do, we'll be rich, famous, and there'll be a path to our door.
>
> Barry Siegel, National Semiconductor

What emerges in these companies is a picture of deep personal engagement and involvement in creating new ideas that address real needs. These people are highly motivated, highly energized toward creating – and highly driven toward creating "successful" ideas, ideas that ultimately sell at a profit. The prime mover is not engineering elegance; instead, it is something akin to playing with new ideas, tempered by a competitive, almost combative desire to best the competition in the marketplace by meeting some customer's need. The thrill of the chase, intrinsic creativity, delight in somehow succeeding around and despite routine responsibilities, pleasure in finagling, satisfaction at demonstrated success against the challenging criterion of the market, beating the opposition – all play important roles. The discipline is provided by marketplace criteria: does the product sell at a profit?

Linked Transfer, from Concept to Product

Practice and theory come together in a linked transfer process – deliberately managed and facilitated passage of nascent ideas through various filters and decision points, to resources, development, and ultimately production, if they are not abandoned. We have already indicated that the notion of "stages" is somewhat misleading. In fact, the "stages" are not nearly so discrete, nor the boundaries between them so clean, as a "stages" model would indicate. Nevertheless, stages offer us a place to begin; we will complicate our vision later.

For any particular new product, we can readily chart the course of rising costs as investment in the innovation accrues, prior to the product's launch into the marketplace; or the rising number of people involved as a product moves from conception into development and on into production. Once a product is into production, a related concept, the learning curve, fairly reliably forecasts the expected reduction of manufacturing costs as unit volume accumulates under traditional manufacturing technologies as a result of increased worker proficiency, process improvements, and perhaps product redesign for easier manufacture as knowledge increases. So-called "S-curves" (Foster, 1986) suggest that such gains eventually level out, and products (as well as technologies) eventually tail off.

These basic ideas suggest the widely established steps of the classic product life cycle, depicted in figure 9.1. Each stage addresses a different task – envisioning the initial concept; refining the concept and blending it with other specialized insight; designing efficient production processes; actually manufacturing it. Each step requires different management skills and perspectives, is governed by different criteria, and, ideally, different organizational emphases.

Our discussion so far has centered on generating innovations. The initial stage, prior to commercial introduction, is necessarily the most creative or innovative stage, where fewest constraints are committed to, most possibilities reside, and the greatest number of ideas is needed as the seedbed for what is ultimately developed. As we have argued, the central issue here is ensuring a free flow of innovative ideas. Continued development of the new idea and product (or process) introduction must follow. For successful products, a growth stage typically sees volume production. Maturity and the wind-down follow, as product sales decline (Kotler, 1980).

Generic Innovation: Technology Families and Generations

Technology families and generations also operate as a form of filter, guiding innovation in broad terms. In our companies, rather than aiming at a single innovation, research focuses on more fundamental, programmatic efforts that will spin off an entire family of products,

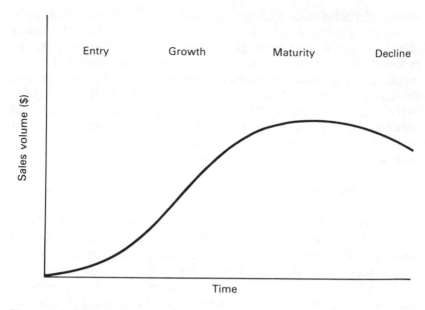

Figure 9.1 Classic Product Life Cycle

through developmental generations over time. For example, Gerry Parker, Intel's Vice President and Director of Technical Development, pointed out why Intel had rejected what had otherwise looked like a hot technology – and what Intel looks for instead in terms of development opportunity:

> It didn't look like a good long-term technology that would be here for ever, and that's one of the things that we try to do. If we're going to go in a direction, we make sure that it's good for more than one product, or one generation. We really like to carry a program. That gives you some continuity and it allows you to continue to develop.
>
> Gerry Parker, Intel

This approach means that longer-horizon, more major technology-based efforts – like the process innovation efforts identified by other manufacturing researchers (e.g. Hayes and Wheelwright, 1984) but linked, here to product families and generations, which are dependent on "technology" or process advances – are interspersed with shorter-term, more incremental efforts that seem to focus more on individual products. The idea is to deliberately wring more benefit from every hard-won technical advance.

The longer-term innovations create technical possibilities; the shorter-term increments assure that these possibilities are fully exploited. In essence, this approach to managing the pace of innovation constitutes an "economies of scope" (Goldhar and Jelinek, 1983) benefit, garnered by re-using knowledge or information inherent in the major innovation in multiple applications to related product families and generations.

To help sustain a continuous stream of product innovations, Intel also strives for constant process improvement, and manages repeated changes in its manufacturing processes. These incremental improvements sustain the logic of a basic technology over time by expanding its capabilities toward their logical limits, persevering rather than being satisfied with an initial success. Incremental process changes also help to extract additional benefits from existing process knowledge, equipment, and experience by expanding their production range. Even with new production processes, and "new technology" products, often not all previous production steps are changed. Instead,

> In a new process, maybe we only change 30 percent to 40 percent of the steps, and then we use the other 60 percent [already in place]. That makes life a little easier. But if you go from a silicon gate to a planar process to a V-MOS process, then go jump to something else yet again [each of these a major technology shift, allowing virtually no retention of prior equipment, steps and expertise], you can't build on a [technology] base. You start from scratch again, and that just takes too long. It's too inefficient. So you have to stick with something that will continue for a while. Our intent is always to achieve our goals with a minimum of perturbation [in the existing process technology].
>
> Gerry Parker, Intel

That inherent conservatism and consistency should exist here, maintained at the edge of the state of the art and amidst persistent technological change, may be somewhat surprising. However, the logic is impeccable: fad and fashion count for far less here than pragmatic accomplishment of very specific goals of better yields, tighter tolerances for circuit width, and the like.

Prior knowledge, pushed by incremental changes, yields an extra dividend in supporting another generation, another member of a developmental product family. Wringing another product, further sales and profits, and the established basis for new efforts from existing commitments levers prior attainments directly into preparation for the future. Given the size of required contemporary investments in technology generations – a wafer fabrication line (a "fab") can run to tens of millions of dollars – it may be that such a paradoxical commitment to innovation via conservatism is essential to survival.

In summary, our sample companies consciously seek to avoid or minimize the costs associated with dramatic shifts in production or product technology, while still maintaining highly advanced capabilities. Their technology development strategy minimizes costs by maximizing the benefits from prior learning, stretched through incremental changes, while constantly looking for the next technology, as well.

One visible pattern is persistence, guided by theoretical understanding:

> [Given the theoretical knowledge that it ought to work], then we *make* it work! A lot of our development is based on theoretical knowledge. We take a look at it, and we say, "Is there any reason why it shouldn't work, for fundamental reasons?" Then we say, "OK, then we should be able to make it work." So, we've gone to much thinner [silicon] gates, very thin gate-type electronics which gives us very high performance. Again, there is no fundamental reason why that shouldn't work.
>
> Gerry Parker, Intel

Innovation is not a matter of intuition or serendipity – although, of course, managers will take that when they can get it. Most of the time, innovation rests on systematic perseverance, guided by scientific theory. When the theory doesn't appear to be working out in practice, Parker asserted, they "keep plugging" on the application, the empirical problem, until they have resolved the roadblock. The same phenomenon, from another perspective, is visible in the pattern of fewer major innovations, interspersed by more, and more frequent, incremental innovations. Persistence insures fuller exploitation of discoveries, and harvests the potential that "pure creativity," or serendipity, or intuition may well have contributed to.

Intel's experience is not unique. Parker's exposition captures an important cluster of characteristics widely visible among successful companies. Our sample companies persist, they rely heavily on theoretical analysis, and they trust their theory, mathematics, and physics – even when problems are recalcitrant:

Occasionally, we do run into problems where it doesn't work. But we say, "There is no reason why in hell it doesn't work." We've got a specific case out at Livermore right now. We were trying to grow thin gates on a new process and the defect densities were enormous on that. We couldn't understand why. It turned out that some equipment we were using was introducing some contamination that we really didn't know about. So, once we fixed that problem, all of a sudden, it's as it should be.

So, in that sense, you try to understand fundamentally and theoretically, "Is the system going to work?" And then you must *make it work*. You really have to at that point solve the manufacturing and engineering problems. When we get an idea or a direction that we want to go with, we pretty much brute force it and say, "We are *going* to make this work." [At this stage] there are very few things that we kill or give up on. If we give up every time we run into problems, then that's no good!

Gerry Parker, Intel

Transcending Stage Barriers

The widely recognized product–process–market stages suggest different emphases, different perspectives, different skills at different points in the innovation process. *De facto* recognition of these differences is to be found in the frequent separation of activities along the developmental time line. Thus research activities are often separated from development, and development from manufacturing, and so on. Activities are separated because those performing them or managing them perceive that the activities are significantly different. Ultimately, however, the separate activities must be re-integrated – a single flow must stretch seamlessly from product concept to the marketplace. Early stages, when new ideas are needed, have been described. We will turn now to later stages of development.

Re-integration is difficult. In most companies, different departments are given responsibility for different development facets. As previous research has shown, different departmental orientations evolve to a mutually reinforcing constellation of other differences. The standard departmentalization of research, development, engineering and manufacturing, and marketing (for instance), has been shown to produce different time horizons, different patterns of authority and interaction, and different views of environments and of environmental uncertainty in older businesses (Chandler, 1967, 1977; Dearborn and Simon, 1958; Lawrence and Lorsch, 1967). Such differences are to be seen even in more recent industries (Litterer et al., 1985; Wilkof, 1988).

These differences can create barriers to innovation. Bridging the gap, in high-technology industries like aerospace, electronics, and computers, is typically the responsibility of project managers. They run development projects to co-ordinate the many specialists and efforts needed to produce a new product. In the aerospace industry, quite often these program managers are co-ordinating administrators who do not contribute to the project's technical development in a material way. By contrast, the semiconductor firms we studied made certain that program managers were also key technical contributors. Their technical expertise was both honed and utilized by development projects, while their managerial skills developed. Technical contributions were an important source of project managers' authority, as Gerry Parker noted:

> [Program managers are] engineers, very definitely from engineering. In that sense, they are expected to contribute technically to the project. It's not what you would call classical administrative management. Usually the program managers are people who were designers or process engineers by training.
>
> Gerry Parker, Intel

Such an emphasis might be considered "routine" in a highly technological company, no more than we should expect in light of the firm's dependence upon science. Yet there is a deeper point here: relevant expertise and task-focused problem solving, not status or hierarchy, are at center stage. Moreover, the engineers in project management positions are steeped in a more inclusive view that goes well beyond their technical background. This is a topic to which we shall return; for the moment, it suffices to mark the interdisciplinary bent of *technically capable* project managers as one important element in transcending barriers that might impede innovation.

Incremental Transfer through Time-Lapped Teams

A closer look at the development and transfer process reveals important cross-functional and cross-unit interfaces, and also uncovers its complex, dynamic character. Kim Kokkonen, an Intel Project

Manager in Static RAM Development cited earlier, described development work on "a new technology" – a new manufacturing process – for which his team was responsible:

> New technologies are defined by starting with a market demand. Where we work is with the Memory Components Division. They say, "We need a new kind of memory, and it has to have these kinds of characteristics." We take that input and try to define some characteristics of the technology which would allow those kind of product characteristics to be achieved.
>
> Kim Kokkonen, Intel

The formal group responsible for generating new product ideas at Intel is part of the Strategic Business Segment (SBS) within which Product Planning Committees reside. Kokkonen described how these committees work, and how they interface with the development activities that he managed:

> These product planning committees . . . are part of the SBS, a formal mechanism that we deal with. For each particular product, there are a couple of documents that are required to be generated as part of the [new product] approval cycle. One is called the POS – for Product Objective Specification – where marketing will put down the characteristics that they see in the marketing study that they've done, and we respond to that with something called the Response to POS. We respond with what we think the technology can do, set up a target specification, [and] schedule a contract. Then those two documents are put together and approved, if they're suitable.

While Technology Development groups respond to Product Planning Committee requests for new technologies and products, Kokkonen explained that sometimes development efforts are modified quite substantially, should market signals shift significantly:

> I guess our biggest problem with marketing is that their job deals with a very inexact science. They're always dealing with a lack of information, a lack of trusted information, to a large extent with rumors and second-hand information . . . As a result, they kind of vacillate, sometimes. And sometimes, with justification, they change their minds. A year into the development of our project, they'll say, "Well, sorry, what we said was totally wrong. The market has changed. We want you to do this, instead of that."

With commendable restraint, he remarked, "Of course, that sort of impedes us." Yet his restraint was unforced, recognizing both the frustrations of unanticipated changes of direction and the ultimate marketplace criterion against which all development efforts would be tested.

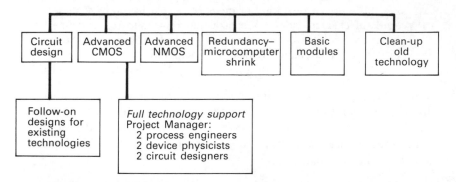

Figure 9.2 SRAM Technology Development Organization

The Static RAM Technology Development department included 35 engineers and "five or six" program managers at any time. Kokkonen's group worked on Advanced CMOS, and he described his responsibilities and groups diagrammatically (see Figure 9.2).

Kokkonen's department included one group working on an advanced CMOS process; a few people working to clean up a technology previously transferred into manufacturing; others working in advanced NMOS but attacking a different market segment; a fourth "doing redundancy" to shrink the number of circuits on a chip; a fifth designing circuits to take advantage of new technologies already developed; and, finally, a basic module development group working on fundamental equipment capabilities, like lithography, to be implemented as part of the technology being developed.

> They [module development people] depend heavily on the type of photo-lithographic capabilities that we have. Like how narrow a line can we make repeatedly, and how good does that look [vis-à-vis upcoming requirements]. These people do nothing but look at new types of optical equipment, trying to make them work well for us. And then, we'll take the sort of thing that they've developed here and implement it as part of the full technology [for a new process].
>
> Kim Kokkonen, Intel

Meticulous attention to each of these facets – developing slightly different versions of the technology; considering different market needs; pushing technical achievements into smaller, more efficient packages; extending basic capabilities; and following up on previous successes to further exploit established capabilities – all witness to systematic attention to harvesting the benefits of each innovation.

These efforts also testify to the importance of the end-game. Here, as in other endeavors, "it isn't over, till it's over:" bringing an innovation into profitable commercialization means attention to the grubby details apparently less glorious than "innovation," but absolutely crucial to realizing its benefits. Pre-product, pre-production activities as well as development well after initial product design and manufacture, all play their roles.

Looking closer still, the development calendar becomes still more complex. To ensure timely innovation within a given area or facet, multiple efforts take place simultaneously, and proceed in an interrelated fashion, Kokkonen noted. Related SRAM projects are started at staggered intervals, avoiding a simultaneous resource demand on auxiliary (but essential) technology support groups.

Figure 9.3 depicts a six-year time horizon. The typical SRAM-TD project's life was three years at the time the chart was drawn. Related follow-on projects were initiated with approximately one-year time-lags. Thus figure 9.3 notes the time-lagged relationships between three projects which have been started at intervals of about a year. More recently, these time intervals have been shortened considerably, as Intel along with the rest of our sample companies strives to hasten the pace of innovation. As circuitry has become more complex, Computer Aided Design (CAD) and Computer Aided Engineering (CAE) have become essential, and have greatly shortened the product development and design cycles, which in turn increases the demand for Technology Development projects. At Intel, Technology Development requires the simultaneous design of at least two new products to test a new technology's capabilities. Kikkonen explained how the projects overlap to work in tandem:

> So let's say that there are three groups here that are working on a full technology at any one time [within Advanced CMOS]. Generally what will happen is that we will stagger them [see figure 9.3]. That is, say this [points] is the "start" and this is the "stop" of a project. A three-year development program is

typically what we have, staggered year by year, so that when mine finishes, we will have learned enough from these next ones down here, and have enough new market inputs that it will be fairly easy to decide what to do here.

Kim Kokkonen, Intel

A "technology" here means a particular production process sequence, intended to produce a particular set of product characteristics. In a very deliberate and systematic way, technology and product are developed simultaneously. As Kokkonen's diagrams and comments suggest, development projects also seek mutual support and interaction, attained by pursuing multiple aspects or possibilities of a technology in parallel. The projects identified in figure 9.3 are related members of a technology family, envisioned as mutually reinforcing, rather than independent efforts. In essence, the activities represented

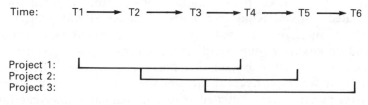

Time: T1 ⟶ T2 ⟶ T3 ⟶ T4 ⟶ T5 ⟶ T6

Project 1:
Project 2:
Project 3:

Figure 9.3 Time Overlaps among Three SRAM Technology Development Projects

by figure 9.3 are one level down in detail from the organization chart of figure 9.2; those in figure 9.4 are down another level yet. As figure 9.3 suggests, the knowledge gained by Project 1 in its first twelve months of development is substantially more than that Kokkonen and his six engineers might have been able to generate working by themselves on the technology. Because two additional groups are working in tandem with his project during the first year – Process Reliability and the Technology Exploitation Group – Project 2 starts up with a much broader, deeper base of knowledge.

Figure 9.4 outlines the fine-grained overlap even more strongly, as Kokkonen looked inside a project for us:

The responsibilities in this time frame [of 24 to 36 months] are split up. NTE (New Technology Engineering) is responsible for any manufacturing sort of experiments. Say they think that a piece of equipment we're using is not the optimum one. They think they have something better. They'd be responsible for evaluating that. Whereas we [the Static RAM Development Project members] would be responsible for completing the reliability qualification, completing the yield requirements, and completing the circuit performance characteristics within this time frame.

When NTE gets involved, there's a meeting which sets up the requirements for transfer, and that's generally a pretty lengthy list of things that we have to complete. It defines who is responsible for what in that last year [of the development calendar]. So here, [at 24 months into the development process] they're making sure that we have a manufacturable technology, and we're making sure that we meet our original development goal, and hopefully, at this time we're reaching something that's relatively close. [By 36 months] that's basically an interface with Fab [Fabrication].

Kim Kokkonen, Intel

Intel's Multiple Simultaneous Clocks

The relationship with NTE was only one of a complicated set of relationships (as sketched in figure 9.4). Throughout this account, Kokkonen stressed interchange among the parties with responsibility for various facets of development, and efforts overlapping in time. Simultaneity and clear responsibility are both visible here:

We do a lot of interfacing with Reliability Engineering. There are a well-defined series of qualifications that any of our new technologies or products have to go through before they can be released to customers. There are two groups. One is called Process Reliability, the other Product Reliability. Again, using this line [the time line in figure 9.4], during about the first year and a half of the project, we will be involved with Process Reliability, because we haven't defined – we haven't actually designed – any products, any technology. All we have are test patterns. Process Reliability is expert in evaluating those sorts of things.

About a year and a half after we're into the project, though, we will have defined our first product, and designed it, and gotten parts out [i.e. manufactured samples]. There will be some overlap period, but from there until the transfer [to Manufacturing], Product Reliability can be involved with us.

We're also involved with Product Engineering, and in this case, this is Portland [Oregon], since the products that we design are always memories, and the Memory Products Division is in Portland. These people will be involved in this time frame here [points to Product Engineering in figure 9.4], and at the point of transfer, they take over responsibility for everything. The responsibility of these people is to define the manufacturing test programs that are used, just to get the product out in the marketplace.

There is also a Technology Development Test Engineering Group. These people supply the test equipment. The very first testing that's done on our new circuits will be done by these people before it ever gets into the actual manufacturing environment. Up until close to transfer, they will also be testing, as part of our evaluation.

                                        Kim Kokkonen, Intel

Kokkonen's description reveals time-lapped teams with simultaneous, yet clear and mutually reinforcing responsibilities designed into a carefully thought-out, rather elaborate process of development. This is purposeful, systematic, and aggressive management of the development process. It is abundantly clear that these efforts are anything but ad hoc or loosely managed. The practices described here are interwoven into a complex web of mutual support, encouragement, and developmental assistance which may be summarized around five points.

Early efforts (1) to begin the process of setting product characteristics, and (2) relating these to process characteristics, long before anything can be exact or precise, lay out some of the directions in which the proposed new product will push existing manufacturing technology. Likewise, efforts (3) to begin identifying relevant limits to existing manufacturing capabilities point to where developmental efforts will be required. The "longer clock" of production technology development translates here into both technology push and market pull. As products create demands, (4) they "pull" technology development; as manufacturing technology is advanced, (5) its capabilities create "push" for the product characteristics enabled by the advances. This interaction involves the concept of related product families and generations, as well as a long-term comprehension within manufacturing of marketplace needs.

The initial design process illustrates some of the interaction. Inherent in some early, fundamental design decisions are implications

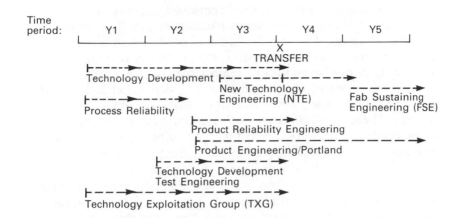

Figure 9.4 Transfer of an SRAM Technology Development Project into Manufacturing

for constraints and demands that will take effect only much later in the design cycle, when manufacturing actually begins. Of course this is true of essentially all design; it is not a characteristic limited to semiconductors. By initiating discussion of manufacturing characteristics simultaneously with product design, Intel maximizes the possibility of interplay to support sound trade-offs, and guarantees its manufacturing staff the longest possible lead-time. This leadtime translates into time for preparation, equipment evaluation, experimentation, reliability requirements, tests and the like. Because development is continual, manufacturing is an equal partner with design, sometimes leading product designers rather than following them.

The benefits of such interactions are equally complex. By initiating simultaneous development in product and process groups – among manufacturing technology and process technology experts at the same time as designers are at work – greater compression of the development calendar can be achieved. Note, too, that having standing groups responsible for on-going attention to improving process capabilities, test capabilities, quality, and yield also pushes capabilities independently of any individual new product design – or of the happenstance of some individual engineer or technical person or manager who might be interested. These formal arrangements institutionalize attention to development tasks for the long term. Such on-going activities sustain an atmosphere of continued improvement.

In semiconductors, well-known parameters like line definition – how fine a circuit line can be reliably produced in an integrated circuit, microprocessor, or memory – seem always relevant. So, too, do ever more precise control of temperature and material purity, or more precise control of gas mixtures and deposition layers. Other industries have other key capabilities that contribute directly to success. These capabilities are both the outcome of "round one" of a new product specification, and the input or baseline for subsequent members of the same product family, sharing a similar architecture and technology; and for subsequent generations, sharing somewhat enhanced characteristics. Only continued attention to relevant details will yield the improvements essential to continued participation in a demanding market, where others too are pushing the technology for competitive advantage.

It would be difficult to overstate the importance of, and the shift from traditional practice embedded in, this description. Existing project administration literature, going well back through the last two decades, has sought clarity and specificity in project or task responsibility, in order to avoid overlap or ambiguity, much as early management literature on "chain of command" did. Implicitly, the hand-off of project responsibility from one group to another constitutes a clean break in responsibilities, with little blurring of boundaries. Implicitly, the criterion for hand-off is sufficient clarity to enable the new group to take up its work independently.

In contrast, the process described here explicitly embraces another view: that overlap is inherent in the process, and that there is no such thing as a clean hand-off, or a determinedly hierarchical management of innovation. Instead, staggered concurrency of development efforts, along with interactive yet defined responsibilities, compels different groups to interface constantly. Overlap, contact, and negotiation are the norms here, with no illusions about chains of command or cleanly distinguished responsibilities.

Rippling Interface: Multiple Masters

Dual charters are obvious in Kokkonen's development group, which simultaneously serves two "product masters:" Memory Components and the Microcomputer Division. As a consequence, his group develops technologies that work both with static RAMs and with microcomputer products. These dual responsibilities entail further simultaneous interfacing with yet another additional set of groups:

> There's a group called TXG, which stands for Technology Exploitation Group, that is part of the Microcomputer Division. Their function is to make sure the technologies we define are suitable for what their product's going to be. They actually get involved very early, right at the beginning of the thing. They are essentially involved throughout the entire development. Basically they attend all our meetings, make sure that what we're doing is consistent with their needs, and also design the first microcomputer products to utilize the technology, to check it out in that sense.
>
> Kim Kokkonen, Intel

The Technology Exploitation Group had additional reciprocal responsibilities, in that they represented Kokkonen's group and its efforts to other groups in the Microcomputer Division, with whom they more directly interfaced in their own divisional project development efforts. Kokkonen appreciated the carefully interwoven network of contacts:

> I think it's an excellent concept for a group. It really helps us because, for example, the process I'm working on now, there are six or seven different microcomputer groups that want to use the technology. If I had to spend time talking every week to all of those different people, I wouldn't get anything done. TXG acts as a kind of funnel – they go off and interface with all the others.
>
> Kim Kokkonen, Intel

The fluency of Kokkonen's description belies the complexity of these interface relations. The web of shared knowledge and technological potential knits the firm's capabilities into a mutually reinforcing fabric of development. Diverse groups, whose chief responsibilities lie in quite different stages of the development process, are blended, and the boundaries between these groups and their responsibilities are deliberately overlapped. Diverse users and uses are taken into account, and communication among them helps to broaden horizons of both operating units and the development group. This also helps to minimize the potential for premature closure in either product or process designers.

Much careful effort is visible here, devoted to eliminating the barriers, boundaries, and walls so evident in earlier literature. Each step of the way from "aha!" to manufacturing is anticipated, then coaxed along, and followed through on. Different users are also integrated: manufacturing (Fab) serves as a primary user, while the Memory Components and Microcomputer Divisions share apparently equal billing. The visible evidence of collaborative effort – in overlapping, time-sharing teams; in meetings and membership across existing organizational boundaries; and in shared responsibilities – testifies to organized attention, not haphazard good fortune.

As with other companies' innovation management processes, Intel's have evolved and been elaborated over time. The groups were created variously over time, as they were needed to solve emerging problems. They did not spring full-blown and complete from some organizing blueprint, but emerged as thoughtful people puzzled over the problems they experienced in the development cycle, and iterated solutions. The NTE group, for example, was created to address perceived difficulties in transferring new technologies directly from development groups into high volume production:

> The NTE group is something that was only created about two or three years ago, in response to a problem. We were having a problem transferring technologies directly from ourselves [in development] into the Sustaining Engineering Group [in fab]. There always seemed to be this period of a couple of years where we wanted to be able to produce things in high volume, but they weren't well specified enough. We hadn't gotten enough of the bugs out to really turn it over just to the Sustaining Group. It just became apparent that they didn't have enough time or the expertise to handle our problems.
>
> The Sustaining Engineering Group is set up such that a Sustaining Engineer will be responsible for a particular area of the process, say diffusion, thin films, [or] lithography. So a particular engineer will be responsible for all the different processes that use lithography in the fab line. I guess the main difficulty we've found is that in transferring a new technology, we needed to deal with a whole number of different people, and that wasn't happening.
>
> Kim Kokkonen, Intel

From Development to Fab: The "Invisible Pilot Line"

Gordon Moore believes that the transfer of a new product or technology out of research and development into manufacturing is the most difficult of the transitions to manage. He is not alone; others too recognize the notorious difficulty of translating "a good idea," even a good research idea, into a viable product. Intel attempts to circumvent this difficulty by removing the interface between development and manufacturing tasks almost entirely. This process depends upon the "invisible pilot line," an in-line, in-process arrangement for producing limited volumes of experimental product amidst routine production:

> The invisible pilot line works quite well to integrate new product developments into an existing [production] technology. More significant problems are encountered in semiconductor manufacturing when entire process or technology changes are introduced. So it's an efficient way of making relatively small changes within the same technology, but it is not a good way to make a dramatic change. Intel has concentrated fairly narrowly on making all of our inventions within the same technology.
>
> Gordon Moore, Intel

Within the same technology, there are also costs associated with this approach:

> The penalty we pay is that we do neither the production nor the original development as efficiently as we would if they were separate. But we do the transfer a lot more efficiently. And I guess I've grown to believe transfer is the more difficult part of the job.
>
> Gordon Moore, Intel

The "invisible pilot line" entails other costs as well; its operation is paradoxically both "straightforward" and fraught with difficulty. Gerry Parker described the straightforward part:

> What happens is that we transfer it one step at a time. There might be a total of – let's say the wafer process has 50 activities total. Maybe 25 of those would be new ones. What you do is transfer each of those 25, one at a time. The first gets documented, and production assigns an operator to it. There is run data; there

is statistical data taken off, and you go through that, one by one, until all 25 [new process steps] are transferred. Then you basically hand the responsibility to the Sustaining Engineers to keep it going.

Gerry Parker, Intel

A perspective closer to the action suggests much finer grained detail. Kim Kokkonen described the transfer of a newly developed CMOS process to fab's personnel as a lengthy process – however straightforward its outcomes. (The three-year time line of figure 9.4 is helpful here.) Development personnel work on the technology well in advance of others, because of the much longer time requirement typically inherent in major process development. (The basic characteristics of coming product need may well have been suggested by earlier limits, however, long before any specific product was conceived.) At year one on the time line, technology development people had been at work for a year, checking out the test pattern, doing very short experiments to check out various elements in the process before trying to put them together. At this point, according to Kokkonen, "Product Engineering hasn't started yet. We don't have Product Engineering involved. We do have Test Engineering involved; we do have TXG [Technology Exploitation Group] involved."

The typical transfer, as Kokkonen described it, was a fairly elaborate process intended to maximize the likelihood of success:

> First, we use different pieces of [new] equipment on the process – several new pieces of equipment. Right now [at the beginning of the transfer process], they're under the control of TD [Technology Development]. We maintain them; we use them; we run them; we develop them. When we get close to transfer – and this is the meaning of the words "Pick up" – fab will pick up the piece of equipment and take over responsibility for maintenance, for its operation. They will actually start doing the processing of the wafers that utilize this new piece of equipment. So pick-up is one major step that has to be covered. That involves our training the fab engineers, the fab maintenance engineers, the fab operators.
>
> Kim Kokkonen, Intel

Here those who will use the equipment are trained by those who have figured out how to make it perform properly *on this particular task*. Although training is often forgotten in other industries – and engineers may be expected to "pick up" knowledge of how to use a

CAD system on their own, or in their spare time, for instance – the quality requirements and time pressures here make training essential. Also noteworthy is the explicit mention of maintenance, another factor now widely recognized as crucial to quality, although long ignored in much American manufacturing. The quickest way to quality production is to take the time to train equipment users to operate and maintain their equipment properly.

Attention to quality extends farther yet, in the remaining steps of the transfer process Kokkonen described:

> The second key part of transfer is Qualification, and that has several facets to it. There's Reliability Qualification, where you have to provide a certain sample material to Reliability, and they beat on it, heat it up, cool it down, and so forth, to make sure that it lasts. Another portion of [Reliability] Qualification is called Process Characterization, where we will do split runs – where we will exercise the process across its expected boundary conditions. That is, there will be normal variation in the process of computer split-runs: "Put one parameter and its variant on this side [of the expected variance range], put the other parameter and its variant on the other side [of the expected variance range], and make sure it will still work." There'll be a series of 20 to 30 runs defined.
>
> Kim Kokkonen, Intel

Drawing on statistical process control theory, each component – material, process, and expected variations – of the new process is examined. All of this is pre-production activity, and all is aimed at ensuring reliable quality output. Finally, as a sort of final test run, the steps are all put together and operated against a concrete standard for performance:

> Then there's a *yield requirement*, where 10 to 20 runs will have to be done, each showing a particular yield for a particular product. If all those occur, then basically transfer is done, although there is also a documentation package.
>
> Kim Kokkonen, Intel

Doing "Well Enough" – Most of the Time

Such exhaustive attention to quality and reliability suggest that somehow Intel at least lives in a charmed world, immune from the pressures of aggressive competitors and the marketplace. Nothing could be further from the truth. Like every one of the major competitors in the semiconductor industry, Intel has booted a few – failed embarrassingly, while others stole a march. Like all US firms, Intel is powerfully aware of the impact of global competition, most particularly from the Japanese.

These dual realities, of marketplace pressure to rush new products to market and of the possibility of genuine failure, create yet another on-going tension that distinguishes the new competition. The constant quality push toward perfection is constrained by the need to "get it out the door now:"

> Intel's philosophy is to "Get it out the door." Go for the 80 percent solution; satisfice, rather than maximize the solution. Get the profit [from the new product] for next year, rather than the year after. Essentially, our innovative ideas must be into manufacturing in two to three years.
>
> Ron Smith, Intel

Smith, an engineering program manager in the Static RAM Development Group, echoed comments by senior managers at Intel. But a bit of care is required – Intel's "80 percent solution" is far more demanding than traditional firms' criteria. And it implies still less clean a transfer than we have been describing, along with increased overlap and interface requirements. Kim Kokkonen identified market pressure as the driver for the faster transfer into high volume production:

> In many cases, the market pressure is such that we will transfer something into Fab's hands in spite of the fact that there are some existing problems with it, because we want two things to happen. First, we need the volume capability of the Fab organization to just pump out a lot of wafers. Second, we need the learning experience, in many cases. The problems are such that they can only be solved by running a massive amount of material . . . So, in many cases, [Technology Development] will allow a transfer of something, then we will have to spend some time with it [in Manufacturing].
>
> Kim Kokkonen, Intel

In the presence of simultaneous, conflicting demands for fast transfer, high quality and technologically aggressive characteristics, products, and processes do transfer into manufacturing, with overlapping responsibilities and interface between the development team and the operational fab team. Insistent competition assures that few transfers are quite so straightforward, so neat, or so unambiguous as to allow the luxury of traditional practice – "throwing the new product over the wall." Here, pitchers and catchers have no wall between them, but a shared obligation to get the product out.

Push is evident, as Smith noted:

> Our schedules are very aggressive to begin with, so if we slip the schedule [because of unforeseen technical problems], we're still ahead of our competition. A schedule is a management tool, but it is difficult to plan for an unforeseen technical problem.
>
> Ron Smith, Intel

Yet success is not guaranteed, for as science elaborates more new technology, companies like Intel face increasing demands. There are many other highly competent firms as adversaries; competition is fierce. Even a highly regarded company like Intel acknowledges limits. Here again, Smith echoed comments voiced by senior executives at the top of the organization:

> What has changed over the past few years is that Intel's technical base is much broader than it was previously. However, the scope of the competition is [also] broader. It is simply tough to be first in everything. We don't have enough resources to be competitive, and first, in every single new product area any more. Whereas historically, Intel was darned near best in all cutting-edge products and technologies, [today] we simply can't be the best in all of them.
>
> Ron Smith, Intel

The tension between "perfection" and "getting it out the door," like the tension between free flowing ideas and guided, chosen courses of innovation, balances efforts over time. If it is less neat or comprehensible than clearly delineated responsibilities and a clean break between design (or development) and manufacturing, Intel's tension is far more in keeping with the company's reality – a reality widely shared nowadays.

Conclusions

This chapter has described the innovation cycle from idea inception through the hand-off to high volume manufacturing. The carefully constructed webs of simultaneous effort, time-lapped teams, and multiple development and manufacturing are complex, both in the telling and in practice. Nonetheless, they thoroughly repay the effort required. These approaches offer enormous leverage to operating managers in managing complex innovation activities and overcoming potential barriers to innovation. They force and foster good innovation practices. In Gordon Moore's words, these practices help Intel to "remove the barrier of transferring new technical knowledge" from one group to another as much as possible.

Intel's efforts are mirrored by other companies in our sample, who face identical demands. Since innovation is so fragile in its early stages, our sample companies strive to eliminate the "transfer" completely. To that end, we discovered that R&D in these companies is heavily decentralized, with 90 to 99 percent of research and development conducted within operating groups – close to, or even actually within, their regular manufacturing facilities. Decentralized R&D provides a sharper market focus for the products being developed, and high usage of those technologies that are developed. The manufacturing technologies on which effort is spent are targeted for multiple product applications, across related generations of products. So their yield of new products successfully manufactured is exceptionally high.

The small residual of R&D that is centralized – the 1 to 10 percent conducted under corporate sponsorship in relatively centralized facilities – provides an economy of scope for longer-term, more broadly applicable R&D in these companies. Innovations requiring longer horizons, perhaps of considerable strategic value and often of substantial applicability across a number of operating units, are explored in corporate-sponsored R&D. So, too, are more basic manufacturing process capabilities (as in HP's basic silicon thrust).

Running through the narrative of decentralized R&D in which barriers between groups are minimized is an explicit philosophy regarding the management of creative individuals. The executives of these continuously innovating companies do not believe that innovation is a random, unmanageable process. Rather, it is very carefully orchestrated; and they manage their engineering, design, and technical resources accordingly. For a corporation to systematically and repeatedly "beat the competition," the efforts of the innovators must be organized and marshalled. Development projects are clearly scheduled, with explicit deadlines and milestones. As Charlie Sporck remarked, "Time is an awesome fact."

While milestone-driven development projects are necessary for timely innovation, there is a dynamic tension between deadlines, on the one hand, and freeing innovators to develop technical ideas of their own creation, on the other. Technical contributors are deliberately given a great deal of design freedom so that they genuinely feel ownership of the problems they choose: problems are "theirs," not "management's." While this appears to impose a certain loss of efficiency in decentralizing technical decisions, it is a cost readily borne, since it is viewed as essential to maintaining a flow of innovation. Moreover, it is widely viewed as essential to overcoming all of the niggling difficulties of detail that intervene between any bright innovative idea and its realization in the cold world of fact.

Technical entrepreneurship is both tolerated and nurtured by management at all levels in these companies. Bootlegging of resources and finagling of time by individual contributors is explicitly condoned. Engineers and scientists are encouraged to bootleg and finagle while they try to shape their initial insights with data. Because the time to experiment is "stolen," they themselves provide the judgment essential to ensure that those projects pursued are technically worthy.

Sanctioned "horsing around" allows innovators to present to management ideas that are more demonstrably useful and thus more defensible because their inevitable rough edges have been polished. Technical horsing around is nurtured and cherished for its contribution to innovation: this is pure pragmatics. Texas Instruments institutionalized technical horsing around in its Wild Hare program; other unscheduled, bootleg technical activities continued as well. Other companies, too, provided funds or managers who were deliberately "blind" to bootleg activities. Still others in our sample institutionalized the same end result by condoning the attitude among engineers that "we're crooks whose hands are always out. We grab serendipitous ideas and horse around with them, with or without management's approval."

Whether formalized or informal, built into systems or winked at, the outcomes are the same: technical contributors are "110 percent" busy, turned on, and engaged in developing ideas they feel are "their own," and to which they are committed. Innovation success and achievement matter personally to these people. Taken together, these elements result in a decentralized, market-cued R&D in which transfer barriers are reduced, minimized or eliminated altogether. The outcome is a vibrant, continually refreshed innovation cycle. A stream of innovative products, manufactured and marketed successfully, testify that innovation is alive and well in our sample of large US microelectronics firms.

This chapter has taken us through several essential phases of the innovation cycle. In the next chapter, we deal with the manufacturing end-game, the final phase of innovation. There we will deal with the perspective of manufacturing personnel who must cope with constant intrusions of change into an environment they struggle to stabilize – one that management practice and theory both argue should be buffered from perturbations. As we have seen in this chapter, research and development people work as fast as they can to produce new products and new technologies. As a consequence, changes, enhancements, and modifications to both manufacturing technologies and products are endless. We shall see that the manufacturing environment in the high-technology companies is the focus of a dynamic tension between change and stability, as manufacturing, too, responds to the impact of competition – striving for ever-faster manufacturing cycle times, higher manufacturing yields, higher quality and persistently aggressive manufacturing performance requirements – amidst ever-changing product characteristics and increasingly complex manufacturing processes. We turn now to the manufacturing end-game.

Notes

1 For some examples of product life cycle literature, see Savich and Thompson (1978) (they cite a voluminous list of references to life cycle forecasts of sales revenues); and Polli and Cook (1969).

   A related line of thought concerns the manufacturing process life cycle, described by Hayes and Wheelwright (1979a, b). Hayes and Wheelwright provide a definitive discussion of this concept in Hayes and Wheelwright (1984), ch. 7. These two concepts relate to the ideas developed in this chapter. However, neither of these models captures the behavioral and managerial complexities of managing innovation in the companies we studied.

2 For the relative rankings of research intensiveness across industries, see "The R&D Scoreboard," *Business Week*, June 20, 1980, pp. 139–62.

10

The Manufacturing End-Game: Sustaining Innovation

We're doing it, number one, primarily because we have to, to be competitive. The reason we have to is because there's already people out there, namely the Japanese, that are apparently able to produce the products at much, much lower manufacturing costs than we do. There's something out there that says, "It can be done."

Ed Boleky, Intel

We won't shy away from commodity products . . .

Fred Heiman, Intel

End-Game Manufacturing: Development and Production

Manufacturing acquires an unexpected importance as technologies and markets "mature." When knowledge and expertise become global, more competitors can match skills formerly rare. The "end-game" of the innovation cycle is where competition is ultimately played out. Because developing new products is only the first step, manufacturing expertise undergoes a subtle shift from simply "delivering the goods" (whatever development or designers have dreamed up), to a central focus for competitive advantage. Manufacturing is, simultaneously, the culmination of new product ideas and the basis for other new products.

Managing this sometimes contradictory task is especially important, because, as the Bible has it, "The race is not always to the swift." It is important to innovate, but innovation in product concept terms alone is not enough. Nor is it possible to always be first in any case. Just how difficult it is to be first all the time is underlined by Intel's problems with the 64K DRAM, a key component that definitively demonstrated that the "new competition" had arrived in semiconductor components.

The 64K Dynamic Random Access Memory was the component on which in 1980 the Japanese beat US makers, including Intel, to the market. By 1981, the Japanese controlled about 70 percent of the 64K DRAM market, although as US firms entered, their share dropped to 56 percent of a market worth $2 billion in 1985 (Walleck, 1985). The significance of their early penetration, however, is that first entry translates to premium profits – devices that sold for $50 in 1980 sold for $1 in 1985: the price of memory chips dropped by an average of 35 percent per year during 1970–85.

Two other insights can be drawn from the US makers' experience with the 64K DRAM. The account illustrates the close interdependence between manufacturing and product design: neither by itself will achieve the desired innovation. US makers could not match Fujitsu's device until almost two years after it appeared on the market. Worse, Intel had continuing problems with the 64K. Finally, the 64K story also throws into sharp relief the pace of technology change in manufacturing – and the importance of its mastery for long-term competitive success.

What is important here is not that "the Japanese succeeded," although that clearly has had continuing consequences. Nor is the fact of difficulties at Intel, then and now widely regarded as the premier US leading-edge firm, in itself of such overriding significance. The task is complex, after all, the competitors closely matched technically, and the opportunities for mis-steps abundant. Of far more importance to our purpose is the clear recognition of the risks in development, the difficulties these firms regularly master, and the nature of the tasks they face to do so. Intel's experience and decisions draw the picture very sharply because the firm is committed to the leading edge; obviously, for firms that do not seek to dominate the most advanced sectors of the market, mastery of volume manufacturing for the end-game has even greater significance.

This chapter will focus on the manufacturing end-game. Here, manufacturing serves two missions. First, it is the ultimate recipient of the fruits of designers' innovation (including any problems in implementation). Manufacturing is also the source of potential competitive advantage in its own right, if the innovation focus can be moved well past the generation of new products, to the generation of new ways of delivering all products. Both missions are critical to success in semiconductor electronics; both missions point the way to survival in global industries of all sorts.

Here again, Intel offers an especially cogent story – its early practice of an "invisible pilot line" and its front-line position as a constantly innovative firm give added sharpness to the contradictions between stability-based efficiency and change-based innovation. The pressures so visible at Intel, for constantly improving efficiency, improving manufacturing capabilities, and generating new products, are replicated in every firm we studied.

The roots of the 64K DRAM lay in the smaller 16K DRAM, first manufactured in volume by Mostek, a US firm, in 1977. Mostek manufactured the device on projection aligners, a new production technology. At the same time, Fujitsu, a leading Japanese manufacturer, was able to produce the 16K device on proximity aligners, an older technology, due to superior clean-room processes and production control. The same superior practices enabled Fujitsu to push the older technology to produce the new generation product, the 64K DRAM, and bring it to the market in volume by 1978 (Walleck, 1985). Fujitsu used proximity alignment, an older, proven technology that was well understood, and pushed that technology to achieve the finer control and definition the new product demanded.

Meanwhile, US manufacturers were struggling to master both the new 64K design and a newer, more complicated production technology at the same time. Their efforts fell behind, and no US 64K devices reached the market until well into 1980. TI and Motorola were the first US producers of the 64K devices, which they produced on a still newer production technology, wafer steppers (Walleck, 1985). In 1981, the Japanese finally began producing on wafer steppers – a generation behind in technology, but well ahead on market share.

Intel's problems appeared to be different. Intel's 64K DRAM was made by quadrupling the underlying 16K design, a common practice. According to Gerry Parker, the error involved a slip in the complex and carefully orchestrated process of innovation we have been describing:

> One reason they got ahead of us is because we did make some mistakes. We tied some very difficult products to some new technologies, and we couldn't get the products running. Our

64K DRAM was sort of a major embarrassment for the corporation. What happened was that we had the process correct on the thing two years before – the process was totally finished and ready to go. We were basically a year ahead of everyone else. What happened was that the 16K design we had didn't work, and we've struggled with the design ever since. That put us behind in that process, so unfortunately the same thing happened in the 64K static [RAM]. The design problem was bigger than we thought.

Gerry Parker, Intel

In essence, according to Parker, the *process* (the manufacturing activity) was ready to go, while the *product* (the underlying design) had problems. However, the interlocking complexity of product and process is crucial; both must be managed, for both are essential to success. Designs can challenge manufacturing capability and push fab's ability to actually produce the item.

Manufacturing Capability

Manufacturing capability in the abstract is in some senses an illusion for these companies. "Process" is intricately married to "product design," and typically the two advance together. If one fails, the other fails . . . and particularly where a new design poses a capability challenge, fixing the problem is not merely a case of redrafting the design. Intel is not alone in experiencing this reality; others testify to the same pressures:

I believe, and everybody in my group believes, you can't develop a process without a product. You don't know if you have the process until you build the product. So we build product, and the whole intent . . . is to prototype product out of this facility. And quantity product.

Jack Saltich, Motorola

Saltich was manager of a development fab at Motorola, in a large facility specifically dedicated to pilot production in quantity – a distinctly different approach from Intel's "invisible pilot line." Where Intel's development fab is already devoted to leading-edge products, Motorola's was more distinctly differentiated for special development work. Despite this tactical difference, however, Saltich's observations corroborate the interdependence we have been describing.

A key issue is the degree of difference required in the new production process, as Saltich noted:

> To adequately serve [the bipolar analog] marketplace, the types of processes that you needed to get the next generation products were evolutionary. Not revolutionary. If it is evolutionary in nature – which means that if you've got a whole bunch of steps, you've only got to alter a couple of them – you can do it inside a [regular production fab] line. But what if it *is* revolutionary? Then what do you do?
>
> Jack Saltich, Motorola

Degree of difference clearly translates here into significantly new operations, new pieces of equipment, or new interfaces between steps or equipment, as Saltich observed:

> It's not a whole new line, but it is unique pieces of equipment. That happens in quantum jumps as you go from optical to photo to steppers, or from wet edging to dry edging, [for instance].
>
> Jack Saltich, Motorola

The specifics of which processes require quantum jumps is not so important here as the distinction in Saltich's account between the evolutionary activities that can be managed by tighter operation of existing equipment while current production continues, and the larger disruption implied by new pieces of equipment and substantial changes. The key difference is that the operations manager, who will still be responsible for current operations, must take on the task of major change – especially difficult if significant development work remains to be done:

> What happens oftentimes is the guy that's running this line, the operations manager, is not too interested in doing that – so that could delay or deter [running pilot production of new products with routine operations].
>
> Jack Saltich, Motorola

Without manufacturing cooperation, new production processes (or, for that matter, new products that require existing production to be disrupted) will not be undertaken.

There are two important ways in which production can go wrong, according to Charles Phipps of Sevin Rosen. First, manufacturing can become a "second class citizen," simply expected to deliver whatever is designed, without regard for the difficulty or problems a particular design creates. This has been far too typical of US manufacturing in general, in an era of financially oriented CEOs, unwilling to invest in manufacturing, maintenance, or new equipment. The second route to difficulties can be even more pernicious. This problem arises when manufacturing investment soars, as it did in the semiconductor business during the mid-1970s: manufacturing became even more decoupled from business strategy, and return on assets dominated thinking in some firms. According to Phipps, "Manufacturing efficiency" ruled, and new processes, which might require three to five years for payback, or new products that might destabilize existing procedures, were resisted.

Neither dismissing manufacturing entirely nor allowing financial and efficiency measures to dominate truly integrates manufacturing into business strategy. Ultimately, only actual, working products that meet real market needs will sell. Yet product design characteristics are tightly linked to the manufacturing steps required to produce them. Much change on either side of the equation carries significant consequences for change on the other side.

Component capacity quadruples, so DRAM generations have gone from 1K to 4K to 16K to 64K to 256K, to 1 Meg (one million bits), 4 Meg and so on. In essence, the larger components have frequently replicated the smaller component design in an expanded format, often with miniaturized line width – so unsolved design problems early on can have persistent repercussions, as in Intel's experience. Since the difficulties were fundamental to the underlying 16K product design, Intel's dilemma implied significant design changes, and thus more time to redevelop production processes as well. Where major changes in design imply major process changes, the problem becomes still more difficult to master.

The manufacturing end-game – on-going and repeated success and survival after initial product innovation – is tightly interlinked with innovation efforts, as we have argued. On the one hand, innovation is imperative; on the other, manufacturing capabilities for both new products and established ones must be constantly pushed. New products, and the new equipment and process steps they often require, must constantly be mastered. Current practices must be refined and advanced. Older products must continue to be manufactured while there is demand for them. And manufacturing capabilities must be developed to provide the platform upon which new products can be developed.

Sometimes this multiple charter intrudes on both innovation and efficiency, as developing a new technology (or even pushing an old one significantly) can slow down the development work required to routinize new production, while working on a new product can encourage fab people to slow down on production changes. Changes needed for new products might imply upsetting already established activities. And, most certainly, pushing manufacturing capabilities by inserting new equipment, new processes, or substantially more demanding process steps will put pressure on output.

The electronics industry's constantly evolving, intensely competitive market persistently pushes these firms toward mastery in both products and processes. Aggressive scheduling in hopes of a marketplace triumph creates pressure for fast transfer. The first mover's advantage is potentially enormous – the first new component to market, because it faces no competition, will sell at a substantial premium. Moreover, the first product to market can well create the industry standard design, guaranteeing a long after-market as the product is built into numerous other products. The shorter the product's cycle (before its replacement by the next generation, more capable product), the greater the pressure to race to market. But too fast a transfer can result in never-finished development efforts, enormous wasted energies, and frustration for both the new product designers and the fab people, as manufacturing laggards – and competitors – prosper. The importance of pushing manufacturing mastery *per se*, as a foundation for competitive advantage that enables demanding product designs, should be clear.

Manufacturing and Development

Timely innovation demands a fast track from development into manufacturing. Too-early transfer can mean that problem after problem must be worked out under (relatively) high volume production conditions. The pressures and frustrations of attempting to meet today's needs while simultaneously coping with tomorrow's are excruciating and unrelenting. High-technology firms are subject to difficulties in this transfer process, just as traditional firms are, according to Intel's Kim Kokkonen:

> Fab is notoriously resistant to accepting transfer of new technology, because it's a pain for them to do it. Eight years ago, all of Intel's development was done in the Mountain View

[California] Fab line. Now we're doing development in three different Fab lines. At the same time those Fab lines are helping us with development, they have requirements for manufacturing output. There's always a conflict between how well they support us [in Development], versus how well they meet their manufacturing output [requirements].

Kim Kokkonen, Intel

From the perspective of the development program managers like Kokkonen, the situation sometimes felt as if it were "Them against us. *All* of them, against few of us." His struggles highlight another aspect of the "invisible pilot line:"

A year or two ago, it was kind of like me fighting against the Fab organization, or [another manager] fighting against the Fab organization. And the *entire* Fab organization, which is massive, and had all the supervisors and operators saying, "Hey, we're judged based on how well we get our production material out, so don't bother us. We'll do you a favor every now and then."

Kim Kokkonen, Intel

Of course, Intel's "invisible pilot line" is only a more obvious example, because pilot production is not sequestered in special facilities, but takes place on "real" production lines. Yet the choice to attempt development on "production" equipment, with production personnel, imposes serious hazards for on-going production. The same difficulties occur in any transfer of new products into manufacturing – in many industries besides semiconductors. "Doing something new" imposes costs that war with the very notion of pushing efficiency by "doing it again."

From the perspective of production managers, the problems are just as frustrating. With Intel's concept of "the invisible pilot line," where development is done directly amidst the normal, high volume production runs, there are conflicting pressures on manufacturing people to maximize simultaneously what some regard as an impossible dichotomy of responsibilities. Moreover, the pace of change keeps accelerating. Ed Boleky, manager of one of three Intel fabrication facilities in California, outlined some of the frustrations of trying to manage under the dual charter:

I think one of the most important things is, it's very, very tough on our people. You've got to figure out ways to keep people from going berserk, especially when they have a dual charter, between optimizing the products that are already in volume production, yet doing a good job on the new technology being developed. That's been brutal.

People keep asking, "Which is more important? Getting today's stuff out the door, or working on the future stuff?" I mean, in my case, I've had times where I had two senior managers in the same room at the same time, and one of them was pulling on one of my legs to optimize today's results, and the other one says, "Hey, you've got to go and make that new technology happen twice as fast as it did before."

Ed Boleky, Intel

People in Boleky's position must deal not only with their own subordinates, but with key constituents across a number of different key interfaces within the company, each of which has an enormous stake in his decision about what to push in his fab lines. This is manufacturing's view of interfaces very much parallel to those Kokkonen described from the design side in chapter 9. For example, the operating managers of two divisions may both have revenues and profits at stake – yet satisfying one may conflict with satisfying the other. The two managers in the scenario described above have conflicting claims on the same fab: one is depending on shipments of established products out of the fab for this month's or this quarter's revenue projections; the other is banking on near-term revenues based on the new technology being brought into high volume production quickly at the same fab. Time and resources spent producing established product output are time and resources unavailable for development work on new technology.

No Easy Answers

An American wit, H. L. Menken, once observed that for every complex problem, there was a clear, elegant, simple solution – which invariably was wrong. So it seems in these companies: because their problems are complex, simple answers don't work. The dual charter of the Intel fabs, to conduct operations and simultaneously to pursue development, is a case in point. The tension between the two tasks was given special potency by Intel's experience with the 64K DRAM and the continuing challenge of Japanese manufacturers, who operate from a protected domestic base market that substantially lowers their risks.

The problems of a small number of Intel development managers and engineers in Technology Development, trying to get "special favors" from those in production, point up the contrast, as Kokkonen observed:

> How long does it take a fab [development] lot to go through the [manufacturing] line? If that's longer than they expected it to be, and if I go beat on somebody's head over there, they say, "Sorry. We can't help you. We can't get it any faster than this." Then I say, "Hey, my entire schedule's going to slide. We're going to lose, compared to the Japanese."
>
> Kim Kokkonen, Intel

In the context of the 64K DRAM, a first approach was quite direct and obvious: push harder. A second solution addressed the most proximate problem, as analysis of the most recent difficulties defined it, in product design. But although the diagnosis of design difficulties was correct, even that was not enough, for the interplay of design and manufacturing was, and is, conspicuous.

New production steps, equipment being used in new ways, and new designs all can introduce production problems, and only careful, step-by-step analysis can sort out the difficulty. Labeling a problem as "a design problem" is foolish – "design" changes imply equally important changes in "production," and both fab and design have clear interests in working through the ultimate performance problem without major design change, if at all possible:

> One of the things we're doing is to totally refocus all of our energies into improving our design capability, because that has been limiting us . . . Plus putting emphasis on getting simpler designs that we know work, so we don't get behind times.
>
> Again, on the step routine, if I had tried to introduce that step routine by going to a whole new design, starting from scratch, it might take a year. And [even] then, I might not have it, because I don't know whether it's the design or the [wafer] stepper [a piece of production equipment, now being run in a new way]. So by using a design I know works, we just went to it, and it works a lot faster. So we're learning as we go.
>
> Gerry Parker, Intel

The balancing act, between "pushing harder" with an existing design and an existing process, versus throwing out the design and with it perhaps significant production development work as well, implies much careful analysis, much hard work. Once a process is well-specified, the advantages of "tweaking" a design to get to the market *now*, are substantial. Above all, self-conscious, self-diagnosing attention to what works and what causes problems must be constant. Both "this product" and "this process," and the broader practices of innovation management must be tracked.

Underlying these observations are the fundamental questions of how fast manufacturing capability is being developed in its own right. Where manufacturing "follows design," only after designers ask for some new capability does manufacturing face that necessity. All too typically in American manufacturing at large, that recognition may come on "job one:" when the new product must be manufactured, in volume; and that, of course, is too late for timely development of new manufacturing capabilities. Equally, however, if manufacturing capabilities restrain design because manufacturing asset returns dominate management thinking, new manufacturing capabilities, equipment, or processes will be brought on-line without regard for market realities.

At Intel, the problems experienced in moving development work were not all solved by identifying "design" problems. The sorts of interactions we have been outlining all take place amid growing time pressure to speed all development to manufacturing transitions. This concern ultimately sent the situation up to Intel Chairman Gordon Moore – and back down again for a negotiated solution. The criterion: it had to be a win–win solution, by which manufacturing could meet its production goals and also provide timely support for new development projects.

The resolution finally put in place seems almost indirect: the managers addressed the performance assessment system. This involved, first, defining performance criteria that reflected manufacturing's dual charter, for development as well as high volume production. Next, it involved recognizing that conflict was implicit in those charters, from time to time. Intel had to assess and reward performance on the basis of both charters in the three development fab lines. From development's point of view, it was imperative to get development work recognized in the development fabs' assessment:

> We're making a transition into defining the absolute goals that these three [Development] Fab lines have to meet to support us right. Those fab lines are now being measured differently in terms of their performance than any other Fab lines in the company. There have been a number of very high level meetings [between senior Development and Fab managers] to define the criteria for what a Development Fab line is. [This is] to make sure that they do get credit for supporting us, and that it is a part of their key results. You know: if they miss a manufacturing indicator, but they did very well for us, then that's good.
>
> Kim Kokkonen, Intel

The necessity of this change in performance assessment criteria becomes obvious in the light of the complex task of moving innovations into production that we have been describing. It is not enough that Fab people occasionally "do favors" for Development; both sides must work very hard, *in concert*, to make the transition work. This higher level of responsiveness to Development needs is neither occasional nor trivial, for the Development Fabs, but a repeated aspect of "business as usual," that simply happens over and above regular production responsibilities.

The new performance assessment arrangements required detailed efforts for successful implementation, across several levels and incorporating the multiple realities of different perspectives. Kokkonen sketched some of the implementation efforts:

> There was a lot of work down at this [project] level in defining indicators [and making] proposals for how things could be made better. It's continuously being worked on. We have weekly meetings now on a couple of levels, where we [Development] talk with Fab. We have meetings on the technician level, between our technicians and the Fab supervisors. Our technicians say, "We need this particular material moved." Or, "What system can we set up that makes this move more smoothly?"
>
> There are meetings also between people on [the project managers'] level and the Fab management, where we set policies basically on how things are to be done. It's a continuing, painful experience. There have been a lot of problems [to work through] within the last year.
>
> Kim Kokkonen, Intel

Shared Management: The General Perspective

Both manufacturing and development people showed a clear grasp of the need not only for co-operation, but for intense, mutually supportive collaboration in solving problems from their different perspectives, to accomplish truly responsive manufacturing– development work. What seems especially noteworthy is a perspective going well beyond either development *per se*, or manufacturing *per se*. This transcendent view was not automatic, nor was it obvious. Rather, it was the deliberately crafted outcome of explicit changes in performance assessment and interaction jointly worked out by operational personnel responsible for the work – and concerted effort. People at several levels were involved; the solution was not simple. Yet throughout, there is evidence of a pervasive awareness of the marketplace consequences of operational success and failure, and of universal commitment to the larger-scale goal of competitive success.

The complex organizational arrangements – in structure, in interaction, in responsibility, in linkages between different groups and the like – are no mystery to the managers involved with them, however elaborate they may appear from the outside, as earlier chapters have documented. Not only do these people understand who they must interact with, what the goals and tasks are, and how they should assess the success of their endeavors. They are also very clear on the ultimate goal – marketplace success, particularly against the most aggressive competitor, the Japanese. There is no ambiguity about competition, or what it takes to succeed.

They are clear, too, about the interim measure that most contributes to success: time to market. In compressing the development cycle by overlapping activities and teams, as we described in chapter 9, our study firms accepted much greater complexity of required relationships and demands. In placing responsibility for creating procedures and assessment criteria in the hands of those who will carry out the work, these firms gain deep understanding and acceptance among their people of what is going on and why, and of how performance is assessed.

To achieve this, they must go well beyond "participative management" as that term is generally defined, to something far more like shared strategic management (Jelinek and Litterer, 1988). This is not perfunctory consultation, cursory problem-sharing, or merely informing people of what their superiors had decided and what they might expect. Instead, by sending the problem back down to where it must be solved, Moore engaged people well down in the organization in responsibility for this solution. Such a pattern, persistently repeated, creates shared responsibility for organizational survival and success. Neither the problem nor the involvement of lower-level people in it is *pro forma*.

Widespread appreciation of the significance of, and need for, aggressive schedules and "push" to market assures a very different sort of collaboration among the parties than would be the case if this were "design's problem," "development's problem," or "manufacturing's problem," as is all too often the case in traditional organizations. Instead, this is "our problem," shared and acknowledged. These managers are clearly alert to how "working their organization" can assist them in solving competitive problems which they recognize as matters of joint responsibility.

In short, what we see might be called a general managerial focus, coupled with awareness of the organization's goals and needs in a broad sense that goes well beyond individual functional specialties and spreads widely through the organization. While Intel's case is especially cogent, we found evidence of similarly widespread general management perspectives in all of the firms we studied. This does not mean there are no turf battles, conflicts over dominance, or struggles for particularistic perspectives in high-technology firms. Nevertheless, such contentions are widely viewed as improper when they do occur. We believe this shared approach to management, operations results, and strategic issues is a key characteristic for innovative success in the turbulent competitive markets of the future.

Manufacturing Cost Containment and Competition

In late 1985, Intel decided that its manufacturing costs needed to fall by 50 percent. This flatly stated goal was targeted amidst a growing recognition that competitive survival in the semiconductor industry, for a company of Intel's size, was no longer feasible by the "cream and abandon" marketing tactics of the past, which we documented in chapter 4.

Formerly, Intel had emphasized being the first into premium-priced markets with leading-edge products, but then abandoning those markets to move on to other, still more advanced products as competitors intruded to push prices down and the markets toward maturity. Unfortunately, the company concluded, such practices preclude the full exploitation of hard-won innovations – and discourage development of the baseline manufacturing skills that must ultimately support advanced products. Surrender allows competitors to harvest fields plowed and seeded by the innovators, and endangers the next crop as well.

Intel's reconsidered decision is noteworthy for three reasons. First, it says that even an accomplished and successful innovator cannot neglect the potentially lucrative later stages of markets and product life cycles. Innovation itself, and the massive investments of time, effort, and treasure required to achieve it, must be utilized to their fullest capacity. These positions are simply too difficult to achieve to warrant abandonment any longer. Second, it points up how important all phases of the innovation cycle are, even to a company on the leading edge of technology. Without the profits contributed by later stages, it may be impossible to fund renewed research and innovation for the next round.

Thirdly, Intel's decision underlines the importance of manufacturing mastery as a fundamental requirement for strategic success. The very same capability that drives costs down and yields up will provide improved capabilities for further product developments and more challenging designs. (The situation is quite parallel to Ford's experience with the Taurus design: "soft shouldered," "jelly-bean" cars, where door and roof meet in a soft curve, require order-of-magnitude closer manufacturing tolerances – or else the roof will leak.) Without superb manufacturing capabilities in place, challenging products cannot be undertaken, whether in semiconductors or in automobiles.

In the past, Intel had been able to escape much of the mature market competition by speedy development of a stream of state-of-the-art products, sometimes with years of lead-time before competitors appeared. As adversaries became more competent, the pace of change accelerated. It was not that Intel's skills had deteriorated – despite the difficulties we have recounted with the 64K DRAM – but rather that competitors had improved. As a result, Intel's lead-time over the competition had diminished. Along with lead-time, the potential to recapture the costs of expensive R&D diminished. The protected window of opportunity during which the first mover enjoyed high margins and no competition decreased – the time frame of the first mover's advantage eroded, for virtually all products:

> We [formerly] substituted process complexity and sophistication as a means [to avoid the need for] lower cost. I guess what we're finding is that we've got to continue to [innovate], but it takes so long and is so difficult to create these great, complex new technologies, that in the meantime we have to [cut costs] – While we're taking this two years to develop this new thing, there's people out there that are absolutely driving the cost of existing [products] down at a tremendous rate. If we don't at least keep up with them while we're developing the new [products and processes], we won't generate enough cash to fund development.
>
> Ed Boleky, Intel

Intel's decision to compete in, rather than abandon, maturing markets required drastically lower production costs. This, in turn, meant organizing the innovation cycle to extend technical attention on into later production stages. Intel's technical talent had to be focused more explicitly on the manufacturing end-game, not just on new products. Intel today is clearly contesting markets longer, and as clearly paying close attention to more competitive products than in the past. For a variety of reasons, some described above, this also meant still more sophisticated management of technology development. Intel's commitment is mirrored by other semiconductor firms we studied, and it is also becoming more visible in other, more traditional industries as well.

This shared commitment to lowering production costs while maintaining extremely high standards of quality and innovation reflects new global standards for competitive cost positioning. All this stands behind Intel's intention to capture more of the innovation cycle margins throughout the active span of a product, product family or production technology, moving from "leading edge" through to "end-game," in innovation cycle terms.

Such a shift in positioning and strategy – from premium, advanced technology markets and early abandonment (Schoonhoven, 1984) to full-spectrum technology exploitation – requires moving to lower production costs, and thus lower prices, to stave off competitors in the end-game. New disciplines become relevant: manufacturing cost control, materials efficiency, equipment usage management, and pushing established technology for further benefits are all involved. New thinking on these issues reflects both tighter competitive circumstances and a commitment to benefit fully from the innovation efforts of the firm:

> It's an attitude, a managerial attitude, not an equipment issue.
> It's an attitude regarding equipment utilization and depreciation
> – that's a significant issue. Keeping our factories filled. We won't
> shy away from commodity products.
>
> Fred Heiman, Intel

At the same time, this decision to contest markets commits the firm to stressing manufacturing *per se* in a new way: manufacturing must be totally integrated with strategy, and it must be developed in concert with product planning. This is not yet so clearly established as a norm in the semiconductor business. According to Charles Phipps of Sevin Rosen:

> Manufacturing is not yet well integrated into business strategy
> in US firms. They are still trying to understand how to use
> manufacturing for competitive advantage, as the Japanese do.
> They have integrated manufacturing capability much more closely
> into business strategy.

Emphasis on higher margin, proprietary products protected Intel from the necessity of competing on "bedrock" manufacturing expertise, so long as the firm could exit contested commodity product markets to go on to something else.

Intel's stated willingness to compete in commodity areas, while simultaneously maintaining its technological leadership and continuing efforts in advanced products, signals a considered response to new realities, most especially the high cost of research and development. For comparison, TI, long famed as a commodity, low-cost producer, had made a parallel decision much earlier, in remaining in the DRAM business, while cutting production costs, (an old strategy) and pushing research even farther than in the past. Hewlett-Packard's increasing attention to computer-based products carries similar strategic implications: computers are a far broader, more commodity-like product with much greater price sensitivity than the premium-priced engineering instruments of HP's past.

For all of these companies, the manufacturing end-game has become far more important than before, for the same reasons. Even those, like Texas Instruments, who had long prided themselves on manufacturing expertise have increased their attention, putting still more pressure on others, who have had to meet the pace. Survival amidst intense competition requires garnering a greater portion of total innovation cycle profits, in order to fund the next round of research and capital investment. Intel's decision also indicates the bite of increasingly stringent global competitive standards, even for a leading-edge company. It is not enough for Intel to beat Motorola's production results, or for Motorola to address TI's, National's, or Intel's. The standards are worldwide, and successful competitors must succeed against the world's best.

Moving Toward Commodity Production

With the decision to contest mature stages of the innovation cycle, Intel committed to lower cost, high quality production. Low cost production had now become an Intel priority. Efficiency and innovation must be simultaneously managed. According to Ed Boleky, this was something akin to the nursery rhyme "Little Engine Who Could," who conquered the mountain by chanting, "I think I can; I think I can!" At Intel, a good deal more work was involved:

> A lot of it has to do, simply, with telling ourselves that it is important. We have not really told ourselves that this was all that important, before. We mostly focused on developing new things – [produced by] the newest process. Before we were really forced to manufacture at extremely low cost, we'd bring on the next advanced process, and try to keep [other] people on a technology treadmill.
>
> Ed Boleky, Intel

A part of the problem was the need to advance in production practices from the craft image of custom production to much more routinely controlled commodity production, according to Boleky:

> We'd gotten ourselves into a mode of custom crafting, adjusting equipment every time a new batch comes through, and thinking that was an okay way to operate, instead of saying, "Hey, what

we really need to do is figure out a way to avoid having to twiddle that knob every time the batch comes through." We need to develop a process where the oven doesn't need to be tweaked every time you make a new batch of cookies.

Such "tweaking" was obsolete because of equipment advances and increased knowledge – and because understanding how to achieve reliable, replicable production without "tweaking" was essential to volume production of increasingly complex technologies. Complexity in the new processes had escalated, completely outstripping the capabilities of the "'tweakers" to control and replicate production processes dependably.

Tweaking had all too commonly been caused by insufficient information in the past, and insufficient time to fully debug a production technology before moving on to something else. These stresses were the consequences of the "cream and abandon" strategy – it often seemed like "skating swiftly over thin ice." It had worked; it had been a source of pride to manufacturing people that Intel could run premature manufacturing processes. Now, though, the requirements were to move away from this "hands on" approach, despite many incentives to do what had worked in the past. It was difficult, simply because the manufacturing people were so adept at making difficult, complex, embryonic technologies work before their time:

> No, no. The requirements of our new technologies are so much more exacting than the old ones that, if anything, there's more of a tendency to tweak things than before. That's another habit that we've gotten ourselves into, because we've specialized in these very new, very difficult technologies. We've gotten into the habit of putting them into production when they're still in the mode where they have to be tweaked. So even when they get very mature, we're still in the habit of diddling with them. It's just a way of life.
>
> Ed Boleky, Intel

Formerly, the better production people were at "tweaking," the more they were heroes, since their work enabled the firm to prosper by beating the opposition. The aura of crisis, the feelings of success and individual contribution were seductive.

Reliable production and dependable replication of highly complex processes require more systematic practices. Intel had to eliminate direct human intervention to make products work because new processes are so very complex and difficult that they are beginning to exceed the "hands on" capabilities of even expert operators. Perhaps even more importantly, the move to volume production meant that production had to be distributed to a larger number of fabs, and that it couldn't be produced only by the "best people." It had to be reliably producible by everyone.

What had formerly been a quite successful approach, depending on extremely skilled operators, carried increasing risks with the decision to seek higher volume, longer production cycles. Intel sought to substitute careful analysis and intensive problem-solving for tweaking, as Boleky commented:

> Our first step is to step back and say, "Hey, we have just got to quit doing that." Starting with our mature technologies that really shouldn't be tweaked, and saying, "'Hey, it's hands off. We're not going to fool around with that oven." Second, if the oven is such that the temperature on the oven drifts, we either have to figure out a way to get an oven whose temperature doesn't drift, or we need to figure out a new cookie [integrated circuit wafer] recipe that will allow a wider range of temperatures and still make good cookies. But we can't have people coming in there and screwing around with the oven all the time, because that costs a lot of money. So it's a whole way of looking at things.

Problems were to be solved and eliminated, in other words, not "tweaked" around.

The issue here is not direct labor cost. In traditional production, often the first target for cost reduction is personnel. Direct labor in operations is often thought to be the source of higher US manufacturing costs. However, as many researchers have pointed out, direct labor is so small a portion of manufacturing cost that even eliminating direct labor entirely would not produce the sorts of cost savings needed to match competitors' lower costs. Direct labor is less than 20 percent of total costs for virtually all manufacturing, and less than 10 percent for most manufacturing. For automobiles, direct labor is about 8 percent; for semiconductors, it is even less (US Department of Labor). It might seem that Intel is barking up the wrong tree by focusing on eliminating production personnel in its efforts to reduce cost:

> The Japanese fabs that we've seen have relatively few people in them. They've engineered their equipment and engineered their process [to the point] where it basically runs by itself. Obviously the cost of doing this, once you get it set up, allows you to build

much cheaper product. We're really getting very serious [about such costs].

Ed Boleky, Intel

But as semiconductor managers recognize, direct labor has a different impact here: the issue is not labor cost *per se*, but human intervention. Labor hours are far less important than their consequences for reliable, replicable production. We have already mentioned increasing process complexity and the need for replicable volume production. Quality factors also enter: most specifically, the more "tweaking," the more potential contact between human operators and the increasingly dense, finely detailed circuitry – and thus the greater potential for contamination.

Removing direct labor's impact on production means ensuring automatic reliability. This, in turn, requires more exhaustive knowledge of production processes. It also requires equipment better suited to the expected production requirements – equipment that doesn't need tweaking, or special intervention:

> [Third], these technologies are really, really touchy. We are pushing the equipment typically past the place where the vendor thinks it ought to be able to run, and that's dangerous. We shouldn't do that. We've got to get back to the place where we let the equipment do what it's capable of doing.
>
> Ed Boleky, Intel

Eliminating direct intervention, no longer having to force the equipment, and ensuring production sequences and product engineering that can be reliably manufactured, all directly affect quality, yield, and thus component cost. Reducing direct labor cost will not provide the needed savings; improving yields can pay substantial dividends, however. Cutting defect rates in half, and cutting them yet again, produces direct profits for the bottom line. A 50 percent reduction in manufacturing cost can only be attained by better, smarter, more consistent manufacturing that produces quality output more frequently – ideally, 100 percent of the time.

Technical Know-How and Skills

Along with running equipment within its tolerance levels, stabilizing production process routines and mastering complex new technologies require broadly expanded technical capabilities. While this is not startling in a company like Intel, operating at the edge of the state of the art, we believe that it will also be increasingly true of all firms, as more information becomes available about production processes (including service production processes). Understanding new, complex processes and running equipment more scientifically is difficult. So, too, is analytically and exhaustively specifying how to replicate the process. So, too, is keeping elaborate new equipment operating properly. Yet all of this is required in keeping up with tough global competitors, now an issue in so many industries. The semiconductor experience offers guides to pressures that many others are also beginning to experience.

Three prime functions in wafer fabrication are production, engineering, and maintenance. Each is essential to successful manufacturing. Production runs the product through equipment. Engineering assists both with specifying the operating sequences to be used, and with debugging and problem-solving (on both new items and on established products). Maintenance ensures that equipment is operating properly, kept in repair, cleaned, and calibrated. These functions are not unlike those in traditional manufacturing; the only real difference is in the complexity of the manufacturing process involved.

In the past, engineers were expected to enter the organization with substantial prior technical education; this was a professional position. Production operators and maintenance people, however, were typically not well trained. Formerly, technical background in these positions was rare. People often learned on the job, and often by the seat of the pants. But as processes become more complex, greater expertise is required. More importantly still, as we have been arguing here, a different sort of expertise is required: knowledge-based, rather than experience-based; and scientific expertise, not "tweaking"-based expertise. Like other firms, Intel is experiencing new needs, the outcome of growing product and process complexity:

> . . . More and more, to be really effective in production, we are having to apply the same kind of discipline and technical approaches to both production and maintenance that we have in the past to engineering. So, we're finding that we need the same kinds of skills, analytical ability, and technical backgrounds in production and maintenance that we do in engineering.
>
> Ed Boleky, Intel

Nor is Intel alone. Texas Instruments is experiencing similar demands.

TI's advanced wafer fab in Dallas began producing 1 Meg DRAMs in 1988, while production projected to over 25 million units; demand for 256K DRAMs also continues strong. Both products are highly demanding; as commodity items, they must be manufactured at low cost, which translates to extremely reliable, high quality production. Training at TI's new facility is constant, and standards for cleanliness, technician skill and the like far exceed those of the past. The other companies in our sample report similarly increased requirements for skill, training, and performance.

TI claims that output and quality at the Richardson, Texas, plant is "quite comparable" to output and quality at the sister plant in Miho, Japan. The Miho plant won the coveted Demming award for quality manufacturing, so its standards are very high. Other sources claim that TI's Richardson plant did not match the Japanese plant's standards. What is clear is that the standards for manufacturing mastery have exploded upwards: survival requires world-class yields, quality, and maintenance, and ever-spiraling manufacturing skills.

State-of-the-art equipment and a growing trend toward low volume, short-run ASICs will still further increase the need for highly competent, technically sophisticated operating personnel in the semiconductor industry. But this only intensifies a trend already clearly visible, the outcome of rapid technological change and product development, as a National Semiconductor manager observed back in 1981:

> The bulk of the products, four and a half years ago, more than half of the product, was built on P-channel metal gate – a very old technology . . . The two [then current best-sellers] weren't even mentioned as a product line or anything – they were in design cycle then. The two fastest growing and largest businesses did not exist about three and a half years ago, and the custom business was much smaller. The custom business has been growing at 50-something percent . . . Now, we have a very large amount of our products introduced on this new N-channel metal gate technology [a more complex and difficult process] . . .
>
> So yes, we've moved very, very rapidly in this time period, from being all low technology to having all engineering go into high technology.
>
> Al LaPierre, National Semiconductor

Even in 1981, new products were being introduced and new processes appearing to be mastered at a very rapid pace. Complexity and tough requirements were facts of life. What LaPierre called "low technology" in 1981 was perhaps "low" by comparison to advanced semiconductors, but already quite complex and demanding in comparison to traditional manufacturing outside the semiconductor industry. Yet the pace of change was perceptibly quickening, even then; people were expected to deal competently with enormous amounts of change.

Intel's Boleky noted that equipment maintenance and repair, like operations, also demanded increasing skills:

> These people have to use a lot of computer tools; they manage their business in a very sophisticated way. The equipment is getting extremely sophisticated; a lot of our microcomputers go right into the kind of equipment that we use to build it. The management of these complex pieces of equipment, and the repair of them, is getting more and more complex. So you need the same kinds of quality-level people in all three of those [fab] organizations [production, maintenance, and engineering].
>
> Ed Boleky, Intel

In short, complexity of several sorts, rapid change, and increasing demands translated into tougher and tougher standards, and higher and higher skill requirements for everyone in production, not just the "professionals" of the past.

The heart of the new demands centers on assuring smooth, successful and repeated development-to-production efforts. A smooth transition from development operations – still partially experimental, and oriented toward debugging and analyzing a new process – to full-scale, high volume production is essential. A smooth transition will speed a new product to market, helping the firm to capture the first mover's advantage. By contrast, a ragged transition can delay effective yield, eroding profits, or even cost a company its market as others beat it into production. This complicated transfer is the culmination of development work:

> It is involved, yes; but I guess it's a measure of how well we do – how good a job we do in our development process. If we do a very good job and solve all the problems, then the transfer can be fairly trouble-free. If we don't, it can be a disaster.
>
> Ed Boleky, Intel

Necessary Documentation

The final step in the transfer process is documentation. Not only must all the bugs be worked out; the specifics of how to manufacture reliably must be detailed so that others can perform them. This is not needless paperwork but essential specificity. Our sample firms manufacture on multiple sites, and development fabs are expected to operate at somewhat lower than commodity volumes. Full-scale production will take more capacity than the fabs can provide – and, for a successful product, ramping up to seize market share can be crucial.

Documentation of new, complex processes must be fastidious, if transfer from development fabs into other production sites is to be smooth:

> We document things – we *really document* the process extremely carefully. It's equivalent to a recipe that you use to cook a meal, except that it's far, far more complex. We have an overall recipe that may have a hundred or so steps. For each step, we have a specification of just how you do it. Then for major new steps in the process, we have a whole, detailed cookbook that has all the history that went into the development. *And* all the things that can go wrong with it. *AND* how you fix them. Plus then we may send people who were involved with the process here – say we're transferring them to Phoenix or New Mexico. We might physically transfer some of the people to serve a tour of duty there, while we're installing the process in the new [high volume] factory.
>
> Ed Boleky, Intel

People in the development fabs, then, must make their organizations accomplish various key tasks – steps in manufacturing to produce specified product characteristics. In addition, they must develop and constantly refine flexibility, to produce a stream of new products. Beyond that, they must push their technical skills, using equipment that keeps getting more complex, to produce products of extraordinary difficulty. Still further, they must capture their insights well enough for others to replicate their achievements elsewhere.

Linked Product and Process Development

Time-lapsed development of product and process, discussed in chapter 9, creates consequences for the manufacturing end-game as well, as the firms push to exploit new manufacturing capabilities. Manufacturing process technology is expected to serve not merely a single product's needs, but the needs of a product family, often with several generations of increasingly demanding characteristics, challenging the newly developed technology as it matures. Intel as a leading-edge producer again highlights the aggressive development work required. To exploit the technology properly, numerous product family members will be in design more or less simultaneously, in expectation of the new technology's readiness:

> Generally when we bring a process up, it's brought up with only one or two [demonstration] products. [Meanwhile], people have been working on these other new products, anticipating when this new process will be in production. Shortly afterward, you're usually inundated with a whole bunch of new products that have been designed in parallel, while we were developing the new process. So you usually get an onslaught – *truly an onslaught* – of new products coming in. You might get a dozen new products within the first year that a new process is in production.
>
> Ed Boleky, Intel

Like the design and development process described previously for new products, add-on members of the same technology family too require extensive interfacing.

Frequent iteration and tight coupling are essential between fab personnel, development personnel, and the designers, who may be in several different divisions at Intel, serving several different sets of end-product and user markets. This complexity results from common manufacturing processes – and heavily capital intensive production facilities. The costs are simply too high to duplicate these facilities in numerous divisions where they would not be fully utilized. Therefore, interface and complexity must be mastered:

> We have product experts in the fab organizations themselves, who specialize in understanding what each product needs to make it have maximum yield. These people work closely with

the designers on the product design, in the product divisions. We [of fab] work with them very closely in introducing a new product, getting masks for it, checking out the new [production] runs.

Then it goes back to the designers, and they check the first samples to see if it works properly. Sometimes, there are revisions to the [photo] masks that go back and forth. Ultimately you end up with a product that meets the market requirements. Then we start increasing our production of it. It's a fairly tight coupling between the product people in the wafer fab organization and the product people in the divisions – the Microcomputer Division, for example.

Ed Boleky, Intel

Development people and manufacturing people at our other firms identified very similar simultaneous efforts, both in product development and in manufacturing, to smooth the complex transition of new products into volume production. The underlying facts stand out across these firms: products and processes must be jointly developed, and close integration is essential for success. The complexities of product and process entail multiple interfaces, many people, and lots of interchange. There is no other way to success.

World-Class Design: Advanced Productivity Tools

The complexities of semiconductor manufacture rest on complex product designs – micron and sub-micron line widths for circuitry painstakingly constructed in meticulously crafted layers. Integrated circuits today can contain hundreds of thousands of miniature components. Designs are so complex that they require computer assistance for design, simulation, and testing, as well as for manufacture. Today's devices are too complex for unaided human design. Burgeoning computer design and simulation capabilities have spun off a whole sub-industry, specializing in custom design. The new twist here is that customers can often design their own custom products, because the computer software can test their ideas and provide the engineering support needed to specify the desired product. According to Fred Heiman, Intel's Director of Corporate Planning:

There is a revolution going on in computer aided design tools within the semiconductor start-ups. The start-ups are [creating such] powerful tools that customers can design their own parts. VLSI and LSI Logic, Wilf Corrigan's company, are creating a gate array business which evolves into a standard cell, which evolves into a full custom part – to 20,000 gates.

Fred Heiman, Intel

The revolution may have even farther-reaching consequences, encouraging still more complex designs, resting on capturing much expert knowledge in programs to assist design. More recently, so-called "silicon compilers" have even hit the cover of *Forbes* magazine, where computer science expert Carver Mead of the California Institute of Technology outlined the impact of an industry in which customers could design their own custom parts. Mead believes that silicon compilers represent the leading edge of a new wave of entrepreneurial activity – stressing user-designed custom products, rather than the high volume standard parts on which the industry has been based up to now (Gilder, 1988).

Whether via silicon compilers and gate arrays, or via other sorts of ASICs, custom products are gaining importance. This means that product runs will be shorter, products must be more carefully keyed to user needs, and therefore that production will become still more complex in the future. For companies like those in our sample, the bottom line is that the design and development process must be speeded still more. In 1981, a three-year design and development cycle was described to us as typical, plus or minus six months. By contrast, in 1987 and 1988, Intel was already pushing the cycle to under a year.

In 1987, Intel created its 82385 cache controller, a complex CHMOS logic circuit containing about 215,000 transistors, in just 46 weeks. The cache controller went from product specification to its first $1 million in revenues in eleven and a half months, at "a pace we would have thought unlikely a few years ago," according to Intel's 1987 Annual Report. The feat is evidence of a blend of advances: state-of-the-art design tools (CAD systems), frequently using software designed in-house; modular design techniques based on ASIC technology; and a broad-based emphasis on "doing it right the first time."

Implications of the End-Game

The marriage of these efforts and tools has resulted in a significant reduction in the time from initial product specification to production of engineering samples at each of the study companies. These firms are able to create chips faster, less expensively and with better quality, even though chip complexity continues to rise rapidly. But the leading-edge, highest-technology firms are not the only ones facing these demands. Similar experiences with computer-aided electronic design in other industries have been reported by others, including instruments (Van Nostrand, 1984), running shoes (Compressed Air, 1985) and automobiles (Mishne, 1988).

When business environments seem especially volatile, new customer needs translate into rapid change in manufacturing. In such circumstances, time to market is often the difference between success and failure. Texas Instruments, long known as a highly effective end-game manufacturer, explicitly elected to remain in DRAM commodity manufacture, rather than ceding the marketplace to the Japanese, because commodity production enabled the firm to hone its manufacturing expertise in support of coming new product developments.

Effective management of the manufacturing end-game, in short, pushes innovation and "routine" production into still closer proximity. At the same time, continued competitive effort into the later stages of the innovation cycle – on to commodity volumes – has become increasingly important even for leading-edge firms like Intel. It is not enough to command the premium prices of early market stages.

For the future, true blending of manufacturing capability into strategic thinking is essential. This means bringing manufacturing development into even closer coupling with strategic thinking, guiding development of capabilities more explicitly in directions that will most likely support anticipated product and technology evolution. This will be a new step for most semiconductor firms – and for most US manufacturing firms in whatever industry. Some firms (Ford is a notable example) already show signs of the shift.

Development costs for continued innovation and equipment costs for the advanced capabilities essential in global markets are so high that only full exploitation of innovation can fund them. Full exploitation means gaining the premium benefits of early entry, but also holding market share in the face of new entrants at later stages.

As others have also argued, staying in the game at all means staying through the end-game (Cohen and Zysman, 1987; Hayes et al., 1988; Ungson, 1987). The manufacturing end-game, no less than the on-going flow of initial product concepts and the complex transition from idea to product design to manufacturing, must be carefully managed. Such is the nature of competitive reality for the high-technology firms we sampled, and, increasingly, such is reality also for more and more firms and industries throughout the US economy.

11
Strong Culture and its Consequences

I think the biggest factor – a very big factor – that is not properly understood (and it probably goes for more than just us, for other companies too, but certainly here), [is] the importance of a very informal atmosphere. That cannot be overestimated. Informal in many ways: not just the hierarchy, but informal in terms of the sets of rules. And that atmosphere – that allows anybody to voice his opinion and to violate "rules" – is conducive to innovation.
Charlie Sporck, National Semiconductor

When I say "turn up the heat," what I sense management is doing – sure as hell what I'm doing, is, I'm trying to knock down all the roadblocks. Let's agree on what it is we're trying to accomplish, let's try to eliminate all the roadblocks, all the bureaucracy. Let's create the right kind of environment, where people are doing it because they *believe* in it, not because they "have to" do it . . . I mean, we *believe* in it!
Pat Weber, Texas Instruments

Strong Culture: Power, but no Panacea

"Strong culture" has been widely lauded in the business press as management's newest tool. It is proposed as a modern, sophisticated means to guide and control employees, ensure their compliance and enthusiasm, and generally serve in place of bureaucratic controls that are viewed as outmoded, if still widely used (Deal and Kennedy, 1982; Peters and Waterman, 1982). But strong culture merits a second look. Do strong cultures really have only unalloyed advantages, and no disadvantages? Our research suggests otherwise.

In this chapter, we will present a more balanced view of strong culture. To do so, we will describe strong culture's attributes and some of the claims made for it. Drawing on our highly innovative companies, which not so incidentally are also among those frequently mentioned as strong culture exemplars, we will highlight some of strong culture's difficulties, before turning to a closer look at how it actually functions. But first, we must define strong culture.

To some degree, all companies have some sort of culture, so what sets strong cultures apart? Strong organization culture has typically been described in terms of widely shared values among organization members. People think well of the same things, and frown on others, in concert. Strong cultures are supposed to be those in which employees from top to bottom share a collective vision of "what the business is all about," as well as deep personal convictions that "the company's success is my business." There may be local goals or views, but these generally coincide with a higher goal, or give precedence to it, in a strong organizational culture (Deal and Kennedy, 1982). Others have noted that shared myths and rituals play a role in corporate culture, that code-words, shared experience, and common memory contribute to a sense of "we" among organization members, contrasting with "them," all those outside (Martin and Powers, 1983; Wilkins, 1983, 1984).

Deal and Kennedy originated the term "strong culture," applying it to a quarter of their sample of 80 companies. The strong culture companies had clearly articulated beliefs in a higher goal, for example, "progress is our most important product" at General Electric. Far more than just a financial target, the higher goal was more of a philosophical guide. These companies were also "uniformly outstanding performers," according to Deal and Kennedy (1982, p. 7), who seem to weld performance and culture together. To date, however, there has been no statistical evidence that strong culture results in outstanding performance, although the notion is certainly attractive, and many anecdotes suggest benefits from strong culture.

Strong culture is described as a powerful lever to guide employee behavior, helping people do their jobs a little better in two ways, according to Deal and Kennedy. First, "a strong culture is a system of informal rules that spells out how people are to behave most of the time." This means that people need not consult formal rules, but can interpret new situations based on their understanding of the culture. Secondly, "a strong culture enables people to feel better about what they do, so they are more likely to work harder" (Deal and Kennedy, 1982, pp. 15–16). Indeed, Deal and Kennedy hoped to instill a new law of business life: "In Culture There Is Strength" (p. 19).

Others share the same persistently upbeat focus on culture. Peters and Waterman (1982) also discussed culture at length, concluding that, "Without exception, the dominance and coherence of culture proved to be an essential quality of the excellent companies" (Peters and Waterman, 1982, p. 75). There is only the briefest mention of difficulties. Mirroring the confusion of Deal and Kennedy, Peters and Waterman also seem to dismiss the idea of strong culture in poorer-performing companies, because these dysfunctional cultures are ". . . usually focused on internal politics rather than on the customer, or they focus on 'the numbers' rather than on the product and the people who make and sell it" (Peters and Waterman, 1982, p. 76). Poorly-run companies, by definition, seem not to have cultures; dysfunctional culture isn't really "strong culture," in the popular press.

Two other possible traps remain. First is the risk that a company's strong culture may blind the firm to dramatic changes in the environment. However, say Peters and Waterman, strong cultures in their excellent companies emphasize being close to the customer, so this trap is unlikely. There is also potential for abuse in the temptation that people will yield to authority in a strong culture in exchange for personal security. This, too, is ignored. So, with scarcely a discouraging word, Peters and Waterman conclude that strong culture makes their companies unique contributors to society.

But defining "strong" culture as "good" culture seems to us to evade the issue. While we found many of the strengths widely advertised for strong culture, our research also suggests that genuine downside risks and costs accompany strong culture, even in companies lauded for both performance and culture. People in the innovative companies we researched were keenly aware of the costs as well as the benefits. Employees in our sample companies praise their companies' cultures, value them deeply, and see many advantages to them. But people within these cultures also bear their costs, and invest much effort to avoid the potential hazards of strong culture.

Some Limitations of Corporate Culture

Corporate culture plays an especially important role in our sample of high-technology firms, with their emphasis on high performance amidst repeated change. By any account, our sample firms are "strong culture" companies, renowned for culture that serves both as "social lubricant" and as "social glue." Because such a culture is both persistent and pervasive, paradoxically, it can facilitate change by maintaining a higher order of stability, in the form of deeply held and slow-to-change values. Thus culture provides a means for new ideas to be taken in. By enabling people to maintain "the sense of continuity that tells us who we are," in Alan Kantrow's evocative phrase, the new can be appropriately related to "what really matters" in the old (Kantrow, 1987).

These observations readily suggest some of strong culture's costs, which are inextricably bound up with its benefits. The same commitment that allows people to invest themselves in their company and its goals also makes them vulnerable to burn-out, renders them less willing to change and abandon what they are doing, and more ready to see the world wholly in terms of the culture's view. Strong culture's pervasiveness within a company means that every act by managers will be interpreted in its light. Real understanding requires a still closer look.

"Strong culture" is said to benefit the firm by making co-ordination easier and motivation stronger. In place of rules and resentment, culture is supposed to enable managers to exert influence more subtly, and thus more acceptably. As practicing managers know, however, the real world is not nearly so simple. "Strong motivation" and co-ordination may serve management's purposes – or they may be directed to other purposes entirely. Corporate culture is not wholly within management's control, it is not completely management's tool, and it is not cost free.

We found these costs being borne on a daily basis by employees. For instance, in the companies we studied, there are relatively high levels of confrontation. Openness and informality in communication mean that people frequently "confront" one another on issues, differences of opinion, or performance results. The style is said to improve innovation and ensure diverse input to decisions, but it can also lead to personal stress. Confrontations intended as impersonal, objective critiques can easily acquire emotional charge, when people have invested themselves in their work. When nascent innovative ideas, extensive project work or potential solutions for vexing problems are involved, the same personal investment that leads to follow-through produces ego involvement – it is tough to separate "my idea" from "me," so that attacks on "it" seem attacks on "me." The following statements are representative:

> It's a battle – an internal selling battle. And it's fought, then, for funds.
>
> Peter Rosenbladt, Hewlett-Packard

> It really hurts [when your program is turned off]. It was a tremendous disappointment. That really hurt because we really had done a thorough job, we'd looked at all the pros and cons, we had come up with a good many innovative technical approaches to solving this problem . . .
>
> Len Donohoe, Texas Instruments

> It's important to keep people not behaving defensively, but to focusing on what the problems are.
>
> Karl Rapp, National Semiconductor

Personality also plays a role. Not all managers, engineers, and scientists are equally skilled in gentle delivery of such criticisms (or in their disinterested receipt). Not all of those who invest themselves heavily are equally able to avoid personal attacks, when "their" project, division, or strategic commitment is challenged. In short, it is not uncommon for critique to be construed as personal, rather than "objective." Equally, lower-level employees also must acquire the skills needed to confront their superiors. Even in an egalitarian environment, one can imagine that the first few times one is expected to openly confront or criticize senior managers, scientists, or technical experts, the experience could well be unsettling.

These are only a few of strong culture's costs. To appreciate corporate culture more fully, we will look more closely at some of its hazards and requirements. Only by recognizing potential problems can managers take effective steps to mitigate them. Only by understanding organizational culture's requirements will managers interact usefully with it.

In summary, our chapter will deal with three broad categories of cost: individual, managerial, and organizational. These downside features are inherent in the very nature of strong culture. They are the mirror images of characteristics that give strong culture its benefits and strengths. We also found yet another cost of the strong cultures in our technology-based companies, one that flows more subtly and pervasively. It is the requirement that executives truly share strategic management and operational details with employees well down into the ranks. This last aspect of strong culture is, like the others, also inseparable from strong culture itself: a strong corporate culture will be shaped by the "foot soldiers" as well as by the "officers," by the "musicians" as well as by the "conductor." In some important ways, this may be the most important and abiding consequence of strong culture upon our ideas of management in the future. We will deal with each of these costs, turning first to the individual costs of strong culture.

High Intensity Management

The first set of strong culture costs are immediately personal. Culture is of value precisely because it produces intense involvement, and deep personal and emotional investment by people in their activities. These outcomes have minuses as well as pluses. People committed to particular goals strive to achieve them – and can resist changes in the goals, regardless of changing organizational circumstances. People devoted to one idea of an organization can resist alternatives. Employees deeply invested in their work can neglect their "outside" lives and families, and "burn out." Strong culture can be all-consuming.

Deep personal involvement is a prime outcome of personal responsibility and informal, open management. It is, on the one hand, highly desirable: it is how people come to care about the outcomes of their efforts. On the other hand, it can be costly. Personal engagement and involvement must be carefully managed. Dan Dooley suggested that socializing newcomers so they could see themselves as contributors was important:

> One of the things I think we've done very, very well – it's either that, or we burn them up – is, we're very good at assimilating college kids [recently graduated new hires]. At least during the

last two years, we've been very encouraged at how quickly they
come up and become contributors.

> Dan Dooley, National Semiconductor

Like the Protestant ethic, the success and participation norms of such
a culture can produce significant stress as well as achievement. In
one major computer firm not in our sample, burnout was especially
visible at the end of the quarter, when people routinely worked
around the clock to make shipping quotas. Our companies also
recognize the potential for burnout, and seek to prevent it. Like
other firms, TI has a broad program of family involvement and
benefits – membership in a TIers country club, for instance – to help
families feel some tangible benefit in return for an employee's deep
involvement.

Hard-nosed, try-harder management is also part of the strong
cultures we studied. It creates pressure. This can be good: it often
produces superlative results. Performance and success are gratifying,
of course, but the pressure can be "consuming." Even the change
that is so widely embraced contributes to pressure, although often
joked about, here in the context of reorganization:

> Every once in a while, they bang on the canaries' cage, and
> throw everything into turmoil.
>
> Anonymous TI Manager (cited in *Fortune*)

Pressure comes because, despite the "turmoil," desired results must
still be achieved.

Sometimes assertions of individual responsibility – both from those
responsible, and from their colleagues – can deny reality as a direct
outgrowth of the tough, can-do attitude built into the culture, and
of hard-nosed, try-harder management. Besides confrontation by
others, the threat of failure provides its own push. Necessarily, the
push of personal investment disciplines people to keep trying; the
other side of the coin is that failure has consequences. Even if some
external factor causes failure, something over which people really
have no control, as one manager put it, "That's no excuse, that is a
failure."

People who thrive in confrontational, high-performance organizations are likely to be quite competitive. They don't like to lose,
whether to external circumstances, "the enemy" (be it the Japanese
or some domestic rival), or even someone else's project inside the
firm. The push – the pressure – is clear. As several others commented:

> Very often people do [get burned out or alienated] – we do. That
> happens to us all the time. You either lick your wounds or give
> up and do something else, or you recognize that somebody had
> a better argument.
>
> Peter Rosenbladt, Hewlett-Packard

Personal responsibility can be carried farther still. Some of the most potent of these hard-nosed, try-harder attitudes do not come from "management" at all: they come from within the individual employee, and from peers. In strong cultures, personal investment also means internalizing the basic attitudes of the culture, including the hard-nosed, try-harder attitude. People are not "driven" by their managers in these firms; far more often, they drive themselves through a combination of excitement, desire to achieve, and the internalized values of trying harder, and "believing in" their company.

In one high-technology firm not in our sample, for instance, people regularly judged any failure as a failure of will or nerve. The typical diagnosis was, "If [Name] had cared enough, s/he could have made it happen." This comment was particularly striking in one instance, when the "failure" involved a railroad car that did not arrive, preventing on-time shipment, due to a major storm washing out track! Ignoring reality also has major potential organizational costs, a topic to which we shall return.

Deep personal investment in achieving the extraordinary, coupled with a personal sense of responsibility, can translate into many "lost weekends," few vacations and little family time, as individuals struggle to deliver superlative results. Silicon Valley is noted for an especially high divorce rate among its inhabitants, and many of those we spoke with mentioned "the astronomical divorce rate" as one outcome of people's investment of themselves in their firms:

> I guess it's a matter of public record that this industry probably
> destroys more marriages than any [other industry] you'll find.
> It's very difficult to avoid taking either the specific issues that
> you're wrestling with, or just the exhaustion, home with you.
>
> Anonymous high-technology manager

The excitement of constant change can be almost addictive, a phenomenon more widely recognized in recent years in the context of addictive interpersonal relationships (Ackerman, 1986). While such relationships are self-destructive, the same dynamics in organizational settings can produce significant achievement and many socially positive outcomes. "High performing organizations" do provide excitement and feelings of accomplishment difficult to find elsewhere (McClelland, 1961; Vail, 1978). High performing individuals, those with an urge to achieve, create high performing organizations by pushing hard to accomplish things others either do not attempt, or abandon as hopeless. Nonetheless, the stress produced by near-constant responsibility for new technology and new knowledge is real. Stress produced by such variety can be positive or negative – perhaps even both simultaneously (Seyle, 1974).

The sheer time pressure too adds to stress, since the marvels of innovation are always confronted with a limited window of opportunity. Decision making under such conditions is difficult, the more so because of uncertainty, tied inescapably to the limited time available:

> It's incredibly stressful. We have to do it fast. We just can't wait until it's more obvious what to do. It's very stressful . . . You can't wait until there's so much information that it would be obvious. It doesn't take a highly paid manager to do that. First, for all of the decisions that we make, there is, at best, marginal information to help you make the decision.
>
> Ed Boleky, Intel

Of course, such time pressure is endemic in the fast-changing environment of our sample companies; it is not limited to Intel. As a manager Motorola commented, somewhat wryly, "animal cunning" plays an important part in innovation, and so does "institutionalized panic" because people do react to the stress:

> Oh, I think that the panic, probably more than anything else, is about the best motivator for innovation . . . Sometimes desperation forces you to seek innovative solutions to problems. I don't want to say that we "institutionalize panic" in the way we do things, but sometimes the pressure of events does force you to come up with things which might not otherwise be conceived. The danger in that is that sometimes, in the present time, you may take an otherwise good idea and just not have time to follow it. These things don't seem to happen by somebody sitting in a room and doing nothing, just dreaming up ideas. Some of this seems to arise out of involvement with practical problems.
>
> Bill Howard, Motorola

The nature of personal costs and difficulties is clear: trying to do what no one else has ever done creates stress as a direct result of personal involvement. People are stressed because they feel personally responsible for things so uncertain and risky that they cannot initially see what to do about them:

> People don't sleep a lot. You'll wake up in the middle of the night, wrestling with something. I personally often have a lot of trouble sleeping on Sunday night. I can block things out Friday night, Saturday, Saturday night and all day Sunday, but [then] I start thinking about what I'm going to walk into on Monday morning.
>
> Anonymous high-technology manager

Pressure does not signal failure, and certainly not incompetence. Rather, it indicates a very realistic awareness of the magnitude of the tasks at hand. Our sample firms confront an extraordinarily challenging environment, and their managers are keenly aware of the challenge. Stress comes from the very personal investment of self in the results of the firm – the very source of strong culture's benefits. People care because they invest themselves; their caring means that they translate the firm's difficulties into their own:

> Staying [ahead], being the leader – even that magnifies the pressure. We're at the top, not just so much from the standpoint of profitability, but we're at the top from the standpoint of trying to stay ahead technologically. We have companies in the States and Japan [with whom we compete] with resources that are five to ten times the resources of this company. The only way we can stay ahead is by being smarter and quicker on our feet [than they are]. There's just really no room for significant errors.
>
> Ed Boleky, Intel

Confronting Culture

Hard-nosed management and the try-harder mentality themselves came in for criticism. Especially revealing – and highly typical of comments by others at all our sample companies – are the comments of Ed Slaughter, General Manager of Intel Development Organization (IDO). Slaughter was brought into a high-level position from the outside, and thus brings a rare objectivity to his comments about Intel's organizational culture. Slaughter's position and the organization he headed were deliberately created outside of Intel's normal operating division structure. Before IDO, development activities took place within a given product line, in the context primarily of product line development; IDO was deliberately set outside traditional organizational lines.

Because he was an outsider, Slaughter, lacking extended contact and familiarity with Intel people, was asked to develop innovations faster and in what appeared to be an "oddball" way – outside existing formats for financial and resource controls. As a result, he was supremely sensitive to Intel methods and their impact on innovation efforts that did not fall into usual Intel practice:

> The 82nd Airborne School of Management is – I have to caricature it – "If there is a hard way to do it, that's probably better than the easy way to do it. If there's a way that's a little more painful, that's probably the way God wants it to be. The fact that it's painful – that's probably good."
>
> Ed Slaughter, Intel

Intel's is not the only culture to embrace confrontation, nor is Slaughter alone in his skepticism. The "push" at these companies is not wholly dependent on top management, or on formal culture indoctrination courses, as we have shown. Yet another manager noted how ingrained confrontation has become at Intel. As in each of the companies we studied, strong culture grew only partly in response to the deliberate attempts of management. This, too, is a downside risk in strong cultures: they may evolve in ways not necessarily foreseen by managers:

> There's a culture [around constructive confrontation] built up independent of the course. It's understood by everyone. That's what happens. That's the Intel culture.
>
> Anonymous Intel manager

Others also commented on the tough facets of strong culture at a number of our companies. Intel's tough culture is only particularly visible in the high value placed on "constructive confrontation." It is so important an element of Intel's problem-solving that a formal course has been constructed around this concept, to explicitly teach the skills involved to the greatest possible number of employees. The senior officers of the firm, including founders Gordon Moore and Andrew Grove, both regularly teach in employee culture classes. Constructive confrontation was described by another of Intel's managers as

> . . . essentially the Intel-approved way of problem-solving, where you are supposed to be very open with people. If you think they have a problem, you're supposed to tell them that you think they're doing something wrong. If you can do it better, you're supposed to tell them. If you think you can help, or if it's partially my problem and I don't think they're doing their job right, I have to tell them to do that and say, "Is there somewhere I can help you organize this?" or "How can we work this out?" It's the Intel-approved way. You're supposed to be very direct, and rude, if necessary.
>
> Anonymous Intel manager

While the behaviors associated with constructive confrontation may be viewed as "rude" by some, the same manager nevertheless felt that constructive confrontation worked very well at Intel:

> It's an effective way to do it. I think the direct way has to be the best way. It puts a burden on us, again in that for a lot of people, it's easier to be polite – to write a memo and say, "Please help me on this," instead of calling up the person and saying, "This is a crock! If you're not doing your job, help me out. How can we do this together?"
>
> Anonymous Intel manager

A very similar style, and quite parallel costs, were described at other firms as well. For instance, "people do a lot of screaming and yelling around here," comments one TI manager, "but it's always about problems. Or almost always around problems." Others described similar direct communications at National Semiconductor and Hewlett-Packard – despite HP's reputation for being "more relaxed."

Strong culture did not mean there were no divergent views, as these quotes suggest. Cultural norms for expressing one's opinion virtually assured diversity – and response. Not all employees embrace this aspect of the company's culture, and not all react well to constructive confrontation. The same anonymous Intel manager continued:

> So it's definitely a developed skill for some people, and some people don't react well to it, either. If you try to use this technique with them, they'll say, "Get off my case. It's my job. Leave me alone." But it is something that Intel tends to push, and I think the direct way has to be the best way.

Being able to openly communicate is an essential skill that was frequently referred to as "part of the culture" in the companies we studied. Whatever it is called, such exchanges can attract an emotional charge when deeply invested people disagree. Such interaction is predictably stressful, regardless of who is confronting whom. We believe such stress is endemic to strong cultures, especially cultures like those we studied that focus on both performance and open communication in highly competitive circumstances. An anonymous TI manager commented about the stress of knowing that one's proposals, and thus one's future, might be on the line in a formal presentation:

> I've seen grown men faint on stage, making an annual planning presentation to Bucy and Shepard, under the pressure.
>
> Anonymous former general manager, TI

Another anonymous Intel manager observed that confrontation could be costly, and might not always be "constructive:"

> They make such a big thing out of the constructive confrontation business that if somebody gets out of hand, it's just confrontation for its own sake. I know of people, some very, very good people who could in fact function quite well at Intel – people who eventually just left. I worked other places where I didn't have this constant interpersonal pushing and shoving, and I got just as much done.
>
> Anonymous manager, Intel

Managers at other firms too commented that people who shouted did so about problems and solutions, rather than as personal attacks. Yet they also reported that often enough, attacks clearly did develop, or were perceived. For all its benefits in problem-solving, clarity and directness, confrontation is one aspect of the strong cultures we studied that entails important personal – and interpersonal – costs.

Informality and Innovation: Shared Control

The personal costs described above are paralleled by special costs borne by managers in these companies, who exist in a very different environment from that typical of traditional firms. The widely reported informality of high-technology firms – a universal pattern, despite some variances – is tied to sharp limits to managers' power. Here, much more so than in traditional firms, subordinates' inputs are recognized as essential to achieving anything.

A third complex facet of strong corporate culture is related to this personal investment; it concerns the sense people make of the organizational world around them, and the impact this has on corporate goals and possibilities. Within a strong culture, communication is facilitated, people understand what their colleagues mean, and speedily share information, visions, and expectations. These shared interpretations and habits of mind, so useful in generating consensus, can be dangerous if they inhibit recognition of new realities. Particularly when a culture values success and effort, it can be difficult to get inconvenient necessity, untenable cost, or even literal impossibility recognized. Instead, people can cling to illusions that are more consistent with their culture.

High-technology companies are noticeably more informal than organizations based on older, more mature technologies. There are, of course, geographic differences: the Route 128 organizations of New England show systematically lower rates of job change, longer tenure, and somewhat more formal standards of dress than the Silicon Valley firms of California, or those in Arizona and Texas, for instance (Weiss and Delbecq, 1988).

This may be due to the task-focused, egalitarian or anti-hierarchical nature of many new firms – where task-relevant knowledge is more important than position in the hierarchy. Some have suggested that since so many high-technology firms are small, this may be a "small company" phenomenon (Tornatzky, 1988). There are variations: some larger, better established high-technology firms are more formal than others; some small firms, despite their maturity, cling to informal modes. But even older, larger, and well established firms like Hewlett-Packard, Digital Equipment, or Texas Instruments persistently tend toward shirtsleeves, shared parking and lunch facilities, first names for all, and other democratic signals (Carlzon, 1987; Jelinek, 1979; Kidder, 1981; Peters and Waterman, 1982).

Informality is built into these firms, and quite deliberately recognized as essential to innovation. Many of our interviews included comments like these, referring to Hewlett-Packard and to Motorola:

> I cannot overemphasize that [informality] as being a very normal trait of the HP company. We depend a lot on this kind of work – the informality is the only thing that allows us to do things

like that. If it was formal, it would be rigid, and it would never work.

Peter Rosenbladt, Hewlett-Packard

One of the reasons I believe Motorola is being more successful than most, is that a lot of freedom is required for innovation. Maybe you can decide on what innovations are required, through something like the [TI] OST system . . . but innovation, I think, is very personal. You've got to have a lot of innovative people, or you don't get innovation. You have to give them enough freedom to work on problems that would interest them. That's kind of a heretical thing to say, because obviously, you've got to direct them to what innovations are needed. But a lot of it is interest . . .

Don Walker, Motorola

The links between informality or freedom and innovation were clearly identified, again and again, in our interviews. The point is that informality facilitates a form of interaction among organization members that deliberately and explicitly de-emphasizes organizational status in favor of task-relevant expertise. Subordinates play different roles here than in more traditional firms; so, too, do superiors. Informality by itself produces nothing. The spontaneous leadership and responsibility by the many that it facilitates, however, can release enormous resources of energy, attention, creativity, and effort.

Informality and Dependency

Another of the costs of strong culture is managers' dependence on subordinates, linked both to the informal atmosphere and business realities. Informality, and the dependency that it signals, are hard to ignore. Informality is more widely observable in these companies than in more traditional industry – in more informal dress for women, as well as men. Often even senior managers and executives appear for work without ties, for instance, and many prefer even formal photographs be taken without jackets. Norms do vary with situations, and these same managers will cheerfully put on suits and ties for meeting guests, important customers, or financial analysts, or for annual meetings. Those more likely to meet the public – receptionists, senior executive secretaries, and managers responsible for day-to-day customer contact – tended toward more elegant dress than those whose activities occurred primarily within the firm. In general, however, informality is a decided preference in dress at all ranks, subtly underlining norms of equality.

Where status differentials are de-emphasized, managers must persuade, reason, explain, and otherwise behave toward nominal subordinates in an egalitarian fashion. Subordinates are not very "subordinate," especially when they possess skills and knowledge that managers lack, or when their efforts are so essential to success. In important ways, managers in firms like our sample of innovative companies are fundamentally and far more explicitly dependent upon their subordinates than is generally acknowledged in more traditional firms.

Equality was also reinforced by norms of informal communication. Managers, scientists, and engineers in each of our companies repeatedly told us that "you can talk to anyone here" with an idea or problem – "anyone at all, including [first name of CEO]." Open communication is deliberately fostered, and not merely for social purposes. It is woven into these firms' daily practices to facilitate business, and particularly to encourage innovation. National's Charles Sporck – widely referred to as "Charlie" throughout the firm – underlined the point:

> *Interviewer*: So it is possible that, if an engineer hasn't gotten the right answer [permission to proceed with a project] the first time, he might go shopping [within the firm]?
>
> *Sporck*: Sure . . . We would want him to, if he feels strongly about it, absolutely. And not just on engineering questions, on any questions.

While this exchange describes National Semiconductor, other firms encourage the same attitude. Norms of "shopping" for the right answer undercut any sense of final, formal authority that a supervisor might have by virtue of budgetary control.

Alternative funding arrangements enable people to seek resources from a range of others in the firm, not just their nominal superiors or the department in which they are assigned. At TI, for instance, any of the TI Fellows around the firm can be approached for on-the-spot funding, and if one says "No," another may say "Yes." As we described earlier, TIers cherish the tale of the engineer who insisted that the laser guided bomb project be pursued, despite being turned down repeatedly by superiors, and even threats of firing. He showed up for work anyway, saying that the project was too important to the company to be terminated. This story was mentioned by a former TI manager at Motorola, with the comment:

> Those examples exist all around the industry, as a matter of fact. Part of my training came under a guy that I worked with in Texas Instruments by the name of Jim Nygard. He never did anything he was told. That's basically it. I don't know how many things we worked on, totally in direct opposition to what [TI Chairman Mark] Shepard had specifically instructed him to do. He said, "Stop this program and go work on that." And we would not stop this program, and we would not go work on the other.
>
> Don Walker, Motorola

At HP, people are expected to involve others in their projects early on, on an informal basis. People are encouraged to talk to those who may be interested in their ideas, rather than just to their direct superiors. There is simply no one single channel for approval, assistance, or resources. There are many similar practices throughout high-technology firms, and they are seen as central to maintaining an innovative atmosphere by those that foster them. Informal, open communication is at the heart of these companies' strong cultures – and it, too, underlines the minimal status and control that attach to managerial rank.

A truly open door, which invites communication, is reinforced by the expectation that individuals *will* communicate with others about their innovative ideas, problems, and concerns in these firms. New product ideas and project proposals are especially matters for speaking out:

> . . . You have to be outspoken and sell your ideas. You don't get it through the numbers – and it's not a formal process. It really takes a lot of initiative to get ideas approved at any level . . . We want people to be agents of change, because we believe that change is absolutely fundamental not only to this company, but also this industry. We want people to be non-complacent.
>
> Peter Rosenbladt, Hewlett-Packard

Similar sentiments were voiced at National by Dan Dooley, who portrayed convincing superiors on "some fundamentally, totally new concept" as very much a matter of course:

> In some cases, one ends up having to sell senior management on
> the idea of funding [a really "new, esoteric" project] long enough
> to where . . . they can get their arms around it.
>
> Dan Dooley, National Semiconductor

Such interchanges are not limited to those inside the firm – and they
are not one-way, as Dooley quickly noted:

> Frankly, if [the new idea] is all that super-duper, we have
> generally pretty good working relationships with key customers,
> and we interface with them. You know – "If you had such a
> thing as this, with these performance criteria, what would it be
> worth to you? How many would you buy? Where would you use
> 'em?" That sort of thing.
>
> Dan Dooley, National Semiconductor

Informal Obligations

An important outcome of informality and open communication is the
constant expectation that those with ideas *will* speak up, as a matter
of course and as part and parcel of their responsibility. In this
light, Dan Dooley described regular innovation meetings including
marketing, engineering and operations people:

> *Dooley*: . . . That is essentially a new product committee, if you
> will, made up of different department managers. They invite
> other people – [like] engineers [for instance] – to sit in. That's
> the forum where, if anybody's got a hot flash, a new concept to
> introduce, they might get it kicked around in those meetings.
>
> *Interviewer*: You really have to have the courage of your
> convictions before you stand up before God and everyone in a
> meeting like that and talk about an idea, though, don't you?
>
> *Dooley*: Not really – it's held pretty informally. As a matter of
> fact, *very* informally. We tend to be a rather informal company.

The informal interchange – among peers, across departments, between
subordinates and superiors, between companies and their customers
– is carefully cherished and fostered, because it is seen as essential
to survival. But it does carry personal responsibility for results. It
quite clearly transcends organizational rank, hierarchy, or structure.
Informality here, while it is a cultural norm, serves a very conscious
purpose: sharing of information and insights where they are needed,

regardless of formal structure or rank. Dooley again highlighted the rationale, and the deeply ingrained marketplace criterion that is inseparable from open communication:

> The problem is that products are no longer simple things, easily conceived and designed and developed. It's very easy to have just a terrific idea, which is a cure looking for a sickness, that nobody wants. It might be a terrific idea.
>
> Dan Dooley, National Semiconductor

These companies are fundamentally dependent upon maintaining their cultural norms of informality, open communication, co-ordinated effort, and sharing of insight. Without it, their complex projects will fail.

Ultimately, the aim is marketplace success. The same criterion was repeatedly voiced over many years in these firms, for assessing ideas and for measuring innovation:

> What is innovation? I'll go back to a Haggerty quote: "An innovation does not exist until you have a commercial success." Right? You can have a lot of good ideas, a lot of good R&D, a lot of neat things that you talk about. But you've got to have a commercial success – because that's the measure of innovation. At least that's the way society measures innovation.
>
> Pat Weber, Texas Instruments

However terrific, the product is useless if it won't sell. The views of Pat Haggerty, who died in 1980, were reiterated in each of our sample companies. Complexity, in product design, production technology, and markets as well, means that many others must be enlisted to ensure any good idea's success in reaching the market.

People who are reticent, or who wait for others to come to them, will not prosper in these firms. Those who are uncomfortable with direct, even confrontational communication about problems, will find these firms' informality highly stressful. Yet managers repeatedly insisted to us that firms that fail to foster the sort of broad interchange and personal responsibility described here will fail to access important innovation capabilities and insights that can contribute quite directly to success or failure of a product in the marketplace.

Depending on Subordinates

Individuals bear significant responsibility in our sample firms for speaking up at need – whether to insist that a project be funded, or to argue for cancellation of one that is unlikely to succeed, or to input their expertise or views along the way. This responsibility gives individuals an important say in and ownership of major projects and in corporate strategy. Beneath this widespread "open communication" policy is a hard fact of life in firms that face high rates of change: management, and senior management in particular, cannot possibly know enough to make unilateral, independent decisions.

This dependency is most directly visible in technical matters. Technology changes too quickly, and there is too much relevant, important information for managers to pretend to control it all. In this vein, another HP manager, Rod Carlson, commented on group-level strategic decision making reviews:

> *Carlson*: If you take the reviews of product strategy that take place at the group level, it's not an approval type thing. No decisions are made in those meetings, obviously.
>
> *Interviewer*: "Obviously?"
>
> *Carlson*: Because they don't have the information, really, to make them. People might think that top managers could come in and see a whole division's presentation on product strategy and make some decisions out of that, but they don't have the knowledge of the customers, of the technology, and so on to make those decisions. What comes back from those [meetings] are [discussion issues and] some written questions, comments, things to consider, and so on.

But the underlying reality is equally true in other aspects of business – the more so in rapidly changing, highly fragmented markets, where competition has intensified and even highly competent and accomplished persons must rely on others' knowledge and specialty expertise. Innovation, technological or otherwise, is not a task for the mythical "only, lonely innovator," in these firms. Consequently, seniors depend fundamentally on those below, whose direct, current and detailed familiarity with product design, material capabilities, marketplace needs and the like must necessarily compose product or project proposals:

The primary proposals for risky propositions [involving inno-
vations] are coming from the bottom up, which is where they've
got to come from.

Peter Rosenbladt, Hewlett-Packard

While senior managers alone can commit the firm to spending the
enormous sums involved in a new fab line, development of a new
technology, or even a significant market expansion, the question of
what to do – Do we need a new fab line? What technology do we
need? What market opportunities are there? – rests firmly on the
concrete specifics of detailed knowledge available only from those
who meet the market, know the technology first-hand, or manufacture
the goods. A part of the problem is comfort with required expertise,
and familiarity with the problems involved, as Gordon Moore of Intel
commented:

> I'm a lot more comfortable spending several million dollars for
> [technology] than I was spending the equivalent amount of money
> for advertising . . . We were coming out of a meeting where we
> approved a major technology program that was about $5 million:
> no trouble at all, [I was] very comfortable with the whole thing.
> I went over and looked at an advertising program that would
> run around $3 million, and my stomach was churning, and I
> started to choke on it. I'm sure that somebody who'd come out
> of the consumer products area might have exactly the opposite
> reaction to the two things.

Gordon Moore, Intel

Moore's comment underlines senior managers' essential dependency,
in high-technology firms, on the expertise of others. Only those who
have the relevant knowledge can say whether existing equipment can
be pushed for one more generation of product, whether current
technologies can deliver what designers suggest, whether "new"
markets justify large advertising budgets, or not. Management
must depend on them, both for ideas and dreams, and for the nitty-
gritty details that will encourage or kill a proposal.

Where senior managers fail to trust their subordinates, real danger
of obsolescence looms. Senior managers who cling to their own
personal experience will almost certainly fail to recognize essential
market changes. For instance, in the computer markets – particularly
for PCs and small workstations – software has been widely identified
as an essential element of strategy. Yet managers whose experience
had turned on hardware capabilities were slow to see how great a

role software played. The reported comment of one senior manager is illuminating:

> [A highly successful senior executive] admonished his managers, "You don't need this software crap – build a better box!" He was really a metal-bender. It took the firm almost ten years to realize how important software was, because the top people had no software experience, and wouldn't bring in any outsiders.

The failure was not isolated: TI, HP, and even Apple have at various times experienced such difficulties in computers – and of course the problem is really quite generic. Any significant shift, unrecognized, can render obsolete older experience and assumptions, as we have argued throughout this book. Where senior managers' experience can become quickly obsolete, their only recourse is to access the more recent insights and experience of their subordinates.

Open Strategic Decisions

Such inescapable dependency produces a more open strategic decision making process. Open decision processes are, as we have argued, characteristic of high performing high-technology firms. They are also quite consistent with the strongly participative corporate cultures we found. Above all, such open processes underline the role of juniors in the strategy sessions on dream creation and vision making, reality testing and "bug detection." Open processes also demand a new role for managers, not as "decision makers," but as askers of inconvenient questions, encouragers of communication and thought, co-ordinators of disparate sources of expertise, and articulators of visions and consequences.

In response, the role of the presenter or project champion also changes. Both senior executives and peers as well must ensure that it does. Rod Carlson, a strategy manager at Hewlett-Packard, described one aspect of the new role this way:

> [You go in] trying to think of the most embarrassing questions you can ask – you know, "Have you thought of this?" and so on. That is really what it is.

At HP and at Intel, and in the other firms in our sample, real strategic direction is exercised by the operating division personnel, well down in the organization, not by remote "senior management." The strategy manager's job is to run strategy review sessions. Senior managers participate by using these review sessions as a means to ensure that ideas are shared, and to test the vision against the best expertise available:

> . . . You want to be sure that if people do have some pretty definite ideas and thoughts, that they are bringing them out to you. And not being so incorrect that you might not really be getting the point or something.
>
> Rod Carlson, Hewlett-Packard

Local Knowledge in High-Technology Firms

Decades ago, it was recognized that managers don't "do." Instead, they depend on others to do, while they see to resources, mind details of co-ordination, keep track of morale and so on. Similarly, it appears that managers for the most part do not make strategic decisions. Instead, their contribution has more to do with co-ordination, management of collaboration and complexity, ensuring widespread input and engagement, and, finally, validating or ratifying the commitment of the firm to a course of action. In short, our high-technology managers recognize quite explicitly that they depend upon their people and their people's "local knowledge" – their detailed expertise in and familiarity with technology, markets, production realities, and all the myriad details of how to understand what is happening, and how to actually implement any plan (Baba, 1988; Geertz, 1983).

Local knowledge, a concept drawn from anthropology, is special knowledge that is context-specific. It exists in discrete pockets, is shared among the "locals" there, and may or may not be noticed, appreciated or acknowledged by those outside the locale. While local knowledge is not a special characteristic of strong cultures, it is an inevitable consequence of differences in expertise, experience, and attention. What is characteristic of strong cultures, and in particular the strong cultures of our sample companies, is that management is deeply respectful of employees' special knowledge. Together with informality, this recognition permeates these firms; they draw upon local knowledge, seek it out, cherish it, and consciously accept their dependence on it as part and parcel of the open, participative culture they strive to maintain.

"Local knowledge" is special knowledge tied intimately to the locale in which it occurs. These firms make particular use of technical knowledge about equipment, procedures, designs, or production processes; and marketplace knowledge – detailed familiarity with a customer's problem or proposed use for a product. This knowledge evolves in only one way: by close contact with the technology (technical local knowledge) or with the customer (local market knowledge). These firms' use of local knowledge is visible in their universal policy of ensuring close contact between engineers and customers, and between designers and manufacturing engineers.

The close contact is explicitly fostered, in order that detailed familiarity can result, and thus be available for problem-solving when needed. The close links between open communication in general in these firms, and access to local knowledge which will be held by lower-level individuals, should be clear. Local knowledge in other industries certainly exists, but it is often ignored. Here, local knowledge is anticipated and counted upon: it is an important contribution from "front line" personnel, those in direct contact with technology or with customers. Perhaps more importantly, because local knowledge is taken seriously and included in decision making, it is ratified and legitimated in our sample firms.

Other forms of local knowledge are also important. One of these is appreciation of a business unit's limitations, knowing what it can or cannot expect to undertake successfully. This knowledge can direct decisions to attempt or to abandon a particular opportunity. Another form of local knowledge is recognition of how developments or discoveries elsewhere apply to the local situation. Because innovation is so often thought of in purely product feature terms, these connections are especially important: they are the almost invisible understanding of the immediate situation that can spell ultimate success or failure in the marketplace.

Just such examples of local knowledge are exquisitely apparent in the context of the decision to launch a major new effort. Dan Dooley at National Semiconductor described one such instance, highlighting the need for varied insights to make success possible in a major technological shift, into optical fiber products. Particularly visible here is the initial appreciation of the organization's limits – what they could or could not expect to succeed at. Knowing what they did not know, they also chose to proceed on more than pure luck. They used existing skills and knowledge to create a test that, in turn, would enable them to proceed more safely:

> The whole area of fiber optics looked like an opportunity. What we actually did, originally [was], we said, "It's too hard a market for us to get our hands around. So why don't we do a product that we know will have general-purpose usefulness, with a fairly low cost for us to put it into the marketplace? It's an incomplete solution, but let's just take and run it in, and see what we get – run it up the flagpole, and see what kind of interest we've got."
>
> Dan Dooley, National Semiconductor

Surely others saw the fiber optic area? Or recognized that lower cable costs changed the economics? Yes; but Dooley's "incomplete solution" approach enabled the team to access *lots* of situation-specific, concrete information:

> From [the trial product effort] we got all sorts of inputs. It turned out that the product we were going to sell was dire, because it *was* an incomplete solution. But, boy, did we learn about the marketplace! People crawled out from underneath rocks and helped the thing. That kind of got us a direction. As a matter of fact, at this point, marketing came up with a rather complete definition of at least one of the products.
>
> Dan Dooley, National Semiconductor

But more collaboration still was required, Dooley recounted. And again, someone's specific insight provided the missing piece. What matters is not what the world knows, but what a specific person, in intimate contact with the problem, can contribute – a very localized knowledge:

> Engineering said, "We don't know how the heck we're going to do that!" At that point was when the breakthrough was made, if you will. An engineer scratched his head one night and said, "Hey! Guess what! I wonder if that will work? Why don't we go and just try a couple of things and see if it works?" And, by golly, it did. Then, you continue to refine it, and refine it, and refine it, and refine it.
>
> Dan Dooley, National Semiconductor

Such ideas are informal, in the sense that they are not written down and result quite directly from the innovator's familiarity with his or her specialty expertise and the problem at hand.

This kind of knowledge is very likely context-specific, even when it is recorded, or a matter of expertise. The problem is that the varieties of insight and expertise that reside in several different potential contributors must be combined. Haggerty of TI and Packard of HP both commented on the importance of "close coupling." Both HP's "Management by Walking Around" and Haggerty's personal "shuttle diplomacy" between the circuit designers and the radio engineers working on the Regency radio were aimed at accessing pockets of local knowledge and linking them up.

"Locality" of knowledge is an unavoidable consequence of increased specialization. As Dooley went on to comment with massive understatement, major innovation like National's fiber optic project "is not without risk." We would add that local knowledge can reduce the risk, and that is why these firms use it; indeed, "such knowledge can become virtually indispensable to the effectiveness of technology-based organizations" (Baba, 1988; Geertz, 1983).

Our sample firms recognize the importance of local knowledge and go far beyond simply opportunistically employing what is available. They deliberately foster its growth and development, and create strong cultural norms to draw it out. In essence, the strong cultures of the firms we studied share an emphasis on local knowledge, task-relevant and specific, as the basis for credibility, contribution, and participation. The cultures are knowledge-based – often local-knowledge-based – rather than status-based.

Local knowledge can be especially important when others in an industry or marketplace "know" otherwise – and are wrong. Local knowledge of this sort represents a strategic opportunity. Dooley's description of fiber optics innovation illustrates this, beginning with widely perceived product needs and an equally widely shared judgment in the marketplace of "reasons why it wouldn't sell." What the National team added was, first, the feeling that some of those reasons were erroneous; and second, swift appreciation of how an external factor would impact their particular innovation effort. There had been many fiber optic product ideas before, according to Dooley:

> They've been there right along. People would recognize it, and they would talk about the future of fiber optics. Unfortunately, a lot of it had never come to fruition, for a whole variety of reasons – about half a dozen reasons. We could see where some of those reasons could be unjust – wrong. One of the key

[reasons], which was completely outside of our control, was that the fiber optic cable costs were coming down phenomenally. They finally got their act together in fiber optic cabling, to where it's going to be competitive with wire. Well, that fact alone is key.

Dan Dooley, National Semiconductor

Dooley's recognition that lower cabling costs would make National's fiber optic product much more viable – "that fact alone is key" – is one example of local knowledge. However, recognition of this sort may be only part of what it takes to successfully innovate. To meet the recognized need, a firm may have to shift its perception of how it participates in its business – it may have to change its strategy, as Intel did in moving into microprocessors, and as National did in its first fiber optic product:

[There was] also the fact that connectors, for making fiber optic connections, are key to the whole thing. There were no good, low-loss fiber optic connectors in the marketplace. So we said, "Well, we'll drive that." So we took a very atypical approach, and said, "We'll drive the packages. We'll not only do everything else [innovate on product and process technology], but we're going to drive the packages." So we came up with a superior connector.

We also said that the problem with fiber optics is that it's hand-crafted. We're not in the hand-crafting business, we're in the "kachunk-kachunk," mass production business. So let's attack it from the equipment end of the thing. Let's lift it out of the hand-crafted [business] and make it a mass production system that we can do our typical thing with – put it in Southeast Asia and turn the crank – from the ground up.

Dan Dooley, National Semiconductor

Recognizing how to adapt a hand-crafted product to a "kachunk-kachunk, mass production" business requires special knowledge. National's clearly articulated strategy was that they were a broad-based supplier of integrated circuits. The choice to move "atypically" into a product where National's contribution was the package, reduced to high volume production in much the same way as their ICs were, accomodates the new idea to existing strengths – it relates a new development to "what we know about ourselves."

In retrospect, Dooley's vision of mass production strategy seems almost obvious, for what is ultimately a mass production business.

Others have done it before, particularly in semiconductors: Dooley's account is very much akin to the observations of Pat Haggerty at Texas Instruments, decades earlier, that semiconductor components had to be produced "like jelly beans," in large numbers. Henry Ford's vision in the early days of the automobile, that what was initially a luxury product with very high cost, specialty applications could be produced at low enough cost to become a commodity, was also similar. These insights were not originally widely shared. Instead, the vision was quite localized. The 20–20 character of hindsight is notorious; Dooley's account makes it quite clear that special knowledge was required.

Dooley articulates clearly the local knowledge within National that "we're not in the hand-crafting business." He is also able to identify when and where it makes sense for the firm to expand its former components focus to include "packages" – the ancillary developments that will enable consumers to make use of the items that National will make in this new technology. Once the "local" knowledge is widely recognized, it ceases to be "localized" in its original site. If very widely accepted, the knowledge may completely drop its "special" character, and the role of local context may no longer be appreciated, as when an industry broadly adopts the leader's view.

Developing Local Knowledge

Developing this local knowledge is an important facet of managing corporate culture. It forms part of the process of socializing juniors into the firm and its culture; one aspect of such socialization, which transforms the juniors from outsiders to insiders, is the acquisition of appropriate perspectives on local knowledge. Local knowledge matters in these firms, it supports innovation, and thus it is to be fostered. By ensuring the transmission of local versions of organizational "common sense" (that "you've got to include the minions," as one wag had it) these firms help to push the essential decision criteria and the wherewithal for decision making well down into the organization.

What is important here is not so much the content of what seniors convey as the process of doing so. Juniors come to recognize that the local, situation-specific knowledge they are expected to acquire is important, that it will be called upon, and that it is their responsibility to develop and communicate it, to be sure it gets into the decision process. Dooley, again, described the process at National, where new engineers are "raised by hand" to develop market sense and strategy sense for how National does business:

> Generally what we do for the engineers that come in [is], we put them up with a senior guy, to go on the system, and bring them up that way . . . Tutoring them, if you will.
>
> Dan Dooley, National Semiconductor

Local knowledge is a key concept here, along with the idea of the strong culture as a pervasive, permeable essence that links people, both within and outside formal systems. Formal systems and checkpoints guide and drive strategy and operations, but only through substantial informal interaction among employees. What knowledge is needed cannot be specified in advance; people must develop it for themselves, must assess it, and must communicate it. In essence, formal systems and procedures *depend on* local knowledge. Thus much time, attention, and effort are devoted to encouraging local knowledge.

Managers in the companies we studied recognize that they depend on the inputs of those who know. Managers cannot tell these people what, specifically, to find out. Thus it is not at all surprising to find managers acknowledging the importance of local knowledge. In stark contrast to much early thinking that assigned the formal systems to management and informal systems to employees – often in adversarial roles (e.g., Dalton, 1950; Gouldner, 1954; Homans, 1950; Roethlisberger and Dickson, 1939; Roy, 1952, 1954; Selznick, 1943), here we see formal systems working closely with informal systems, relying on local knowledge. Indeed, these firms cannot operate without it, because knowledge is developing too fast – by the time it's written down and formalized, it's obsolete. So they capture "enough" in the documentation, and rely on local knowledge for the rest. Equally, the firms cannot ensure that decisions will be made according to what they see as appropriate criteria unless those criteria are built into the decision process. This means, of course, that the criteria must be widely disseminated and widely accepted.

Shared criteria also constitute a double-edged sword: once those criteria are widely shared, people are able to recognize the importance of their local knowledge. Recognizing it, they will feel entitled to consideration in strategic decisions. If people are to accept responsibility for outcomes, they will insist upon being substantively included in the decision process. They will have, and will articulate, their opinions and insights. Only by broadly and substantively including people can innovation be fostered (Carlzon, 1987; Kanter, 1983).

Our research shows that local knowledge can be encouraged: people can be sensitized to the need for it via congruent formal and informal means. And strong cultural norms of open participation, shared communication, and emphasis on task-relevant knowledge as the basis for credibility and authority provide a vehicle for bringing the local knowledge into decision making. In other words, local knowledge can contribute essential strength to decisions, but it requires a different management style, and a surrender of older ideas about hierarchy and status if it is to function properly. Intense personal involvement is another outcome of depending on local knowledge; and that also carries costs, as we have shown.

Dependency Costs for Managers

Two important sources of stress for managers in our sample companies are technological change and dependency on subordinates. It isn't always easy for North American managers to live with constant change, and with the dependency on those whom they supervise that that change implies. At one company, a technical manager described "the Screaming Room." This person's manager, who had profit and loss responsibility for a large division within the company, was warmly and favorably described as "non-political:"

> [That] means he's very honest. It means he can see. He doesn't do things for stupid personal reasons. He can see good and bad. He tends to be very pragmatic.
>
> Anonymous high-technology manager

Yet nevertheless, this well-regarded manager occasionally succumbs to the pressure, and subordinates bear the brunt:

> Suddenly the human part of him is falling apart. He's bitching at me all of the time, he's complaining, and he's apt to be yelling at me, too. I'm not a yeller, but the only way I can handle him if he gets like that is, I yell back. We had a room built for him, which we call "the Screaming Room." I said "[Name], if you've

got to scream, would you run for the room, so we don't disrupt the whole area?" When he would start this [yelling], productivity would drop to zero, and I don't like the effect on the people.

In such a case, subordinates must manage the boss's reaction to pressure, and this manager did:

Finally, it got to the point where he was driving me nuts, because I couldn't even find out the reason he was screaming so. He would give a reason, but that wasn't the real reason. At first, I was missing it, but then I finally realized: "Oh, yeah. He's really uncomfortable [technologically] with the program." So I said, "I think we need some tutorials. We're going to spend four hours a week, and I'm going to sit down . . . and give you educational lectures." This guy, [whom] I had worked with for seven years, is really very bright. He's a really good man, who is suffering from "technology shock," and reacting by some heavy psychological things. I do a big education job for management, [when it's needed].

"Training up" is notoriously difficult, and "training" *per se* is not an explicit part of this anonymous manager's job. Nevertheless, it was independently undertaken, in a very matter-of-fact way, to assist a respected superior in coping. Such efforts are, of course, eminently consistent with local knowledge in the open communication culture we have been describing, in terms of shared expertise and taking personal responsibility, and also in terms of managerial dependency. They are also quite atypical of large-company manager–subordinate relations in traditional firms.

Managers and executives faced with their own likely technical obsolescence are in some senses confronted with their own professional mortality. Understandably, this is a difficult recognition to make, and not all acknowledge it, or accept it gracefully. We might expect such a recognition to be especially difficult in strong cultures, where investment of self in the work of the firm is most profound. The cost to a superior involves the humbling experience of admitting limits, further undercutting the status differentials captured in organizational hierarchy and calling them further into question. The cost to subordinates, beyond the frustrations of trying to communicate past erroneous assumptions and obsolete knowledge, may include contending with training. All is not roses in high-technology firms; people work hard at working well with one another.

Time to Manage Culture Costs

The effort to deliberately manage culture is necessarily expensive of managerial time. To begin with, it is an attempt to influence a great deal that is beyond management's direct sphere of influence. As one anthropologist suggested:

> To an anthropologist, the conscious creation of a culture by management is amusing, because all human groups have culture by nature, and these systems of values and beliefs are shaped by experience, tradition, class position, and political circumstances – all powerful forces that are extremely refractory to directed change, particularly by occasional committee.
>
> Reynolds, 1986

In our sample firms, the "occasional committee" Reynolds mentions was not even considered as the mode of culture management. Instead, the effort to build and manage culture was a serious, constant, iterative, "hands on" activity. It entailed enormous amounts of time spent in communicating to people, sharing ideas and views, articulating goals, encouraging, and hearing out. Of course, organizational culture will emerge even without management attention, regardless of management's wishes. Its values and norms, in that instance, may be very different from those management would have chosen. Seeking to influence corporate culture, management in our sample companies must invest substantial amounts of time, energy, attention, and conscious effort. "Endless meetings" and "endless explanations" are symptoms of this cost category.

Even so, culture will not be wholly within management's control. External culture (ethnic culture, the national culture within which the firm operates, and the like) also play a generally underappreciated role (Hofstede, 1984). Although we will not spend time on it, "external culture" enters our sample firm in the form of enormous variety – personnel on a production line speaking ten or more languages other than English, for instance. This reality creates very different culture problems for North American managers in, say, California, than for Japanese managers in Tokyo facing an essentially homogeneous workforce. These complexities are only one item of culture's cost for managers in our sample companies.

The management of innovation efforts, particularly in terminating activities that do not make business sense, can be delicate as well as time-consuming – the more so since administrative fiat is not an acceptable solution. An account from Motorola highlights the difficulty, and the consummate care of the managers for their innovative contributor:

> It turns out that we went far enough with [an experimental project] to determine that, unfortunately, it was going to be too expensive and could not be made large enough to approach the market as a whole. What we did at that point, was to get together a task force of people to examine the idea and where it was going: the people doing the work and the people who were likely to understand the most likely market – put them together in one room to reason their way through to the fact that we really ought to drop the project. It turns out the inventor by then had come to the conclusion that "I really ought to go off and look at something else now." It was sort of a group kind of thing, but there wasn't somebody telling him, "You can't do that." It was an attempt to lead him to the realization that this was something that wouldn't work . . .
>
> You don't want to turn him off, because his next winner might be a real winner . . . It turned out that he was the one who made the presentation and suggested we get out of it.
>
> Bill Howard, Motorola

Meetings, and time for them, are a serious management expense in strong culture organizations. Because so much communication is deliberately informal, it is not recorded on paper. Thus it involves massive amounts of reporting, in person or on paper, to keep everyone up to date:

> Fifty to eighty percent of my time goes to meetings, either with one of my engineers or in development meetings, or in planning functions, or – we have a series of meetings set up with this group since they provide a service to us – and oh, I don't know – ten to twenty percent of my time [is spent] on the phone . . . and the rest of my time, either in filling out forms that I have to fill out or thinking, sometimes. That's a rough estimate.
>
> Kim Kokkonen, Intel

Constant meetings and interface requirements exacerbate time pressure, widely recognized as exasperating. Multiple meetings, among parties with differing agendas and often conflicting needs, are also a source of stress and "interaction fatigue," as well as time-expensive.

As to formal written reports, in our sample firms we also saw efforts to reduce the number of them, and to facilitate their production – for instance, by substituting computer programs for manual information collection and transmittal. Nevertheless, despite such efforts, the management effort required to co-ordinate, collaborate and integrate innovation activities is great:

> There are a number of mechanisms in place that are good by themselves, but when I add it together, it's a very large time segment that we are always fighting. That's something that we've argued about a lot. I personally don't feel that all the indicators [reports and briefings, based on data collected and analyzed] we do are essential. However, there is a strong proponent for each indicator in upper-level management.
>
> Kim Kokkonen, Intel

Shared information is the foundation of participation in decisions, yet as the number of people to be co-ordinated rises, the number of potential communication links, be they by computer, telephone, paper or in person, rises dramatically. Ultimately, the cost is overload, and the response of people to overload is stress, prioritizing, queuing of information (or problems), and, ultimately, degraded performance.

Some portion of these costs must be due to the particular sort of culture – surprisingly uniform, across these very different companies – that our sample firms sought to induce: a highly participative one. Nevertheless, the old aphorism applies here, "TANSTAAFL" – There Ain't No Such Thing As A Free Lunch. Especially in trying to foster a culture of open communication and widely shared ideas, managers and others must spend enormous time communicating and sharing ideas. *Too much* time is spent on committees, teams, and meetings, according to some.

As noted earlier, Les Vadasz remarked that pruning committees and interfaces was somewhat difficult. His comment is worthy of attention, especially in the context of such high change organizations as those we studied. Even there, even with all the change, people find it difficult to cut back on activities in which they have invested themselves over time.

Committees and complex, multiple reporting relationships, which are necessary, can get out of hand. This danger, and the maintenance task of overseeing organizational arrangements and seeing to them, are very real costs of a strong culture. Time and attention must be expended in managing these relationships. Yet it can seem burdensome, or even dysfunctional. According to Vadasz – and, we might add, many other managers we talked to in our sample firms – cutting back to avoid "meeting overload" and an over-elaborate structure of relationships is a never-ending task:

> We try to do that. We're more conscious of these things than we used to be, before. But in fact, we had one senior individual in the company who was spending most of his time trying to clean up some organizational messes. That doesn't make sense. But, you know, when you explain these concepts to the people who are part of that committee, or they are the chairman of that committee – it's very easy to say, "Yeah, that other committee is really bad. It's not me. It's them."
>
> Les Vadasz, Intel

The phenomenon of meeting overload highlights another managerial cost to the sort of culture we have been describing. The committees and working groups are certainly participative, and are intended to be arenas for wide input from a variety of sources. However, they cannot be allowed to operate as completely autonomous or ad hoc bodies. Their functioning must be managed, and this takes management time. As Vadasz noted, "somebody has to do the supervising."

In essence, managerial time – supervisory effort – is being put in as the transaction cost to ensure effective committee efforts. The dual tasks of supervising committee operation and pruning committees and other such relationships back when they are no longer necessary are real management costs in strong culture firms. The alternative, allowing individuals or individual committees to operate without supervision, would also incur costs. The firms we studied have universally decided that ad hoc, undirected teams are simply too expensive in terms of creative effort and participative input. Therefore they elect to manage these activities.

What we see here are costs brought into management's account: an internal structuring cost, via committees; an on-going maintenance cost, for repeated pruning; and an internalized transaction cost, via management time. These costs, formerly borne by the individual employees if the necessary co-ordination was to take place, now accrue to their managers. This makes sense if and only if these committees and interfaces produce more innovation and more efficient innovation than the alternatives. Of course, committees can fail. The participants can fail to express their views, the experts' expertise can be withheld, people can fail to attend, fail to contribute, or fail to follow through. All these contributions and more, in addition to the required time, must be forthcoming if the committees and interfaces are in fact to produce the close coupling and co-ordinated collaboration these firms need.

Values, norms, and expectations – the very stuff of culture – must provide a context within which open communication, personal responsibility for outcomes, and shared focus on problem-solving can occur. Local knowledge can be brought to bear, but only if its possessors share with management a common vision that values contribution of one's special understanding, particularly when that understanding is different from that of others. Scattered experts will contribute to complex team interfaces, but only if frequent pruning ensures that their scarce time isn't wasted on needless meetings. In short, management of values, and management consistent with values, is a constant, and difficult, task.

The management of corporate culture is expensive of time to *do* it – the endless meetings that people participate in. It is also expensive of *management time* – the careful fostering of innovation's context, of the value of listening, and the patient explanation of goals and norms and targets, and the willing "open association" policy, even at very senior levels. Managing culture comes full circle: the need to instill values is driven by the need for those values to be available to guide people's activities.

Conclusion

The tour of cultures contained in this chapter has highlighted the costs of strong culture and methods for its management. Strong culture's benefits do not come unalloyed, nor without cost. Our discussion has centered upon individual costs – particularly personal and interpersonal costs – and managerial costs, as well as organizational cost. While we have touched upon organizational costs, a further discussion of this topic remains to be dealt with in our next and final chapter.

12

Living in Turbulent Times

"May you live in interesting times."

Ancient Chinese curse

Predictions are always difficult – especially about the future.

Niels Bohr

You won't have innovation or success with the customer unless you have the right leadership, the right set of objectives and goals, and the right environment for innovation to occur. That's all very fundamental.

Pat Weber, Texas Instruments

"Who's Excellent Now?" is Not the Question

During 1985 and 1986, the US semiconductor industry companies collectively lost roughly $500 million in the most recent of this volatile industry's sharp downturns. By the same period most US firms had exited the DRAM market in droves, leaving behind only TI and tiny Micron to face Japanese competitors reputed to hold "substantially all" of the market in some commodity products. This prompted *Business Week* to ask in its issue of 18 August 1986, "Is it Too Late to Save the US Semiconductor Industry?"

The semiconductor industry has always been highly cyclical, depending as it has primarily upon sales to other manufacturers. As a result, semiconductor components makers in particular are the first to feel the pinch as other manufacturers prepare for downturns by cutting their components orders, and the last to recover when business turns back up, as OEMs work off any old inventory before ordering again. Even sharp market downturns are nothing new in semiconductors: in 1960, between April and October, estimates of the total semiconductor market the following year fell by about 18 percent. Price volatility also plays a role: by 1962, the industry was shipping twice as many units as it had in 1960, but for 3 percent fewer dollars.

Price declines have traditionally been the norm in semiconductors, coupled with constantly increasing functionality in products. Transistor prices, as a percentage of the preceding year's prices, increased from an index figure of 80 in 1956 to 112 by 1959 – only to plunge to 70 by 1961 and again in 1963–4 to 60. Recessions struck the industry in 1960–1, 1970–1, 1974–5, 1980, and 1983. Recovery in 1984 produced a banner year, but recession returned to the industry in 1985–6, with 1986 sales almost flat. More recently, in 1985–7, worldwide overcapacity has exacerbated the latest downturn.

Alarmist articles like that from *Business Week* quoted above serve only to intensify American business's much lamented orientation toward short-term results. The semiconductor rollercoaster is not new, and such articles offer little insight because they ignore the industry's history. Perhaps an even more regrettable example was the *Business Week* cover story entitled "Oops!," which reviewed performance of Peters and Waterman's "excellent" companies. The article suggested that of the 43 companies singled out in their book, 14 had "not been doing so well lately," and had lost their luster. Thus presumably the firms' methods weren't very good, after all. A key word in the assessment is "lately," which seems to mean today, right now and very recently. Short-term results are an inappropriate focus.

Some context suggests a richer interpretation. Each of our companies has been affected by the swings, to varying degrees. Yet throughout the history of the industry, the functionality of components and devices has increased with the number of components on an integrated circuit chip roughly doubling each year. Moreover, each of these companies has not only survived but grown against this backdrop, continuing to innovate and dominate specified areas of endeavor despite volatility, downturns, and competition. Results over the longer term are obviously far more revealing than swings up or down in any single year.

Our companies are identified by name, and no doubt they will again, from time to time, experience setbacks, market downturns and the like, as they have in the past. These will be widely reported, of course: the drama of their struggle is big news, and US electronics firms have not emerged unscathed from their struggles. But while it will be easy to point the finger at their difficulties, no company's occasional problem undercuts the overall success of its methods in remarkably challenging circumstances. It would be naive to insist that excellence required no slips, no setbacks, and no competitive downturns – especially in so intensely demanding and highly volatile an industry as semiconductors. Such a perspective understates the lasting value of deliberately undertaken short-term investment or concession strategies, and unrealistically anticipates instant returns. Worse still, it ignores the potential for learning from past successes and failures on which the real world turns.

No firm in our sample has avoided significant setbacks or major market misses; nobody bats 1.000. We might observe that the idols have feet of clay – but a more important insight is that these firms don't surrender. They retrieve their losses, examine their difficulties, and learn from experience. *That* these firms learn from their experience is important. *How* they do it, and how their practices connect with repeated innovation, is still more important, for their competitive world is increasingly the world of most firms.

Beyond the High-Technology Firms

Volatility, intense competition, and dramatic price declines coupled with equally dramatic surges in performance requirements, unanticipated surges and sags in demand, and rapid technological change characterize competition today for all companies, not just for semiconductor firms. We live in turbulent circumstances, in "interesting times," as the ancient Chinese curse had it. While the semiconductor firms exist at the leading edge of these stresses and strains, today it seems that virtually every industry is being battered upon the same reefs and shoals, ranging from technological change and hitherto unexpected global competitors to the unsteady dollar to unanticipated interconnections among industries. Turbulence appears to be the new norm; and this impression is not ill founded, as some data will suggest.

Looking primarily to the US for the moment, there are numerous indicators of economic turbulence (see figure 12.1). Bankruptcies are

---

Banks: 1987 was the banks' worst year since the Great Depression. For 13,700 federally insured banks in 1987:

Assets:	$3 trillion
Earnings	$3.7 billion
Return on assets	0.13%
Failed:	184
Unprofitable:	2,366

Source: Federal Deposit Insurance Corp.

Machine Tool Industry: A bellwether industry, machine tools dropped roughly in half between 1981 and 1985. Figures are in millions of dollars; the apparent recovery in exports reflects changes in the value of the dollar against major trading currencies.

	1981	1983	1985
Production	5,111	2,132	2,500
Exports	949	359	450
Imports	1,431	921	1,700
Consumption	5,593	2,695	3,800
Imports as percent of market	25%	34%	45%

Figure 12.1 Some Indicators of US Economic Turbulence

at historically high levels, equalling the rates seen during the Great Depression of the 1930s. Bank and Savings-and-Loan failures are at similarly high rates. But the turbulence ranges more widely. Exchange rates for the dollar against major trading partners' currencies – the yen, the pound, the Deutschmark and so on – are volatile, having fallen precipitously in recent months after years of historic highs. The yen moved from a high of about 260 to the dollar in 1985, to about 150 per dollar – a drop of roughly 40 percent – just over a year later. Japanese industries too are facing challenges – from Korean competitors like Goldstar in consumer electronics, for instance. It is easy to understand why, for business people, these seem like very turbulent times indeed.

In the US, this turbulence has been reflected in, and ultimately intensified by, lower US investment in business. Consistently lower investments in new equipment are visible in the average age of US manufacturing plant overall, and in the proportion of advanced equipment in use here. In both, we have lagged our global competitors. Although US capital investment has recently been increasing, major trading partners invest far more in capital equipment. Capital investment as a percentage of GNP in France and West Germany was more than 20 percent greater than that in the US, where the rate fell to only 2.6 percent of GNP during the late 1970s. During the same period, Japan's rate was almost double ours (Hayes and Wheelwright, 1984; Eckstein et al., 1984).

Lower investment is also visible in figures on R&D as a percentage of sales: for US industry as a whole, this figure has hovered at or below 3 percent, with some old-line businesses like steel investing less than 0.5 percent. While US spending on R&D as a percentage of GNP has declined, rates of R&D spending among our major trading partners have continued to increase. While many explanations could be offered – pointing to taxes that discourage R&D and investments in plant and equipment, for instance – the fact of comparative underinvestment remains.

Firms in our sample of innovators are again leading in changing this situation: they have invested much more in R&D than the US industrial norm, as a look back at figure 4.1 (page 115) illustrates. Repeatedly, the high-technology firms have insisted that innovation is crucial, and that substantive investment in R&D and capital equipment is essential to that continued innovation. As previous chapters have described, these firms' investment is not limited to dollars in plant or to R&D; instead, they have carefully fostered and deliberately sustained complex, and at times costly, organizational cultures and management styles. All of this effort has aimed at supporting repeated innovation. The need for innovation, so urgent here, seems increasingly urgent in mature industries as well.

The Ford Example

The new rules of competition are by no means limited to high-technology firms or to glamorous, go-go industries like semiconductors, as we have repeatedly maintained. Ford and GM have both invested significant sums in advanced technology: they have had little choice, because machine tool and assembly equipment has been revolutionized by electronics, while factory practice has also radically shifted toward vastly improved efficiency. In mature industries especially, companies will either meet the new global standards – often requiring major change – or lose ground to their competitors.

GM's declining market share in the mid-1980s, Ford's visible efforts to redirect manufacturing, and the successes of Honda and Toyota offer excellent examples to testify that these same dynamics exist now in a thoroughly mature, century-old industry. The automobile industry is currently experiencing changes and challenges very similar to those of the semiconductor industry: competition is increasingly global, with major competitors from the Pacific Rim (Japan and Korea), as well as from Europe and within the US; and the industry has undergone a technological revolution, with the advent of robotics, CAD, new materials, lasers and a host of other marvels.

One other widely recognized consequence of global competition (and especially the advent of the Japanese into American markets) has been vastly increased standards of manufacturing control and product quality. At Ford, the visible result of this challenge has been significant change in operating philosophies, management style, and manufacturing practices carried out during the past decade. Such approaches as statistical process control (SPC) and line-stop by operators who see difficulties have become routine at Ford. These practices are far distant from the traditional "beat to fit and ship it" manufacturing practices of the past (Mishne, 1988). Manufacturing practice is changing because it has to. Competitors ever-increasing manufacturing competence demands response.

The depth and breadth of the changes under way testify to the difficulties facing this mature industry. Total quality control and SPC, reorganized new product development teams and a revamped culture are not quick or simple answers. For Ford managers, one plant manager commented, the difficulties only began at initial implementation. Since this was not a temporary "project" but a change in fundamental approach, continuity and persistence were essential. As product quality went up relative to past performance, the problem was how to maintain people's interest and attention, how to keep them actively pushing for more. After all, people can quite accurately say already that "this is the best product we've ever made."

Serious attention by the plant manager to daily SPC reports, frequent conferences with departmental and divisional management, plus detailed follow-up on commitments and action plans to solve identified difficulties all constitute a different, more systematic and problem-focused approach. So, too, do continued "benchmarking" and comparisons with the best of the competition and "world-class" standards for everything from defects to inventory turns to price-feature ratios.

"Change management" and "innovation" were central to attaining the manufacturing control and stability so desperately neeeded for competitive success. Stabilizing and controlling manufacturing translates directly into sustainable, long-term competitive advantage in automobiles. They mean quality output, lower waste and rework, and more reliable product performance: all essential features for survival against competitors like Honda, Toyota, and Nissan, whose better "fit and finish," fuel economy, and price have translated into almost 25 percent of the US domestic market – revolutionary indeed, for a "mature" industry (Wheelwright, 1985).

For Ford, these changes have required some nine years of persistent effort and on-going commitment to the new strategy of quality – a balancing act that reconstituted core values, assumptions, and beliefs through explicit systems, then pushed hard to keep the systems from degenerating into mere form. The push is not over yet, nor is the battle won. This, too, mirrors the high-technology experience.

Renewing Systems – the On-going Challenge

Ford's problem is quite analogous to TI's difficulties with its OST system. Having experienced some significant successes through the 1970s, TI's problem was to retain "that old-time religion," as times changed and challenges mounted. The firm was slow to field MOS technology – so slow that some despairing managers spun off their own firm, MOStek, to pursue the innovation. Serious investment and effort in TI's advanced scientific computer produced some successes – but did not translate into any solid position for TI outside its specialized niches.

In the 1980s, the changes and challenges stalled TI's progress – "another plateau, just like some we had hit earlier," commented several TI managers in 1986. But the stall of the mid 1980s was longer and deeper than previous ones. The firm experienced a major product embarrassment in home computers, along with losses and layoffs as its internal difficulties coincided with the worst industry downturn in decades. TI seemed no better able to respond to these challenges than other US firms, and surrendered first place in semiconductor components to arch-rival Motorola, while it battled the Japanese for market share in key product areas.

TI's faltering was widely attributed by outsiders to the OST itself, and to what was described as its "inevitable" slide toward a overly rigid and mechanistically controlled mode of management that stifled innovation. Months were added to the new product development cycle, as essential information exchange was frustrated by bureaucracy. Others blamed senior management, noting that TI's difficulties began after its revered chairman, Patrick Haggerty, had retired. Haggerty's unexpected death, shortly after his retirement, threw the company's managers back entirely on their own resources.

Under Haggerty, the OST had attained significant successes, both in product innovations and in company growth. After these successes, under other managers somehow the focus seemed to be on the system itself, rather than the innovation it was expected to generate. The OST was thoroughly institutionalized, and other elaborate OST-like systems were also put in place. As we have recounted elsewhere, performance assessment and reward were also tied to the OST. This became "how we run the company," with plans and numeric "model" goals for businesses acquiring overwhelming importance. Reaching model goals (those built into mathematical models of anticipated performance) seemed to cost TI its innovative spark. Such procedures also became the source of significant stress, as we have noted, for the OST presentation put one's proposals, and thus one's future, on the line. There was some talk, inside TI and out, that the system had failed.

But Haggerty's philosophy was not abandoned. By 1988, almost a decade after his death, both Haggerty's impact and the OST were back. Managers repeatedly quoted him, and repeatedly insisted, as William P. Weber did, that the OST was alive and well:

> What I'm trying to tell you is that the fundamentals of TI's approach to management, in themselves, have not changed. What has changed is the understanding of how we implement them. This is not only a fundamental shift within TI, but the market *demanded* – absolutely demanded – that we shift with it, in terms of the way we apply these systems, these fundamentals. I sure don't want to mislead you that we've turned a new coin, that it's "Whoops! That was wrong! We're gonna have a new system, and do this, this, and this." That's not so.
>
> Pat Weber, Texas Instruments

As head of TI's Semiconductor Group, Pat Weber presided over roughly half of TI's business revenues in 1988. He had been with the company for many years, with experience in marketing and R&D in addition to operational responsibility. Particularly noticeable are the tone and fervor of his assertions, and the power of their obvious linkage, for him, with TI's past successes. His assertion that "nothing fundamental has changed" was elaborated further:

> Let me tell you, because I tested that when I came over here [to head the Semiconductor Group] . . . We challenged everything we'd ever done. And we needed to challenge everything we'd done, because the marketplace was telling us we were doing something wrong – OK? – because the [performance] numbers were not good. That's the measure. So we challenged every damn thing that we'd done or that had been done. And what came out of that was very fundamentally . . . "There's nothing wrong with the systems. So don't try to change the systems. Go back and reinforce the systems." Right?
>
> *"Talk about* why they're right. *Talk about* what's good about them. Right? And then go back and *look at how you have applied them*, what went wrong with the way you were applying them, and what needs to change in the way you're applying them."
>
> Pat Weber, Texas Instruments

What Weber is describing with such evangelistic fervor, in tones reminiscent of an old-time revival meeting, is a return to the meaning, philosophy, and underlying values that the OST represented – Haggerty's values. These values are more persistent than any formalism into which the sytem may have fallen. Weber's engagement underlines the importance both of values and of top management commitment to them – quite over and above any formal system. With such commitment, the values serve as a highly motivating guide. Without it, the system becomes merely mechanistic.

The application of the systems necessarily changes, as situations and personnel, market needs and challenges change, according to Weber. What was the error in TI's use of the systems? Weber's answer was direct:

> We made 'em bureaucratic. We used the systems as a control tool, rather than a facilitating tool. That's the difference. And that's why I get back to top management. Top management should not use [strategic] systems to control. They should use

the systems as an indication and a framework for the way they
want the business to be managed. Not for the way they want
the business to be controlled . . . Something clicked within TI
that had [the OST] as more of a control system than a set of
tools to go innovate, to go market . . .

                                        Pat Weber, Texas Instruments

When people perceived that the OST system was being used for
control, rather than for encouraging innovation, the same "high
visibility" for strategic projects that made the system so valuable for
managing strategy meant that people felt very much at risk. Worse,
they felt betrayed by what many saw as an improper use of the
system. The predictable result was rigid adherence to forms and
formats, *pro forma* or "dog and pony show" presentations, and
alienation among those who felt unjustly controlled.

This view was also voiced by a number of former TI managers
who had gone on to positions in other firms. One former TIer
explained his defection this way:

I had a desire at TI for a long, long time to kind of do my own
thing. In a way I still have that – that is a driving force . . .
because they're so well disciplined and so well organized, they
sort of, if you will, discourage doing your own thing – because
they're so regimented and so disciplined. If there's one thing
that I think I could critique [at TI], it would be that overmanaged
aspect of things. The P&L business manager or division manager
many times has to really do what the company wants him to . . .

    That's a critique I have against TI: it's too regimented, and
as a result, you do not have that flexibility.

                                        Anonymous former TI manager

Like virtually every ex-TIer who spoke with us, this person was
careful to give abundant credit to the systematics of TI's approach,
even while criticizing, particularly in comparing TI's discipline to
other firms' far less disciplined practices:

While I admire TI, and still do think very, very fondly of their
discipline, it does discourage some of the innovation for the
individual.

                                        Anonymous former TI manager

Another former TI manager analyzed the difficulties in terms very
similar to those Weber had used:

The Objectives–Strategies–Tactics concept is excellent, and that was how Haggerty conceived it: "We need to have an overall objective, and we need to put strategies together to support that objective, and you have got to have tactics, or you'll never make the strategies happen." What happened was that it became institutionalized and formalized to the extent that it became "another TI program." Its intent was to catch you at something, rather than lead you through the right process of "Are your strategies in support of the Corporate or Sector Group Objective?" and "Do your Tactics make sense?" and "Are you going and doing those things, and what progress are you making?"

Anonymous former TI manager

The close interactions between system and spirit, and between feelings of autonomy or ownership and innovation, are also evident in another former manager's description:

Overcontrol was the TI problem . . . Then [too] the Haggerty successor, Mark Shepard, was a very strong manager, but didn't have obviously either the foresight or strategic mind that Haggerty did, certainly did not have the vision that Haggerty did. So he was more of an implementor and a controller. They then picked the next guy under Shepard, Bucy. His whole reason for existence was that he had an iron grip on everything that happened. Once Haggerty was out of active management, and certainly once he died, we lost vision completely. The whole job became one of control, and that basically killed the whole semiconductor operation, and almost the corporation.

Junkins is a lot more straightforward. Junkins was a good choice for that – he is a lot more straightforward guy, and he is pretty well the no-nonsense type. But he can think strategically, and he will begin to add the strategic thinking process back into Texas Instruments.

Anonymous former TI manager

A Hard Act to Follow

A certain amount of dissatisfaction is, of course, to be anticipated in *former* employees' description of their ex-employer. These former managers were clearly dissatisfied enough with the company to leave. But an important underlying problem also merits attention, and potentially contributes to dissatisfaction: the succession issue *per se* in a strong culture.

Haggerty had been a charismatic leader, difficult for anyone to follow. His impact is clearly visible in the accounts by a number of managers, and Pat Weber's version is representative, both in content and tone, of numerous others' descriptions of Haggerty and his impact:

> Let me tell you the beauty about Haggerty; we can all relate to this, any of us who were around and can remember him: he was a visionary. He was also a spellbinder – OK? Because he could talk about his vision, and you'd get the picture. You were right there with him, and you were relating to everything he would say.
>
> I can remember when he would make talks to us in the auditorium. It was always spontaneous – at the end of some planning session, or whatever. He didn't have any charts, or a speech – that's not the way he was. He didn't need somebody to write for him. He didn't need CRD&E [Corporate Research, Development, and Engineering] either. And . . . you'd sit there on the edge of your seat. You could hear a pin drop, waiting for every word to come out of his mouth. Because you believed in him, and he had that vision, and he was that philosopher and that leader that everybody wanted to follow.
>
> Pat Weber, Texas Instruments

Weber's account was mirrored in the very similar comments of a former TI manager, whose personal account also stressed the emotional impact of Haggerty's charisma:

> When he would come out on the floor once in a while, especially during his younger days, and my younger days, he could really generate excitement. In fact, even without coming out on the floor, during the time when he was very active as Chairman, just in the annual meeting – he was always the summary speaker at the annual planning conference. He could get us ready to go out there and take on the world.
>
> He retired, and the two speeches that you heard at the end were from Bucy and Shepard, and when I left [after their speeches], I wondered if I wanted to stay with the company, because it was not motivating. Actually, it was demotivating, especially to those of us who had ever heard a Haggerty speech, which was very straight to the point and very motivating.

Shepard's speech would be an attempt to do that. Bucy's speech would be "If you don't do that, we are going to beat the hell out of you." And, boy, that just doesn't do it.

Anonymous former TI manager

It is easy to discount TI's difficulties in the post-Haggerty era as simply due to top management's insufficiencies, or to stylistics. This diagnosis is by far too facile: like the short-term focus of the popular press, it ignores what is potentially far more important. Haggerty's impact was profound, and it has survived among so many managers for so long that we cannot doubt its power. Charisma like Haggerty's is necessarily difficult to match. Market downturns and business difficulties do aggravate the potential for unkind comparisons. Together with the genuine warmth of feeling so evident among those that knew Haggerty, this created a real possibility of invidious comparisons for his successors in the best of times. And, of course, the 1980s has not been the best of times for semiconductors.

Since every successfully innovative company begins with a visionary leader, the quandary is a general one: who will follow? Who will succeed? How will the old vision be transcended or renewed? How can new visions flourish, especially since succeeding managers necessarily stand in the shadow of their accomplished predecessors? Each of the firms in our sample face this difficulty.

Adapting Systems by Adapting Culture

Successful succession, in our companies, appears to be paradoxically "conservative," in that continued innovation relies on maintaining or returning to "old-time" virtues. At the same time, new circumstances require reconsideration of just what the old virtues are – it is not enough to simply iterate mindlessly what worked before. Haggerty and TI offer an illustration. The almost indelible mark that Haggerty left in the fabric of the company also assisted change.

Both among those still at TI and those who left, many senior managers who had worked closely with Haggerty were clearly deeply moved by the memory of this man. They not only spoke of him with great fondness, but also relied on his spirit as a touchstone for guiding their efforts. They did so in a thoughtful, analytical fashion – not simply reproducing "What Pat did," but trying to puzzle through "What Pat would do, in our circumstances." In other words, the culture's talismans themselves can assist change – but only if senior managers are confident and adroit enough to use them.

Note the paradox: since the corporation *was* experiencing difficulties, its systems and practices were legitimately to be questioned. But too great a shift away from the past, especially abandonment of basic tenets of belief and past success, would deny the truths gained from experience and alienate those who believed. The answer, according to TI managers, was adaptation, to provide a framework for excellence:

> That's a moving target. Managers have got to be able to adapt to that moving target. But that doesn't mean that you completely turn over. I've always said that if you've got a good strategy, it doesn't change. Right? You only change a strategy when it's a bad strategy. I'll also tell you this: many managers change strategy because what they're doing is not working – right? – when in fact the strategy is probably good, but their application, and the way that they're managing is bad. See my point?
>
> Pat Weber, Texas Instruments

The day-to-day "changes," according to Weber, must be underpinned by a long-term philosophy, a vision based on fundamentals that rarely change. In terms of culture, the basic beliefs and commitments rarely change, but their application to new situations must be repeatedly re-examined and reinterpreted:

> The *cores* don't change – the core systems, the core philosophies. But you've got to be flexible enough to recognize that there's always got to be changes and improvements. [But] the cores don't change.
>
> Pat Weber, Texas Instruments

"Who's excellent now?" is not the question, for momentary and cross-sectional slices of performance in so volatile an industry as electronics highlight only ephemeral prospects. That question may sell magazines, but it cannot guide managers. Systems can become bureaucratic; even good innovation systems can be subverted for purposes of control. Used in ways that heighten feelings of risk, they quickly stifle the sort of openness, free communication, iconoclasm, and risk-taking that are essential to repeated innovation. The more telling assessment of innovation must accept occasional problems to ask, "What do these companies *do* when they encounter periodic difficulties?"

This question is the more important because, if established

businesses are to adapt to changing times, they must change within the context of prior culture, prior systems, prior expectations, and prior practices. The so-called "greenfield option" of starting over from scratch may be attractive: it surely seems easier not to contend with organizational inertia, the residues of past commitments or mistakes, and the lingering resentments of past failures. But for most organizations, "greenfield" is simply not an option. Instead, managers must somehow face the challenge of balancing stability and change, managing simultaneous control and innovation, and evolving a more open and participative management style, despite the fears and limitations of the past.

As manufacturing expertise (or, equally, detailed mastery of service delivery) and quality become increasingly important, these challenges will proliferate through most industries. In place of the assumed stability of the past, managers will face the need to innovate repeatedly, in response to new opportunities as well as new threats. But rather than pursuing innovation as an isolated, single, untrammeled goal, managers will also have to guide their firms' activities in the service of a coherent strategy.

In short, it is not only high-technology firms that face challenging circumstances, that must adapt to turbulence and change. Today it seems that change, turbulence, and the need for repeated self-renewal by means of innovation are universal. So, too, we argue, is the need to reconsider a whole host of long-accepted management practices, ideas, and notions. What works in these highly innovative firms is different from traditional practice, and calls it sharply into question. Deficient older notions of innovation, technology, structure, participation and control, organizational culture and leadership from the past are no longer adequate to meet the challenges of the future.

Challenges for the Future: Innovation and Change Management as Survival Strategies

Established Firms Can Innovate

The first lesson to be learned from our sample of high-technology firms is that *innovation can be maintained in large firms – but not*

by traditional bureaucratic management methods. Our sample firms'
experience suggests powerfully that innovation and change management are essential survival strategies. Without effective change
management, firms will be swamped by the changes around them.
Change and innovation are not simply ordered by fiat, however, nor
are they a simple matter of throwing R&D dollars at specific problems.
Instead, successful innovation management has entailed a broad,
interconnected web of shifts in management practices.

It is no secret that "bureaucracy" stifles innovation (see, e.g.,
Morison, 1966; March and Simon, 1958; Gouldner, 1954). The new
elements here are specific practices and rationales that go beyond
complaint to action. The high-technology firms have developed
methods to fight bureaucracy by painful experience, careful reassess-
ment, and constant attention. The methods work, although they do
not guarantee perfection. The methods also require constant attention,
constant openness, and constant commitment.

Stability and Change in Dynamic Tension

The second lesson is that *these firms are not ad hoc.* Innovation is
central, but it is neither random nor undirected. Continued research
is important; both complex manufacturing and market knowledge
development require persistent effort over time. So, too, does the
development of local knowledge and personal expertise. So, too, does
the careful nurturing of the complex linkages among organizational
interfaces, close and trusting interpersonal relations among superiors
and subordinates, and tight coupling of vendors with suppliers and
customers.

"Strategy du Jour" is *not* appropriate for any of these needs.
Successful management of innovation and change is a long-term
endeavor. Nevertheless, firms must be prepared to change important
elements like products, markets, positioning, and structure of the
firm to attain the ultimate goal of strategic innovation. The strategy
of innovation itself does not change, but much else is frequently up
for reconsideration.

Dramatic structural volatility – organizing for innovation by
repeatedly reorganizing – suggests that managers in these firms see
"structure" differently. Where traditional management practice seems

to assume permanence (e.g. Burrell and Morgan, 1979), highly innovative firms seem to assume change. Yet "change" acquires a different flavor here: it's "no fault" and adaptive, not a renunciation of the past. A decision that the firm must change today does not impeach the decision that made sense yesterday, for competitive circumstances, markets, technology, and skills are all dynamic, too. "No fault" objectivity is easier to advise than to implement, of course, particularly in cultures where people routinely invest themselves in their work. But however difficult, it is clearly the target.

Dynamic, volatile structure permits these firms to reconfigure themselves in response to changing needs and opportunities. If current structure doesn't work well, or seems to impede desirable interfaces and links, it will be changed. Willingness to change structure is a visible outcome of listening to employees' observations about what makes their tasks unduly difficult, distracts attention, or obstructs necessary collaboration. The third insight, then, is that *stability and change exist in dynamic tension in these firms*. Changeable structure allows these firms to stress first one set of linkages and interfaces, then another, as needs change over time.

Both response to changing needs and attention to the consequences of existing structure are far more actively acknowledged in our sample than in traditional firms. In contrast, traditional notions of "structure" as permanent are deficient; they undercut organization members' ability to deploy their attention and communication resources effectively as needs change.

Maintaining Stability amidst Change

Despite frequent, repeated structural change, endemic changes in products, processes, and technology, people do need some sense of stability. Our fourth insight is that *internal stability in these firms derives from strong, carefully nurtured organizational culture*. Culture provides boundaries for interpretation and expectation that help people to know what to count on, how to make sense of changes, and how to reinterpret their changing organization. Some things – "the fundamentals" – never change, however much products, processes, or organization structure may shift.

A host of formal and informal practices contribute to the aura of stability that these firms enjoy amidst change. People tend to sign on to stay in these firms, and many long-timers are visible. Status differentials are minimal, while contribution is admired and appreciated, regardless of the perpetrator's rank. The widespread roots of innovation – "from everywhere" – and the universally acknowledged primacy of the marketplace as ultimate arbiter both contribute to common goals and criteria. A fifth insight can be derived from these features: *innovation must be broadly rooted, and the criteria of success as broadly recognized.*

Innovation Nurturance and Choice

Broadly shared criteria are essential in these firms because, as our sample of high-technology managers repeatedly insisted to us, "There is no only, lonely inventor:" ideas combine and interact and hybridize many times on the route from "aha!" to the marketplace. Again and again, ideas must capture the imagination of people whose push and personal commitment are essential for ultimate success. *Only by pushing the criteria down into the roots of the organization can innovation be effectively fostered – and effectively filtered at the same time.*

Innovation can be managed and directed in this fashion, but the management and direction are broadly shared and far less "directive" and "managerial" than traditional modes of management or leadership. Leadership in these organizations is far more a question of maintaining "an environment that fosters innovation," as several managers put it, than of "deciding." The atmosphere is important: "innovation is delicate," as Gordon Moore observed, but it is also a crucial matter of competitive survival. Jerry Sanders of Advanced Micro Devices put it this way:

> In the electronics industry, competition is global: the market is the world. Mere survival – let alone growth and prosperity – depends upon creating and exploiting a competitive edge through innovation. Virtually all other considerations are secondary.
> W. J. Sanders, III, Advanced Micro Devices

Keeping innovation flowing depends not only on a broadly shared set of criteria for judging innovations, but also on both explicitly permitting deviations and explicitly corroborating established directions. Squeeze too hard, insisting on one direction only, and creativity will dry up. Squeeze too little, allowing scarce resources to bleed off for "anything and everything," and anaemia will set in: no-one will take innovation or criteria very seriously, even if resources suffice to keep anybody around for long. *Innovation demands a careful balance between challenge and support, encouragement and demanding standards.*

To strike that balance, our sample firms made innovation each person's business. *Managers open and share the decision processes,* especially around innovation, simply because innovations are so crucial to survival. To keep a pool of good ideas available for choice, a great many more ideas than can be developed must be examined and tested, shaped or discarded, adapted or reconfigured, each in specific and intimate detail. This task is simply too enormous and too nuanced for "management" to perform. It must be performed by the only people who can, those who have the ideas in the first place, and those who will execute them, throughout the firm.

Because even such an open process can miss some ideas, our successful high-technology firms also create and maintain alternative channels for "legitimated subversion" by new ideas for products, processes, and strategies. Alternatives need not be formalized; "bootlegging" is alive and well here. Attention to exceptions, consciously entertaining invitations to change, and praising good ideas regardless of their source all help to keep the system honest. Alternative sources for funding and support contribute to a balanced, high-tension system: shared choice is counterpoised by shared commitment to common goals.

Shared Criteria

Such a system needs realistic criteria – market-related, generally accepted as non-political, visibly utilitarian and fairly objective: *marketplace success* is the ultimate criterion in these firms. In its turn, the market criterion depends on an "open culture" and shared rationales. Managers must explain and share their specific criteria, and their choices. They cannot make arbitrary decisions – about products, changes, structures – by fiat. Yet this is not ad hoc, not uncontrolled. It is not "management by serendipity." The controls are real, because the market outcomes are real.

These organizations also believe they need to provide for second chances and "soft landings" for failure, depending on its cause. You cannot shoot the messenger, or bad news won't get through. You cannot penalize any failure with eternal damnation, or risk-taking will fade, and ho-hum, pedestrian results will rule. Here, again, the balance is delicate, in not letting people off the hook too easily, while also not stamping out risk-taking. Control is exercised by getting people to internalize "the hook" in their own judgment, using their conviction as the incentive. This "soft landing" model seems to have some universality:

> We constantly have several alternative projects going. Before the competition is over, before there is a complete loss, we try to smell the potential outcome and begin to prepare for that result as early as possible. Even after we have consensus, we may wait for several months to give the others a chance. Then we begin to give important jobs [on other programs] to members of the losing groups.
>
> If your team doesn't win, you may still be evaluated as performing well. Such people have often received my "crystal award" for outstanding work. We never talk badly about these people. Ibuka's [Sony's founder] principle is that doing something, even if it fails, is better than doing nothing. A strike-out at Sony is OK, but you must not just stand there. You must swing at the ball as best you can.
>
> Sony's top R&D manager, quoted in Quinn, 1985

Messages for Managers

The messages are clear, if paradoxical when viewed from the simplistic perspectives of the past. Paradoxically, innovation is controlled only by opening up the process of strategic management and sharing control. Discipline is exercised best in a freer process by not punishing mistakes. People have real power, and their mistakes carry consequences for the firm. Managers in these firms share participation in their most crucial activities, knowing full well that they risk the company on their people's judgment – because they must. The alternative is stagnation. *Shared strategic management gives people genuine power to steer and influence the organization – because no other method works.*

Like Kanter's (1983) notions of "empowerment," the sort of participation we found is widespread, woven into the firm, and seen by its managers as essential. In our sample of successful firms it was specifically oriented toward innovation, explicitly aimed at creating the future of the firm. It was also richly elaborated into a mutually reinforcing set of checks and balances that maintain the dynamic tension between innovation and stability, participation and control, short-term and long-term. Strategy and innovation are no more ad hoc than was structure, in these firms. Instead, managers in our sample firms are adept at steering by shared criteria, common values, widely communicated aims, and open decision processes. In short, *innovation can be managed through culture; but culture alone won't do it.*

Steering by culture entails much informal guidance, shaped and evolved over time. It rests upon acquaintance and familiarity among members. "Innovation as a state of mind," resting on shared values and a shared vision of "who we are, what is right, how we do things," is at the heart of these very different firms' cultures. Strong culture of this sort carries numerous benefits. It offers such control as independent professionals find bearable, which enables them to collaborate successfully. Strong culture engenders feelings of potency and ownership among organization members, as well as flexibility to shift into innovations, while maintaining a sense of direction.

Strong culture, however, carries costs as well, including almost constant intensity and the potential for tunnel vision and "true believership", where paradigms govern what can be perceived. Without careful attention to the costs, culture can mislead. The senior management role subtly shifts, from "decider" or "actor" to "keeper of the culture." But "keeping" a culture is a paradoxical task, as we have been noting. Culture cannot be kept unchanged, nor simply institutionalized into formal systems. Instead, it must be "kept vital" by constant re-examination and reinterpretation, consistent with its deepest values. Senior management must embody the spirit of the culture, especially in succeeding such charismatic leaders as Hewlett and Packard, Noyce and Moore, Haggerty, and other such giants – whether in high-technology firms or elsewhere.

This suggests another insight: *Modern management is far more complex than the "leadership and decision making" models of the past.* Structures, systems, and styles all need to shift – perhaps as Peter Drucker suggests:

> We need to move from the traditional, military-style command structure to one that is more like a symphony orchestra. With the number of people the New York Philharmonic needs on stage to play Mahler's Seventh Symphony, traditional

organizational structure would require deputy conductors, assistant conductors, and section conductors to bring it off. But that's not the model for that organization. Instead, all of the players report directly to the conductor. And the reason that's possible is because the conductor and the individual players all know the score.

Drucker, 1987

Vision – visionary leadership – seems far more important than "making decisions" as the central task of leaders in complex firms. Cultural evolution, cheerleading, and linking diverse pockets of local knowledge seem far more effective than traditional "taking charge," "planning" in the usual sense, or "organizing," in so far as that implies unchanging structure. "Controlling" is scarcely recognizable in comparison with the conventional version, and "staffing" seems to have a great deal more to do with managing a paradoxical blend of acculturation and iconoclasm than with simply bringing numbers of people into the firm.

Managers in all industries can learn much from high-technology firms. They can learn how to manage an organization as a high-intensity, high-innovation change engine without giving up control or responsibility, by sharing control and increasing others' sense of responsibility. They can learn how to keep the flow of innovation going, recognizing that innovation is both delicate and increasingly important. They can learn how to share judgment and the strategic steering process, both essential in complex and turbulent times like ours.

Managers can also learn from the high-technology sample how to mind the process, and guide content, while opening content up. Content will come mostly through others, the more so as more technical and local knowledge play their proper role. The manager's central responsibility is to sustain an environment in which innovation can flourish, watching for the need to change structure or systems, or to reinvigorate culture. Above all, managers must ensure that the "true religion" of shared criteria and challenging, legitimate marketplace demands is widely communicated, to fuel effective participation, involvement and ownership. As Jerry Sanders of Advanced Micro Devices is fond of repeating, "knowledge is power," in innovative organizations and strategies as elsewhere.

What High-Technology Firms Need to Learn

Managers in mature and established industries also have something to teach, a lesson they, too are re-learning: managing the manufacturing end-game. While the pace of product innovation continues unabated in the semiconductor industry, the competitive game seems to be being decided "in the last quarter:" by manufacturing mastery, as much as by design panache. The more interesting designs and innovative products, as always, require higher-order manufacturing skills. Today, widespread manufacturing competence translates to higher skills simply to stay in the game. Survival is determined by yield, and pulling one more product family out of horrendously costly equipment can spell hundreds of millions of dollars in sales, market position, and profit. In short, *dominance is in the details.*

Advances Needed in Management

The nature of high technology, and increasingly, as we have argued, the nature of competitive reality for most businesses, requires different management practices to deal with changed demands and new complexities. Old static, linear, rigid approaches simply cannot provide the flexibility and responsiveness necessary in a changeable, volatile, fluid competitive and technical environment. Ad hoc organizational practices, too, also fall short of what is needed: precision, control, and meticulous management of a multitude of details are also essential, in the design process as in manufacturing, in marketing and in environmental scanning, in integrating functional activities and more. What we have been describing is clearly not "loose" management in any meaningful sense, albeit very different from the structured rigidities of past bureaucratic practice.

Current theory, and even current management vocabulary, are insufficient to comprehend the complexity managers increasingly face. Many concepts are woefully impoverished in usage and theory, and offer managers inadequate tools for reasoning about the challenges they face:

Technology is all too often seen as static, linear, or unitary. Instead, in electronics first and foremost, but also in an ever-widening circle of related technologies of product or process, technology changes almost constantly. These changes are significant; they produce not only incremental improvements, but truly extraordinary advances. Technology changes, and with a fair degree of frequency changes in ways that make wholly new activities feasible or even mandatory.

As but one example, computer-controlled metal cutting, a product of developments in computers and electronics, makes possible degrees of precision in small, inexpensive machine tools that were simply inconceiveable not long ago. As a result, closer tolerances at much lower prices can be expected as the norm – and those unable to provide them will lose out to more advanced competitors. Equally important, as prices fall even small firms will be able to provide such new standards of precision.

Most organizations – and certainly those we have described here, including those producing the "simplest" and "least complex" products are vitally concerned with multiple technologies at any instant. Such multiple technologies evolve or mature at different rates, and interact in significant ways. Any given product may draw upon several underlying production technologies, and multiple options for creating the product's characteristics may be available. Both the product and its evolution, and the processes and their evolution are significant.

In high-technology firms particularly, managing a so-called "technology strategy" involves more than simply cranking out new products incorporating incremental improvements or enhancements, although that may also be required. Chapter 9 described the innovation cycle, suggesting a highly desirable sequence of innovation projects. But incremental improvements are not enough, and not every project travels smoothly to completion – even in good companies. Technological change is far more uncertain than this. So instead of sure bets, investment in R&D, particularly in the early stages of investigation, constitutes hedging – placing bets to ensure options, not guarantees. If such bets are not placed, the company may well forgo participation in some new technology.

Where the new technology is central, or provides some crucial advantage, the company may be compelled to purchase it from others (perhaps at an exorbitant price), or exit its chosen markets. Surprise developments by others, unanticipated by a firm committed to existing technology for products and processes, can invite "technological mugging" – disastrous disadvantages in products or production capabilities, price, or quality that can destroy market share.

Managing multiple technologies means managing multiple time horizons and multiple development clocks: exploratory efforts are not necessarily predictable, although in contrast targeted development can be highly structured, with end-points well specified. Both sorts of activity are necessary in highly volatile environments, thus managers must be able to think more complexly about technology and its management.

Structure in high-technology firms is more a flexible tool for realignment than a rigid or confining skeleton. High-technology firms use structure, anticipate that it will change, and shift from one structural arrangement to another. While the structure is in place, however, it does indeed specify quite explicitly who shall report to whom, who has responsibility for decisions, what a given entity's field of action is, and so on.

Unlike structure in standard bureaucratic organizations, high-technology structure does change frequently. Consequently, there seems to be both a greater tolerance for structural explicitness, and higher expectation that structure shall match intention. Contemporary management theory has suggested that where structure fails to support *de facto* strategies and intentions, "informal structural arrangements" will take over. Informal structure may even subvert the espoused strategies and intentions of the firm, where these differ significantly from the strategies and intentions actually enacted or signaled by practice.

In high-technology firms, there seems less of this subversion, and a closer linkage between intentions and actual practice. Two reasons suggest themselves: the role of "informal" practices and the frequent shifts of structure to improve alignment. What might have to be accomplished informally in a less change-tolerant, more bureaucratic organization can be in fact enacted in structure, where formal structure is a volatile, changeable tool.

Since much of the independent action that traditional firms forbid is actively encouraged in the high-technology firms, there is less necessity for undermining existing practices in order to accomplish something new. Indeed, there are multiple legitimate paths to resources, for instance. At the same time, no firm we investigated did not have a full complement of undercover activities and "bootlegging" going on – some officially acknowledged, and some deliberately ignored to preserve the bootleggers' own autonomy. All this suggests that our notions of formality, informal action, "legal" and "prohibited" activities need substantial reconsideration. The role of informal practices is less a matter of structure than of control and participation, to which we now will turn.

Control and participation are both concepts inadequately defined and accorded insufficient explanatory power in current management theory and practice. While it is clear that control is essential in a highly complex business, typical bureaucratic methods are insufficient to achieve this. Participation is desirable, to ensure "ownership" and maintain engagement by key professionals in high-technology firms. But "participation" as this term is usually understood is simply not adequate: it is too directed, too limited, and too condescending. Where managers and executives are so dependent on subordinates' expertise and knowledge, "participation" is no longer an altruistic luxury.

Similarly, what is dismissed or deprecated as "informal" and thereby relegated to purely socio-emotional orientations in other firms takes a far more central role in well-run high-technology firms. Local knowledge, grass-roots insights, and broadly shared responsibility for outcomes entail new methods of control, new demands upon both employees and managers, and different approaches to the web of communication and interchange that is the firm.

Lessons from High-Technology Firms

What lessons can be learned from the high-technology firms? The innovation management process is complex, although typically its aim is simple: keep innovation happening effectively. Its complexity comes from a variety of constant contradictions and tensions which must be held in balance through culture, norms, attitudes and understandings, systems and formal arrangements, and, above all, through managers' attention. These tensions reflect genuinely conflicting demands at the heart of successful innovation strategy; they are the source of its vitality, as well as the source of its difficulty.

High-technology firms are not the only innovative companies, nor even the first companies to make use of the approaches we have been outlining. "Team management," explicit attention to innovation, "strong culture," even structural change and many other aspects of these firms' innovation management methods are to be found elsewhere. In any single technique, these firms are not unique. As we have shown, however, they do provide an especially challenging environment, where the tensions of managing innovation are easily visible, and effective practices to deal with them have emerged.

What can be learned from these firms are their clear patterns of innovation management, their visible methods for coping in the innovation marathon. Both the need for innovation and the potential for turning it to competitive advantage are, we argue, increasingly general. Our sample companies' successes suggest approaches that might be adopted by others. While simple transplant is unlikely to succeed, the patterns visible here can be adapted to other firms in other industries: self-renewal is a matter of growing urgency for American industry.

We believe the high-technology firms' emphasis on innovation carries important insights for other industries for the future, especially conspicuous in the light of changing manufacturing technology in more traditional businesses. As electronics penetrates deeper into older, more established products and processes, more mature businesses become more like electronics.

The technology is, to some extent, a driver of change. But technology does not offer a deterministic future so much as a changed set of competitive realities: more intense competition; more interconnected, global markets, and yet more fragmented opportunities; a much increased science base upon which to reconfigure even more mature businesses. Such new realities offer opportunity, as well as threat.

More mature traditional businesses are now experiencing the full pressure of global competition – much as the electronics firms have, for some time. We believe that electronics firms have valuable lessons to teach about competing in a global market. The high-technology firms' management practices are distinctly different from standard management, and seem inextricably intertwined with their need for, and practice of, innovation. But the more traditional industries' experience in global competition carries lessons for the high-technology firms as well, particularly in the importance of persistence and attention to the end-game of manufacturing. As the race is not always to the swift, so competitive survival in modern times is complex, and goes well beyond technological innovation.

Appendix

Research Methods

We elected to study how organizations produce a stream of innovations over time by investigating high-technology firms in the electronics industry. Because our concern is with repeated innovation over time, the research is an empirical investigation in the field, spanning the period 1981 to 1988. The research is based on a multiple case study design, and data are collected longitudinally. In the paragraphs which follow, we will describe the research setting, the research design, data sources, interview techniques, and data analysis methods.

Research Setting

Our research was conducted in five multi-billion-dollar high-technology firms in the electronics industry: Hewlett-Packard, Intel, Motorola, National Semiconductor and Texas Instruments. All are diversified across a range of related products and markets within the electronics industry, and compete in the merchant semiconductor market as well as in related markets such as systems, computers, and electronics instruments. All firms are publicly held.

The firms were chosen as an intentional sample of cases from a population of US electronic firms. Since we wished to understand the innovation process in detail over time, we selected firms embedded in an industry characterized by rapid innovation, preferably in both product and process. Electronics provides such a context. All of our sample firms are engaged in the design and manufacture of semiconductor components – an industry in which rapid technological change is well documented. Also, all our chosen firms are participants in the broader computer industry in some way, whether through the manufacture of memory and logic components for computers, through design and production of computer systems, or by means of computer sub-systems that drive other equipment – or all of these.

The computer and semiconductor industries have been among the most research and development intensive of all US industries for the past fifteen years.[1] For example, in 1987, the figure for US all-industry composite investment in research and development as a percent of sales was 3.4 percent. In contrast, the computer industry composite figure was 8.2 percent and the semiconductor industry composite figure was 9.6 percent.[2] The firms we have studied are highly research intensive: one indicator of the extent to which they focus on innovation.

The firms we studied have also survived long enough, and prospered persistently enough, to offer experience across a range of business and technology cycles. They do vary in age, size and number of employees. Table A.1 lists the age, size, and research intensiveness of our sample firms at three points in time: at the beginning (1981), the mid-point (1984), and toward the end (1987) of our research.

Study Design: Research Cases at Multiple Levels of Analysis

The research is based primarily on original qualitative data gathered on-site at each of the study companies, using a multiple case study design.[3] Yin has defined a case research study as "an empirical inquiry that investigates a contemporary phenomenon within its real-life context, when the boundaries between phenomenon and context are not clearly evident, and in which multiple sources of evidence are used" (1984, p. 23). The multiple case study design is appropriate for those research questions where the organizational context is important, and where no single source of data on its own is likely to be sufficient. Several data sources are tapped within the organization, because the phenomenon under investigation is complex and must be viewed from multiple perspectives. This research design is especially appropriate for understanding and theorizing about dynamic processes, where a "how" or "why" question is being asked about a set of events (Yin, 1984, p. 13).

Table A.1 Characteristics of the sample companies

Firm	Year founded	Age in 1987	Research intensiveness (%)			Size in revenues ($ m)		
			1981	1984	1987	1981	1984	1987
Hewlett-Packard	1939	48	9.9	9.8	11.1	3576	6044	8090
Intel	1968	19	14.7	11.0	13.6	789	1629	1907
Motorola	1928	58	7.0	7.6	7.8	3570	5534	6710
National Semiconductor	1959	28	8.6	9.5	11.7	1110	1655	1868
Texas Instruments	1941	46	5.2	6.4	7.6	4206	5742	5595

Case studies have been appropriately criticized over the years for what have been called "non-scientific," "non-systematic" methods. This is because most cases were written for teaching purposes, not for research. Recent work on the case method has distinguished between case studies designed for teaching purposes (their traditional application) and those designed for research. Leonard-Barton (1988c) has described the shortcomings of teaching cases when evaluated from a research perspective:

> [Teaching cases] are illustrative business situations posed as managerial dilemmas for the students to . . . wrestle with . . . and . . . deliberately leave the story only partially told . . . for pedagogical reasons. . . . Fidelity to detail depends upon how critical is that detail to the teaching purpose. While teaching cases often provide managerial insight, they are not methodologically rigorous.
>
> Leonard-Barton, 1988c, pp. 5–6

Research methods experts such as Campbell (1975) and Yin (1984) have helped researchers distinguish adequate from inadequate research case methods. Recent work published by Leonard-Barton (1987, 1988a, 1988b) and Eisenhardt and Bourgeois (1988) illustrates the contemporary application of the more rigorous research case methods.

Using the research case design allows a replication logic (Yin, 1984), with a series of cases being treated as a series of "experiments" in which each case serves to confirm or refute inferences drawn from the previous ones. While the multiple case design is more demanding than a single case, it permits the induction of more reliable and richer insights by which to inform theory.

Our research also employs an "embedded" design, where multiple levels of analysis are included (Yin, 1981a; 1984). Rather than examining only the top management perspective or overall firm strategic decision making as a monolithic entity, we studied multiple levels of organizational functioning. Our study includes four levels of analysis: (1) the organization level of analysis (overall corporate strategy, organization, and performance); (2) the sub-unit level of analysis (divisions and business units); (3) the team level of analysis (multifunctional, cross-disciplinary development teams); and (4) individual level perceptions, rationales, and actions (how individuals function within the larger team, sub-unit, and organizational context).

We also examine the relationships between these levels. For example, how do resources held by top-level managers reach individual engineers and scientists so that innovative ideas are eventually funded? This is a question about the flow of resources across various levels. We also study the "glues" which hold these various levels together: organizational culture, systems, and management attention.

While gathering data at multiple levels of analysis is regarded as an important research strategy for those doing quantitative research, its significance has only recently been acknowledged by qualitative researchers. Its advantages are that it provides a greater richness to the data base and also taps into multiple perspectives from which to view the phenomenon. Understanding the perspectives on innovation at all four of these levels enables us to compare up and down levels within a single firm, and at the same level across the firms studied intensively.

Our research design is longitudinal, both in that it tracks sequences of events that unfolded over time, and in that data were gathered in separate waves. The first wave of data was gathered on-site from the summer of 1981 through 1982. The second wave of data was gathered on-site between January 1985 and continued through 1986. Additional interviews were conducted at Texas Instruments and Motorola in 1987 and 1988 to follow up high-level changes in management and their implications for innovation. In the periods between on-site interviews and after the second wave of data, published data were provided by the firms themselves. Business press reports were also collected. In all, the book covers the period from 1981 through 1988 intensively, although accounts of earlier events are also given as background.

Data Sources and Research Methods

We accessed three sources of data for this research: (1) systematic interviews on-site with the founders,[4] chairmen, the chief executives, vice-presidents and general managers, functional managers, and on down to research and development engineers and bench scientists throughout the organization; (2) documents collected from the companies regarding internal functioning; and (3) publicly available information obtained from several sources including the companies themselves, Computstat® data tapes, annual reports, and 10Ks. Case study research designs rely variously on qualitative and quantitative evidence derived from field work, archival records, verbal reports, and other such sources (Yin, 1981b, p. 58).

Our field research methods were to enter each organization and to systematically interview a knowledge–based sample of people involved in the research process and its management. Each organization was entered by first identifying the founders and highest-level officers, contacting one of them, and requesting an interview. In all cases that interview was granted, although in two cases a follow-up letter was required which formally described our research.[5] Whether by letter, by telephone, or in person, our research was described as:

> . . . Investigating how some firms continuously innovate products and manufacturing processes over time, and how they bring those innovations to high volume production and commercial success. Our research design focuses on successful firms like yours, for insight into the management of innovation and as a guide to the future that many managers and corporations face.

Thus at Hewlett-Packard, for example, our first interview was with David Packard, one of its two founders, then serving as Chairman of the Board. At Intel, the first interview was with Dr Gordon Moore, a founder, Chairman of the Board and then Chief Executive Officer.

Each interview followed a semi-structured protocol which allowed for open-ended responses. Interviews lasted from 45 minutes to two and a half hours, and averaged an hour and a half. All interviews were conducted by the authors and were tape recorded for later transcription. Interviews began by asking about innovation-related processes. The following topics were covered:

- genesis of ideas for new products and processes;
- acquisition of resources for innovation;
- project evaluation, selection, and management;
- opposition and disagreements, and how these were dealt with;
- the organization of the firm, and its R&D efforts;
- reorganization and organizational change;
- strategic planning and its relationship to innovation;
- the path of new ideas through development to manufacturing;
- interdepartmental and interfunctional relationships;
- how the simultaneous needs for innovation and efficiency are balanced;
- the respondent's education, experience, job responsibilities, and the structure of the department where located.

Top-level people were asked to identify and describe a strategic change related to an innovation, while those further down in the organization were asked about these specific innovations, as well as about innovation processes in general.

A strength of the semi-structured interview format and the open-ended responses it evokes is that it guides topics generally, but its openness allows respondents to cognitively structure the inquiry. Thus, for example, a question about the genesis and sources of innovative ideas might be quickly transformed by the respondent to enrich the inquiry: "Ideas come from everywhere, but the best ideas are technical and require extensive collaboration and interaction across functions and technical specialties." Respondents' own issues of concern, ideas, conceptions of the topics and structuring of the innovation phenomena they experienced can come forth. As a consequence, a second strength of this field research method is its ability to capture new data, topics, and perspectives. Because we believed that innovation was inadequately understood through the filters of existing theory, we sought to remain open to such expansions, rather than to prematurely close on a limited set of relations rigidly guided by *a priori* theory. Semi-structured interviews with open-ended responses allowed us to achieve our purpose.

Taken together, the interviews addressed a set of targeted concepts with all respondents, regardless of position held or level in the hierarchy. For instance, all were asked about the sources of innovative ideas, organization structure and reorganizations, interfaces between functions and units, the phases of development, project selection, resource flows, strategy and strategic planning, and so on. At lower organization levels, greater depth and detail was gathered from informants' generally greater specific knowledge, as would be expected. For example, when a manufacturing manager was interviewed, additional questions focused on the flow of new technology and products from development into manufacturing, and on the ramp-up to higher volume production.

We used a knowledge-based sampling method. All people interviewed were asked to suggest others with whom we should speak, who *had knowledge of*, or *were intimately involved in* aspects of innovation and its management. "Who else was involved?" was a key inquiry. By asking explicitly for the names of others with knowledge of these activities, knowledge-based sampling elicited representation of the functions involved in innovation within each company, regardless of the local title or position in the subject company.

Table A.2 Number of people interviewed, by position

Position	Total
Top management	
Chairman of Board or CEO	8
Senior/Executive VP	7
Operating management:	
Group Director or Division General Manager	15
Strategic Planning	
Corporate and Operating Group	9
R&D Functional Managers	
R&D Managers (VP to Project Leader):	26
Engineers or scientists	9
Manufacturing functional managers	10
Total number of interviews	92
Total hours of tape	138
Total transcribed pages	2760

While this method yielded roughly equivalent positions across companies, a more important outcome was knowledge equivalence. In all, we interviewed people in the following positions: founders, chief executives, executive vice presidents, high-level technical experts, division general managers, strategic planning managers, R&D managers, project managers, development engineers, production and operations managers, and manufacturing engineers. Table A.2 displays the distribution of informants by position. This display highlights the multiple levels of respondents, and the richness of data.

As table A.2 indicates, these research methods resulted in 92 interviews in total. The tape recorded interviews produced some 138 hours of audio tape time. Transcription pages numbered 2760. The systematic interviewing, recording, and transcription have created the same interview database for each company.

Data Analysis

Because we conducted original interviews in the field and also gathered archival and secondary data, two methods of analysis were employed.

Qualitative and quantitative data were independently analyzed. Our motive here was to stay as close as possible to the model of independent, triangulated data analysis (Jick, 1979), and to explicitly use documentary and archival material as a check on memory and perception.

The quantitative data reported in chapter 4 documents the extent of strategic decision making in eleven high-technology semiconductor firms on the basis of objective, external data over time. This analysis addresses the extent to which measures of strategy and financial performance are correlated over time. These data were derived from existing public data sources, such as annual reports, 10Ks, and Compustat® tapes. In two of the eleven firms, data for two years were provided by knowledgeable insiders. (As these two firms were acquired during the investigation period, their data were not reported publicly as independent organizations from their parent for two years during the investigated time span.) The quantitative data were analyzed by calculating percentages, growth in sales performance over time, and Pearson correlation coefficients for tests of significance between variables (more detail on these methods is reported in Schoonhoven, 1984).

Our analysis of qualitative data from the interviews builds on the techniques of others (e.g., Glaser and Strauss, 1967; Miles and Huberman, 1984; Yin, 1981, 1984). A common problem in field work which yields qualitative data is the danger that the researcher will take incomplete notes, or later erroneously paraphrase the respondent. Either problem can lead to inappropriate inferences, since the basic data are of variable fidelity and may be incomplete. Others warn of the danger of not being able to distinguish note-taking from narrative-writing (Yin, 1981, p. 60).

We avoided these threats to the accuracy of our data by tape recording[6] interviews and having them transcribed verbatim. As a consequence, there was no second-hand reworking of the field notes; the directly transcribed interviews provided the data. The researchers checked for accurate transcription and corrected typographical errors by listening again to the tapes.

Unlike hypothesis testing research, inductive analysis of qualitative data does not have a generally accepted model. In the absence of such a standard, we used the following approach. We began with a set of concepts – a conceptual framework – around which interview questions were designed. The questions were intentionally open-ended, as previously described. We also frequently tested our comprehension of respondents' meaning by restating our understanding to them. One then asks, around which topics should the evidence be further organized and integrated, given that new information was revealed in the interviews?

Following the lead of others, we collected interview segments from several respondents on the same topic or concept, and compared these for similarities and differences, both within firms and across firms (Jick, 1979; Yin, 1980). In essence, we conducted an intensive search for patterns in the data, combing through the transcripts, highlighting information on key concepts, and comparing that information to that of others in the same organization, across levels and positions for similarities and differences. The same intense search for patterns was also applied across firms.

In integrating data by topic and concept, we were concerned to make adequate allowance for potential differences in perception within the firms, when employees in different positions and at different levels of the hierarchy were queried on the same topic. For example, we compared the organization structure described for us by people at different levels within the same organization. As others have reported with this methodology of comparison, however, differences found in this sort of data are primarily due to the addition of new events, or new information on known events (Bourgeois and Eisenhardt, 1988; Eisenhardt and Bourgeois, 1988).

This comparison method documented a key finding in our research: the clear structures encountered across the organizations we studied. As described in chapter 9, for example, an engineering project manager and his superior four levels above in the organization described precisely the same formal structure at Intel. For much of the data, however, "fact" (the number of structural levels, for example) is not the issue. Perceptions of events and interpretations of them are central to people's understanding and to their choice of actions, regardless of whether they agree with others' perceptions and actions. We found many shared perceptions, as well as shared descriptions. These shared perceptions, like the clear, shared structural descriptions, provide a significant finding in our research not reported elsewhere in the management of innovation literature, where amorphous, ambiguous structures and hierarchically dominated perceptions are assumed.

To analyze the cross-case data, we used the case-comparison

approach (Yin, 1981, p. 62). Since our interest was in developing a deep understanding of a complex phenomenon, we traded off a large number of cases in favor of an in-depth, longitudinal knowledge of the five cases studied. The case-comparison method has been likened to more generalized theory-building, and has been used to construct a common explanation for phenomena observed in several studies (Derthick, 1972; Yin, 1981).

With the cross-case comparison approach, the researcher must provide a chain of evidence consisting of the explicit citation of particular pieces of evidence, as one shifts from data collection to within-case analysis to cross-case analysis and to overall findings and conclusions (Yin, 1979, p. xii). We have used this methodology throughout the book. As Yin observed, much case study research "has failed to establish an explicit chain" (Yin, 1981b, p. 64). The chain of evidence in this book is in the numerous direct quotations from our informants, who have been liberally cited throughout the book as evidence for a particular conclusion regarding what is important in the management of innovation.

In analyzing qualitative data, it seemed important to pay attention to the time dimension, to consistency and change over time in key variables. Were it not for the longitudinal design of the study, we would not have detected the frequent reorganizations, the consistent self-analysis and organizational re-examination so characteristic of these firms. Intensive, pervasive dissatisfaction with the status quo was only observable over time. To our knowledge, few case method research projects have taken a longitudinal perspective on qualitative data gathering, although this appears to be emerging as an important research strategy (e.g. Leonard-Barton, 1988c).

From the intense search for patterns, tentative relationships between variables have been developed. These are offered in the final chapter as implications for management. Because managers cannot wait for five to fifteen years for the results of the knowledge-accumulation process that drives academic research, we offer our insights as a set of working hypotheses. In another vehicle, we will report on these relationships as hypotheses to be confirmed by larger-scale comparative research – the next logical step in the accumulation of knowledge about a given set of relationships. However, it will be literally years before we and others are able to gather data of this quality on the internal functioning of a large number of firms. This is the research challenge.

In the meantime, of course, consistency of our findings with other accounts, "the ring of truth" in our account, if there be any, and the testing of these ideas against readers' experience must serve. As our working hypotheses became firmer in our minds, a next step was to compare them with the extant literature. We sought to identify both similarities and contradictions, and to understand why some of our findings differed from earlier results. Conflicting literature is important to theory development, because understanding the nature of the conflict typically produces a better theory in the long run. While we have spared our executive and managerial target audiences an extensive trip through this literature in the text, it has been important to note along the way how our findings differ from previous research on the management of innovation.

Limitations of this Research

Different research methods produce different problems regarding the reliability and validity of their findings. A challenge in all research is to ensure reliability and validity, nowhere moreso than in case research (Yin, 1984). These are among the more troublesome elements for research conducted in the field, away from the controlled circumstances of experimental laboratories (Campbell and Stanley, 1966). The purpose of our research was to learn about continuous innovation in a field setting from those who are actually innovating. Our intent was to remain open rather than to prematurely close on a limited set of relationships rigidly guided by *a priori* theory. The multiple case method was ideally suited to the inductive research, developmental perspectives, and rich knowledge we sought.

The question of reliability was addressed directly by using a research protocol in which all firms and informants were subject to the same sequence of entry and exit procedures. The data base for each firm was organized and constructed in the same way. One threat to reliability hinges on the concept of replicability. Would different researchers find the same results if they were to repeat (or replicate) the research methods? In quantitative research, statistical tests help to assess the degree of confidence appropriate for the data, by calculating inter-rater reliability coefficients, for example. Assessing reliability in this way is a problem for qualitative research. In our study, however, multiple levels of analysis and an explicit search for convergent and divergent patterns across multiple respondents on common topics minimize the risk of systematic bias in the findings. The use of archival data provides further insurance. Taken together, these precautions and research methods enhance reliability.

External validity in the experimental methods literature refers to generalizability: the expansion to other populations, settings, treatment variables and measurement variables of the findings (Campbell and Stanley, 1966). When applied to research case methods, we are concerned with whether our findings may be generalized or applied to any other organizational settings. We have approached external validity through the *multiple* case design of the research: rather than a single firm, five independent organizations have been intensely studied. A larger number of cases helps counter any concern that the findings are in some way limited to the special setting of the research.

Because our five firms are in the broader electronics industry, are public firms, and face broadly similar environmental conditions, we are more confident that our results are not particularistic. This selection technique "controls for" variables in a quasi-experimental way, where real control is not possible, as it may be in an experimental study. The firms do vary in size and age, however (see table A.2).

What is especially important is the nature of the environment in which these firms compete. Theirs are "high velocity" (Bourgeois and Eisenhardt, 1988) or "turbulent" environments (Emery and Trist, 1963), where rapid, discontinuous changes take place in demand, competitors, technology, regulation, and other important areas. Information is often unavailable, incomplete, inaccurate, or obsolete. Such conditions produce constant instability and discontinuous change. Using this definition, such diverse industries as some consumer products, biotechnology, banking, microcomputers, savings and loans, semiconductors and airlines participate in high velocity environments, as do our sample firms.

Many argue that most industries today are moving into rapid and discontinuous change – conditions similar to those of our sample firms. We argue that the conditions facing the electronics industry today prevail in an increasingly broad array of industries. Competition is increasingly global, and increasingly dependent upon innovation in products and manufacturing (or service delivery) processes. To the extent that an organization competes within a turbulent or high velocity environment, we would argue that our findings generalize to that organization. As Mintzberg observed, if no one ever generalized beyond her or his data, there would be no interesting hypotheses to test. Every theory requires a creative leap, however small, to break away from the expected and describe something new (Mintzberg, 1979b, p. 584).

Since our research design called for a knowledge-based sample of organization members well informed about the innovation process, rather than randomly selected respondents to a rigid questionnaire, some bias might be expected in the data, from traditional experimental-research perspectives. One potential bias of some concern is the danger of obtaining a "power-related" sample of persons linked to the dominant executives through whom we made our initial contacts. When researchers begin at the top of an organization and interview down through it using any non-random selection method, there is danger the information will simply conform with the prevailing management view. This concern is valid, from a statistical point of view. However, it assumes to some extent that organizational participants are automatons, who mimic and reflect only what more powerful others expect, and are without views of their own. The outspoken commentary we received from respondents suggests otherwise.

The design of our research is deliberately multi-level. As one moves through multiple levels and across sub-units, the links between top management and the lower levels of the organization become more remote in any case. Indeed, much research has shown that people in different positions at different levels of an organization invariably have access to different information, which in turn influences their perspectives. This is referred to as "loose-coupling" in organizations (Weick, 1976), organizational "differentiation" (Lawrence and Lorsch, 1967), and "local knowledge" (Baba, 1988). We deliberately sought multi-level informants to tap into these information differences.

As we have shown, especially in chapter 11 on the costs and benefits of strong culture, the criticisms expressed within these firms are extensive and freely offered; there was no sign of censorship. Researchers should be wary when they encounter universally sunny representations. Our informants were openly self-critical, and critical of their organizations and their operations as well. Their critiques were not cynical or unduly negative, but considered, specific, backed up with data, and articulate. Such multi-level perspectives and their character allayed our concerns about potential power-related sample bias.

Conclusions

The framework described here includes the key features of our research design, research methods, and data analysis. Inductive research is creative in some ways. It requires constant iteration and overlap between steps, and between concepts, data, and literature (Mintzberg, 1979a; Miles and Huberman, 1984). Overall, the anticipated result of this work will be the creation of a theoretical framework, with a set of testable hypotheses, and possibly what academics call a "mid-range" theory.

All of these will be linked to our research questions about how some firms produce a stream of innovations over time, which ultimately bring commercial success in the marketplace. Our goal has been to provide new insights into the management of innovation, and thereby to contribute to contemporary management. Today's managers are faced with global markets, widespread competence in competitors who are themselves innovating, and a pace of change in technology and markets that seems to cry out for continuous innovation as the only feasible response for industrial success – in the United States and elsewhere, in the future as well as here and now.

Notes

1 See the "R&D Scoreboard" published by *Business Week* for comparative figures on research intensiveness across all US industries.
2 "R&D Scoreboard," *Business Week*, 20 June 1988, pp. 139–62.
3 Greater depth on the methodological foundations of our research can be found in: Glaser and Strauss (1967); Pettigrew (1979); and Mohr (1982).
4 The original founders of Texas Instruments and Motorola are no longer living. Motorola's Chairman is the son of the founder, however. Hewlett-Packard's founders have been much less active in the business in recent years, although David Packard was Chairman at the time of our interviews. Intel is still managed by its founders. Charles Sporck is so intimately identified with National Semiconductor that he is widely believed to have been an original founder. Instead, he is the author of National's "second birth," in the words of Pierre LaMonde, National's Vice President and Technical Director (1981):

> [National] was actually founded in 1959 and did very poorly until 1967. To put things in perspective, in 1967 the company

had sales of $7 million – an eight-year-old company with sales of $7 million! You know, Fairchild had been founded a year earlier, and had sales well in excess of $100 million by then. So the *second birth* took place when Charlie Sporck and a group of us joined the company in February 1967, and we moved it very fast to a profitable position.

5 A sixth firm initially participated in the research project in a limited way. Founded in the late 1960s, this firm increased the number of younger firms in our sample and added a second firm whose primary business was semiconductor products. This firm was somewhat comparable to Intel in age, size, and business focus. One of its founders consented to participate and was interviewed. However, through its public relations office, the firm's CEO declined to participate, citing internal and external business pressures, thereby truncating further research at the firm.

6 All people interviewed were told that confidential or proprietary data would be removed or not directly attributed; any information they deemed to be "sensitive" but publishable would be reported anonymously. The tape recorder was switched off during private telephone calls. These safeguards to proprietary data and confidentiality, as needed, helped to assure participants that they could speak openly, while providing accurate data.

Bibliography

Abegglen, James C. and Stalk, George, Jr., 1985. *Kaisha: The Japanese Corporation*. New York: Basic Books.

Abell, Derek F. and Hammond, John S., 1979. *Strategic Market Planning: Problems and Analytical Approaches*. Englewood Cliffs, NJ: Prentice-Hall.

Abernathy, William J., 1978. *The Productivity Dilemma: Roadblock to Innovation in the Automobile Industry*. Baltimore: Johns Hopkins University Press.

Abernathy, William J., Clark, Kim B. and Kantrow, Alan M., 1983. *Industrial Renaissance*. New York: Basic Books.

Ackerman, Robert J., ed., 1986. *Growing in the Shadow: Children of Alcoholics*. Pompano Beach, FL: Health Communications, Inc.

Aldrich, Howard E., 1979. *Organizations and Environments*. Englewood Cliffs, NJ: Prentice-Hall.

Allison, Graham T., 1971. *The Essence of Decision*. Boston: Little Brown.

Andrews, Kenneth R., 1971. *The Concept of Corporate Strategy*. Homewood, IL: Dow Jones/Irwin.

Anthony, Robert N., 1987. "We Don't Have the Accounting Concepts We Need," *Harvard Business Review* 65:1 (January –February), 75–83.

Ashby, W. Ross, 1971. *An Introduction to Cybernetics*. London: University Paperbacks (Methuen & Co.).

Baba, Marietta L., 1988. "The Local Knowledge Content of Technology-Based Firms." Presentation at the University of Colorado Conference on Managing High Technology Firms, January.

Battista, John R., 1982. "Holographic Model, Holistic Paradigm, Information Theory and Consciousness," *The Holographic Paradigm*, ed. Ken Wilber. Boston: New Science Library, 143–9.

Berger, Peter and Luckmann, Thomas, 1967. *The Social Construction of Reality*. New York: Penguin.

Bernstein, Jeremy, 1984. *Three Degrees Above Zero: Bell Labs in the Information Age*. New York: Charles Scribner's Sons.

Blau, Peter M., 1955. *The Dynamics of Bureaucracy*. Chicago: University of

Chicago Press.

Borysenko, Joan, 1987. *Minding the Body, Mending the Mind*. Reading, MA: Addison-Wesley.

Boston Consulting Group, 1972. *Perspectives on Experience*. Boston.

Bourgeois, L. J., and Eisenhardt, K. M., 1988. "Strategic Decision Processes in High Velocity Environments: Four Cases in the Microcomputer Industry," *Management Science* 34:7, (July) 816–35.

Bower, Joseph L., 1986. *When Markets Quake*. Boston, MA: Harvard Business School Press.

Buffa, Elwood, 1984. *Meeting the Competitive Challenge: Manufacturing Strategy for US Companies*. Homewood, IL: Dow Jones/Irwin.

Burgelman, Robert A., 1983. "Corporate Entrepreneurship and Strategic Management: Insights from a Process Study," *Management Science* 29:12 (December), 1349–64.

Burgelman, Robert A., 1988. "Strategy Making as a Social Learning Process: The Case of Internal Corporate Venturing," *Interfaces* 18:3 (May–June), 74–85.

Burgelman, Robert A. and Sayles, Leonard R., 1986. *Inside Corporate Innovation*. New York: The Free Press, 204, n.2.

Burns, Alan, 1981. *The Microchip: Appropriate or Inappropriate Technology?* Chichester, UK: Ellis Horwood, Ltd.; New York: Halsted Press, A Division of John Wiley & Sons.

Burns, Tom and Stalker, G. M., 1971. *The Management of Innovation*. London: Tavistock. (First published in 1961.)

Burrell, G. and Morgan, Gareth, 1979. *Sociological Paradigms and Organizational Analysis*. London: Heinemann.

Business Week, 1975. "Plugging in a new team at Motorola," 12 May, 27.

Business Week, 1984. "Why Hewlett-Packard Overhauled Its Management," 30 July, 111–12.

Business Week, 1984. "Who's Excellent Now?" 5 November, 76–8.

Business Week, 1988. "R&D Scoreboard," 20 June, 139–62.

Campbell, Donald T., 1975. "'Degrees of Freedom' and the Case Study," *Comparative Political Studies* 8:2, 178–93.

Business Week, 1988. "R&D Scoreboard," 20 June, 139–62.

Campbell, Donald T. and Stanley, J. C., 1966. *Experimental and Quasi-Experimental Designs for Research*. Chicago: Rand McNally.

Carlzon, Jan, 1987. *Moments of Truth*. Cambridge, MA: Ballinger.

Carroll, Paul B. and Gilman, Hank, 1987. "Big Blues: Mainframe Slowdown and Stiff Competition Put Pressure on IBM," *Wall Street Journal* 69:29 (23 November), 1, 18.

Chaffee, E. E., 1985. "Three Models of Strategy," *Academy of Management Review* 10:1, 89–98.

Chandler, Alfred D., Jr., 1967. *Strategy and Structure: Chapters in the History of Industrial Enterprise.* Cambridge, MA: MIT Press.

Chandler, Alfred D., Jr., 1977. *The Visible Hand: The Managerial Revolution in American Business.* Cambridge, MA: The Belnap Press of Harvard University.

Child, John D., 1972. "Organizational Structure, Environment and Performance: The Role of Strategic Choice," *Sociology* 6:1 (January 1967.) 1–22.

Clark, Kim B., Chew, W. Bruce and Fujimoto, Takahiro, 1988. "Product Development in the World Auto Industry: Strategy, Organization and Performance." Research report prepared at the Harvard University Graduate School of Business. Not dated, but reported at the 1988 Atlanta meeting of the Society of Manufacturing Engineers.

Clifford, Jack R., Pettingill, Stewart A., Marcus, Philip and McLennan, Norman D., 1979. *A Report on the US Semiconductor Industry.* Washington, DC: US Department of Commerce, Industry and Trade Administration, Office of Producer Goods, September.

Cohen, M. D., March, James G. and Olsen, J. P., 1972. "A Garbage Can Model of Organization Choice," *Administrative Science Quarterly* 17:1, 1–25.

Cohen, Stephen S. and Zysman, John, 1987. *Manufacturing Matters: The Myth of a Post-Industrial Economy.* New York: Basic Books.

Compressed Air, 1985. "The Great Race in Running Shoes," 90:7 (July), 10–15.

Connor, Patrick E., 1980. *Organizations: Theory and Design.* Chicago: SRA Associates.

Cooper, Arnold C. and Bruno, Albert, 1977. "Success Among High Technology Firms," *Business Horizons* 20:2 (April).

Cooper, Robin and Kaplan, Robert S., 1988. "Measure Costs Right: Make the Right Decision", *Harvard Business Review* 66 (September–October), 96–105.

Daft, Richard L., 1983. "Symbols in Organizations: a Dual-Content Framework for Analysis," *Organizational Symbolism*, ed. Pondy, Louis R., Frost, Peter, Morgan, Gareth and Dandridge, Thomas C. Greenwich, CT: JAI Press.

Dallmeyer, Dorinda G., 1987. "National Security and the Semiconductor Industry," *Technology Review* 90:8 (November–December), 46–55.

Dalton, Melville, 1950. "Conflicts Between Staff and Line Managerial Officers," *American Sociological Review* 15 (June), 342–51.

Davidson, William H., 1984. *The Amazing Race: Winning the Technorivalry with Japan.* New York: John Wiley & Sons.

Deal, T. and Kennedy, A., 1982. *Corporate Cultures: The Rites and Rituals of Corporate Life.* Reading, MA: Addison-Wesley.

Dean, James W., Jr., 1987. "Building the Future: The Justification Process for New Technology," *New Technology as Organizational Innovation*, ed.

Johannes Pennings and Arend Buitendam. Cambridge, MA: Ballinger.

Dearborn, DeWitt C. and Simon, Herbert A., 1958. "Selective Perception: A Note on the Departmental Identification of Executives," *Sociometry* 21, 140–4.

Defense Science Board. Report on the Semiconductor Industry. (Cited in Dallmeyer, 1987.)

Delbecq, Andre L. and Mills, Peter K., 1985. "Managerial Practices that Enhance Innovation," *Organizational Dynamics* 14:1 (Summer), 24–34.

Derthick, Martha, 1972. *New Towns In-Town: Why a Federal Program Failed*. Washington, DC: The Urban Institute, 1972.

Drucker, Peter F., 1986. "Productivity: Today's New Meaning." Address delivered at the annual Peter F. Drucker Symposium, New York University Graduate School of Business Administration, 7 May. Excerpted in *The Consultant Forum*, 4, (3) (1987), 2–5.

Eckstein, Otto, Caton, Christopher, Brinner, Roger, and Duprey, Peter, 1984. *The DRI Report on US Manufacturing Industries*. New York: McGraw-Hill.

Eisenhardt, K. M. and Bourgeois, L. J., 1988. "The Politics of Strategic Decision Making in Top Management Teams: A Study in the Microcomputer Industry," *Academy of Management Journal* 31:4 (December), 737–70.

Emery, F. E. and Trist, Eric L., 1963. "The Causal Texture of Organizational Environments," *Human Relations* 18 (August), 20–6.

Ettlie, John E. and Bridges, William P., 1987. "Technology Policy and Innovation in Organizations," *New Technology as Organizational Innovation*, ed. Johannes Pennings and Arend Buitendam. Cambridge, MA: Ballinger.

Fahey, Liam, 1981. "On Strategic Management Decision Processes," *Strategic Management Journal* 2:1, 43–60.

Farnum, Gregory T., 1987. "Profiles: Tradition and Necessity," *Manufacturing Engineering* 98:4 (April), 60–1.

Festinger, L., 1954. "A Theory of Cognitive Dissonance," *Human Relations* 7, 117–40.

Fleck, L., 1979. *Genesis and Development of a Scientific Fact: Introduction to the Study of Thoughtstyle and Thoughtcollectives*, ed. T. J. Trenn and R. Merton. Chicago: University of Chicago Press. (First published in German, 1935).

Forbes, 1979: "Credit where credit is due," 1 October, 121.

Forester, Tom, 1981. *The Microelectronic Revolution*. Cambridge MA: The MIT Press.

Fortune, 1975. "Here Comes the Second Computer Revolution," 92 (November), 134–9, 182, 184.

Foster, Richard N., 1986. *Innovation: the Attacker's Advantage*. New York: Summit Books.

Galbraith, Jay, 1973. *Designing Complex Organizations*. Reading, MA: Addison-Wesley.

Garvin, David A., 1984. "What Does 'Product Quality' Really Mean?" *Sloan Management Review* 25:3 (Fall), 25–43.

Garvin, David A., 1987. "Competing on the Eight Dimensions of Quality," *Harvard Business Review* 65:6 (November–December), 101–9.

Garvin, David A., 1988. *Managing Quality: The Strategic and Competitive Edge*. New York: The Free Press.

Geertz, Clifford, 1983. *Local Knowledge*. New York: Basic Books.

Gilder, George, 1988. "You Ain't Seen Nothing Yet," *Forbes* 141:7 (4 April), 88–93.

Glaser, J. and Strauss, A. L., 1967. *The Discovery of Grounded Theory*. Aldine: Chicago.

Gold, Bela, 1982. "CAM Sets New Rules for Production," *Harvard Business Review* 60:6 (November–December), 88–94.

Goldhar, Joel D. and Jelinek, Mariann, 1983. "Plan for Economies of Scope," *Harvard Business Review* (November–December).

Gouldner, Alvin W., 1954. *Patterns of Industrial Bureaucracy*. New York: The Free Press.

Grove, Andrew S., 1983. *High Output Management*. New York: Random House.

Hambrick, Donald C., 1980. "Operationalizing the Concept of Business-Level Strategy in Research," *Academy of Management Review* 5:4 (October), 567.

Harris, J. M., Shaw, R. W. and Sommers, W. P., 1983. "The Strategic Management of Technology," *Planning Review* (January).

Hatch, M. J., 1987. "Physical Barriers, Task Characteristics, and Interaction Activity in Research and Development Firms", *Administrative Science Quarterly*, 32 (3) (September), 387–99.

Hayes, Robert H. and Abernathy, William J., 1980. "Managing Our Way to Economic Decline," *Harvard Business Review* 58:4 (July–August), 67–77.

Hayes, Robert H. and Clark, Kim, 1986. "Why Some Factories are More Productive Than Others," *Harvard Business Review* 64:5 (September–October), 66–73.

Hayes, Robert H. and Wheelwright, Steven C., 1979b. "The Dynamics of Process – Product Life Cycles," *Harvard Business Review* (March–April), 127–36.

Hayes, Robert H. and Wheelwright, Steven C., 1979a. "Link Manufacturing Process and Product Life Cycles," *Harvard Business Review* (January–February), 133–40.

Hayes, Robert H. and Wheelwright, Steven C., 1984. *Restoring Our Competitive Edge: Competing Through Manufacturing*. New York: John Wiley.

Hayes, Robert H., Wheelwright, Steven C. and Clark, Kim B., 1988. *Dynamic Manufacturing*. New York: Free Press.

High Technology Business, "Interview with GM Vice Chairman Donald J. Atwood on the New Auto Industry," 7, (10) (October), 42–5.

Hofer, Charles W. and Schendel, Dan, 1978. *Strategy Formulation: Analytical Concepts*. St Paul, MN: West Publishing Co.

Hofstede, Geert, 1984. *Culture's Consequences*. Cross-Cultural Research and Methodology Series, 5. Beverly Hills, CA: Sage.

Homans, George C., 1950. *The Human Group*. New York: Harcourt, Brace & World.

IBM Canada, Ltd, 1978. *Report on the Computer Industry*. Montreal.

International Monetary Fund, 1984. *International Financial Statistics* (March) 264.

Janis, Irving L., 1972. *Victims of Groupthink*. Boston: Houghton Mifflin.

Janis, Irving L. and Mann, Leon, 1977. *Decision Making*. New York: The Free Press.

Jeffrey, Brian, 1986. "IBM's Protean Ways," *Datamation* 32:1 (January), 62–8.

Jelinek, Mariann, 1979. *Institutionalizing Innovation*. New York: John Wiley & Sons.

Jelinek, Mariann, 1987. "Production Innovation and Economies of Scope: Beyond the 'Technological Fix'," *Engineering Costs and Production Economics* 12, 315–26.

Jelinek, Mariann and Goldhar, Joel D., 1985. "A Whole New World of Manufacturing: Strategic and Organizational Implications of Advanced Manufacturing Techniques," Paper presented at the TIMS/ORSA Annual Meeting, Atlanta, Georgia, November.

Jelinek, Mariann and Litterer, Joseph A., 1988. "Why OD Must Become Strategic," *Research in Organization Change and Development*, 2, ed. Richard W. Woodman and William R. Pasmore. Greenwich, CT: JAI Press.

Jelinek, Mariann, Litterer, Joseph A. and Miles, Raymond E., eds, 1986. *Organizations by Design: Theory and Practice*, 2nd edn. Plano, TX: Business Publications, Inc.

Jennings, D. F. and Sexton, D. H., 1985. "Managing Innovation in Established Firms: Issues, Problems and the Impact on Economic Growth and Employment." *Proceedings of the Conference on Industrial Science and Technological Innovation*, sponsored by National Science Foundation. The Center for Research and Development, Publishers, State University of New York at Albany, New York.

Jick, Todd D., 1979. "Mixing Qualitative and Quantitative Methods: Triangulation in Action," *Administrative Science Quarterly* 24: 602–11.

Johnson, Gerry, 1988. "Rethinking Incrementalism," *Strategic Management Journal* 9:1, 75–91.

Johnson, H. Thomas and Kaplan, Robert S., 1987. *Relevance Lost: The Rise and Fall of Management Accounting*. Boston, MA: Harvard Business School Press.

Kanter, Rosabeth Moss, 1983. *The Change Masters: Innovation for Productivity in the American Corporation*. New York: Simon and Schuster.

Kantrow, Alan M., 1987. *The Constraints of Corporate Tradition*. New York: Harper & Row.

Kaplan, Robert S., 1986. "Must CIM Be Justified by Faith Alone?" *Harvard Business Review* 64:2 (March–April), 87–93.

Kennedy, Mary M., 1979. "Generalizing from Single Case Studies," *Evaluation Quarterly* 3, 661–78.

Kidder, Tracy, 1981. *Soul of a New Machine*. Boston: Little, Brown.

Kiesler, Sara and Sproull, Lee, 1982. "Managerial Response to Changing Environments: Perspectives on Problem Solving from Social Cognition," *Administrative Science Quarterly* 27, 548–70.

Kotler, Philip, 1980. *Principles of Marketing*. Englewood Cliffs, NJ: Prentice-Hall.

Kuhn, Thomas, 1970. *The Structure of Scientific Revolutions*. 2nd edn. Chicago: University of Chicago Press.

Langer, Ellen and Piper, Alison, 1987. "The Prevention of Mindlessness," *Journal of Personality and Social Psychology* 53:2, 280–7.

Larson, Erik, 1987. "The Best-Laid Plans," *INC*. 9:2 (February), 60–4.

Latham, Gary P. and Locke, Edwin A., 1979. "Goal Setting – A Motivational Technique That Works," *Organizational Dynamics* (Autumn), 68–80.

Lawrence, Paul R. and Dyer, Davis, 1983. *Renewing American Industry*. New York: The Free Press.

Lawrence, Paul R. and Lorsch, Jay W., 1967. *Organization and Environment*. Boston: Harvard University Press.

Leavitt, Harold J., 1958. *Managerial Psychology*. Chicago: University of Chicago Press.

Leonard-Barton, Dorothy, 1988a. "Implementation as Mutual Adaptation of Technology and Organization," *Research Policy* 17:5.

Leonard-Barton, Dorothy, 1988b. "Implementation Characteristics in Organizational Innovations," *Communication Research* 17:5.

Leonard-Barton, Dorothy, 1988c. "Synergistic Design for Case Studies: Longitudinal Single-Site and Replicated Multiple Site." Paper presented at National Science Foundation Conference on Field Research Methods, Austin, Texas, 16 September.

Litterer, Joseph A. and Jelinek, Mariann, 1987. "Implementing Global Strategies: New Forms of Participation." Paper presented at the Eastern Academy of Management's Second International Conference, Athens, Greece, August.

Litterer, Joseph A. and Jelinek, Mariann, 1988. "Strategic Participation in the Global Firm." Paper presented at the Strategic Management Society meeting, Amsterdam, October.

Litterer, Joseph A. and Miyamoto, Lance, Teitelbaum, Helene and Voyer, John, 1985. "Managing New Product Development: The Challenge of Guiding Innovation." Unpublished manuscript presented at the Strategic Management Society meeting, Barcelona, Spain.

Lundstedt, S. B. and Colglazier, E. W., Jr., 1982. *Managing Innovation*. New York: Pergamon Press.

Lynn, Leonard, 1988. "Comparing US and Japanese Engineering Careers." Unpublished manuscript.

Madhn, Swaminathan, 1985. *Electronics: Circuits and Systems*. Indianapolis, IN: Howard W. Sams & Co.

Magaziner, Ira C. and Reich, Robert B., 1983. *Minding America's Business*. New York: Vantage/Random House.

March, James G. and Simon, Herbert A., 1958. *Organizations*. New York: John Wiley & Sons.

Martin, Joanne and Powers, M., 1983. "Organizational Stories: More Vivid and Persuasive than Quantitative Data," *Psychological Foundations of Organizational Behavior*, ed. B. Staw. Glenview, IL: Scott, Foresman, 161–68.

McClelland, David C., 1961. *The Achieving Society*. Princeton, NJ: Van Nostrand.

McManus, George, 1987. "Steel Shortage: What Happened to the World's Surplus?" *Iron Age* (December), 14–19.

Merryfield, B., 1983. "Forces of Change Affecting High Technology Industries," *National Journal*, 29 January, 255.

Meyer, J. W. and Rowan, B., 1977. "Institutional Organizations: Formal Structures as Myth and Ceremony," *American Journal of Sociology* 83, 340–63.

Meyer, Mark H. and Roberts, Edward B., 1986. "New Product Strategy in Small Technology-Based Firms: A Pilot Study," *Management Science* 32:7 (July), 806–21.

Miles, Matthew B. and Huberman, A. M., 1984. *Qualitative Data Analysis: A Sourcebook of New Methods*. Beverly Hills, CA: Sage Publications.

Miles, Raymond E. and Snow, Charles C., 1984. "Fit, Failure and the Hall of Fame," *Strategy and Organization: A West Coast Perspective*, ed. Glenn Carroll and David Vogel. Boston: Pitman with the *California Management Review*.

Miles, Raymond E. and Snow, Charles C., 1978. *Organizational Strategy, Structure, and Process*. New York: 1978.

Miller, Danny and Friesen, Peter, 1980. "Momentum and Revolution in Organizational Adaptation," *Academy of Management Journal* 23:4, 591–614.

Mintzberg, Henry, 1977. "Strategy Formulation as a Historical Process," *International Studies of Management and Organization* VII:2, 28–40.

Mintzberg, Henry, 1978. "Patterns in Strategy Formation," *Management Science* 24, 934–48.

Mintzberg, Henry, 1979a. "An Emerging Strategy of 'Direct' Research," *Administrative Science Quarterly* 24:4 (December), 582–9.

Mintzberg, Henry, 1979b. *The Structuring of Organizations*. Englewood Cliffs, NJ: Prentice-Hall.

Mintzberg, Henry and McHugh A., 1985. "Strategy formulation in an Adhocracy", *Administrative Science Quarterly* 30, 160–97.

Mintzberg, Henry, Raisinghani, O. and Theoret, A., 1976. "The Structure of Unstructured Decision Processes," *Administrative Science Quarterly* 21, 246–75.

Mintzberg, Henry and Waters, James A., 1985. "Of Strategies, Deliberate and Emergent," *Strategic Management Journal* 6:3 (July–September), 257–72.

Mishne, Patricia P., 1988. "A Passion for Perfection," *Manufacturing Engineering* (November), 46–58.

Mitroff, Ian and Mason, Richard, 1981. *Challenging Strategic Planning Assumptions*. New York: John Wiley & Sons.

Mohr, Lawrence, 1982. *Explaining Organizational Behavior*. San Francisco, Jossey-Bass.

Morgan, Gareth, 1986. *Images of Organizations*. Beverly Hills: Sage Publications.

Morison, Elting E. 1966. *Men, Machines and Modern Times*. Cambridge: MIT Press.

Patz, Alan L., 1981. *Strategic Decision Analysis*. Boston: Little, Brown and Co.

Perrow, Charles, 1984. *Normal Accidents*. New York: Basic Books.

Perrow, Charles, 1970. *Organizational Analysis*. Belmont, California: Brooks/Cole, 258.

Peters, Thomas J. and Waterman, Robert H., Jr., 1982. *In Search of Excellence*. New York: Harper & Row.

Pettigrew, Andrew M., 1979. "On Studying Organization Cultures," *Administrative Science Quarterly* 24.

Pfeffer, Jeffrey, 1981. "Management as Symbolic Action: the Creation and Maintenance of Organizational Paradigms." *Research in Organizational Behavior*, 3, ed. Larry L. Cummings and Barry M. Staw. Greenwich, CT: JAI Press, 1–15.

Pfeffer, Jeffrey and Salancik, Gerald R., 1978. *The External Control of Organizations*. New York: Harper & Row.

Pollack, Andrew, 1984. "A Move Into Microprocessors," *New York Times*, 5 January.

Polli, Rolando and Cook, Victor, 1969. "Validity of the Product Life Cycle," *Journal of Business*, October.

Popper, Karl, 1965. *Conjectures and Refutations*. New York: Harper Torch Books.

Porter, Michael E., 1980. *Competitive Strategy*. New York: The Free Press.

Prestowitz, Clyde V., Jr., 1988. *Trading Places: How We Allowed Japan to Take the Lead*. New York: Basic Books.

Quinn, James Brian, 1985. "Innovation as Controlled Chaos," *Harvard Business Review* 63:3 (May–June), 73–84.

Quinn, James Brian, 1980. *Strategies for Change: Logical Incrementalism*. Homewood, IL: Richard D. Irwin.

Reynolds, Peter C. 1986. "Corporate Culture on the Rocks," *Across the Board* 23:10 (October), 51–6.

Richman, Louis S., 1987. "Lessons From German Managers," *Fortune* 115:9 (27 April) 267, 270, 274, 278.

Ricklefs, Roger, 1986. "Upward Mobility: Many Wine-Makers in France Are Striving to Improve Quality," *Wall Street Journal*, (16 January), 1, 16.

Roberts, Edward B., 1977. "Generating Effective Corporate Innovation," *Technology Review* (October–November).

Roethlisberger, Fritz J. and Dickson, William J., 1939. *Management and the Worker*. Cambridge, MA: Harvard University Press.

Romanelli, Elaine and Tushman, Michael L., 1986. "Inertia, Environment and Strategic Choice: A Quasi-Experimental Design for Comparative–Longitudinal Research," *Management Science* 32:5 (May), 608–20.

Roy, Donald, 1952. "Quota Restriction and Goldbricking in a Machine Shop," *American Journal of Sociology* 57:5 (March), 430–7.

Roy, Donald, 1954. "Efficiency and 'The Fix': Informal Intergroup Relations in a Piecework Machine Shop," *American Journal of Sociology* 60:3, 255–66.

Rumelt, Richard P., 1974. *Strategy, Structure and Economic Performance*. Boston: Graduate School of Business Administration, Harvard University.

Saporito, Bill, 1984. "Hewlett-Packard Discovers Marketing," *Fortune* (1 October), 50–6.

Saporito, Bill, 1987. "The Smokestacks Won't Tumble," *Fortune* 115:3 (2 February), 30–2.

Savich, Richard S. and Laurence A. Thompson, 1978. "Resource Allocation Within the Product Life Cycle," *MSU Business Topics* 26:4 (Autumn).

Servan-Schreiber, Jean Jacques, 1968. *The American Challenge*. New York: Atheneum.

Schoeffler, Sidney, Buzzell, R. and Heany, D. F., 1974. "Impact of Strategic Planning on Profit Performance," *Harvard Business Review* 52:2

(March–April), 137–45.

Schon, Donald, A., 1963. "Champions for Radical New Inventions," *Harvard Business Review* 40:2 (March–April).

Schon, Donald A., 1967. *Technology and Change: The New Heraclitus*. New York: Delacorte Press.

Schonberger, Richard J., 1986. *World Class Manufacturing: The Lessons of Simplicity Applied*. New York: The Free Press.

Schoonhoven, Claudia Bird, 1980. "Volatile Environments, Structure and Effectiveness in High Technology Corporations." Paper presented at the Pacific Sociological Association meeting, San Francisco, April.

Schoonhoven, Claudia Bird, 1984. "High Technology Firms: Where Strategy Really Pays Off," *Columbia Journal of World Business* (Winter), pp. 5–16.

Schoonhoven, Claudia Bird, 1987. "A Time Series Analysis of Strategy and Performance in High Technology Organizations," *Planning Review*.

Schoonhoven, Claudia Bird and K. M. Eisenhardt, 1985. "Influence of Organizational, Entrepreneurial, and Environmental Factors on the Growth and Development of Technology – Based Start Up Firms." Funded proposal to US Department of Commerce, July 1985.

Selznick, Phillip, 1949. *TVA and the Grass Roots*. Berkeley, CA: University of California Press.

Selznick, Philip, 1943. "An Approach to a Theory of Bureaucracy," *American Sociological Review* 8, 47–57.

Seyle, Hans, 1974. *The Stress of Life*. New York: McGraw-Hill.

Sharpe, Henry, 1977. Cited in Farnum, 1987.

Skinner, Wickham, 1985. *Manufacturing: The Formidable Competitive Weapon*. New York: John Wiley & Sons.

Szakonyl, Robert, 1987. "Worlds Apart – Bridging R&D and Manufacturing," *Manufacturing Engineering* 99:6 (December), 71–4.

Thom, Rene, 1980. *Structural Stability and Morphogenesis*. Reading, MA: The Benjamin/Cummings Publishing Co.

Thompson, Donald B., 1987. "A Tale of Two Plants," *Industry Week* 235:2 (19 October), 54–8.

Thompson, James D., 1967. *Organizations in Action*. New York: McGraw-Hill.

Thurow, Lester, 1985. *The Zero-Sum Solution*. New York: Simon and Schuster.

Tilton, John, 1971. *International Diffusion of Technology: The Case of Semiconductors*. Washington, DC: The Brookings Institution.

Toffler, Alvin, 1970. *Future Shock*. New York: Random House.

Tornatzsky, Louis G., 1988. "Transitioning to Advanced Manufacturing Technologies: Industry Structure, Organizational Structure, and Work Group Design." Presentation at the University of Colorado Conference on Managing High Technology Firms, January.

Tornatzsky, Louis G., Eveland, J. D., Boylan, Myles G., Hetzner, W. A., Johnson, E. C., Roitman, D. and Schneider, J., 1983. *The Process of Technological Innovation: Reviewing the Literature*. National Science Foundation, Washington DC, May.

Tushman, M. L. and Anderson, P., 1986. "Technological Discontinuities and Organizational Environments", *Administrative Science Quarterly* 31, 439–65.

Tushman, M. L. and Moore, W. L., 1982. *Readings in the Management of Innovation*. Boston: Pitman Publishers.

Ungson, Gerrardo R., 1987. "Developing Flexible Infrastructures: Responding to the Japanese High Technology Challenge." Paper presented at the Strategic Management Society meeting, Boston, MA, October.

Uttal, Bro, 1987. "How US Chipmakers Can Survive," *Fortune* 115:8 (13 April).

Vail, Peter, 1978. "Toward a Behavioral Description of High Performing Systems," *Leadership: Where Else Can We Go?*, ed. Morgan W. McCall, Jr. and Michael M. Lombardo. Durham, NC: Duke University Press.

Van de Ven, Andrew H., 1986. "Central Problems in the Management of Innovation," *Management Science* (May).

Van de Ven, Andrew H., 1988. "Processes of Innovation and Organizational Change." Proposal to the National Science Foundation for the Minnesota Innovation Research Program, Technical Report of the Strategic Management Research Center, University of Minnesota, February.

Van Nostrand, Roland, 1984. "A Case Study of Justifying CAD," *CIM Review* 1:1 (Fall), 45–52.

von Hippel, Eric, 1986. "Lead Users: A Source of Novel Product Concepts," *Management Science* 32:7 (July), 791–805.

Walleck, Steven, 1985. "Strategic Manufacturing Provides the Competitive Edge," *Electronic Business* (1 April), 93–137.

Webbink, Douglas W., 1977. *The Semiconductor Industry: A Survey of Structure, Conduct and Performance*. Staff Report to the Federal Trade Commission, Washington, DC.

Weick, Karl, 1976. "Educational Organizations as Loosely Coupled Systems," *Administrative Science Quarterly* 21:1 (March), 1–19.

Weick, Karl, 1977. "Organizational Design: Organizations as Self Designing Systems", *Organization Dynamics* (Autumn), 31–46.

Weigner, Kathleen K., 1988. "No More Hubris," *Forbes* 141:4 (22 February), 65–6.

Weiss, Joseph W. and Delbecq, Andre, 1988. "A Regional Culture Perspective on High-Technology Management." Presentation at the University of Colorado Conference on Managing High Technology Firms, January.

Weissmann, Gerald, 1985. *The Woods Hole Contata*. Boston: Houghton Mifflin Co.

Bibliography

Wheelwright, Steven, 1986. "New Product Project Teams." Remarks at a symposium on manufacturing sponsored by McKinsey & Co., Boston, September.

Wheelwright, Steven C., 1985. "Product Development and Manufacturing Start-Up," *Manufacturing Issues 1985*. New York: Booz-Allen & Hamilton.

Wilkins, Alan L. 1983. "Organizational Stories as Symbols Which Control the Organization," *Organizational Symbolism*, ed. L. Pondy, P. Frost, G. Morgan and T. Dandridge. Greenwich, CT: JAI Press.

Wilkins, Alan L. 1984. "The Creation of Company Cultures: The Role of Stories and Human Resource Systems," *Human Resource Management* 23:1 (Spring), 41–60.

Wilkof, Marcia, 1988. "A Socio-Technical Analysis of an Attempted Innovation: The Clash of Cultures," *Managing the High Technology Firm: Proceedings of the 1988 University of Colorado Conference on Managing the High Technology Firm*. Boulder, CO, January.

Wrapp, H. Edward, 1967. "Good Managers Don't Make Policy Decisions," *Harvard Business Review* (September–October).

Yin, R. K., 1979. *Changing Urban Bureaucracies*. Lexington, MA: Lexington Books.

Yin, R. K., 1980. *Studying the Implementation of Public Programs*. Golden, CO: Solar Energy Research Institute.

Yin, R. K., 1981a. "The Case Study as a Serious Research Strategy," *Knowledge* 3, 97–114.

Yin, R. K., 1981b. "The Case Study Crisis: Some Answers," *Administrative Science Quarterly* 26:1 (March), 58–65.

Yin, R. K., 1984. *Case Study Research*. Applied Social Research Methods Series, 5. Beverly Hills, CA: Sage Publications.

Glossary

ASIC Application-Specific Integrated Circuit. A semi-custom or custom chip, designed especially for the particular use to which it will be put (e.g. for automobile engine pollution control, for a particular family of industrial products, etc.). Such circuits are more efficient in operation, but require more precise manufacturing capability, as fewer of them will be manufactured than of a comparable general purpose circuit.

CAD Computer Aided Design.

Chip The commonly used term for integrated circuit.

CMOS Complementary Metal Oxide Semiconductor.

DRAM Dynamic Random Access Memory. A standard computer memory component used in a wide variety of applications for storing data, instructions, and so on. The information disappears when power to the circuit is turned off. DRAMs are one of the largest volume products in semiconductors, selling well into millions of units. DRAMs typically come in sizes designated as "K" (for kilobytes of memory), e.g., 128K, 256K, or as "Meg" (for millions of bytes). (*See also* EPROM, PROM, ROM, SRAM.)

EPROM Erasable Programmable Read Only Memory. This standard memory component is typically erasable by exposure to ultraviolet light. When first introduced, it was an advance, because it could be "reprogrammed." However, the ultraviolet mechanism is less convenient than subsequent electronic methods. *See* EEPROM.

EEPROM Electronically Erasable Programmable Read Only Memory. EEPROMS are far more convenient and easy to use than PROMs that require ultraviolet light, because EEPROMs can be reprogrammed "from the keyboard."

Gate array　An integrated cirucit with a regular array of logic sites, each one an identical collection of transistors, resistors, diodes, etc. The logic sites are surrounded by input and output devices for off-chip connections.

Gate array design　A method of customizing a chip by activating connections in a partially-finished gate array with predefined logic sites.

Integrated circuit　A small, compact, electronic circuit packaged in a minute unit (typically about 7.5 to 50 mm square), varying in complexity. ICs were initially quite simple, but have become increasingly powerful and dense as more and more devices (transistors, resistors, diodes and so on) are added to the circuit. An IC can be put onto a single silicon (or gallium arsenide) substrate to create a monolithic IC or several circuits can be connected in a hybrid package.

Microcomputer　A system based on microprocessors, including the essential power circuitry, memory, and input–output control devices necessary to constitute complete "computer" functionality.

Microprocessor　A programmable large-scale-integrated circuit containing all the elements of a miniature computer. Occasionally referred to as "microcomputer," especially when input–output control interfaces, power circuitry and memory are added. This device is essentially "a computer on a chip," including capabilities for basic arithmetic and logical operations as well as control functions.

MOS　Metal Oxide Semiconductor.

PROM　Programmable Read Only Memory. A standard component that can be programmed with information, instructions or data by the supplier, but "Read Only" by the user. The common varieties include EPROMs (Erasable PROMs, typically erasable by exposure to ultraviolet) and EEPROMs (Electronically Erasable PROMs, which are far more convenient and easy to use because they can be reprogrammed by computer instruction).

RAM　Random Access Memory. A memory device that a programmer can access directly, without having to read sequentially through its contents (as with a tape recorder tape, for instance). RAM is usually a larger space in a computer than ROM.

ROM　Read Only Memory. A memory that can be read from, but cannot be written to, by the user. ROM cannot be modified or reprogrammed.

SRAM　Static Random Access Memory. A standard computer memory component that is "static" or "nonvolatile" because it retains its instructions when the equipment is turned off. By contrast, volatile memory must be continually refreshed, requiring power, and thus loses its contents when the power supply is turned off.

VLSI (circuit) Very Large Scale Integrated (circuit). A high-density, tightly packed, complex circuit, typically incorporating 10,000 to 100,000 gates, or logic circuits. This device is so complex that it requires CAD (computer aided design).

Wafer A slice of silicon on which integrated circuits are produced. Usual practice is for a large number of identical circuits to be reproduced on the same wafer. Wafer size is generally inversely proportional to yields, the proportion of good circuits per wafer. However, if manufacturing can be very tightly controlled, larger wafers enable the manufacture of more ICs with one pass through the production process.

Index